ASTROLOG I:

LIFE AND MEANING

Bruno and Louise Huber et al

HopeWell
Knutsford, England

A selection of articles first published in German
in the magazine *Astrolog* over the period 1990-2007

This first English translation published by HopeWell 2008

HopeWell,
PO Box 118, Knutsford
Cheshire WA16 8TG, U.K.

Translated by Heather Ross
Edited by Barry Hopewell

Jacket design by Barry Hopewell
Jacket photograph by Bruno Huber

ISBN 0-9547680-7-8

In memory of Agnes Shellens

1921 – 2005

*Her generous bequest made possible
the publication of this book.*

Symbols of the Planets

Sun	☉	♂	Mars
Moon	☽	♃	Jupiter
Saturn	♄	♅	Uranus
Mercury	☿	♆	Neptune
Venus	♀	♇	Pluto
ascending Moon Node	☊		

Symbols of the Signs

Aries	♈	♎	Libra
Taurus	♉	♏	Scorpio
Gemini	♊	♐	Sagittarius
Cancer	♋	♑	Capricorn
Leo	♌	♒	Aquarius
Virgo	♍	♓	Pisces

Abbreviations

AC	=	Ascendant	HC	=	House Cusp
IC	=	Imum Coeli	LP	=	Low Point
DC	=	Descendant	BP	=	Balance Point
MC	=	Medium Coeli	GM	=	Golden Mean

Aspects

Green	Semi-sextile	Angle of 30°	⌄
	Quincunx	Angle of 150°	⊼
Blue	Sextile	Angle of 60°	✳
	Trine	Angle of 120°	△
Red	Square	Angle of 90°	□
	Opposition	Angle of 180°	☍
Orange	Conjunction	Angle of 0°	☌

Contents

Introduction

Along with the development of psychology, the 20th century saw
the emergence of psychological approaches to astrology, through
pioneers such as Fankhauser, Ring and Rudhyar. In the 1950s the
young Bruno and Louise Huber developed their own system of
astrological psychology after extensive research done in collaboration
with Roberto Assagioli at his Institute of Psychosynthesis. In what
became known as the 'Huber Method' they aimed to combine the
best of astrology, depth psychology and the discoveries coming from
their own research.

In 1964 Bruno and Louise founded the Astrological Psychology
Institute (API) in Zurich, and devoted their lives to counselling,
teaching and further research into this approach. Since then over ten
thousand students have been trained with API, many achieving the
Institute's professional Diploma.

In 1981 the German-language magazine *Astrolog* was established, and
has been published bi-monthly since then. Each of the now-over-
150 issues of *Astrolog* contains articles by contributors who include
the Hubers, API teachers, students and Diploma holders, many of
whom are professionals in other disciplines. Subjects have included
amplification of aspects of the Huber Method, new ideas and
research, practical experience, including relating to other disciplines,
case studies etc. There is thus a large volume of experience and
knowledge embedded in the past issues of *Astrolog*.

In 1983 an English-language school, API(UK), was established by
Richard Llewellyn and Pam Tyler. API(UK) has since enrolled over
1000 students, many of whom have gained their own Diplomas
and continue to use astrological psychology, either on its own or in
conjunction with other disciplines. In the meantime, the Hubers' eight
books on astrological psychology have become available in English
and are sold across the world. There are thus now many people
interested in this practical and proven approach.

Agnes Shellens was supportive of API(UK) from the early days, and
helped its development, translating a number of articles from *Astrolog*
into English, plus Bruno Huber's book *Astrological Psychosynthesis*.
Agnes was unfortunately unable to continue this work in her later
years, and it was with sadness that we learned of her death in 2005.

It was a pleasant surprise, some time later, to learn that Agnes had left a sum of money as a bequest to API(UK). It was deemed appropriate that this money should be used to make available in the English language more of that treasury of information in the back issues of *Astrolog*. This book is the first fruit of Agnes's final generous demonstration of her support.

The set of articles selected for this book was chosen with a view to including material which would be of most value and interest, in the context of what is already available in the Hubers' books and the various publications produced by API(UK). We also aimed to include a reasonably wide selection of different authors.

All the articles have been translated by Heather Ross, who will be familiar to many as the translator of the books *Aspect Pattern Astrology* and *The Planets and their Psychological Meaning*.

Special thanks are due to Joyce Hopewell and David Kerr for their efforts in checking through the results of Heather's excellent translations plus my editorial adjustments.

The book has been structured into four parts, each containing articles related to a specific theme:

> Part 1: Astrological Psychology
> Part 2: Life and Meaning
> Part 3: Age Progression
> Part 4: Growth and Transformation

At the beginning of each part you will find a brief introduction to the articles contained therein.

We intend to publish a companion volume with further articles on the broad theme of *Family, Relationships and Health*, and hope that you will find these two volumes a valuable resource and a fitting memorial to the generosity of spirit of Agnes Shellens.

Barry Hopewell

Editor

Part 1: Astrological Psychology

This first part of the book contains three overview articles related to astrological psychology, the approach to personal development pioneered by Bruno and Louise Huber, which will be of particular interest to readers who are not familiar with the subject.

Astrological Psychology, **by Bruno Huber**
Briefly highlights most of the essential features of astrological psychology, a 'holistic approach to human problems'.

The Meaning and Value of a Horoscope Reading, **by Louise Huber**
Briefly outlines the purpose and benefits of this approach to individual consultation and psychological development.

Psychosynthesis and Astrology, **by Bruno Huber**
Outlines the influences of Freud, Jung and Assagioli in the development of astrological psychology.

These are followed by features on the Moon and Saturn's rings, and three articles on the implications of recent astronomical discoveries and Pluto.

The Moon in the Twelve Houses, **by Louise Huber**
Expands on material in the book *The Planets and their Psychological Meaning* by considering the interpretation of the Moon's position in the different areas of each of the houses.

Lean Years, **by Bruno Huber**
Considers the significance of Saturn's rings, their effect on the brightness of the planet and the astrological implications.

Pluto and the Transneptunian Planets, **by Harald Zittlau**
Takes a look at recent advances in astronomy and their astrological implications.

Is Pluto a Planet?, **by Bruno Huber**
This brief article, written in 1985 but still relevant today, considers the question of whether Pluto really is a planet.

Pluto's Transformations, **by Wolfhard König**
Considers the astrological-psychological implications of the smaller planetary objects in the solar system.

Readers who are unfamiliar with astrological psychology and seek further introductory material may like to go on to one of the following books, which have been found particularly effective in introducing the Hubers' approach:

The Cosmic Egg Timer, by Joyce Hopewell and Richard Llewellyn
    A basic introduction suitable for beginners.

Astrological Psychosynthesis, by Bruno Huber
    A psychological introduction.

Further information on the astrological-psychological implications of the planets can be found in:

The Planets and their Psychological Meaning, by Bruno & Louise Huber

Astrological Psychology

Bruno Huber

*First published in 'Astrolog' Issue 60, February 1991,
and subsequently in Bruno's uncompleted 'Astro-Glossarium'.*

Astrological Psychology is a type of psychology that uses astrology as a (diagnostic) tool. Its psychological background is firstly the findings of depth psychology, but also humanistic and transpersonal psychology. Its concept is closest to the psychosynthesis of Roberto Assagioli.

Astrological psychology is based on the concept of an organic, self-regulating and therefore subjective healthy being, not on patterns of illness, as in most types of psychology. "A person is only ill if they think they are ill". Finding the reason for "feeling ill" is the main focus of astrological-psychology.

Astrological psychology is based on the clear motivation of increasing people's learning aptitude through its teaching, counselling or therapeutic activities, i.e. stimulating them to think for themselves, not prescribing formulae or offering quick fixes. In brief, it involves allowing the person to get to know themselves using an appropriate tool, so that the person accepts themselves and can become freer, happier and more creative.

Its first and most important concern is the holistic approach to human problems. This not only applies to the psychological concept, but also to the choice of astrological techniques and how they are implemented.

The astrological-psychological method therefore follows the holistic claim, that all its parts must be integrated in a mutually complementary way. As such, it is a self-contained method, but is not closed to further developments and improvements. However, this is why the elimination of some techniques of traditional astrology was unavoidable. They are logical and consistent in themselves, but they stand in isolation. This mainly concerns those techniques that can limit people's freedom and independence, and those that cause a "magnifying effect", by distorting the proportion of the human image in the eyes of the observer.

A special mention here goes to a variety of classic and modern prognosis techniques, which all work on parts instead of the whole and usually only take into account external events. However, the experiences of the interior world of the personality are the real active forces that determine which external events we subjectively perceive and how we experience, assess and respond to them. The **Age Progression** used in astrological psychology deals with this world of experience. It is a way of showing how we move through our own horoscope, and, by extension, how we work through our whole character during the course of our lives.

Simplification is the real, organic requirement that has also influenced the choice of technical method. A basic trait of the modern human intellect is logical, linear causal thinking, which is essentially analytical. Its basic tendency is therefore to separate the whole into its parts, i.e. into multiplicity and ultimately into the complicated unmanageability of its own means and ends. Many techniques do not solve the current problems in reading a chart – in actual fact they make it more difficult to do. In astrology, we are often taught that a reading can only be accurate if it is achieved through several different techniques. The principle of astrological psychology is the opposite: if several readings are necessary to gain clarity, the primary resources have not been sufficiently exhausted.

In this sense, the primary elements are clearly defined: they were stated by Ptolemy and can be grouped into four levels:

The aspect figure with aspects of the 30° sequence:
  - the motivation level
The ten planets and the moon node:
  - the functional or living organs
The twelve zodiac signs:
  - the genetic make-up – the archetypes
The twelve houses or fields:
  - conditioning – learned behaviour.

These few elements, the four 'levels of existence', are used rigorously, and applied with great subtlety and precision. Some characteristic features of the method of astrological psychology are listed below:

A clear horoscope chart graphic is an essential requirement to enable sensory perception of the horoscope's qualities and proportionality. The levels mentioned above are each shown in a separate space and the use of colour enables a quick, visual understanding of the way the qualities are distributed.

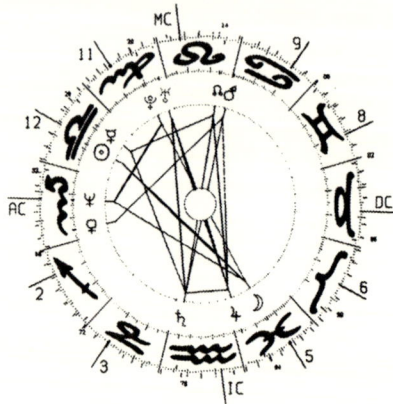

Definition of Planetary Terms. The wording of the meaning of the planetary symbols has been more and more reduced to their essential contents after years of experience, so that there is no longer any overlapping of planetary definitions. This has proved vital for research purposes, as otherwise confusion occurs, which makes it impossible to obtain clear results.

Aspect Figures. The interpretation of individual aspects has proved problematic, as the linear proximity of such definitions inevitably leads to inconsistencies, even to irresolvable contradictions. Because in normal cases, a planet is aspected not only to one but to two or more other planets, they must also be interpreted as a group, as the individual aspects of a figure affect each other. However, in reality it is impossible to conceptually merge several aspect interpretations. The solution lies in the fact that aspect figures (triangles, quadrilaterals and polygons) already have meaning in their own right, without the planets. These provide a generic context for the planets they contain. In astrological psychology the horoscope is therefore basically analysed in terms of its aspect structure. Planets, signs and houses are only interpreted in the context of the aspect structure as organs of implementation and working spaces. This gives rise to a naturally proportioned reading (character pattern).

Intensity curve. Extensive research has shown that in every house, there is an intensity curve like a sine curve, which shows how the effectiveness of a planet changes according to its position in the house. The maximum is shown at the peak, the minimum after the middle of the house (low point). The curve allows an accurate understanding of the energy available for each planet that can be transferred into daily life, which is essential for a differentiated psychological diagnosis.

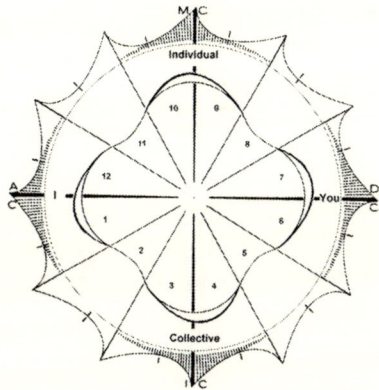

House horoscope, dynamic counting and **dynamic quadrant** are innovations in astrology, whose development only became possible thanks to the discovery of the intensity curve. They enable a distinction to be made that is not easy to make in psychology between **innate behaviour** (nature, genetic make-up) on the one hand, and **learnt behaviour** (nurture, environmental influences, conditioning) on the other.

One of the main focuses of psychological problems can therefore be solved using these tools: the conflicts and pressures which arise during childhood and youth from the contrast between the environmental nurturing efforts of adults and the primordial character traits of the child. Further subtle definitions arise if we include the personal, family space:

The Family Model, the horoscope position of the Sun, Moon and Saturn. It shows the subjective experience of the child's relationships with its parents, or others responsible for raising the child. It enables the understanding of relationships with the mother and father, as well as a potentially destructive attitude towards the opposite sex, which can show itself in problems with a partner. It also reveals the real roots of the person's attitude towards power and society.

The **role model for the adult personality** is also derived from the same planetary positions. The identity and integrity of the three-fold personality (mind, emotions, body) develops in childhood under the influence of the family model (father, child and mother roles), as derived from the positions and aspects of the Sun, Moon and Saturn.

It is common practice in modern astrological psychology to **work with three horoscopes**: radix, house and moon node horoscope; the latter includes an additional dimension of the unconscious, which C.G. Jung called the "shadow".

ɑ ɑ ɑ ɑ ɑ

The Meaning and Value
of a Horoscope Reading

Louise Huber

First published in 'Astrolog' Issue 60, February 1991

An astrological-psychological reading is a fascinating new way to find the path to our inner selves. Using a personal horoscope, and with the aid of newly-developed psychological interpretation methods, it is possible to get to the root of individual problems, a result that test psychologists only achieve after many sessions. The individual horoscope as a diagnostic pattern can be understood at a glance and problems quickly identified. Normally, a horoscope reading lasts two hours. The conversation is recorded on a tape recorder so that the client can listen to it again later in peace.

Methods of Psychosynthesis

In an astrological psychological consultation, methods of psychosynthesis are used in order to raise up deeper life issues, mental endeavours and spiritual motivation forces into the consciousness. Astrological synthesis enables both a differentiated understanding of the personality and the integration and reshaping of the whole person. The causality of human behaviour is understood at the root; psychological and spiritual contexts are revealed. This is relevant to the modern human condition.

Causes instead of Symptoms

Most people do not like being judged by their symptoms or their behaviour. They want to know why they react in one way and not in another. They want to be acknowledged and understood in their innermost being and to discover the deeper meaning of a problem. The searching for causes is a concern of our times and the principal objective of the astrological psychology reading.

Astrology is a valuable tool for Self-Help

In an astrological psychology reading, the personal horoscope is experienced as a mirror to the self and provides a new sense of identity, a certainty that one really exists. The integration of cosmic laws leads to a higher mental and emotional dimension. One gains a new attitude towards many things, and difficulties and conflicts take on their correct proportion.One achieves the necessary perspective and therefore a greater objectivity and power of judgement. The causes of problems in choosing a career, bringing up children, in marriage and partnership as well as one's own spiritual development are related to the character as a whole.

Horoscope Reading as a Process

A horoscope reading is a consultation process that aims to increase the person's freedom and awaken their spiritual potential. Careful and discreet personal questions and the corresponding life issues are addressed using the individual horoscope. The psychologically trained astrologer does not just direct the person who confides in him, he treats him much more as a partner whom he leads through a process of self-discovery and creates the conversational atmosphere that encourages the client to open up. He aims for an overall understanding and psychosynthesis of the personality, for the activation of the client's own developmental and constructive powers. He concentrates not on weaknesses and mistakes, but on strengths and abilities. Valuations like "good" and "bad" are strictly avoided. The concept of astrological psychology is based on a positive image of the individual person. It assumes that the person is healthy in the core of his being, that his inner potential can be awoken by approval and has a self-healing effect.

New Questions

It is a trend that more and more people are consulting astrologers to find answers to deeper life issues. With the help of the astrologer, they hope to find a meaning for their life, their true identity or their higher self. They want to get to the bottom of the meaning and purpose of their life, identify their karma and learn about their true vocation and the purpose of their incarnation. Others seek further spiritual development and are trying to change misguided ideas and behaviour patterns. A holistic and spiritually oriented horoscope reading deals with the following questions:

"Who am I – where do I come from – where am I going?"

An astrological-psychological reading is therefore a tool that enables penetration deep into the core of the person's own being. If we help ourselves with a sense of responsibility, we soon discover that we gain insights that lead to a comprehensive understanding of our existence that can be life-changing.

◻ ◻ ◻ ◻ ◻

Psychosynthesis and Astrology

A broad-ranging, differentiated concept

Bruno Huber

Originally a lecture by Bruno, edited by Rita Keller and first published in 'Astrolog' Issue 134, June 2003.

Psychosynthesis is not a collection of techniques; it is primarily a way of thinking intended to help people with their psychological problems. It is essentially a particular attitude to a particularly important task.

We lived with Roberto Assagioli, the founder of psychosynthesis, for 3 years, and got to know his theories, ideas and methods. Assagioli said: "Methods are of secondary importance. There is no clearly defined group of psychosynthetic methods."

Basically, Assagioli himself was always trying out new methods and never restricted himself. He started from the principle that there were no universally valid methods for all human problems. Each person must be treated totally individually, with methods chosen and combined especially for him. The patient's own collaboration in this process is essential.

I can only confirm these statements out of personal experience, for every person has their quite individual story and therefore needs a personally tailored approach in order to be successful.

This often contradicts other types of psychology and is a theme that is usually suppressed by psychosynthesists (followers of Assagioli), because it does not suit their psychological landscape and they don't feel comfortable with this requirement.

What is Psychosynthesis?

What are its aims and what does it offer? That is the key question.

Every psychologist and every psychological school has its own image of man. The psychosynthetic image is a psychosynthetic one, but what does this mean? It means "seeing the person as a whole", unconditionally, impartially, without having any preconceived theories of what a person should be like. Again, no fixed ideas, just an openness on the part of the therapist and a desire to understand what kind of "wonderful universe" each client represents and contains within them.

One important thing that I learnt from Assagioli, which is a positive therapeutic tool, is that every day I can be surprised again, for there is no encounter that is not new, even with the people I already know, but most people do not realise this. The desire to be surprised and amazed, to constantly reassimilate and try to understand whom one is dealing with is a fundamental prerequisite to really be able to help people.

Usually, we have our own fixed model of what people should be like; we have certain ideas, without really being aware of this. We philosophise and measure with our own individual measuring system, which often consists of impulses of which we are initially unaware, but which are characteristic of us. We can divide the impulses into two main parts. They are provided from a personal point of view by the character, with regard to both people and the world in general. Because we as individuals want something from the world and have a life purpose, there is a certain one-sidedness in our perspective, of which we are not always fully aware.

If different people consider a landscape, one sees the trees in front of the mountains, another sees the distant horizon and a third notices the blue sky. These are different points of view, but in reality everything we see is part of the whole, but what we notice is different depending on our interests.

That is one part, those innate qualities that are closely connected to life motivations and which produce a certain one-sidedness. We carry the other part around with us unconsciously, and it comes from the environment we grew up in. Here there were a lot of dogmas, basic conceptions of how we should see and judge life that influenced us in our childhood and youth. The result of this is that we have a certain way of evaluating life and judging according to certain standards, for behind this lies a certain morality and a certain environmentally-typical philosophy. When seen in this way, the world looks different to everyone.

A problem that psychology has had to deal with since Freud is that we can never know for sure whom we have in front of us. Sigmund Freud addressed this problem by letting his clients free associate; they just had to talk about their lives. His role as therapist was to listen without influencing the patient by suggestive questioning, but to observe them attentively in order to find out where their problem lay and what could have caused it. This is acknowledged to be a long-drawn-out process that can last years and one never quite knows where one really is, and there are always certain misleading contradictions.

C.G. Jung adopted this process for some time, and later varied it somewhat, but the problem was that knowing that people and their ways of measuring were different meant that they could not always be helped with the same procedures. Also, one was labouring under a delusion; under no circumstances did one want to admit that people could be influenced by suggestion. To avoid this happening, long-drawn-out processes were used so that no influence could occur, however this was no guarantee, just an attempt on the part of the therapist. This could actually give rise to a lack of concept or idea of what the person could be like.

Jung went one step further; he had a definite concept, which was very cautious and to some extent anxious as far as the science was concerned. Jung postulated again and again that there could be a higher self or an inner essence but he never formulated it clearly, for its existence could not be proven.

Roberto Assagioli's concept took this yet another step further. He said "People have manifestly spiritual reactions and develop spiritual drives". He called it this to distinguish from the Freudian notion of drive.

He assumed that that the person also is or has a spiritual essence and was quite open about it, and this spiritual concept of man had to be integrated. By doing this, he became the founder of the now extremely popular movement of transpersonal psychology. Transpersonal psychology presupposes that man also has spiritual drives with which to transcend his habitual, normal, worldly viewpoint and lifestyle and strive for greater meaning, look for enlightenment and undergo peak experiences. For Assagioli and transpersonal psychology, these ideas are central features of the idea of man. One can say that there are three conceptual steps between Freud and Assagioli.

For Freud, everything was reduced to drives. *(This was true until about 1920. With Ego Psychology and particularly with modern Self Psychology, psychoanalysis formulated other non drive-conditioned areas of motivation.)* These were, it has to be said, almost uniquely masculine drives. As far as Freud was concerned, there were no feminine drives at all. *(This is true until about 1920. Modern psychoanalysis has a detailed formulation of the development of masculine and feminine drives.)* Women were just the victims of masculine drives. Jung expanded this; he had enlarged the concept of anima and animus and postulated a masculine and feminine polarity. Above all, he had assumed more causal human functions than Freud, where everything was traced back to drives, to the famous libido. With Jung, we have a concept of the personality that also already has a notion of spiritual drives, although this was not really official. *(Jung eventually formulated the Archetypes as vital driving forces.)* With Assagioli, the concept of the spiritual person has been incorporated, and once this has been done, it becomes obvious that there is no longer any universally valid formula, but that every case is different.

From the human spirit come movements and conscious and deliberate decisions, which just cannot be explained by a narrow concept, and universal formulae are no longer valid either. As long as the person is conditioned by drives, as with Freud; as long as he follows physical concept structures, he is basically predictable; one can put him in a given situation and he will always react in the same way.

This makes man predictable, i.e. one can determine what he will do next, make forecasts and pin him down, which can become quite dangerous. Astrologers are often reproached for this kind of thing, because their forecasts can cause dependency and addiction. However, this only happens if one has a narrow concept oneself and is controlled by instincts. If a person's concept structures are hard-wired in their reactions, then the person has no free will. His ability to make his own decisions is therefore limited; the answers and decisions he gives are determined by his inner drive and instinctual structures.

This process lasts until a new, spiritual perspective enables the person to escape from this structure, and this is provided by Psychosynthesis. Self-transcendence is possible, and there are plenty of examples of this in human history. Roberto Assagioli assumed that every person has a broad, free, inner space inside them, from which unexpected reactions can emerge and where decisions can be made. That is a quite crucial point that was a new departure for psychology. One could say that it conceptualised, incorporated and defined human freedom. It is supposed to be a large, open space in which the individual can lay foundations and where he has the freedom to decide to adopt a new perspective. We are therefore presented with a new human duality; on the one hand we are controlled by instincts and on the other hand we are able to gain quite a good understanding of what is going on. Astrological psychology is helpful in identifying drive and instinct structures.

Astrological Psychology

The horoscope is a kind of diagram of human nature, which sums up what we are able to comprehend of the human character here on earth, i.e. it shows determining factors that establish how we want to react in certain situations. In this respect, the horoscope is seemingly Freudian and Jungian. However, this is not the only thing we can see in the horoscope; there are also empty spaces where one can exercise one's own free will and authority, giving a different result from that which can be seen in the fixed structures of the horoscope. So there are visible fixed structures in the horoscope, but they are not at all represented in a way that always allows a person's reactions to be predicted with certainty, and this is revealed very clearly in consultations, when it would be advantageous to be able to predict in advance when and how someone will react.

A very important discovery for me over the years has been that even people who do not know themselves very well and who have little self-awareness still have access to this free space. It is always present and visible in all horoscopes, is unique to the individual and used in different ways by everyone.

The behaviour of people who do not make use of it can be predicted quite accurately. One can therefore make very accurate predictions for some people, however for those people who are aware it does not work as well, and for an even smaller group, it hardly works at all. This shows that there are gradual differences. These were important results for me and I found that psychosynthesis can enable the consciousness to access this free space, because it makes one aware of its determining structures. It enables the creation of greater self awareness and to the extent that this happens the deterministic aspect of the horoscope is reduced, which means that astrology is a science which exists to make itself redundant. However, there is a long process to go though before the horoscope is no longer necessary, and because it would then be rendered invalid, it is questionable whether this is a desirable state from a human perspective. We are born on this Earth and have a task here which requires a certain amount of structuring that can be understood and used in this world; that is our nature. This was a small philosophical leap.

Assagioli postulated that a psychology that is not also a philosophy has no value. There were three psychologists who were decisive in my own development as a person and as a psychologist. For me, everything started with Freud, I discovered Jung at university, and nobody had ever told me about Assagioli, and it was not until later that I deliberately met him.

Sigmund Freud 06.05.1856, 09:17, Freiberg (Mähren), Austria

In Freud's horoscope, Mars stands out as the tension ruler, which explains why the libido was so important for him, and the masculine one at that. If it were not for Mars, it would be a very top-heavy horoscope with a small upper figure, but Mars at the bottom constantly draws our attention downwards. This is a strong theme which has a very compulsive dualistic nature and represents Freud's own character, and also his methods and theories.

Jung's horoscope is larger with more aspects. An interesting phenomenon is that there are three figures in the aspect pattern.

Jung himself expressed two personalities, and possibly also a third as one was subdivided into two further parts, and this corresponds

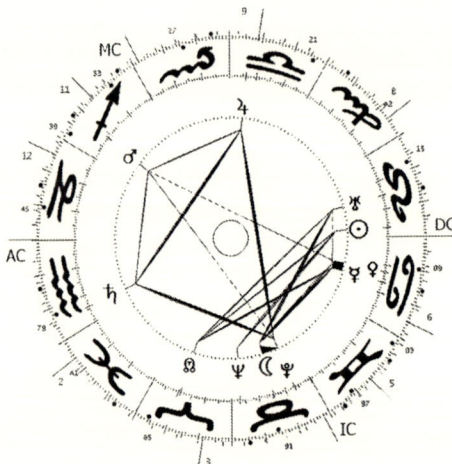

C.G. Jung 26.07.1875, 19.32, Kesswil, CH

exactly to his aspect pattern. So we can clearly see one great concept, but there is also a less obvious duality and there would even be a threefold division, except that two figures are connected to the Moon/Pluto conjunction.

In my dealings with Jung, I always had trouble with his incomprehensible duality; I always had the feeling that it constituted a ditch that I had to jump over – it was a more expanded and freer concept. Freud was able to bring everything under one denominator: problems were caused by the libido. This is relatively easy to grasp and he always focused on this reference point. Jung went further and developed a more comprehensive concept.

Assagioli worked with Jung as his assistant in Burghölzli and knew his theories. He often discussed this duality with Jung and did not agree with it. This was actually an important reason why he looked for a broader concept that was not divided.

Assagioli's horoscope is larger still and I don't think it is a coincidence that the size of the concepts of the three psychologists is reflected in the size of their aspect patterns.

I would like to emphasise that this should not be understood to be a judgemental statement though. The size of an aspect pattern does not indicate the size of a person's intellect/spirit. However, it is interesting that the concepts of Freud, Jung and Assagioli are so clearly reflected in their aspect patterns.

It is often difficult for a person with an unusually large aspect pattern to get an overview of the whole. But for me the point is that psychosynthesis enables a large space to be opened up for spiritual development.

Roberto Assagioli 27.02.1888, 12.03, Venice, Italy

I would not like to give the impression that we are able to find a quick fix with simple theories. Human problems are complex and require a wide-ranging, differentiated concept, without which a solution cannot be found.

Simplistic theories may help us to solve certain problems, but there is a danger of problems being suppressed and shifted to other areas. We know that this also happens in the case of physical illnesses, which are often caused by psychological problems.

If psychosomatic illnesses are then only cured by medicine, i.e. by fighting the symptoms, the cause of the illness may reappear somewhere else. Often the connection is not noticed and the spiritual problem is not cured and overcome. We may feel much better, but new problems will appear and the connection will again not be made. Problems can therefore migrate and appear as other symptoms.

Psychosynthesis is fundamentally holistic, and that is why Assagioli gave his concept this name, because he wanted to clearly distance himself from psychoanalysis and analytical psychology.

It is interesting that both Freud and Jung use these similar but different terms. It is almost a play on words, but the two theories are actually more different than one may suppose.

Both methods are analytical in their approach to problems; they try to analyse them in their component parts. In order to understand the background, questions are asked as to when this complex was understood and which circumstances have triggered it. That is an analytical approach.

Assagioli thought "synthetically", i.e. he did not want to "dissect" people into separate parts, but to unify them. This was his basic idea

Bruno Huber 29.11.1930, 12:55, Zürich, CH

and is why the term synthesis is accurate, for the person is only healthy from a psychosynthetic point of view when the whole functions.

However, I must add that Assagioli was not against analysis, for he himself used analytical methods, e.g. the Jungian Association Test, a classic analytical tool, which identifies disturbing factors by using word association. It allows the determination of where difficult areas are, and often also how they originated. Selected terms are used that complement each other and zero in on certain themes, so that the overall results reveal where any problems may lie.

At the start of a therapeutic process, Assagioli first required a patient to talk about his life and to write a biography. A biography offers a really broad overview of a long period of time, including childhood experiences and reveals whether certain themes appear again and again in different forms during the patient's lifetime.

This produces large-scale structures, expands the person's image, shows that a certain problem has an environment to which it organically belongs and ensures that this is not seen and analysed in isolation, but rather as a part of this environment. This can often provide initial approaches for healing. This synthetic standpoint enables the whole to be seen and any connections to be seen. In other words, the visible problem is only the tip of the iceberg and the really important thing is that the whole iceberg is investigated and not only the visible, troublesome part on the surface.

This can lead to quite different healing approaches, and very often no drastic healing methods are necessary, just a clear dialogue and productive processes. Assagioli advised his clients to paint and play music and included musical elements during the therapy itself to encourage the holistic process.

Basic Research

During my stay with Assagioli, I had the opportunity to undertake basic research and had contact with people who had been in therapy with Assagioli. He always encouraged me in my research because he thought that astrology could enrich psychology. He knew little about astrology himself, and in certain cases I drew up people's horoscope to give him a better idea of the person's nature as I saw it.

At this time, I developed new ways of drawing the horoscope, i.e. in colour, with clearly separated spaces, aspect patterns, planets, signs and houses, and the five layers emerged. Inspired by psychosynthesis, I wanted to be able to see the horoscope as a whole at a glance. This was a decisive point. If I had not attempted to draw the horoscope more clearly and distinctly, my research would probably not have been so successful. I would probably have returned again and again to particular areas and considered them to be important, but the new way of drawing largely prevented this from happening. It was therefore not just an aesthetic detail but a quite key prerequisite for synthetic horoscope work.

We stipulate that no individual elements, not even individual aspects between planets, are interpreted. There is admittedly some astrological literature which does advocate the interpretation of details, but this is analytical and at the end of the day it cannot be right, because it is not a holistic evaluation. They are considered and interpreted in isolation, and that just cannot be correct. In order to gain insight, the whole psyche must be transparent, which is why a horoscope that makes this possible is required. In this respect, the methods of astrological psychology as we understand it make it a psychosynthetic astrology.

Although I was surrounded by analytical psychology, I always tended to think synthetically; I just couldn't really put it into words. Only thanks to Assagioli was I able to gain some clarity around this for myself, for his concept was fully-developed and he had extracted the essential points from each different branch. This enabled me to undertake a new kind of astrological research.

I owe an incredible amount to this fact, for the concept we use would hardly have arisen without this key development. That is why it is quite true that I can no longer separate astrology and psychology; for me they are just two different ways of looking at the same thing.

When I look at a horoscope, I immediately have psychological ideas and when I hear people talking about psychology, I see planets and aspects, i.e. I can no longer keep them apart. They have become one, logically and organically.

Anyone who deals with people will find that the same problem crops up again and again on different levels and with different facets, but it always looks different depending on one's perspective.

Assagioli once said: "You must always let people dance before you for a while; let them twist and turn so that you can see all their facets. They may need a little help to be able to twist and turn, to come out of their shells and start to move. Then you can see the problem from different angles and gain an overall picture."

Mental Alertness

This is how we want to consider the horoscope, not rigidly staring at something in particular that catches our eye. It is a question of expanding our viewpoint, whether we are now using astrology or psychosynthesis, so that we can really understand. Our mind should be alert and open to people, with an all-encompassing view that sees everything as connected.

People can adopt deceptive roles. Fears are controlled consciously or by the subconscious, for the subconscious has quite specific ideas about how to present itself in order to give the best impression, i.e. the therapist can be misled by illusions and manipulation from the subconscious.

The psychologist should therefore take more notice of, for example, body language and he must be able to see through any deception. This is not that easy, for there are people who are incredibly clever in the way they present themselves.

The horoscope provides a completely different starting point; it is a kind of neutral or objective mirror. We must be able to read the horoscope accurately though, for here too, mistakes can occur and we must try to acknowledge that by not looking at it analytically, but holistically.

As the three example horoscopes show, the interpretation of the aspect pattern is helpful. It is the synthetic key to the horoscope. It shows the proportions, the emphasis and the purpose and is the most individually accessible part of the horoscope. That is why we place great value on the differentiated interpretation of the aspect pattern.

Planets, houses and signs bring colourful, concrete detail; they make it real. It is important to see that there is a psychosynthetic concept in the horoscope that is reflected in the way it is drawn. We know that the layers, the aspect pattern, the planets and signs and the houses around the outside represent a holistic concept of man. Elements jostle against each other, the alignment of the planets changes, sometimes they are in groups or sometimes wide apart; there are an infinite number of individual variations. The combinations of every horoscope are as unique as we are.

The Uniqueness of the Individual

A concept is therefore just a kind of structure. Very precise, exact and very restricted concepts of people used to be made. The concept of psychosynthesis is that no two people are the same.

Meanwhile, in the social sciences, the prevailing view is that it does not make sense to have a concept of man, as it will be restricted by culturally-conditioned standards. Such models would be one-sided and would put pressure on the personality.

Assagioli said again and again that every person has a self-contained universe within them with its own natural laws. We can only help people when we can see and accept them as "functional universes". Certain areas in such a universe would naturally be neglected, because the milieu did not encourage or even repressed certain talents of the child when it was growing up. That can lead to problems that we could term deficiencies or imbalances of the system. The system does not work in equilibrium; certain parts are no longer supplied with blood, to compare it with the body. The affected organs are no longer able to function properly and cause disruptions in the life process of the whole psyche.

He considered a person to be organically healthy if he was able to live by self-motivation; a view that is also expressed by psychosynthesis. It considers a person to be healthy if he can stand on his own two feet and make his own decision. I would like to emphasise this point: we are all healthy, we are all here of our own volition, fear factors could have held us back, and maybe they did discourage some people. Health therefore exists the moment we are able to survive in this world and do not perish.

Perfection and Dysfunction

In this world, perfection is not found in nature, and every person must also naturally carry a certain ratio of dysfunction that stimulates human development and prompts our consciousness to change. Dysfunctions are part of life and exist to trigger certain tendencies to self perfection due to imbalances. What Assagioli established, and what I have noticed in my practice, is that they are the problems that drive a person forwards in their development. It would therefore be wrong to believe that only spiritual development is right; the material level is just as important for us, otherwise we would lose touch with reality. Every person is a reality because he is a universe. We must study our own natural laws and understand their workings and their significance so that we are better able to comprehend and clarify the imbalances and problems.

The point is not therefore to find out how ill one is, but what is wrong with one's health. Dysfunctions, I must emphasis, are inconsistencies, imbalances in one's own system and problems with the environment. They are system failures within me, and the environment prompts me to relate better to myself, to want to know myself better. It stimulates me to confront myself in order to discover how I can become more aware in my relationship with myself and with the environment. This is a key view in psychosynthesis: the aspiration to grow and the quest for higher insight is a vital life impulse, just as crucial as the drive for self-preservation or other drives that we can express according to Freud and others. The aspiration to grow can become just as strong and powerful if I accept it and have a concept of it.

There are, however, social backgrounds that do not accept that human spiritual aspirations exist. As long as a person adapts, functions as well as he can socially and is therefore accepted, no spiritual aspiration can exist or be awakened. He will ultimately interpret, represent and explain everything by this self-sufficient, self-perpetuating system that revolves around himself. However, according to psychosynthesis, these spiritual drives do exist, and are awakened if he can admit that he is not functioning correctly and that there are short circuits and wiring that is lying idle. As soon as he recognises this, spiritual development can begin. It is not a question of how big a problem is, but rather it is the insight that something could be better that initiates the search for meaning. He must be able to take the higher ground, for the environment will usually encourage our dysfunctionality. For if others also live in this rather dysfunctional paradigm, then the whole continues to function and the need for the status quo to change is questioned.

So everything remains the same, he dysfunctions with conviction in a well-dysfunctioning system, everything is ok. This world wants to preserve itself and there will always be mutually corrupting dysfunctionality so that the scenario remains the same, for this is the basis of survival. It is the drive imperative, and as soon as he starts to realise that something is wrong, he is no longer a "blindly" functioning member. He starts to observe himself, setting in motion chain reactions in the consciousness that cannot be stopped.

He can therefore wish, for example, that he had never got involved with astrology, in order to become completely "normal" again. However, it will not work, and definitely not in the long term. It does not even need to be astrology; it can also be something different that can lead to new insights. So the established equilibrium system of human society changes and is disturbed in a different way, emanating from the spiritual level. The disturbance from the drive area is familiar, for the whole is able to function due to mutual support, but disturbances from the level of spirituality bring upheaval. From the point of view of psychosynthesis, the growth drives can be observed as phenomena in society. In every society, throughout cultural history, it can be observed that a couple of troublemakers with new ideas can change society and allow new standards to enter people's minds. It has always been minorities that have significantly influenced the social system with new ideas. Often, this creates difficult situations, for one has to take responsibility for one's ideas, account for them, and be prepared to suffer personal disadvantage. Previously, such people were burnt for their heretical ideas; today we live in a relatively safe, free-thinking world.

Drive for Spiritual Growth

Interested people start to see that many things are wrong, and that is the point that I have previously mentioned, where the drive for spiritual growth is awakened because one starts to question oneself. This is happening on a wide scale, and can be read about in the media, and we talk of a New Age. The phenomenon that we are questioning as a society is an alarm signal in the context of psychosynthesis.

It is an alarm signal, because something is now starting to grow out of mankind itself, otherwise these ideas would not appear in the mass media; at the most they would be published in philosophical books. Mankind is striving for new insights, sensing that something is not right. How quickly solutions can be found is another matter, but what is happening is organic, something healthy and something that will change history in a relatively short time from a historical perspective. So the way that individuals can change in a matter of weeks will change humanity in a matter of decades – because one can honestly say that we have made massive mistakes, and that many things need to be changed.

In my evaluation of the world based on its symptoms, here I will use the same prerequisite as Assagioli did with people. He said that each person is a universe that is healthy in itself because it functions, and I assume that mankind is healthy, even if it has created many problems. Now, where it is starting to realise this, it is healthy. Of course, there are also people who are negative about everything, but they too are necessary. There are even people who recognise that mistakes have been made, who proclaim this loudly and clearly and create anxiety.

We live in very interesting times, and never before have so many people been interested in astrology during its entire history.

In the early days of astrology, it was the preserve of a few members of the upper classes, for they made the decisions. It used to be a well-protected science; today astrology is accessible to all.

We should take a positive view of this beautiful world in which we live and recognise that man and therefore his world is healthy although not everything is running as smoothly as it might.

□ □ □ □ □

The Moon in the Twelve Houses

Louise Huber

First published in 'Astrolog' Issues 144-147, March – September 2005

In this article we describe the different positions of the Moon in the twelve houses. This was done for the Sun and Saturn in *The Planets and their Psychological Meaning*, also for the Moon in the zodiac signs.

The Threefold Personality

Before looking at the detail of the Moon in the houses, we briefly summarise what we mean by the "threefold personality". In this structure the Moon represents the emotional-feeling self; it has a connecting function because of its central position. So it is important for us to consider the three levels of life experience, or selves, on which our personality is anchored. We distinguish between:

1. The physical self: Saturn
2. The emotional-feeling self: Moon
3. The autonomous-thinking self: Sun

These three areas of experience of the self are relatively easy to understand for our normal human consciousness. They are immediately understandable and enlightening because they are organic. We can all sense them in ourselves and find them to be real. You can read more about them in *Astrological Psychosynthesis* Part 2 "Personality and Integration" and in *The Planets and their Psychological Meaning*.

The Physical Self: Saturn

In the structure of the threefold personality, Saturn represents the physical self, or physical awareness. Saturn has always been considered as the principle of form, of delimitation. Physicality is a limited form and is the visible, material part of our personality structure. We can see and touch the body. The skin outlines its form and forms a boundary against the environment. As well as being able to touch and feel, it also has a protective function.

The Emotional-Feeling Self: Moon

The second level is the emotional world, which can be compared to water. Our Moon self is reflected in it, as is everything to do with our emotions. In this article, we describe the position of the Moon in three areas of each house. On the feeling level, everything is experienced in a subjective way. We need lively contact, relationships, love, harmony and beauty around us. Only then do we feel loved, accepted and cared for.

The Autonomous-Thinking Self: Sun

Unlike the Moon, the Sun radiates its own light. It is autonomous and does not need acknowledgement from anyone. The conscious self can say "I think therefore I am". This self is the "ego on the mental level", i.e. pure self-awareness and therefore the most important element of the personality.

Position in the Houses

One of the most productive ways of interpreting the planets and especially the ego planets is their position in the house system. This starts at the ascendant with the first house and goes in an anticlockwise direction around the zodiac. From a psychological point of view, the houses represent environmental influences and are depicted around the outer edge of the horoscope. They represent twelve areas of experience that we live through daily, and where we have to prove ourselves. They show our acquired behaviour patterns shaped by environmental influences, which we can consciously deploy in life with the help of our horoscope.

Three Areas in one House: Cardinal, Fixed, Mutable

From experience, we know that it is not enough just to describe the planets in a house. An accurate description of the planets can only be obtained by sub-dividing each house into three areas. Attributing one of the three cross qualities (cardinal, fixed, mutable) to each area aids interpretation and the intensity curve, described in *The Astrological Houses*, also helps us to evaluate the three areas.

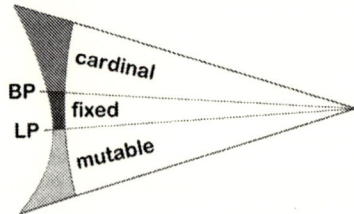

To obtain this differentiated interpretation of the planets, we subdivide each house into three areas. The first extends from the house cusp to the balance point (house size times 0.382), and is related to the cardinal principle. This is the strongest position for the Sun, which corresponds to the cardinal principle. The next area from balance point to low point corresponds to the fixed principle. Here Saturn is at its strongest as the fixed principle is saturnine. The area from the low point to the next house cusp corresponds to the mutable quality, comparable to the quality of the Moon. This is also called the stress area of the house, because planets situated there have to serve two rulers. In the Huber method, we work with the so-called dynamic house system in which the next house already starts [psychologically] at the low point, so there is a double function until the next house cusp.

Overlapping

In the following descriptions of the Moon in the three areas, we can assume that the described properties can also be felt in the other areas. The area boundaries are not abrupt, there is always some overlap. We should also not forget that the sign in which the Moon is situated also affects the interpretation, and in the process we should note whether this is compatible with the area as far as cross and temperament are concerned. Last, but not least, every astrologer should refine the interpretation still further by referring to the whole horoscope.

MOON   The Emotional-Feeling Self

As mentioned above, the second level of our three-fold personality is the emotional world, comparable to water. Here is reflected our feeling self and everything that appeals to our emotions. The reproductive or sex drive is associated with the Moon as the contact planet. The Moon drives us to connect with a You, a loved one. On this emotional level, our experience is subjective. We need living contact, relationships, love, harmony and beauty around us. Only then do we feel loved, accepted and cared for. We do not perceive ourselves on the emotional level without contact, the environment and other people. If someone approaches us openly and warmly, we rejoice and are happy; if we go unnoticed and are ignored, our feeling self suffers.

The feeling level is a world of opposites. Feelings of joy and pain, of sympathy and antipathy ebb and flow, symbolised by the changing Moon phases. The Moon has no light of its own; only the light received from the Sun makes it visible. There are new Moons, full Moons and positions in between. Nothing is stable, all is in flux. Our feeling self is just the same, depending on sign and house position, it is unstable, changeable, moody and dependent on the environment. We want to be loved, acknowledged and admired by others.

We are afraid of being alone and of having to live without love. If we are left alone, our reactions are often negative, dismissive, cold-hearted or too subjective, i.e. egocentric. We have often hurt other people in the process and it is our fault that they left us.

The Moon's position in the horoscope tells us how we react to the ups and downs and the opposites on this level. Do we swing from one extreme to the other, from activity to passivity, from love to hate, from attraction to rejection, or do we remain serene? Do we lose ourselves completely in other people because we are emotionally dependent and don't want to grow up? How do we cope with disappointments in love? Do we still believe in love despite negative experiences and remain sociable and able to love, or do we close up and become embittered and plot revenge? Do we learn from experience and try to escape from this swinging to and fro and gain some stability and balance? What consequences do we draw from the pairs of opposites and how do we overcome the subjectivity of the feeling self? All these questions are answered when we look at the position of the Moon in the horoscope, where we can learn about the person's sociability.

Moon in the 1ˢᵗ House

In the first house of self-manifestation, the Moon reacts subjectively and selfishly. It does everything it can to be loved. This Moon position produces a restless nature, continually yearning for change, depending on the sign quality.

In the cardinal area of the first house, the self-portrayal is that of: "a good, sweet person; come to me and be nice to me". A person with this Moon position knows instinctively that they need people's love to survive. They therefore go all out to gain sympathy, are sweet and adaptable, so that they get what they need emotionally. The Moon self in the first house learns to pick up on other people's signals and to react to them so that things go well for them. In the cardinal area, depending on the impulse energy, there are very often ulterior motives involved. The Moon self is busy with its own needs, feelings and desires, so it is difficult to see others objectively. In extreme cases, depending on sign and aspects, these people focus so much on their own needs that they are unable to behave altruistically. Everything revolves around them, making them develop narcissistic traits.

In the fixed area, the Moon self looks for security. If it is trusted, it feels reassured and thrives, approaches others with sensitivity and can empathise with them. It has a kind of childlike openness that attracts others. Its own feelings are strong and unchanging, depending on the sign. However, someone with this Moon position is also adaptable and good company. He has a sense of which contacts can bring him something and also feels in danger if something is not in order. Although liking to talk fancifully about himself, he is also a good listener, according to the sign. But if someone doubts or mistrusts him, he retreats. The trust placed in him by other people is extremely important for his well-being, and possible misunderstandings must be eliminated again and again.

At the low point of the first house, the Moon becomes "invisible"; it retreats and avoids close contact, afraid of being hurt. It cannot tolerate the pain of rejection, coldness or feeling exposed as they make it suffer deeply. It will also show this pain, either as self-pity or by reacting sensitively to everything. Depending on sign, it is easily offended, accuses other people and likes to talk at length about its emotional experiences and about how badly it has been treated.

In the mutable area, it is very changeable. As the Moon is a mutable principle, moods do not last long here. A person with the Moon in the stress area before the second house is never in a bad mood for long, especially if his self-esteem is boosted. He quickly cheers up if praised and told he is good at something. He cannot stay in the background for long, for he is only really in touch with himself when others pay attention to him. He is always courting love and attention, either by doing nice things for people or by declaring his longing for affection. His love usually has selfish overtones, but he is unable to believe this as he wants to see himself as worthy of being loved. Depending on the sign, love does motivate much of what he does though. He needs relationships with other people who confirm his existence through their friendliness, esteem and love.

The transformed Moon is freed from the immature longing to use other people to satisfy his feelings. He has realised that he must take responsibility for his own feelings, and must first show love and understanding to others before they can reciprocate.

Moon in the 2nd House

The Moon, the feeling self, looks for encounters and needs to experience itself through others. The fixed principle of the second house reduces its ability to make contact spontaneously. It feels the need to control relationships according to standards of quantity. That is why it is cautious in encounters, for this gives a boundary to protect its security. The way this manifests psychologically is that the person places conditions on potential encounters. That can restrict emotional and contact needs,

Moon landscape

particularly when this Moon is in a mutable sign. It is well known that it is oriented towards this kind of contact and in the fixed second house one cannot do as one pleases due to the need for security.

In the cardinal area, feelings are dependent on ideas and criteria. Feelings of affection can only really develop when all is in order and there are no disturbing factors to be afraid of. So the Moon sets conditions for security, which usually, depending on sign, must be met by acquisition and provision of material means. He is concerned that the people he meets should not jeopardise his own resources, and if possible should help to increase them. If advantages can be expected from a relationship, the feeling self unfolds itself with passion and is devoted, loyal and always available. If acknowledgement and security are lacking, then the feelings cool and complaints and reproaches are made and new conditions are set that must be met.

In the fixed area of the second house, the Moon is usually possessive towards people it loves and whom it has allowed into its personal space. If it also lies in a fixed sign, those people are in a way assimilated into the person's existence and from then on belong to him. A symbiotic claim can easily arise, leading to clinginess. Such a person has great trouble detaching themselves and giving other people freedom. This emotional inflexibility in the fixed area of the house makes the person very dependent on emotional habits.

Especially **at the low point** relationships should always follow similar patterns. Depending on sign, emotional satisfaction can only occur through controlled repetition of experiences. If relationships are not structured as he would like, emotional rigidity can result. He feels cheated of pleasure, leading to emotional frustration.

In the mutable area, the stress area before the third house cusp, the feeling self must serve two masters, the fixed second house and the mutable third house. The Moon finds this very unsettling; it has to deal with changes but it still tries to avoid them. It is torn in two directions, loses strength and stability and becomes impressionable. As the mutable principle, it has more affinity with the third house and gives the impression of being unreliable. A possible compensation is following current trends; he does something because most others are doing it. If he is conditioned by collective norms, he will frequently change his mind. If he is more determined by the fixed principle, he can stubbornly and conservatively defend old values.

A transformed Moon has savoured many things; it is satisfied and has no more needs. He trusts himself and the goodness of nature and knows that he has enough to satisfy everyone's needs. He gives as much as he can.

Moon in the 3rd House

As a mutable principle, the Moon is in its element in the mutable third house. The feeling self tends to reflect everything in its vicinity, it identifies with the everyday environment, with the banalities and everyday tasks of life. This naturally includes (depending on sign quality) a strong bond with people around, such as siblings and relatives. Love and loyalty, adaptation, real openness – sometimes too much – are characteristic. The person is easily influenced in the early years, gullible as a child, believing everything she is told. She thinks that if others see things in a certain way, they must be right.

There is an evident dependency on collective thought, plus an openness and a need to always have someone to share impressions with. She is talkative and tends to confide in the wrong people, who often use information given in confidence against her. Tension aspects often show this kind of disappointing experience, which is why she must learn to discriminate and know when to hold her tongue. This is after all the house of learning, where we accumulate experience and knowledge; but this Moon position does not guarantee that she learns from them, or develops the ability to discriminate.

In the cardinal area of the third house the Moon is hyperactive (depending on sign), always looking for new people and new opportunities to learn. She is never still, always on the go (usually on short trips), running around and always busy, be it with everyday tasks or devouring books or meeting lots of people, so that she is constantly learning new things. She approaches people and wants to learn something from them and keep up to date. This can be advantageous for a journalist, who can get what she wants from others thanks to her sympathetic, innocent and open manner, i.e. she gets them to tell her things that they would not normally share so quickly with others.

In the fixed area the need for security prevails. The Moon loses some of its spontaneity, making her less likely to approach others; she has finally learnt a little reserve. However, she still wants contact with her fellows, needs them to talk about her experiences and what moves her emotionally, but other people often don't realise this.

Especially **at the low point**, she does not easily inspire trust in her immediate circle. She does not present herself in the right way and has trouble clearly expressing things as they actually are. The verbally oriented Gemini house with its tendency to be conceptual is not really compatible with the emotional quality of the Moon. That is why the knowledge and intelligence here is often too generalised and diffuse. Depending on the sign, what she says appears to be rather vague, unsure, too general or schematic. As a result, the truth is not very accurately grasped or passed on.

In the mutable (stress) area, we find compensation mechanisms. Some people make a great effort with their family and children, in others the imagination can become fanciful, which can be fascinating for the purposes of written or poetic expression, but slightly dangerous. When it comes to describing facts, the truth is often misrepresented. If another aspect of Mercury (ruler of Gemini) is also involved, this can easily degenerate into falsehoods or lies. Often such a person just does not realise that she relays things incorrectly. In classical astrology, tension aspects between Mercury and the Moon are indeed known as lying aspects. She does not choose her words carefully enough and therefore runs the risk of being misunderstood. In the representation of events from the past, the subjective Moon impression all too easily takes over and objective clarity soon disappears. She is rebuked by the environment and is no longer taken seriously.

A transformed Moon in the third house is concerned with self control, is able to observe itself and to try to see and describe reality as it really is. It is then able to be creative and can relay knowledge and impressions accurately and in an interesting way.

Moon in the 4th House

As ruler of the sign of Cancer, the Moon is at home in the fourth house. The Moon is the child, a subjective being that is influenced by the environment, particularly emotionally. Relatives are the priority in the fourth house experience. There is an intense emotional relationship with them, be it good or bad. In the fourth house, the gift of fantasy is extraordinarily rich; it operates in the world of symbols and creates from archetypal depths. The Moon near the IC (collective area) enables archetypal and collective-unconscious material to be brought to the surface.

In the cardinal area, the main experience of the Moon is in the collective and the family, which are intended to nourish its feelings of belonging. It clings to these people and does all it can for them. They are its natural protection against the outside world, and a person with this Moon position must always feel safe and protected in their nest. However, the Moon as the changeable principle is not able to guarantee that in this house. If there is a danger of losing the home, the feeling self seizes up in advance. If such a person ever has to go far away from home, he suffers badly from homesickness. Depending on sign, this Moon reacts very sensitively to emotional insecurity or changes. He only loves those who belong to him, clings to them, while treating strangers with suspicion. Just as the child loves his environment from a very early age and rejects anything outside it, these people's reactions in emotional relationships will be like this for a lifetime.

In the fixed area, primal human needs for protection, affection and warmth are particularly pronounced. Insecurity and unfulfilled desires destroy faith in life. He has particularly strong subjective reactions to affection, rejection or neglect. In the fixed area, his priority is also protecting himself against strangers. He only accepts those he knows well; anyone else is rejected. At most they are checked over, to see if they are worth getting to know. These values are established subjectively in early childhood and from then on are applied to all encounters with others. These are the roots of chauvinism and xenophobia.

On the other hand, someone with this Moon will not forget emotional experiences; they are retained in the well of memory. If they were negative experiences, he will talk about them repeatedly and burden loved ones with them. If something has not gone right in the family, they are usually made painfully aware of it, much more consciously than if something had not gone right in the third house.

A Moon **at the low point** clings to existing relationships. It is afraid of falling out of the warm nest and remains childlike for as long as possible. It never stops longing for protection and expects or requires eternal emotional devotion. Although it clings to the trusted environment, it also has to grow up. At the fourth house low point all experiences go very deep. An emotional injury from childhood can last a lifetime. The roots of depressive moods are also found here. At the low point, the Moon is pulled into the centre of being, there it must give up subjectivity, give itself security and find protection in its core being.

In the mutable area, the Moon becomes lighter and more independent. The feeling self does not want to be held back forever, it is already looking towards the fifth house where it can make its own experiences. But nevertheless, the Moon is still connected to the fourth house and oscillates between the feeling of wanting to be free and the need to retain the security of the bosom of the family. His own self-worth is dependent on the people he loves, and he wants to be with them forever. The appearance of rivals is viewed with jealousy, and if they do appear they are intimidated by threats and chased away. If he is left anyway, his world collapses.

The transformed Moon will have to learn that he cannot own other people. He must give them freedom otherwise they will leave. Childish expectations are converted into creative visions.

Moon in the 5th House

The Moon self is also the child self, which has its territory here in the fifth house. Here we want to remain as children and often refuse to grow up. Depending on the sign, we don't want to take responsibility for ourselves and would rather lean on someone strong. On the other hand, being childlike means remaining young and gives the possibility of being creative. The fifth house is indeed in this sense the playing field on which we should cavort and react spontaneously. In the field of creative education, we have discovered that creativity is attained by cultivating this carefree childlike awareness. Creativity therefore has an affinity with the fifth house. Having the courage to experiment, to react spontaneously and to take risks all encourage creativity. It is essential to overstep boundaries here.

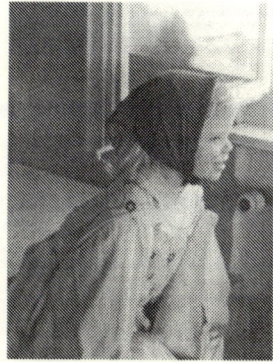

In the cardinal area, she wants to experience relationships or the experience of love in quite a specific way. She reacts subjectively and wilfully. Inner impulses run in quite a specific direction and also have an important role to play in sexual matters. With the Moon in the fifth house reflexes and controlling behaviour in relationships are typical. For without a certain amount of standardised behaviour, she cannot keep her "love life" under control. She should be able to trust certain reflexes, otherwise each time she is in a new situation, she must first think about what she should do and how she should behave. Not everyone can handle such a complicated way of experiencing relationships. It is therefore good to have templates, but these of course harbour tricky traps. One can react stereotypically, but comes across as affected and phoney.

With the **Moon in the Fixed Area** there is a contradiction. The motivation of the fifth house is for security and boundary setting, but it also involves spontaneous reactions, caused by the Moon and the fire temperament. Spontaneity, emotional changeability, adaptation and intuition are quite the opposite of conservative. Such feelings are always trying to assert themselves. However, the fixed principle is stronger in this area. Sexual matters are also included here, which naturally has certain rules, partly innate and partly acquired. There is no area of human nature where stereotypical behaviour plays such an important role as here. Let us just think of the impulses responsible for sexual arousal. These impulses are totally individual. They are determined by the positions of Mars, Venus and the Moon and are essentially the product of childhood experiences. They are then further shaped by morality and in the course of a lifetime they create an emotional dependency on these reflex templates.

At the low point the emotional templates according to which relationships must proceed assume a definitive form, which cannot easily be broken out of. Dissolving such structures later on means a lot of work. It requires careful self-observation and much effort to break loose from these forms engraved in consciousness. The automatic nature of the reflexes makes critical self-reflection difficult. Although she has habitually reacted in a certain way, this can also be wrong – and in certain situations she may lose touch with reality. Reactions may sometimes be inappropriate, but they are automatic. She wonders what other people say about her, or how strangely they behave, not at all nicely, and the Moon naturally makes her contrite. After all, she needs other people's love and approval to meet her needs.

In the mutable area, feelings are compensative; she is often devoted and self-sacrificing and does a lot for those she loves in order to be loved in return. That is why she often feels used or abused. The problem lies in striking a balance between altruism and egotism. Some people do everything to gain other people's favour, humiliating themselves to avoid losing love. Faced with conflict, they back down so as not to provoke the anger of their adversary. They are afraid of doing something wrong and often do things that they should not do or promise to do things they cannot do.

Depending on whether spiritual planets are connected to it before the sixth cusp, **the transformed Moon** can here sublimate subjective motivations into a higher motivation of helping and healing.

Moon in the 6th House

With the contact self in the You area, we are emotionally focussed on those around us. The sensitive feeling self picks up the smallest nuances of mood in the environment. That is why the Moon will often suffer in this house, because it reacts to everything that touches it; it is often abandoned by the environment without protection.

The person with this Moon position is mainly interested in other people, has a humanitarian outlook, is helpful, ready to serve and able to create a friendly and humanitarian atmosphere, to improve the workplace so that everyone feels good. The productivity of this house is of less importance than personal relationships. Social injustice can burden the subjective Moon self unduly, even hurt it; he takes everything personally, but puts himself out for the wellbeing of others. Someone with this Moon position should use their special sensitivity in a caring, social or healing profession.

In the cardinal area he relies on and listens to his feelings. He would like to do what interests him most, what fascinates him, what he enjoys and what he reacts spontaneously to. He has a natural willingness to serve, can offer positive support to other people, by focussing on them emotionally and being there for them, particularly in times of need. Helping others is the greatest fulfilment for this Moon position. It is the best way for the feeling self to affirm itself. However, this can become a "helper syndrome".

In the fixed area the contact self does not react so spontaneously, and is more subject to the duty mechanisms of this house. He then suffers from the pressure or constant demands of the environment and feels used. On the other hand, with this Moon position, he is always ready to take everything on himself, to sacrifice himself for others and carry their burden. His self esteem, even his reason for living, depends on how much he is needed. If this is not valued he is deeply hurt. So he is also dependent on relationships with work colleagues and the behaviour of his superiors. If there are problems here, he suffers spiritually and may become ill, because the sixth house is clearly prone to psychosomatic processes.

At the low point, depending on sign, he passively allows himself to be used, offering no resistance. If he loves another person, he does all he can not to lose them; he does what they want, easily making him a victim of the environment or of his need for affection. If he has nobody to care for, he feels useless; the feeling self stagnates, leading to depression. Also at work, he does all he is asked to do, he is servile, subservient and allows himself to be used. Such a person can easily develop psychosomatic illnesses, for in a way he takes the suffering of the environment upon himself. He often believes that the suffering of others is his own. It is hard to set boundaries between himself and others. Sometimes such a Moon absorbs the disagreements of the environment. This is the wrong kind of pity, which increases suffering by doubling it.

In the mutable area, the Moon wants to learn a lot. He has a strong interest in people and relationships. This is what pushes him again and again to look for new contacts, because it is fascinating for him to learn from them and to be creative. In a form of compensation, he wants to attract other people's attention by any means possible, by doing everything he can to make himself liked. He has the urgent desire to be seen as a loveable and good person by the You and does all he can to create this impression. He has the feeling that this is the only way that the contact self can exist.

The transformed Moon functions correctly when it is a catalyser for the suffering of others, without being burdened by it. He shouldn't count on feedback (e.g. gratitude), as transformation themes require him to renounce praise so that the subjective Moon self is freed from ego desires.

Moon in the 7th House

Our feeling and contact self feels at home in the contact area of the horoscope. The whole You field is available to it, for the seventh house is associated with relationships that have a legal character, into which the Moon enters playfully. However, it is hard for the Moon to take real responsibility for the You with which it is connected. As long as all goes well, and the Moon gains enjoyment and wellbeing from the relationship, it reveals its best qualities. As soon as something goes wrong, and it is not loved or spoilt as much as the childlike Moon self would like, the Moon will complain, feel aggrieved and move on to other relationships.

In the cardinal area contacts will not be lacking. On the contrary, the Moon will throw itself into changing relationships and accept every self affirmation with joy. It can adapt spontaneously to the current situation and nearly always reacts appropriately. At the cusp of the seventh house, it has an excessive need for stimulation and social interaction and is therefore dependent on it. She cannot resist the intensity of her feelings and always finds someone who can satisfy her desires. Here too there is great manipulative ability, it is however not, as in the case of the Sun, used to achieve common goals, but for the purpose of satisfying personal desires and wishes.

In the fixed area, the Moon will have more self-restraint; it seeks security and subjective pleasure, until the you-affirmation is completely exhausted, hence its intense dependence on a relationship, in which it is ready to give everything that it itself needs: love, understanding, tenderness and dependency. But here too a conscious or unconscious egoism is at work, i.e. the wish that everything she gives will be returned to her in abundance. Even with the spontaneous Moon, she must accept this selfish motivation, otherwise she is not being honest with herself. Who is not looking for selfish protection from a partner, who does not want to be protected and feel safe in a relationship? In principle, every relationship in the seventh house has some kind of legal character, and is governed by some kind of contract or agreement. The Moon must therefore accept this fact and still be ready for love, even if it is disappointed. It is nearly always its own projections and insecurities that are reflected in the partnership and in other relationships that make it suffer. Realising this is difficult for the Moon self though, because it can only experience itself in projection, in its reflection in other people.

Especially **at the low point**, the Moon must collect its wits and evolve. Constantly courting sympathy for herself does not work here. She must take rejection in her stride and think deeply about communication, about giving and taking, about the laws of exchange and equal rights in partnership. Injured vanity, pride and broken relationships affect the spiritual balance and it is hard to restore the You's damaged trust. Without a basic transformation of life motivation, it cannot usually be done.

In the mutable area the Moon initially has a compensative function. In the shadow of cusp eight, it tends to take advantage of others. This Moon is constantly looking for sympathy. It is often extremely personable, and adapts itself to requirements only in order to complain about it later. It likes to blame other people and justifies itself enthusiastically to other people. It is always dealing with people, and is also involved in bringing people together or reuniting them. There is often an obsessive drive to make contact, to experience new relationships and then to run away, continually changing. That can even lead to a loss of self on the part of the Moon, especially when the Sun is not in a very strong position in the horoscope. There is also a danger of the loss of self when all three ego planets are in the You area, particularly in stressful situations. Where there are hard aspects to the Moon, there is an intriguing tendency to burden emotional bonds with unresolved psychic factors that already belong to the eighth house.

The transformed Moon in the seventh house will take responsibility for its relationships. It is better able to cope with its own feelings and no longer burdens the You with unfulfilled wishes and infantile addictions. This is also demonstrated by the fact that it cares about the wellbeing of others, thinks first of the You and only then thinks of itself. It must be honest and show its true colours and admit and transform its dependencies and expectations.

Moon in the 8ᵗʰ House

This Moon position would like to be popular with everyone. He can easily adapt if necessary, is conciliatory, friendly and tries to make sure that every contact situation goes as well as possible. Emotions are kept hidden and under control until he is sure that others are worthy, decent and reliable. Expressions of emotion often seem studied and clichéd. The flexibility and spontaneity of the Moon as feeling and contact self are reduced in this fixed house, where, particularly in childhood, it must totally adapt to prevailing behavioural structures, which restricts its ability to socialise. It is also dependent on internal and external pressures, on sympathy and aversion and controlled by prohibitions or the desire to take advantage. The childlike feeling self is here at the mercy of the rules and conventionality of the collective, the social environment, finding it difficult to disregard them. If someone with this Moon position breaks out of the established order, everyone attacks him. He must be friendly, kind and nice so that nobody can hold anything against him; everyone is inspired by him and thinks he is great.

In the cardinal area emotions are turned actively outwards and are especially responsive to useful contacts. Although controlled, the amount of friendliness and openness shown is always dictated by the environment. If the other is helpful, the feeling self will devote itself fully and sensitively to them. If someone is not helpful, they will be punished, usually by the withdrawal of love. Judgements here are almost always subjective. If we have something to reproach others for, if they have not been decent and friendly, the feeling self can just as easily turn away and close up. If relationships are excessively one-sided, it soon loses patience. The give and take must remain in a state of flux. In the eighth house the feeling self is strongly influenced by the economic principle of supply and demand. It does not just want to give, but also to take. Love, money, sympathy, increased wellbeing, relationships with a good "fit" and a quick return on investment are the ideal concepts of this Moon. It instinctively attracts to itself everything it can have, has a particular ability to turn situations to its own advantage. Depending on sign and aspects, there is a danger of manipulating the You and twisting laws so that they work to one's own advantage. Such people are capable of deceiving others in order to get what they want, and there is always a price to be paid. Usually, in the eighth house, the bill for improper behaviour is settled later. In this "karmic field", everyone gets what they deserve in the end.

In the fixed area, possessiveness and a tendency to acquisitiveness due to security motivations play an important, if often unconscious, role. The Moon would like to benefit as much as possible from the laws, structures and people he knows. With cleverness, sometimes even by unfair means, this Moon is able to get ahead in life. He believes he can gain advantage using the existing laws, without making any effort himself. In traditional astrology, the eighth house is also associated with money that has not been earned, e.g. inheritances, gifts, disability pension, etc.

The nearer the Moon is to the low point, the more such a person has the feeling that he does not have enough, does not possess what is apparently due to him, and that he should therefore take all he can. If he has to renounce contact, love and the praise due to him, he plots revenge. The vindictiveness of the eighth house is well known, as is its jealousy. In situations of acute rivalry, he begrudges others their enjoyment of life, advantages, love and sympathy. Some wait a lifetime for an inheritance and gamble it away. Meanwhile, others must give up, sell out to benefactors and let themselves be exploited or misused by those they love. Most people with Moon in the fixed area of the eighth house confuse possession with love and have a money problem. Depending on sign and aspects, they want more than they have and suffer from constant jealousy. That is why they also experience many rejections, restrictions and limitations, which should stabilise the capricious feeling self.

At the low point the Moon is sandwiched between contradictory structures and attitudes, which can often make it difficult to relate to others. Although it does manage to make contacts, this Moon remains lonely on the inside. At the low point it is influenced by the transforming forces of the inner self, which call for introspection. Here he is often frustrated and discouraged; his own inadequacies, calculated approach and desires for profit rebound on him. The boomerang effect comes into force, separating him from people on whom he depends and whom he himself has frustrated or misunderstood. That is why he usually suffers from the fear of loss, that people he trusts will leave him or that positions or functions could be taken away from him. But the very nature of the self is transformed here too; even the Moon cannot escape the death and rebirth process of this purification field. That usually requires expansion, transgression and a casting off of the protective and yet restricting skin of a previously attained state. We may have reached this state by belonging to an influential community, a particular worldview or to individuals we love. This means that in the eighth house, we must give up our emotional dependence on apparent securities, e.g. societal structures, clinging to loved ones, material wellbeing, opinions, regulations, taboos, etc. In letting go of these things, we broaden our consciousness and our spiritual capacity expands into a constantly growing whole. In this transformation process, the feeling self has the impression that it is at one with creation.

In the mutable area the Moon has a particular aptitude for learning. Experiences are reflected, processed and relayed. In the shadow of the ninth cusp, the experience of the Moon in the stress area is compensative. In both social and romantic relationships there is an underlying motivation for security and profit-mindedness, along with the claims for freedom and independence of the ninth house. Previously established contacts are clung to frantically and anxiously. He watches over the other so that they do not escape, and imposes regulations and restrictions on them, while taking advantage of all possible freedoms for himself. The compensation hides his own inability, and he claims the right to use or abuse others' means. The appropriation of other people's things is the problem, above all if they are used as his own. When the great transformation begins, he is usually left alone and without resources, and it becomes very clear which real resources are actually at his disposal.

The transformed Moon is purified and transformed by the cleansing process of the eighth house. It will now only serve the truth and advocates justice and freedom, authenticity and honesty. In the transformation process it has liberated itself from the different pseudo-self forms of its emotional nature, so that it is now able to work on transpersonal tasks with love and devotion.

Moon in the 9th House

As a mutable principle, the Moon has an affinity with the mutable ninth house. This Moon is spontaneous, stimulating and lively. In the house of independent thought, subjective emotional preferences influence most thought processes and judgements. Love, not autonomy, is its strength. It is fickle, interested in everything, pursues every thought, lets itself be distracted, is dissipated, absent-minded and busy with many different things, not just those it has a duty to fulfil. A person with this Moon position is interested in foreign countries and inspired by large-scale ideals transcending the mundane. But when it comes to actually putting things into practice, depending on sign or aspects, it is equally quick to move on.

In the cardinal area it is alert and active, has a broad range of interests and takes a keen interest in everything. It is also adaptable and loves to live footloose and fancy-free, to enjoy freedom and likes to be influenced spontaneously. It loves to travel and would like to be in many places at the same time. It is always dreaming of foreign lands, of the people it could love and paints a picture of the world as it would like it to be. It sometimes lets itself be carried away, pursues false ideals and is then often disappointed. It loves things that make life enjoyable. It often makes subjective judgements and is only interested in itself and its own enjoyment, but afterwards it can quickly change and work very devotedly for humanitarian ideals.

In the fixed area it is able to separate itself more effectively from the mutable quality. It is looking for security by trying to discover or feel out the true nature of both itself and other people. It intuitively knows the laws of life and constantly seeks personal growth. Broadening of the emotional nature is its principal and greatest need. Travelling abroad and making contact with people from other countries and with unusual people allow it to do this. It is interested in everything that makes life worth living, looks for harmony and connections in togetherness, can daydream, talk and think about ideas and ideals for hours on end, and depending on sign or aspects, reflect upon them. It is very selective. Although basically liking coming into contact with new people, it does tend to seek out friends and contacts who are on a high spiritual level.

At the low point it can close up, cling to principles, reiterate truisms, stubbornly champion false ideas and concoct a "pocketbook philosophy" that it brings up at every appropriate and not so appropriate opportunity. But then it loses credibility with the environment, especially when ideas borrowed from the collective are involved. He too must undergo the transformation of the self at the low point; he should develop his own depths and values, so that he can be more his own person. He often feels misunderstood, expresses himself awkwardly, clumsily and, depending on sign or aspects, is emotionally inept. But the point here is to extract the deeper meaning from this house.

In the mutable area, in the shadow of the MC, a compensative attitude towards relationships leads the Moon to develop an exaggerated sense of its own importance. The Moon is all about having intense relationships with the environment. Such a Moon must have many contacts one after the other, not at the same time. The demanding and intense way he relates to people can be overpowering, and often egocentric, depending on sign and aspects. He always needs somebody and always manages to find somebody. Above all, he wants to be loved and admired, so puts a lot of effort into being important and popular. The best compensation for this Moon is on the stage. Many actors have Moon before or after the MC. They play their role as well as possible, sometimes even outstandingly, because they need others to feel validated.

The transformed Moon in the ninth house feels a deep love for all living things, for nature and for the whole of creation. The transpersonal life sense of this house can allow the Moon to become a real philanthropist. The subjective Moon self can transform itself and find security in higher consciousness. Teachers with this Moon position win the hearts of their pupils; they are particularly valued because they are able to relate to and inspire children in a way few others can.

Moon in the 10th House

As the reflecting principle and the feeling self, the Moon is not so readily able to cope with the demands of the tenth house, because it cannot adopt the position of the Sun. The Moon will not be able to replace the Sun without outside help, i.e. planetary connections supporting the Moon. The Moon is naturally a fickle element that is buffeted by environmental influences, making it unsuited to pursuing the clear goal-setting required in the tenth house. It cannot remain constantly at the planning stage, hence the frequent appearance of uncertainties with respect to career direction and social position, as well as a certain changeability and moodiness.

The tenth house requires inner strength, integrity and steadfastness from a self-contained personality. The Moon, on the other hand, is looking for love, adoration, help and approval. That is why this Moon is often afflicted by a desire for popularity that drives their whole personality. She is capable of pushing herself to the limit in an inspired and brilliant way in order to gain applause.

In the cardinal area, the contact self can adapt to any situation. Active intervention and rapid reactions to favourable opportunities mean that the person makes useful contacts that raise their social status. Here, depending on sign and aspects, they work skilfully and cleverly on those around them to ensure approval. They usually succeed for a while, but not in the long run. If they are criticised or fail, they quickly give up and "throw in the towel". As friends they are very popular; they are witty and funny and cheer up those around them. Depending on sign and aspects, they can win others over by flattering them and affirming their uniqueness. Many actors have this Moon position, an association noted in traditional astrology.

In the fixed area she finds that the collective is a variable factor; one cannot have public approval forever. In her efforts to secure the sympathy of the public, family, superiors or those in power, she is afraid of losing them or of losing ground and falling back from the level already reached. That is why she clings to strong people and needs their support, makes compromises and, depending on sign and aspects, even allows herself to be blackmailed. Everywhere she looks for people who will find her good and unique and admire her. That is why she is susceptible to flattery, she needs a role model, someone who will be her rock or set an example that she can emulate.

The fixed area is about looking for something to cling to. The Moon needs support for its affairs. It either finds a strong person, someone in authority, who gives stability to its fickle individual aspirations, or it falls victim to inner fears and insecurities, constantly losing stability because it cannot and will not hold on anywhere. At best, it simulates the security of the tenth house to others. But the nearer the low point, the more dependent it is on approval from the environment.

At the low point of the tenth house, the Moon feels exposed, misunderstood and dependent, but is unable to free itself from this situation. Sometimes feelings of guilt arise if external circumstances hinder the striving for autonomy and, despite good intentions, the desire for popularity makes her dependent, and inner goals are neglected to avoid making waves. So the feeling self must constantly be reoriented inwards, which means renouncing external success. Liberation of the emotional nature from any search for approval on the path to personal inner strength is the goal of this Moon position. This transformation process is helped by any spiritual planets that are connected by aspect.

In the mutable area in the shadow of the eleventh cusp, the Moon as the feeling self also compensates with respect to either pride or high ideals of popularity. Close acquaintances, friends and lovers are the focus of projection of her ideal concept of what people and relationships should be like. She is looking out for special relationships and drops the names of influential people with whom she would like to have a friendly relationship in order to raise her self esteem.

There is often a childlike aspiration to originality, she wants to be as great and famous as those she admires, and to emulate and copy them. However, adorning herself with borrowed plumes is dishonest, leading to the fear that the fraud will be exposed. Nobody can be trusted and she isolates herself out of fear that her helplessness will be discovered and self esteem lost. Here too, it is a question of placing her humble Moon self at the service of a higher task, without turning it into an exercise in self aggrandizement.

The transformed Moon in the tenth house fights for noble humanitarian ideals. Her own authority is used to do good for others and stand up for those in need. Depending on sign and aspects, the desire for popularity is overcome and she rises above any flattery or attacks from the collective, fully absorbed in her task. Here she serves the collective, she wants to do something to make the world a better place and goes about it with passion and commitment.

Moon in the 11th House

The Moon symbolises our feeling self, which wants to feel protected, as though in a cosy nest. It will feel isolated and exposed in the lofty heights of the eleventh house, so quickly seeks out friends to redress the situation. The more he has, the better he feels. The ego requires friendships and several deeper relationships to feel appreciated. The feeling of self-worth is, depending on sign, more or less dependent on how many influential and high-standing friends he has. These should also raise his own status by virtue of their rank and name. Some namedrop that yesterday they had lunch with actress X or professor Y. He therefore associates with influential, powerful personalities to bathe in their reflected glory.

Some find Moon in the eleventh house to be emotionally cold, because there is too much premeditation and too little spontaneity, although naturally the sign also plays a role here. The emotions are contradictory, for on the one hand he needs affection and closeness and to feel accepted and protected, but on the other hand he does not want to give up his individual liberties. This Moon projects the ideal view of what a person should be onto friends, until he is disappointed and understands that ideality must begin with himself.

In the cardinal area, the subjectivity of the Moon is revealed in the desire for autonomy and originality. Most people with the Moon after the eleventh house cusp have a social awareness and feel a calling to support like-minded or disadvantaged people. They promote good ideas and support gifted younger people where they can. They devotedly stand up for their protégés and people affected by pain or injustice. They like to work on the restoration of justice and order. The exhilaration of transcendence makes them receptive to what is good in other people and they enjoy assisting them in a collaborative manner.

For the Moon as feeling self, the quality of human relationships is crucial; he is less interested in identifying with ideas, much more with the people who represent these ideas. He wants friendly, stimulating relationships, nurtures them intensively and is always a good friend in times of need. He likes to work in a team and to feel part of a group. But his need for attachment also makes him really jealous, for he wants to preserve relationships at any cost. In the personal area, this fear of losing loved ones tends to make him clingy. Usually, trust is demanded of those he gets close to. Someone with this Moon position can also (a side that one would hardly have expected from the Moon) become a secret manipulator in the group and pull the strings of sympathy and antipathy in the background. This can have unpleasant consequences, but does not happen without the appropriate aspects.

Defiant behaviour can also be observed. If he does not get something he wants, or has to do something that is beneath him, he entrenches himself behind a mask of arrogance. The desire for freedom, which is so natural for the Sun, often functions in a childish and immature way with the Moon. The elevation and breadth of this house precludes passionate and deep emotions. Love and emotions must have some kind of intellectual foundation. As with the Sun, a noble and pure disposition is the result, a "good soul", who is incapable of thinking bad thoughts and can stride unsullied through the morass of life.

In the fixed area of the eleventh house, personal input in teamwork or within the circle of friends is acknowledged by gratitude. There is a great need for security and the desire for plentiful, optimal reflection. Some make it a point of principle that everyone should be valued. Many feel called upon to make sure that nobody is badly treated, that everyone gets what they need and that the world's resources are shared equally. They fight for the disadvantaged and even suffer with them. At times, people with this Moon position become passionate about religious, fanatical or, in extreme cases, even terrorist ideas. They are seduced by ideal visions of the future and also want to implement ideas that involve great personal sacrifice.

Many are unable to decide whether an idea is right or wrong. If the idea is inspiring and emotionally appealing, he supports it unquestioningly. In this fixed area in a fixed house the Moon is restricted and must stick to the circle of friends to which it belongs and try hard to ensure their support, for only they can satisfy its need for sympathy. But as the Moon is a changeable principle, sympathy can suddenly switch to antipathy. If the group, or part of the group, does something that it does not like, it reacts by exerting organisational or financial control. For example, it takes over the financial management in order to make itself indispensable to others.

At the low point, the feeling self projects onto friends everything that it would like to be, but is unable to. Someone with this Moon position has a fixed, ethical view of their friends, contacts and relationships. If they do not behave as he would like, he closes up or is capable of ending the friendship overnight. As long as his wish projection is fulfilled, he is delighted, because his ideal vision is still intact. If he is disappointed, he clams up and wants nothing more to do with them. If they have behaved wrongly, contravened etiquette or principles, he can be as cold as ice. His emotional devotion dies if his idea is proven to be wrong. He has no more feelings for them, is frustrated and deeply offended that his ideal vision has not been reflected by reality.

As the emotions are also refined and transformed here, selfish emotional concepts must adapt to reality. He must realise that disappointments in friendships are useful for personal development in that they help us to overcome personal subjectivity. Then even the Moon can achieve objectivity, scale the observation post of the eleventh house and gain an overview from which he can issue groundbreaking advice to others. But with the Moon a trace of subjectivity always remains, which is precisely why they give advice to others from this overview situation that they simply do not want. Some interfere in the affairs of others without being asked, force their dogma and help onto others, typical of the so-called "helper syndrome". The lesson to be learned here is that personal ego demands, wishes and projections must be withdrawn and he should cultivate an observant, understanding and forgiving attitude towards friends or peers.

In the mutable area in the shadow of the twelfth cusp, he compensates his demands and ideas onto friends. For example, if someone with this Moon position does something for a friend, he requires just as much if not more in return. Many only associate with people who have something to give materially or spiritually; other people just don't count. The roots of this compensative behaviour lie in childhood. This Moon indicates a lonely child who did not receive enough affection and who now cannot get enough of it.

The unconscious pressure to use friendships for his own ends naturally puts people off and he will eventually be left alone. Although plagued by the fear of losing people he loves and who have given him something, he still makes mistakes with people and is rejected as a result. If he is too demanding and exacting and abuses friendships or relationships for selfish ends, he is quickly dropped and excluded from groups, circles and communities. That is the most painful experience that a Moon can undergo here, at any rate until egocentric, immature actions are sublimated into transpersonal goals.

With **the transformed Moon** in the eleventh house we find real, deep emotional values, which help to create a coexistence based upon a noble, humane ethic. It is all about cultivating true love, tolerance, helpfulness and comprehensive understanding. This usually involves some idealism; he joins forces with others to come nearer to the implementation of the ideal human image through love. Such a Moon strives for unconditional love and believes in human goodness.

Moon in the 12th House

Our feeling self feels an affinity with the water element and need for belonging of the twelfth house. Depending on sign and aspects, there is a tendency to withdraw and retreat if others declare more urgent needs. Such people deliberately put themselves in second place, and accept that their own wishes will not be satisfied if necessary.

Empirical evidence shows that this Moon position indicates a neglected child. It never learnt social skills, because it usually has too little contact with children of its own age, or with anyone at all. Some felt rejected in childhood and that their emotional needs were not understood. Others were pushed aside by the environment for some reason and isolated in a room, where they constructed their own fantasy world, into which they retreated whenever they were let them down by those around them. As a result, it is difficult for such people to fully develop their social skills. Depending on the aspects involved, the lack of human contact during childhood and youth that is nearly always experienced by a twelfth house Moon, frequently also leads to psychic repression with social phobias or inhibitions that are hard to get rid of.

In the cardinal area and on the twelfth cusp, these people are actually aware of their own wishes and needs, but are prepared to give way to others and help them. They usually anticipate the wishes of others even before they think of them themselves. Depending on sign, they are modest and apparently easy to please. Many sacrifice themselves in order to feel valued, as nurse for a doctor, as secretary for a boss, as wife for a husband, even the other way around.

Many become addicted to being needed; the so-called "helper syndrome" is associated with this Moon position. Depending on sign and aspects, they act out of a kind of devoted love, without ever asking for deserved praise. Some look up to others and belittle themselves, because everyone appears to be much too important and unapproachable. They project their own ideas onto others and are disappointed if others do not correspond to their expectations. A very variable position of the Moon, then, encompassing a wide range of possibilities.

In the fixed area people like to cut themselves off; they create a fantasy world into which they can escape if the world outside seems too unkind and they don't want to react. They feel secure in their interior world and, depending on sign and aspects, build there a safe haven where nobody can disturb them. They want to be left in peace to indulge in their own visions, dreams and images. Deep inside they are afraid of rejection, exposure and humiliation, depending on the aspects involved. Many never find the deep contact with people that they passionately crave and fantasise about, but can never bring to fruition. They all too easily feel misunderstood, misjudged and disappointed. In the case of insurmountable problems, others escape into illness in order to gain love and sympathy from the environment.

This introversion is most pronounced **at the low point**. Many do not really come out of their shells and cannot show their feelings. They do not give themselves a chance to get close to people, as they are afraid of losing themselves. Other people comment: "What is the matter with him; he doesn't react correctly at all, in fact he underreacts." There is often a great fear of being hurt and also of devotion. For many, depending on the sign quality, this becomes a fear of contact that stops them from letting others get close to them. Many have never learnt how to make contact spontaneously.

This Moon should work more in the area of love for humanity than love for individuals. Usually, these people are looking for a career in which they can help to implement humanitarian goals. This Moon position is also a good precondition for people who are creative in some way and who do not need to be too interested in detail. The transformation at the low point does not happen by itself though. It is true that the Moon is the childlike feeling self, which is still capable of being very subjective. That is why in the twelfth house she initially feels as though she is placed in a corner, which she does not want to accept and which could be called a "sulky Moon". Depending on sign and aspects this Moon is full of self-pity, and close to the AC narcissistic tendencies can also arise.

In the mutable area, in the shadow of the AC, compensative forces are at work, which the Moon, the most subjective of the ego planets, makes it hard for us to acknowledge. She bullies the environment and projects unfulfilled wishes onto it, leaving others no peace because she so much wants to attract attention by transferring her frustrations onto the world. Such people are hard to please; they always feel like victims, misjudged and getting a raw deal, complaining about the coldness of the environment and feeling misunderstood and unloved. Compensative self-love (narcissism) is most likely refined or transformed by a dramatic love affair with one person. This can lead to the profound fragmentation of the egocentricity and to transformation crises, which the esoteric psychology of Alice Bailey called the "2nd initiation of the baptism" or which Roberto Assagioli called the "dark night of the soul".

The transformed Moon in the twelfth house has undergone this kind of spiritual experience, which allows the development of love as a conscious life motivation, so that such people develop a real helping and healing skill. It is important to clarify whether, in the process, the person is still anchored in the ego level or whether she already has a notion of the transformation into the higher self. Only then can she gain access to universal healing energies that she can use. It is precisely in the twelfth house that she can easily fall victim to self-deception, hence the need for a change of motivation which in the case of the ego planets is always imperative. Only after this will her Moon allow her to access transcendence, the return to the great protection of the state of being. The best way for this Moon to transform is to develop the principle of universal, transpersonal love.

▢ ▢ ▢ ▢ ▢

Lean Years

When Saturn loses its Rings

Bruno Huber

First published in 'Astrolog' Issue 87, August 1995

Saturn, the upholder and securer of our existence, undergoes significant oscillations in brightness and hence visibility from earth. It is currently (August 1995) in its dimmest phase, which always happens when, as now, it transits the sign of Pisces, or that of Virgo.

Previous generations of astrologers, back into antiquity, spoke of "seven fat years and seven lean years", and numerous legends were woven around this phenomenon. The word "lean" indicates that these were understood as seven years of lean living, i.e. poor harvests, poor business, possibly crisis. Although we live in a prosperous society (compared with past centuries), mass psychological symptoms of the fear of the lean years can still be observed today. At these times, most people have a degree of existential angst, whether there are rational reasons for it or not. They think they have to cut back spending on non-essential items and invest their money in material assets.

In this case, there is actually an astronomical law behind the phenomenon. The fat years are the seven bright years of Saturn, which are always followed by seven dim (lean) years. But why does Saturn, to which we attribute steadiness and regularity, show this "temperamental" oscillation?

The famous Dutch astronomer and telescope maker **Huygens** found the solution in 1655. The phenomenon of varying brightness is related to Saturn's rings, whose existence was unknown before Huygens. He discovered that Saturn (in his words translated): "is surrounded by a ring that is flat and unsupported and inclined towards the ecliptic".

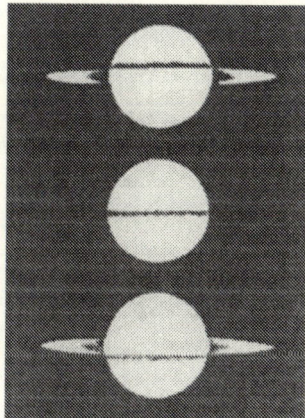

First sighting of Saturn's ring as it disappears and reappears in the hand drawing of Huygens; top: March 1655, centre: January 1656, bottom: October 1656

Nowadays, we are all familiar with the beautiful photos of Saturn provided by space probes: a ball surrounded by a flat ring. Most of these images show it from the same angle – from diagonally above.

This image is not always available to us on Earth though, for in its orbit of the Sun, lasting nearly 30 years (29.457 years), it shows us all its sides. Saturn's axis, around which the planet rotates in 10 hours and 14 minutes, is like the Earth's axis inclined towards the ecliptic (Sun's orbit), which also leads to the existence of seasons. And not only this: its rings are at a right angle to its axis and therefore also form an angle with the ecliptic, i.e. they are highly tilted in our line of sight.

Reflections

During its orbit of the Sun, Saturn's axis remains firmly aligned to the signs of Gemini and Sagittarius. **Saturn's Equinoxes and Solstices** (cardinal points) therefore do not lie in the cardinal cross but **in the mutable cross.**

If now in its passage it arrives in Sagittarius, we see its rings in the greatest possible inclination from above. And when about 15 years later it has reached Gemini, we get an optimal view of them from below. The effect of this is that the planet and rings together reflect the sunlight. That is the full (or even "fat") light of Saturn. When it is half-way between these two signs, in Virgo or Pisces, we see the rings edgeways on. Seen from the earth, they are then no more than extremely thin lines that can only be seen with a powerful telescope. They are no longer visible with the naked eye. Now the rings do not reflect sunlight to us, only the planet itself acting as a reflector. From our point of view, Saturn has temporarily lost its rings, which results in a much dimmer light. Sometimes we can only see it in the second half of the night. At these times, we must know which of the visible stars is Saturn, for it does not stand out particularly from the surrounding fixed stars. At the other extreme, in its "fattest" times, Saturn can put even the brightest fixed stars in the shade. This happened seven years ago (about 1988) in Sagittarius, and will happen again in another seven years when it passes through Gemini.

Strangely enough, the quarter in which Saturn is at its brightest also contains the highest number and brightest fixed stars (the quarters where the Milky Way crosses the ecliptic in the constellations Taurus/Gemini and Scorpio/Sagittarius). In the lean years, however, it traverses a to-the-naked-eye poorly populated and dim quarter of the zodiac (the constellations Virgo, Libra, Aquarius and Pisces).

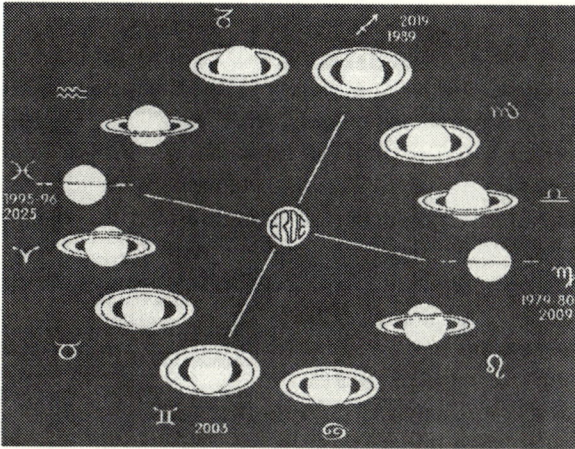

Existential Angst

The **Virgo-Pisces** axis is known as the **existence axis** of the zodiac. When Saturn passes through one of these signs and is also at its dimmest, then more or less obvious symptoms of existential angst can be observed in the human collective. That can be expressed in very different ways by different ethnic groups and by different people. The scale of angst ranges from the feeling of being threatened by fate, by society or by individuals, through to simple pessimism or general defeatism to aggression or even, as projection or defence mechanism, to the willingness to go to war (crusade reaction).

Strangely enough, on closer inspection, these forms of angst often cannot be clearly traced back to truly threatening concomitant circumstances. It appears to be more a kind of mass psychosis, of which most people are largely unaware. The reaction is also usually different during the transits of Pisces and Virgo. In Pisces, one feels oneself to be the victim of unfortunate/evil circumstances. The feeling of helplessness overcomes one and resignation can also be observed. In Virgo, the moans can also be heard, but there is much more a tendency to take action against the threat. Many proposed solutions and one-size-fits-all philosophies are put forward, from which however in retrospect some turn out to be unrealistic "tilting at windmills".

Corresponding ways of reacting as personal character traits can also be observed in people born during these periods, thus having Saturn in Pisces or Virgo in their horoscope. Naturally the character traits are modified in their personal characteristics by their different house positions (environmental influences). Furthermore, the different aspecting of these Saturn positions indicate a correspondingly different personal interpretation and transfer of such Saturn qualities that is unique to the individual.

"Ringlessness"

The above-mentioned properties are most visible, both in contemporary collective events and in the character of the Saturn in Pisces/ Saturn in Virgo people, when Saturn is "ringless", i.e. in the shorter or longer period during which its rings are not visible. The length of this phase differs depending on whether they are near the opposition or conjunction with the Sun. In the vicinity of the conjunction, the "ringless" phase lasts about three or four months, while near the opposition it lasts between nine and thirteen months.

Out of the seven "ringless" phases in this century, only one (1950) was a shorter one (see table). The current one will last from March 1995 until March 1996, i.e. around 12 months. The absolute zero point (when it is invisible even with a ten inch telescope) is repeated three times: on 22.5.95, 10.8.95 and 12.2.96. Already in May 96, the attentive observer may notice a marked increase in Saturn's brightness when Saturn would not already have passed over in the sky during the daytime.

9-13 months	3-4 months
1907/8	1950
1920/21	2009
1936/37	2025
1966/67	
1979/80	
1995/96	
2038/39	

'Ringless' phases from 1900

As a rule of thumb, in order to establish the phase of "ringlessness" in a personal horoscope, one can assume: *if Saturn is either in Pisces or Virgo and simultaneously in conjunction or opposition to the Sun.*

One can assume that the period of poorest luminosity lasts about 2 years, which corresponds almost exactly to the transit through Pisces or Virgo. The lean years in total though last between 6 and 8 years.

Occurrences of the "edge-on position of Saturn" – as astronomers call it – are about 13.75 years apart when it is moving from Pisces via Gemini to Virgo, or 15.75 years on its journey from Virgo via Sagittarius to Pisces. In the middle of these phases lie the roughly seven "fat years". The next occurrence will be from 1998 – 2005.

To sum up, we can say that: **When Saturn "loses" its rings, it reacts with irritation and anxiety, for the rings represent its ability to keep danger at bay (protective ring) and therefore in mankind there arises a loss of confidence in its ability to protect itself (existential insecurity), which just eats away at self-confidence.**

□ □ □ □ □

Pluto and the Transneptunian Planets

Harald Zittlau

First published in 'Astrolog' Issue 155, January 2007

We have all followed the story in the media; in 2006 Pluto ceased to be considered one of the fully-fledged planets in our solar system. This was the result of a decision taken at the 26th Plenary Meeting of the International Astronomical Union (IAU) in Prague in August 2006, where criteria for the classification of bodies in the solar system were established. This was necessitated by the discovery of a whole series of new planet-like objects in the solar system.

In order to be granted the status of **fully-fledged planet**, a body must meet the following criteria; it must:
- Be on a Keplerian orbit around the Sun
- Have sufficient mass so that it is made almost spherical by its own gravity (hydrostatic equilibrium)
- Have cleared its neighbourhood of other debris

An astronomical object is a **dwarf or small planet** if it:
- Orbits the Sun
- Has sufficient mass so that the force of its own gravity makes it almost spherical by (hydrostatic equilibrium)
- Has not cleared its neighbourhood of debris and
- Is not a moon/satellite

According to this definition, all newly-found objects (and also, incidentally, Pluto), are small planets, and our solar system once more contains 8 fully-fledged planets.

The decision of the IAU also has a particular significance for the world of astrology, for it will, like other decisions the organisation has made, sooner or later be accepted as the universally-held agreement (as was the establishing of the limits of the 88 constellations, 1922/1928, for example). What effects will this decision have on astrological interpretation theory in general and on astrological psychology in particular? Let us just play with a couple of ideas that are relevant to the current discussion.

Until the discovery of Uranus in the late 18th century, astronomy had developed a stable relationship to the known (visible with the naked eye) bodies of the solar system. Discoveries and physical model theories were given more or less the same importance as spiritual or mythological valuations.

Since the split into two disciplines, astrology has repeatedly faced the challenge of integrating the facts and discoveries of astronomy and fending off scientific criticism of its methods.

For most astrological interpretation theories, the Ptolemaic foundations from the early 3rd century AD were predominantly valid (and are still valid for many schools today).

As a result of the growing freedom of opinion and the public diffusion of theories and opinions since the start of the 20th century, there has been a significant diversification in the revival of astrological thought. There has been the greatest development and expansion of astrological theories, schools and approaches to interpretation ever witnessed in the history of astrology.

Typically, nearly all authors of this time initially borrow, almost untouched, the core elements from the Ptolemaic interpretation theory of the seven classical planets, but clothe them in the language of their social era.

At the same time, there was a great propensity for experimentation, for inserting additional elements into astrological interpretation, in order to fill in the gaps. A real mania for calculation and proof emerged, in order to be able to substantiate the desired astrological statements with allocateable (visible) horoscope factors (enhancement of the type of aspect, introduction of mirror points, half sums, resonance axes, hypothetical planets, sensitive points, countless direction, transit and prognosis calculations, etc.). Was this an unconscious concession to the scientific concept?

Some astrological theories were more ignorant of the state of astronomical knowledge than others. As an example, let us consider on the one hand the Hamburg School with its "hypothetical planets" and on the other hand astrological psychology, which as far as possible tries to integrate the elementary astronomical facts into its methodology.

As far as the planets Uranus, Neptune and Pluto are concerned, there is little information in the literature as to which author or esoteric group with which point of view drew up the first guidelines for interpretation. It is much easier to establish that circulating interpretations from most authors were readily copied and updated.

From the beginnings of the astrological search for contexts in cosmic events to the present day, man was able to learn to observe and evaluate countless complete orbits of the classical planets. Since the discovery of the new planets, though, we should not forget that Uranus has made only three orbits of the Sun, Neptune only one and Pluto less than half an orbit.

For many astrologers, e.g. the discovery of the small body Chiron (discovered in 1977, diameter about 140 km), has been more important than the classical planets.

In recent decades, astronomy has been coming up with new heavenly bodies and discoveries that may have long-term relevance for astrology in increasingly rapid succession. Let us therefore look at the current state of astronomical research as far as classification of the bodies belonging to the solar system is concerned:

- In the centre of the solar system lies our Sun. It (still) concentrates more than 99 per cent of all matter of the entire solar system in its sphere, and measures 1.4 million km in diameter. All matter in the solar system orbits our central star. The Sun's gravitational field extends up to 1.5 light years out into the universe.

- All solar system bodies hitherto discovered and described by astronomy move in a maximal radius of 5 light days around the Sun!

- The solar system is currently divided into 5 different principal zones:

1) The **inner solar system** with the earth-like (terrestrial) planets Mercury, Venus, Earth and Mars. So far astronomy has been unable to locate a planet that orbits between the Sun and Mercury (Vulcan); however a few asteroids have been found, known as the near earth asteroids.

2) The **asteroid belt** between Mars and Jupiter. There are currently about 340,000 asteroids catalogued, with diameters of less than

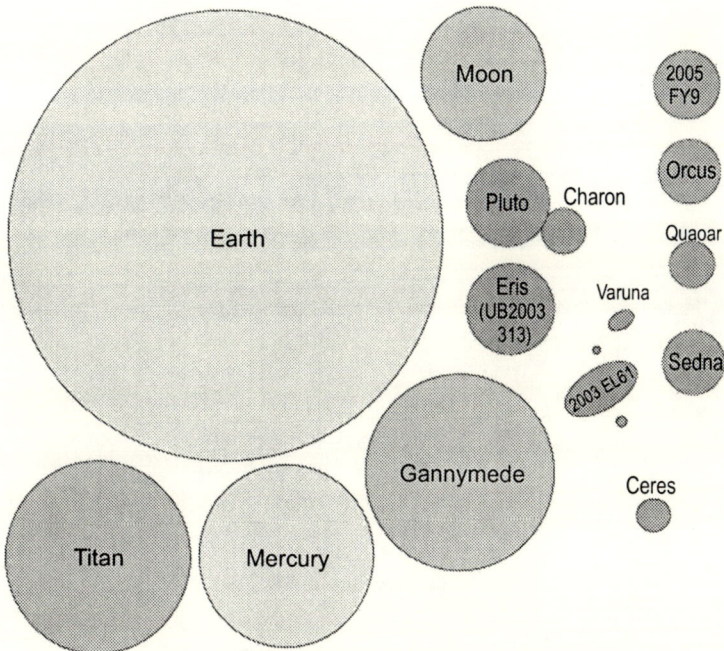

Size comparison of the Earth, Mercury, Jupiter Moon, Saturn Moon and Transneptunian Bodies.

100m to almost 1000 km. The actual number goes into the millions, according to astronomers' estimates. About 90 per cent of known asteroids (or planetoids) are found here. The largest object, Ceres (discovered in 1801), has a diameter of just under 1000 km and is now classified in the group of small planets by the IAU.

Other well-known asteroids are Vesta, Juno, Pallas or Astraea. For a while after their discovery (1804 to 1845), they were even considered to be planets. At the time of its discovery in 1846, Neptune was the thirteenth planet in the solar system!

However, the discovery of other small bodies meant that a distinction had to be made, so that from 1850 the number of fully-fledged planets was reduced back to eight again.

After the discovery of Pluto in 1930, which was initially considered to be the ninth planet, its status as a fully-fledged planet was contested from the start in some astronomical circles.

Another group of asteroids are Trojans, small bodies that follow the orbits of planets around the Sun. The so-called Mars, Jupiter and Neptune Trojans are well-known. Further information is available in the literature or on internet for those interested.

3) The **outer solar system** with the Gas planets Jupiter, Saturn, Uranus and Neptune. Asteroids are also found in the area between the orbits of Jupiter to Neptune. The most famous belong to the Centauri class, e.g. Chiron, Pholos and Nessus. We assume that they originate from the Kuiper Belt and are dead comets. (In the case of Chiron, a weak comet tail was recently discovered.)

4) The so-called **Kuiper Belt** or area of the Transneptunian Objects (TNO) is a zone of the solar system beyond Neptune's orbit. Most of the objects discovered in recent years are in this region, which ultimately led to the current discussion of planetary status:

Name	Discovered	Diameter
Varuna	28.11.2000	450-750 km
Quaoar	04.06.2002	ca. 1250 km
2003 EL61	07.03.2003	ca. 2200/1100 km elliptical
Eris*	21.10.2003	ca. 2500 km
Sedna	14.11.2003	ca. 1700 km
Orcus	22.11.2004	1600 – 1800 km
2005 FY9	31.05.2005	ca. 1800 km

Transneptunian Objects

*Eris was first called 2003 UB313 (and according to the astronomical naming of new discoveries of heavenly bodies the number 139199). Then it was given the name Xena, and finally Eris. It has a moon that was discovered later, initially called Gabrielle and now called Dysmonia.

5) The inner and outer **Oort Clouds** is a postulated spherical area surrounding the solar system at the edge of the Sun's gravitational field. The suspected distance from the Sun is between 300 (inner area) and about 100,000 (outer area) astronomical units (1 astronomical unit (AU) = distance Earth-Sun, ca. 150 million km or ca. 8 light minutes).

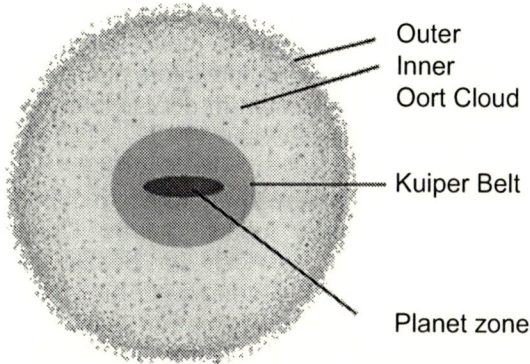

The Oort Cloud contains large amounts of dust dating from the origin of the solar system right up to larger bodies of rocks and ice. It is assumed that matter is continually being lost from this area, which moves towards the centre of the solar system in the form of asteroids to small planets. It is further assumed that the inner area of the Oort Cloud merges into the Kuiper Belt.

With improvement in astronomical observation techniques, further discoveries and larger bodies are expected in the future. Current research cannot foresee whether other fully-fledged planets could be located at the edge of the solar system. Neither is there any indication as to whether our central star has a possible companion ca. 1.5 to 3 light years away, as occasionally postulated by theoretical astronomers.

A legitimate question that e.g. astronomers or interested non-astrologers could sometimes be justified in asking would be why some of the bodies discovered in recent decades are now included in horoscope interpretations, yet others are not. Actually, the criteria for the choice are not just the pure size or mass of the found objects. Furthermore, other elements are included and interpreted in the horoscope for which astronomical evidence is completely lacking (e.g. Lilith as the sensitive point, the above-mentioned hypothetical planet of the Hamburg School, etc.)

Let us now take a look at the heavenly bodies that various schools of astrology consider to be worth including in interpretations, again with respect to their astronomical relevance. This produces some interesting relations:

- The planet Mercury is exceeded in size and mass by Jupiter's moon Ganymede and Saturn's moon Titan. Here it is plausible to argue that Jupiter and Saturn are taken as whole systems, inclusive of all their satellites.

- Pluto and all previously found Trans-Neptunian Objects are considerably smaller than the Earth's Moon. It is also extremely far away.

- The same could justifiably be said for Vesta and Chiron. Why does e.g. Vesta appear in horoscopes, when the larger object Ceres does not?

Such questions and considerations are as old as the dispute between the two sisters: astronomy and astrology, dating from the time they became separate disciplines. Each wants to explain everything in its own way.

Somehow it seems fascinating that, from time to time, exotic interpretations usually find favourable acceptance among their astrological or astronomical "consumers" by being constantly reiterated.

Distances and dimensions of orbits and areas in the solar system

Million km

7000 — Kuiper Belt

6000

5000

4000 — Neptune

3000 — Uranus

2000

1000 — Saturn

— Jupiter

— Asteroid belt

Mars
Venus   Earth
0 ——————————— Mercury

Would it not therefore be better to ask ourselves whether astrology has its own research agenda? Are we wrong in the way we interpret celestial objects in horoscopes? Should we reinterpret Pluto's significance for astrological psychology?

A Couple of Thoughts on this Topic

Unlike astronomy, astrology has no worldwide recognised body that sets the rules for horoscope interpretation and the integration of newly discovered celestial objects.

It is a fact that astrological wisdom and accurate interpretation is only established after long-term observation, many-sided case studies and the consolidation of communicated experience. There has been enormous progress made in this area since the last third of the last century. For the first time in the history of astrology, the attempt was

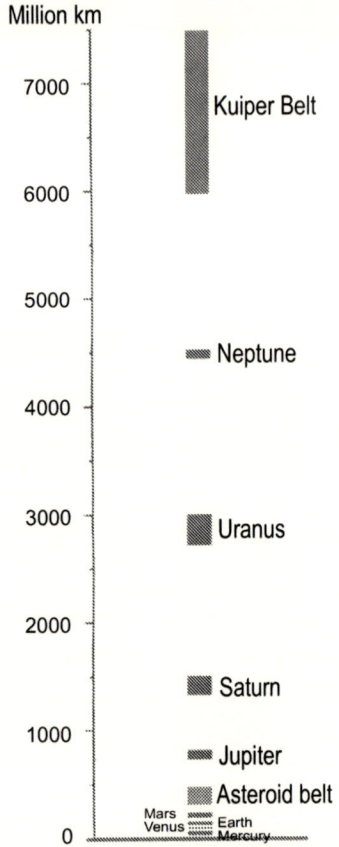

successfully made to place modern man at the centre of interpretation and to liberate him from mediaeval determinism.

Impressive, humanistic discoveries were made, particularly those which combined psychology with astrological symbolism, thereby making available an instrument of individual self-discovery.

Trial and error and above all decades of practical verification of the findings have been crucial in this process.

The aim of astrology is to help to solve mankind's eternal questions regarding what life and the universe are all about. In the process, it goes beyond the boundaries of the purely material approach, as usually preferred in the natural sciences.

Astrology prefers the holistic approach, which essentially says that possible spiritual laws exist that it is worth knowing, because they may be the central key to unlocking and developing mankind's latent potential. Many people now accept that everything in the universe is connected, and this idea is now also shared by some representatives of cutting-edge research in physics.

As far as our astrological search for knowledge is concerned, and with respect to the celestial bodies that we choose to interpret, this means that we see the complete solar system as an organic whole. We therefore welcome every extension of the horizon of knowledge, because it brings us greater insight into the realities of the universe. The demotion of Pluto into a newly created category of small planets is a formal measure. It should help to bring a little more order into the different functions of the components of a system.

This does not affect the knowledge we have gained of Plutonian symbolism. Now at most there is an increased challenge to welcome the newly founded members of the family and to establish which part they can play in the future in the expansion of our consciousness. Much patience and hard work will be required to ensure continued gradual development.

I see a provisional main problem being a kind of "uncertainty principle" of the human mind, which is incapable of meaningfully interpreting what is observed. The following example can illustrate what I mean by this:

We are (still) not able to penetrate to the deep spiritual understanding of a phenomenon to the same extent that we can determine externally accurate standards. That is why it (still) makes no sense e.g. to calculate a planetary position or the start of house to a fraction of an arc second (which would in principle be possible): we lack the spiritual means to make a differentiated interpretation of formal differences beyond a certain limit. The progress of evolution will hopefully enable mankind to close these gaps some day.

Here lies perhaps also a reason why caution is advisable when it comes to using the smaller members of the cosmic family for the

purposes of interpretation. It is therefore in no way wrong to deal
with Chiron, but it would be unwise to place the conclusions drawn
from it in unreasonable relation to proven interpretation factors.

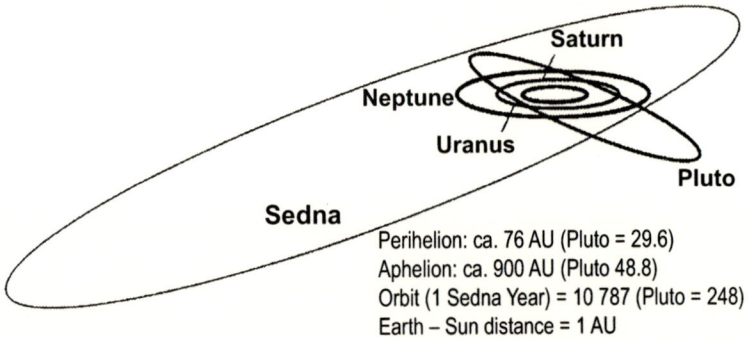

Saturn
Neptune
Uranus
Pluto
Sedna

Perihelion: ca. 76 AU (Pluto = 29.6)
Aphelion: ca. 900 AU (Pluto 48.8)
Orbit (1 Sedna Year) = 10 787 (Pluto = 248)
Earth – Sun distance = 1 AU

Conclusion

What is opening up in the way of new knowledge about our solar
system is extremely exciting. We should therefore start to deal with
the new facts.

It does not mean that all previously acquired knowledge must be
revised; it can be expanded. It will require some time, for we only learn
from experience and repeated qualitative observations. The physical
size of a celestial body is still not the only criterion for interpretation
and quality!

Many suggestions have been made as to how to deal with the new
celestial bodies. We should, as always, observe with the required caution
and keeping people in mind, whether and how new dimensions of
consciousness are manifested. As I said before, we need a little time.
Sedna, the most exotic of the newly-found heavenly bodies, takes ca.
10,780 years to orbit the Sun, according to initial calculations!

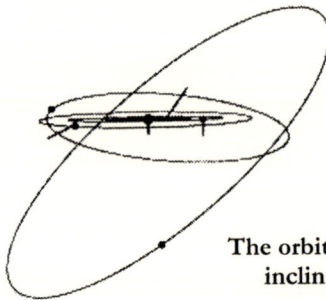

The orbit of Eris has an
inclination of 40°

❏ ❏ ❏ ❏ ❏

Is Pluto a Planet?

Bruno Huber

First published in 'Astrolog' in 1985; reprinted in Issue 155, January 2007

Not long ago, a rumour circulated in the world of astrology. At the 26th General Assembly of the International Astronomical Union in August 2006 in Prague, the decision was made to strip Pluto of its planetary status and to recategorise it as a dwarf planet. Since then, Pluto has been known as "Minor Planet 134340".

At this convention, attended by scientists from 75 different countries, the criteria for determining what is and what is not a planet were formally established for the first time. Prior to this there had been no definitive criteria. That is why we reprint this article by Bruno Huber, previously published in Astrolog in 1985.

Already right after its discovery in 1930, a few astronomers expressed the view that Pluto could not really be called a planet. There were good reasons for this, e.g. the extreme inclination of its orbit: 17 degrees is otherwise only found in the case of planetoids (asteroids) and comets, and the eccentricity of its orbit. Its size too (or lack of it) was a factor; hitherto it had been compared to the smallest in the solar system. Only recently was it was found that its diameter could only be around 6000km (compared to a diameter of 6770km for Mars and only 4840 for Mercury).

Expert opinion was divided and the issue was temporarily shelved. However, the most recent findings have reopened the debate in a wider context. The creation of another class of bodies in the solar system is being considered, that of the "Trans-Neptunian Objects". While the classical planets (up to and including Neptune) move exactly on their almost circular orbits approximately concentrically around the Sun, and therefore can never touch each other, there are a few that do not obey these rules and whose orbits touch or cross those of the classical planets. Pluto is one of these.

Then there are some planetoids that do not keep to their allocated space between Mars and Jupiter, but whose eccentric orbits bring them close to the Earth or even Venus (Eros, Amor, Apollo, Adonis, Hermes, etc...) or, like Hidalgo, cause them to venture outwards towards the orbit of Saturn.

And then there is Chiron, first discovered in 1977, which orbits the Sun in the space between Saturn and Uranus. We should actually say oscillates, for, like Pluto, it is quite eccentric and touches the orbits of both Saturn and Uranus.

And finally a completely new finding came into the equation; Pluto had a moon! In the photo, Pluto can be seen for the first time as a disc instead of just a point. On the right, its moon, Charon, which takes about 20,000km to orbit Pluto. This photo was made possible by the development of a new electronic-photographic procedure (Speckle Interferometry), in which a few thousand photos of the same object are superimposed on top of each other by computer. This makes the light a million times brighter, enabling astronomers to see even the faintest of heavenly bodies in great detail. The apparent gap between Pluto and Charon on this photo is only half an arcsecond (that is a 7200th of a degree – try to enter that in a horoscope chart!) Even the largest optical instruments on earth (e.g. 5m mirror, Mt Palomar) can only visually distinguish objects that are more than one degree apart. This state-of-the-art technology will definitely bring yet more astronomical eureka experiences.

The bottom line is that we now know that Pluto can only have a diameter of between two and three thousand kilometres [about 2300km – Ed], making it the smallest "planet" in the solar system – having more in common in terms of size with a moon. The other planets have seven moons that are all larger than Pluto, with diameters of between 3200 and 5400 km.

We now have a class of bodies in the solar system that are smaller than 3000km and also all have eccentric orbits. Pluto meets both criteria, as does the newly discovered Chiron. Since the discovery of the latter, both astronomers and astrologers have disputed whether it is a planet or a planetoid (minor planet or asteroid). For both, we could therefore use the following criteria for potential astrological interpretation:

Exceeding boundaries – entering occupied areas (particularly in the case of Pluto) – the uniting of opposites (in the case of Chiron) – bringing new dimensions into the realm of the familiar – daring to break the rules, etc.

This new approach may be confusing at first. But it fits the definitions above, and corresponds to our experience so far with Pluto. It also means that we deal with the other body that is similar to Pluto – Chiron. In American astrological circles, this process is well underway. There have been ephemeredes for Chiron since 1978 and recently also the first publication of interpretation literature.

◻ ◻ ◻ ◻ ◻.

Pluto's Transformations

Or: The Celestial Revolution of the 21st Century

A Few Basic Astrological, Psychological and Philosophical Reflections

Wolfhard König

First published in 'Astrolog' Issue 155, January 2007

I. New Elements

In a previous article [page 53], Harald Zittlau explained the new facts about the universe; the latest scientific and astronomical findings that we must deal with.

Astronomers (and astrologers) must have had a similar sensation in 1781 after the discovery of Uranus. At first, the discoverer Herschel believed for months that he had discovered a comet, so outrageous did it seem to disturb the "sacred seven", the planetary order that could be traced back to the Sumerians, Babylonians and Greeks.

In any case, we must separate the **astronomical discovery** and the astrological interpretation, i.e. the **astrological-psychological significance** of an astronomical object.

Only in the case of the seven classical planets can we assume that there is a fundamental consistency between their naming, mythological associations and astrological-psychological interpretations. This was the result of centuries of observation on the part of the ancient civilisations mentioned above, the so-called mythical cultures (J. Gebser).

How can we now, in our modern scientific world, establish whether newly discovered astronomical bodies possess sufficient astrological-psychological significance and if they do, what that significance is?

When Quaoar was discovered in June 2002, it was given a name and mythological significance just weeks later and in November 2002 a "book on demand" was published on internet: "Quaoar – the tenth planet", in which astrological interpretations were derived from its hastily attributed name and mythological association. Our ancestors would surely have called this hubris.

Following the example of Pluto: what does an empirical, practical procedure involve? We must start by incorporating a newly-discovered astronomical body, e.g. Pluto, in as many horoscopes as possible.

Using computers and modern data files, it is now possible to do this in tens of thousands of known horoscopes.

Then we must select a number of horoscopes, perhaps a few hundred and in the second run a few thousand, in which this new element is in a particularly strong position, e.g. on main axes, strong in the sign and with many aspects, or even as tension ruler.

And then comes the crucial pragmatic-psychological question: Is there something in the life and the biography of this person that cannot be adequately explained using the classical ten elements, but which the new elements would allow us to do much better? Let us assume that the new planet is exposed at the MC. The question would be: Is there something on this person's path to the self, on his individuation path (MC), that can be more convincingly explained by this new planet in this position?

With respect to Chiron, for example, Bruno Huber already established that the same information that can be derived from Chiron can also be derived from Neptune (possibly together with the Moon). Then Chiron would be at most a clarification of this existing connection.

Only after a pragmatic examination of a person's life history and life style can valid deductions be made as to what a new planet means, explains or indicates in the way of a person's psychological abilities. And only then can it be judged whether its recently-given name and mythological association are consistent with it.

Astrologically, where there is doubt, the astrological-psychological examination of the significance found in people always takes precedence.

For the new planets, Uranus, Neptune and Pluto, this means:

- The mythology associated with Uranus makes sense if the whole mythologem of Uranus is attributed to Gaia (Gaia is the revolutionary)
- In the case of Neptune, the mythology of an archaic, brutal Poseidon is unfounded, and is completely inconsistent with the significance of Neptune as the Christ imago or empathy. Therefore, other mythologies must be attributed, like Dionysos (god mythology), or Orpheus (hero mythology) or Amor and Psyche (god and hero mythologies).
- If one attributes to Pluto the Demeter-Persephone-Hades mythology (the leading of Persephone through Hades and her development after detachment from maternal symbiosis), it is very consistent with Pluto's effect, which is one of individuation.

For an in-depth explanation of the names and mythologies of the three spiritual planets, see *Astrolog* issues 77 (general), 78 (Uranus), 86 and 88 (Neptune), 91 (Pluto) and 92 (Why is it called Pluto?).

So the Sumerians, the originators of astrology, observed that if a boy was born while Mars was rising in the East (Mars at the AC), he often became a reckless warrior, or if he was born when Mars culminated (Mars at the MC), he often tended to become a great commander of men, etc. These connections are basically statistical, but also empirical.

When the discoverer (Mike Brown, California Institute of Technology) exercised his right to name object 2003 UB 313 Xena (and the moon Gabrielle), it may well have been his right, but Xena does not come from mythology but from a Hollywood film series, in which a wild female warrior has (thoroughly exciting) adventures, and the mythology of Hollywood is freely marketed. It gives us no indication of the possible astrological interpretation of the planets or planetoids. The discoverer of the next new planet could call it Donald Duck, and what would that mean for astrology?

It is clear then that only careful long-term observation of the significance of a new astrological element in the horoscope can allow an accurate, valid astrological-psychological interpretation to be made. We should therefore allow ourselves sufficient time to research each new element.

II. Reflection

As the particular significance of the ten heavenly bodies (8 planets, the Sun and the Moon) is clear and there is therefore no doubt as to the great astrological-psychological significance of Pluto in the 76 years since its discovery, we could limit ourselves to these ten elements. We could make an exception for Pluto, as even though it is only a small planet, it is a less recent discovery (1930), and leave it at that.

This may be obvious and a good idea if we are preparing a radix horoscope and want to focus on the aspect pattern in a consultation, for the aspect orb and the aspect figures involving the ten planets are already proven. If we also include ten asteroids (from Ceres to Xena), then nearly everyone has a number of aspect figures in their horoscope and if we add enough elements, then each one has a diamond in their horoscope. The aspect pattern then loses its meaning.

However, can we really eliminate all new heavenly bodies and their possible astrological significance forever?

I actually think that every heavenly body is not only an astronomical object but also has astrological significance, that therefore every heavenly body may always give an external and internal orientation. Externally in astronomical navigation they act as signposts and internally they reflect part of our psychological make-up.

Today, we no longer assume the mediaeval notion of the planets exerting forces on people (e.g. Mars in transit radiates powers on to me and makes me quite aggressive or nervous), as this influencing theory has proved to be both psychologically (man develops by learning processes, i.e. by the effects of information), and physically (the forces concerned have never been measured) obsolete.

However, we do assume that there is a mirroring, so that Mars in transit indicates that I must confront the theme of aggression in my life and in the process may undergo new experiences and developments. This is what Jung meant by his term synchronicity (acausal coincidence) e.g. of a person's Mars position and aggression experiences. Bruno Huber always said that a horoscope is like a voltmeter: it shows the tension in a power point, but does not make the voltage, which comes from the power station.

Let us therefore assume that every heavenly body also has a reflective dimension, i.e. it reproduces or shows something about our interior world.

Then absolutely every asteroid would also have this dimension, from Ceres to Pholus to Xena (which now is thankfully called Eris, which is at least a Greek goddess, albeit the goddess of discord who ultimately caused great misfortune by triggering the Trojan War).

It would also otherwise be difficult to set boundaries: which astronomical elements have two sides, i.e. an astrological side as well as an astronomical one, and which do not and why not?

If we then consider every heavenly body to be a smaller or larger mirror and search for the elements most suited to be astrological reflectors, the question arises, how many mirrors do we need and which mirrors work well together to give a harmonious image?

III. Test Psychology

At this point it may be interesting to note that similar questions and problems also exist in psychology, particularly in test psychology. Psychologists are also confronted by the question of how to find out as much as possible about the patient, about his consciousness and his unconscious. Usually the experienced test psychologist uses a so-called **test battery**, a bundle of psychological tests that fit together and complement each other (every test is a kind of mirror).

Usually this includes the MMPI (Minnesota Multiphasic Personality Inventory): a **questionnaire** containing about six hundred questions (with answers to tick) which was invented in the USA in 1940. It is definitely the most thorough questionnaire, but nowadays is sometimes rejected as old-fashioned, even though it has been revised.

However, the problem of every questionnaire is that it can only measure what the patient is aware of. If he considers himself to be very friendly and that is why he has a low score on the aggression scale, it is indeed his opinion, but it can be that a partner or neighbour has had a completely different experience and would give him a high aggression score, which is also objectively correct. But the questionnaire itself only measures what the patient thinks.

If we also want to use tests to learn something about the patient's unconscious, we must use so-called **"projective tests"**. Here the patient is offered so-called anchor stimuli onto which he must project the contents of his unconscious. The most famous projective test (and the oldest) is surely the Rorschach Test, which was developed back in 1921 by the Swiss psychiatrist Rorschach with reference to Freud's psychoanalysis. Here the person is shown the famous ink spot images and must spontaneously describe what they remind him of, i.e. project the contents of his unconscious. Great experience is required to evaluate these tests.

Also well known are TAT tests (Thematic Apperception Tests, apperception: perception based on past experience). In 1935, H. Murray originally drew 30 illustrations that depicted people in different gestures or social situations. The patient has to make up a story about them. Another popular method is also to provide the start of a sentence as an anchor stimulus, e.g. "One lovely afternoon, I go for a walk in the park, it is slowly getting dark. Then suddenly…" The patient must now finish telling the story, e.g. "Then suddenly, I meet my best friend…" or: "Then, suddenly there is a rustling in the undergrowth and a robber jumps out at me…"

The projective test is concerned with the interpretation of symbols, like in a dream, but instead the symbols (e.g. stories) are externally activated by a stimulus. It does show which contents of the unconscious are readily available though.

Finally, we should mention the Lüscher Colour Test, which allows the patient to choose their favourite (or least favourite) colour from colour tables. The choice of colour allows the personality to be interpreted (including the unconscious parts). We can see that the choice of colour reveals much about our inner life and its deeply unconscious sides in the use of colour dialogues and the interpretation of its images.

In the interpretation of symbols, there can be no clear results of the evaluation, but the fact that unconscious elements are involved is what makes them different from the questionnaires. A good psychologist will nevertheless still conduct one or more personal discussions (medical history) and make notes. A test battery only exists when e.g. a questionnaire, a projective test, a colour test and the results of the discussion are evaluated together in a report.

There is another experience that I find interesting. Sometimes magazines contain short tests for their readers, a typical test may be called "Are you jealous?" They hope that many readers want to do the test and buy the magazine. Naturally, a serious (scientific test) should not be expected and the test is usually limited to two pages. The amazing thing is that these very simple and short tests are not completely wrong.

The test writer/ psychologist must initially think up a series of concise questions on the subject. One question could be: "Your partner stares at another man/woman on the train in your presence. How do you react?" answer a) not at all, b) I would be nervous, c) I would be furious. Each answer scores a certain number of points.

There are often five or six such questions on a page of the magazine, each with three possible answers. One must then add up the total number of points. On the second page, there are then e.g. three or four interpretation tests: a) 0-20 points: you are unusually tolerant. b) 21 – 40 points: you are very jealous, c) 41 – 60 points: you are dangerously jealous, etc.

One could take such a test just for fun, but readers often feel they have been accurately evaluated.

Even such a simple test, if cleverly constructed, can therefore reveal (reflect) something, however limited.

IV. Conclusion

One could perhaps say that if such a simple test can reflect something of a person's interior world, then equally even a small planet or asteroid can reflect something of a person, a facet, a certain personality component, if only in a limited fashion.

In a battery of tests, it is important to assemble the right tests that fit together and illuminate as many aspects as possible of the person, understand him as holistically as possible. The right number should also be chosen; 2 is far too few and 25 is too many to evaluate meaningfully, not in the time available anyway.

In the case of the horoscope, on the one hand the key proven elements (the existing ten planets) should be used. However, if we award every cosmic element a certain value (a little piece of reflection), then at the very least we can experiment with the small planets. We may find that they capture something specific or corroborate or modify certain findings. In other words, we can assemble many mirrors and it really comes down to what we want to experience, from which question we proceed.

We can draw two conclusions from this:

1) We should not reject out of hand small planets around the same size as Pluto, that may arrive in the future, perhaps even in greater numbers, from the Kuiper Belt or even the Oort Cloud. This would also contradict any spirit of research. We should test according to

the above-mentioned criteria, whether they reflect astrologically meaningful connections (about people) and if so, to what extent.

2) In astrological-psychological consultation, we should then proceed in two phases; firstly a thorough analysis of the basic horoscope with the "ten classical planets" and a clear aspect pattern is necessary. Then an analysis with the three horoscopes is very helpful. Every creative astrologer should then be at liberty to experiment with other mirrors.

Perhaps in the future, every astrologer will have to find his own variation of astrology; perhaps in the second step some will include the Sabian symbols, conduct degree astrology (which Bruno tended to do), or find that some planetoids are suitable elements of reflection.

It will perhaps lead to the often-invoked "harmony of the originals" in which every experienced astrologer is an original – and harmony is what we should hope for.

V. Empathy and Intuition – the subjective, personal choice

There is yet another point that we should consider: there are astrologers who are able to obtain very good, sophisticated interpretation results using degree astrology, the sensitive points (luck point, health point, etc., cf. Brandler-Pracht) or by including fixed stars (cf. Erbertin/ Hoffmann). I personally could never really start to use these elements, perhaps because they do not correspond to how my intuition and empathy work.

There is another experience from psychology that could perhaps help us further. Already before the war, in the University of Munich an interesting experiment was carried out (quoted according to Prof. Müller): a scientific psychological team wanted to find out whether there was any substance to iridology (diagnosis of the iris of the eye). It asked three healing practitioners and three psychologists to follow all the rules of the art of iridology as accurately as possible. In the ensuing patient test, the three psychologists failed, yet the three healing practitioners achieved astonishing results.

The explanation is simple, but very important: The three healing practitioners combined their intuition with the methods of iridology and employed the rules empathetically and sensitively and put their hearts and minds into this process. Therefore, it may just be that the iris gives clues that can only be interpreted under intuitive and empathetic contact with the patient, leading to correct diagnosis. Spontaneous ideas during a sitting (countertransference) are also of great importance for therapists.

So if an astrologer puts "his heart" into a supplementary method, if he trains and develops his intuition e.g. in the use of the sensitive points, then he can perhaps find personal interpretations there that are particularly coherent, i.e. also reach and help the client. Perhaps other astrologers would achieve similar results by using other elements.

It is similar in the case of depth psychological dream interpretation: interpretations according to Freud, Jung or Adler are basically not really so different, despite approaching the patient's theme from different angles. Seen in this way, an astrologer could choose to use different planetoids and be able to find them personally and intuitively useful.

Astrology should therefore become more varied and individual in the future – and hopefully lead to the harmony of the originals.

◻ ◻ ◻ ◻ ◻

Part 2: Life and Meaning

In this second part of the book we have grouped five articles related to life and its meaning.

Career, Vocation and the Meaning of Life, by **Louise Huber**
Addresses the question of what is the meaning of life, and how understanding of this can be helped through use of the horoscope.

Searching for the Life Myth, by **Gabriele Gertz**
How our personal life myth, life patterns, traumas and chronic physical symptoms may be reflected in our dreams and in the horoscope, starting from the perspective of process-oriented psychology.

The Trinity – Ideality, Reality, Hope, by **Wolfhard König**
Psychologist Wolfhard König, long-time friend and collaborator of the Hubers, considers the basic psychological mechanism, at an individual and cultural level, whereby new ideas and ideals become accepted in everyday reality, and shows how these are reflected in the horoscope.

Moon Node – Ascendant, by **Ruth Schmidhauser**
API tutor Ruth Schmidhauser takes a detailed look at the interpretation of the Moon Node and its role of indicating the next step in life towards the theme of the ascendant.

Sagittarius Sun and AC Signs, by **Bruno Huber**
Considers the significance of the sign at the ascendant, traditionally indicating an aiming quality for our lives, and its relationship with the Sun's sign and house position – using the particular example of the Sagittarius Sun, Bruno's own Sun sign.

Photo: Bruno Huber

Career, Vocation and the Meaning of Life

Louise Huber

Published in 'Astrolog' Issues 65-68, December 1991 to June 1992

The Meaning Question

I would like to begin this subject with the search for meaning in life, for this should be central. Solving the question of meaning in a philosophical, astrological, religious and psychological sense is connected to the questions: "Who am I? Where do I come from? Where am I going?" It is also the question that motivates most people when they start to study astrology. The meaning question cannot be answered with an intellectual or philosophical idea, but with an experience of reality in which one experiences oneself as a part of the whole and becomes aware that one is not an isolated "I" without intrinsic connection to the environment, the cosmos, to God and to one's own soul. Such an "I" lives separated from the great whole, cut off from the protection of interpersonal relationships, from love and basic trust, it lives in absurdity. ("Satanas" in Sanskrit means the separated one.) Meaning can only therefore be experienced in the presence of love, which in turn requires a connection with the environment and to the whole. We are not monads with closed doors, not isolated I-entities for all eternity. We all have an open window within us; we have the feeling that we are connected to the world. We need this open window so that we can go out into the world and look for tasks that give us joy and meaning as we carry them out. We must take risks and have the courage and desire to look for new experiences to find our way out of meaningless isolation. But we ourselves must make the effort to seek contact with the world in a process of self-actualisation that gives lasting meaning to our lives.

A good way of solving the meaning question is via holistic understanding of the horoscope to which we aspire. This depends on our perceptual capacity, i.e. our visual imagination and our sensory alertness. We have senses that are directed outwards, the eyes, ears, taste, hearing, speaking; we also have senses that are directed inwards, like our inner perceptual capacity, the inner ear, the experience of our interior world. Many of us also have a certain sixth or seventh sense. How we answer the question of the meaning of life therefore depends on our inner perceptual capacity, i.e. to what extent we can draw our senses inward. This usually only occurs when we are at peace and the outside world is sleeping, when we enter our inner space during deep meditation or when we call for help in a state of spiritual distress. From a psychological point of view, the meaning question always starts at zero; we fall into an identity crisis that we cannot solve with our rational mind and cannot find answers to our questions. From a spiritual point of view, though, we must fall back again and again into this so-called "zero state" to long for a deeper meaning in the first place!

Every person has a strong inner need for a meaningful life. Some people are always looking, some in the wrong direction. If they believe that meaning lies in external success, in a powerful position, in finding an intellectual structure, in technology, tactics, dialectics, logic, then they will be disappointed. Real meaning can be found in consciously perceiving every moment, in the here and now, in the present, in the objective sensory perception of the world. By being alert and having a vital relationship with the environment, we can perceive possible ways of structuring our lives. This creative affirmation of life can even enable us to change reality and make a new and better world for ourselves. This is the task that we have to do in this moment, that when accomplished will give us meaning and joy, and that can even mean freedom and truth. Truth is the real and clear perception of the world.

We must work on keeping the meaning of life alive on a daily basis. We should not let ourselves go, never give up or get stuck in the rut of a daily routine. It is important to go inwards, to meditate, to confront the meaning of life everyday, always checking whether we are still living from the centre of our hearts, and creating our power from the unity of all things.

The Meaning Question in the horoscope

The personal meaning question can be derived from the character and therefore from the horoscope, which tells us how a person relates to the environment and which special abilities and relationships exist in his house system. The orientation of the hair-cross shows how far a person has distanced themselves from their environment and from love, and how much he has to struggle to sort out these relationships and also what kind of special tasks he must accomplish to achieve a more rounded character.

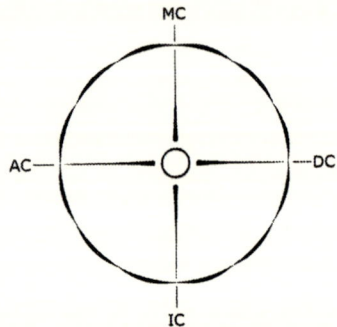

In the horoscope we can see the relationship to the environment from the vertical or horizontal orientation of the aspect pattern. The horizontal relationship is on the I-You axis, the vertical axis shows the tension between the individual and the collective, or the path from the root in the divine source to the independent personality. We are born into these two polarities. The power within us pushes in two directions, which can torment us, drive us onwards and be contradictory.

There are other elements in the horoscope that help us to resolve the meaning question. One of these is the ascending moon node, which always represents the first step, and the ascendant sign, which shows the individual's developmental aim. This is the signpost, the goal that we should achieve and that constitutes the task that gives meaning to our life. It is obvious that when we ask about the meaning of our existence, we need to use different methods than when we want to know what the future holds! We are not just defining a constellation on one level, for this is just one part of the truth; our objective is always to interpret the horoscope on three or four levels.

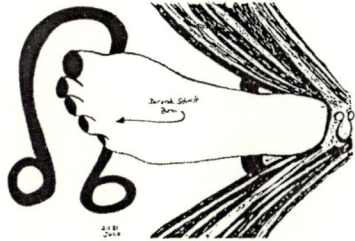

The Meaning Question and Three-Dimensionality

The theory of the trinity appears in all fields of philosophy, culture and religion. Even in physics and biology, many things can only be correctly understood from the point of view of the trinity. For example, a married couple only becomes fertile when a child comes along to make three. When two people are fighting, a third can usually calm things down, and so on. When there are two opposing sides, only a third objective pole can provide balance; in the case of an opposition, tension is dissipated by an aligned aspect, or channelled into creativity. There are many more examples, such as the three-step creative process. The trinity always represents wholeness, it symbolises an underlying ordering of our lives, which indicates a three-phase creative process that is inherent in all living processes, and is therefore organic. Everyone can identify with it, and understand connections that were previously obscure and contradictory. A new dimension of love and understanding can allow the meaning of what causes suffering, worry and anxiety in a dualistic worldview to be understood, and also bring enlightenment and liberation.

We have now moved on from the dualistic mediaeval view, where good opposed evil, or God and the world were separate, and most people know that in modern astrology it is unthinkable to talk about horoscope or aspects in terms of good and bad. New psychologically refined interpretation methods now allow us to find the cause and meaning of a problem, and the three-dimensional approach allows us to establish differences in quality that correspond to the people concerned.

The Theory of Relativity

From a historical point of view, we have only been able to understand the effect of the third pole since Albert Einstein published his Theory of Relativity, which changed our philosophical, religious and physical worldview. In astrology, we are familiar with tripolarity e.g. in the three-fold personality structure and in the aspects following the addition of green aspects – previously, in line with the black and white thinking of the time, only the red and blue aspects were shown in the horoscope. Today, we can use the green aspects to understand the relativity, cause and meaning of a person's destiny. Men have changed in line with the laws of evolution; they have become more intelligent. A one-sided understanding of the world and the environment is increasingly being replaced by a holistic image of people who freely and independently understand their destiny with the aid of their horoscope and can either consciously embrace it as a learning process or dismiss it.

The Meaning Question and the Three-Fold Personality

The question of meaning can also be addressed using other astrological hypotheses. One of these is the gradual development in the five layers of the horoscope; the other corresponds to the construction of the three-fold personality, a concept of psychosynthesis and the esoteric psychology of Alice Bailey. This assumes that we all have a body and live in a physical reality, which is the material, physical and visible level, which corresponds to Saturn. But we also live in an emotional world, which we experience through the Moon 'I', and are also active on a thinking level, ruled by the Sun 'I'. The fourth dimension concerns our inner essence, our self or soul, as the unifying principle. Below we analyse these four stages or levels with regard to the meaning question.

  1st Level: It is easiest to understand the quality of this level if we compare it with Saturn, the ruler of form, crystallisation and matter. It rules the level of physical reality. This limits us, determines and forces physical realities upon us. It shows us our dependence on the laws of nature, on material conditionalities and on boundaries. This level is ruled by themes of continuity, stability and preservation. One does not want to change, clings to the status quo and wants to be sure of the future. This level can be compared to the fixed principle and leads us to absurdity and ultimately to the recognition of meaninglessness when death knocks at the door.

  2nd Level: This level corresponds to the Moon, the emotions and the alternating experiences of joy and suffering. The law of causality, of cause and effect, of guilt and atonement, punishment and reward, ebb and flow, of good and evil rule on this level. It is the experience of duality, the conflict between the I and the You, the discrepancy between inside and outside, between above and below, the swinging back and forth between the polarities of existence that often worries us needlessly. Through tension in the pairs of opposites, through pain, suffering and conflict, we learn to distinguish between good and evil, right and wrong. This level is comparable to the analytical one and corresponds to the mutable cross. Here there are many absurdities, contradictions and unnecessary sufferings.

3rd Level: On this level, the mental principle is in its element. In astrological terms, it corresponds to the qualities of the Sun. Here we learn that to establish the truth, there are not only two sides, but three or more. We recognise that different elements belong together, that all forms of relationship are interconnected and the deeper connections of life and death. Although here we can lose ourselves in diversity, we are aiming for a rounded character, for integration and self actualisation, for unity. On this level, on the one hand we experience the highest form of individuality, and on the other we become increasingly aware that we are a part of the whole. This experience corresponds to the cardinal principle and the Sun. Here we ask why and look for deeper connections.

4th Level: On this level, the consciousness of the soul prevails, which we can only imagine because a higher perceptual capacity, a meditative alignment, is required to know when we are in touch with our soul. The core, in the circle at the centre of the horoscope, is the place where life itself is anchored, and where the meaning of our existence is hidden. By living out of the core of our being, all diverging forces come together in ourselves or through ourselves, enabling us to attain unity and find meaning. The three spiritual planets as transpersonal general principles of the soul and the circle in the centre of the horoscope correspond to this level.

According to this reasoning, the meaning question cannot be answered with intellectual or philosophical concepts, but with a meaningful and authentic experience of the soul, in which one recognises oneself as part of the whole and is constantly developing oneself in the process of evolution. The answer to the meaning question depends therefore on our relationship with the environment, on our ability to perceive the environment as it really is with our sensory organs, while at the same time connecting with our soul, which brings us into contact with the eternal now and keeps us in contact with the source of our existence.

People who study astrology these days are usually concerned with deeper issues, like questions about vocation and meaning, which means that they cannot really avoid considering the theory of reincarnation,

The Meaning Question
from the Point of View of Astrological Psychology

**Development in the four layers in the horoscope,
four stages or levels, symbolised by planets**

1ˢᵗ Level: Unconscious acceptance of destiny   *meaninglessness*
         (corresponds to the house system or the Saturn level)

> Primitive, instinctive life experience, self-preservation. The person is to a great extent determined and does what he is told. It does not occur to him that he can free himself from obligations; he just takes this situation for granted.

2ⁿᵈ Level: The struggle for meaning, for the why   *absurdity*
         (corresponds to the zodiac signs or the Moon level)

> It is the rebellion against internal and external pressures. The person tries to free himself from the determinants, which are starting to make him suffer. Level of acute conflicts, of learning periods and contradictions. It is a fruitful learning period that is used to gain more information about reality.

3ʳᵈ Level: Finding Meaning by Complying with Laws   *finding meaning*
         (corresponds to the aspect pattern or the Sun level)

> Here one identifies with one's own self and individual means of expression. One recognises the true nature of one's being. A period of positive self acceptance and identification with personal destiny, one embraces it as something unique to oneself, develops undeluded awareness of reality and acts according to acknowledged laws of nature.

4ᵗʰ Level: Meaningful Existence in Creativity   *achieving meaning*
         (corresponds to the central core, the whole horoscope and the three spiritual planets)

> Meaning lies even deeper, in one's own creative potential. Here the person learns that he is part of eternity, part of the whole. He recognises that he must make a contribution to the whole, as otherwise life will be meaningless. He creates a new reality for himself and for others, a new world, and becomes free from all determinants. He discovers the power of the soul and true love, liberates himself from the shackles of the threefold world and achieves universal awareness.

understanding the idea of evolution and going back to the origins of things. When we search for meaning, we initially find that problematic experiences, strokes of fate, crises, suffering, hard times and painful transformation processes are all part of the growth process and aid development. We recognise the deeper hidden meaning in creative and evolutionary processes and can see them in a positive light because they cannot be avoided anyway.

The Way to the Self

We know from our inner being that our soul is the ultimate source of our existence. Our soul incarnates again and again on earth in order to achieve perfection. For we mortals, this means that our souls are eternal. Soul awareness could be described as a focus of consciousness in the "here and now, which moves through time and space", where past and future flow together. Esoterically, this focus is called the "angel of the presence" and corresponds to the 4th causal plane, astrologically to the circle in the centre of the horoscope symbolising the soul. It is a state of awareness in which meaning can be found.

We all know that the way to the self is a long and painful journey, full of crises, transformation processes and changes. The process of broadening awareness does not stop with our relationship with the environment and finding meaning in our lives, but also the vertical orientation which is related to the evolution of the self. It is symbolised by the hair cross mentioned above; this is the orientation cross in which we find ourselves. From the I to the You we find meaning through love, from our roots (4th house: background, evolution ideas, where do I come from?) to the top (MC, where am I going?) we find the meaning in our inner vocation. The symbol of this cardinal cross then converges in the centre, where the core of being can become aware. Astrological psychological synthesis shows us the way to the self, for psychosynthesis means nothing other than becoming whole. We are actually always whole, we just don't realise it!

The Astrological Way

Astrologically, we can address the meaning question in these steps:
1. Meaning can be found from a holistic horoscope chart.
2. Beginning and end of the time dimension, the Age Progression
3. Evolution, karma, cause and effect, conversion and change
4. Relationship to the whole
5. Experience of oneness and individuation
6. Creative consciousness, universality
7. The cross-hair: the two pushing directions:
   I-You / Collective-Individual
   And the circle in the centre

Here is a brief reiteration of the four stages of the experience of meaning:

1st stage (houses): experience of meaninglessness, unconscious acceptance of destiny, dependence on the environment (Saturn). We can wake up when we experience meaninglessness here.

2nd stage (planets and signs): struggle for meaning, for the why, acute conflict, fight against absurdity (Moon)

3rd stage (aspect structure): saying yes to life and to its tasks, finding meaning through conscious integration (Sun)

4th stage (centre circle, whole horoscope): meaningful existence in creativity, undertaking a task for the collective (world, mankind, earth), finding meaning.

To identify vocation requires an even closer examination of the psychological and spiritual significance of these stages or levels of awareness. The description can be expanded at will, for every person has his own individual experiences. That is how it should be, for the way to individuality requires self-awareness.

Existence Level

On the first level, life is all about survival. This is necessary, because we want and need to exist. Up to a certain point, it is also legitimate to be concerned with personal survival and to take responsibility for ourself and for our own existence. For the meaning question is automatically related to the existence question! It just has different layers, through which we must pass and form our own point of view, in order to find the way to our inner vocation. The idea of vocation is not there from the outset, it comes as awareness develops! Initially we are only interested in material things, like money, for the purposes of survival. At this stage we also have material reasons for practising astrology, we want to use it to make money! Here we want to know something about the future; we go to the clairvoyant, to the fortune-teller or to the prognostic astrologer. But because we do want to think holistically, we see that as just a stage and our consciousness evolves to the next level.

Polarity Level

On the second level, we start to wonder about the meaning of destiny, although we are still completely trapped in the polarities. That is the Moon level, the reflecting level where we first experience ourselves in a contact situation as "I" when we are touched by something emotional and experience acknowledgement. When we are loved and in contact with others, when we are told that we are good, or that we are bad, we react in a highly personal way, i.e. a subjective and "lunar" reaction. When we react sensitively to criticism or reprimand we are on this second level. Here we are easily irritated, hurt or wounded and do our utmost to get revenge. On this level things always go up and down, back and forth; reactions are volatile. We react automatically with retaliation or become defensive if someone attacks us. The score absolutely has to be settled, or we cannot be at peace.

However, at a certain point we start to ask: why is he criticising me, why doesn't he love me, why does he find something in me that he doesn't like? I therefore begin to study myself. I ask myself why I have problems in situations of conflict, in problems with my relationship, with my children, relatives or with workmates. Then, from the polarity level, a process of cognition occurs; we strive for meaning and find there is none, for this question cannot be answered on this level! As the saying goes: "you can't put out a fire with gasoline". On the polarity level everything is always black or white! That is why when we are in polarity we are unable to understand the truth or to find meaning! So we then fall into absurdity. In this situation of struggle and conflict, a relationship, for example, suddenly becomes absurd. Everything that used to be so beautiful loses its charm; it becomes meaningless because love has gone.

Love and Rejection

On the horizontal axis there is only meaning in love, in the harmonious relationship of the I and the You. It is the embracing, understanding love that leads to wholeness. Wholeness can only be understood when we experience everything as a part of ourselves. And we can only integrate something into ourselves or allow it to synthesise, when we love it and perceive it as good, meaningful and right! If we don't think it's right, we reject it. Rejection on this level is a natural reaction to anything absurd. On this polarity level we oscillate back and forth between pairs of opposites and experience the good and the bad, the beautiful and the ugly as realities! If, for example, we turn against our job because the boss is always giving us dirty looks or does not say hello in the morning – a detail in the contact situation that bothers us – then we enter a state of aversion, we just reject the boss, our work and anything connected with it. Rejection is, of course, the polar opposite of acceptance. One can also accept everything because it is positive and beautiful, because on the Moon level it corresponds to wishful thinking, or because it is the easiest way to live without making an effort.

Ultimately they both bring problems on this level, in any case until we can differentiate between the opposites and recognise the underlying meaning or laws. The opposite experiences of approval or criticism, love or rejection, etc. belong to this learning process. Nobody can really avoid this learning process, firstly because everyone on this level has an I-component, i.e. their Moon, and secondly because according to the laws of evolution, no stage or level can be skipped or left out. That is why we are all more or less actively trapped in the experience of polarity, because that is our reference to the environment. But we can change our position, broaden our awareness and learn to understand what is going on. The study of astrology, for example, can help us with this. From a superior or cosmic position, we can survey the situation, recognise the connections and therefore the meaning.

The Absurdity of War

Oscillating judgements between friend and foe are another example of the polarity level. Wars also arise from this principle, actually from the simple formula "we are the good guys and you are the bad guys", which we believe gives us the right to destroy others. Even in our enlightened times, such concepts of enemies are still created. On this level we experience the absurdity of war and arms, of which people are becoming more and more aware. Through the absurdity of this level, we reach a desperate situation from which there seems to be no escape, in which there is nothing more for us to expect, because everything we expect never happens! This desperation and agonising unhappiness in polarity is also the zero point as mentioned above, a state that Roberto Assagioli called "the dark night of the soul". Only in this absolute nothingness does our consciousness start to free itself from polarities! When we can find no more answers in this little game of good and evil, we seek help and a higher meaning.

The Peak of the Crisis

Whether in career or relationships, we only reach this zero state when the crisis reaches its peak. At this peak we can evolve into the next dimension up. That is a process of death and rebirth, without which we cannot reach a transformation or a higher level! Only in this zero state does the consciousness ask about meaning, then we want to know it and we start to study e.g. astrology or esotericism, or we start to become acquainted with the idea of evolution and to understand that there may be a karmic component involved in our situation. Then we dig deeper and want to know why and how. These questions can only be asked by the Sun, for the either-or principle, the revenge attitude prevails on the Moon level. Only on the third level do we find 'why' questions. Murderers used to be hanged without further ado; today we ask: "why did he do that?", examine his psyche to find a plausible reason for his behaviour; we want to understand and explain.

Autonomy

On the third stage, in the Sun consciousness, i.e. with the Sun that functions autonomously and can decide things for itself, we first realise that day and night, good and evil, love and hate are changing principles that are always in flux and therefore constitute a law. Then we realise that everything can be turned around. Suddenly we can also see what was actually bad as good! There we see that on this level our independent thinking, the autonomous Sun principle, has a certain power over destiny. Depending on our level of knowledge, we can give everything meaning, significance, value. We even suddenly realise that there is meaning in so-called bad, conflictive situations – every experience can teach us something!

Now we start to investigate, now we want to know! That is our Sun-I, the thinking self, that now starts to function and can achieve the ability to discriminate, initially because it is not totally at the mercy of polarities. It is, of course, impossible to live without polarities, for they are part of "being free". But on this level, we are not so completely involved with them. By behaving intelligently, we can avoid being caught up in this process of death and rebirth all the time. This is where spiritual development really begins, in this moment where we realise that we have the freedom to say "yes" or "no"! So we just say "no" to the little games and avoid them and study some fringe area or go travelling to see and experience the world and to feel everything with our senses again, so that we escape the meaninglessness of the polarity experience. We can only end this process ourselves by deciding whether we want to say "yes" or "no".

If we go to a guru and ask him what to do, all he can do is give us an antidote on the polarity level again. Or if we look into behavioural psychology, or investigate transactional analysis or other psychological methods, then we are just replacing one thing with another. Breaking down one programme and constructing another one is not the answer either. Then we realise, after two or three years of doing and trying everything, that it is not the solution, it still does not provide us with meaning, does not put us in touch with our inner self and does not free us from this state of being trapped in polarities where everything is divided! This great division still exists, even if the third pole is already very effective. All of humanity can only be born into the Age of Aquarius if they can think three-dimensionally. A manifestation of this is the increasing willingness to talk together, as is already happening on the international political stage! The polarity model is mediaeval, we have had it instilled in us for 2000 years, and it has failed.

The Third Level

Today people need a more intelligent philosophy. It is the third level, the Sun, with which we can bring together the finding of meaning and the way to the self, the holistic perspective or psychosynthesis (they are all the same thing). Spiritual development begins when we ask about meaning, because this is when we start to think macrocosmically. It is astrology that brings us this higher, universal way of thinking, not science. Until now, only astrology has embraced this new micro-macrocosmic philosophy, which in this time of change can bring about a spiritual revolution. For astrology, as the mirror of the cosmos in our horoscope, is the ordering principle. We can look into it and find everything that gives us meaningful answers if we can understand the connections, not just from the position of the Sun, Moon and aspects, but by understanding the deepest meaning of the horoscope as a whole.

The Zero Point

We now return to the basic idea of finding meaning, that we can only find meaning when we reach the zero point, for at this point we have lost everything and only our true self remains. At this point we have a spiritual experience, in which the "I am" is the only reality. There is nothing left to stop us entering the light of the soul. There, even our love for our children, partner, career, hobbies and friends can become meaningless. It is the so-called identity crisis, which often occurs at low point 9 as an absolute zero experience. I have often described this experience as "It doesn't get any worse than this!"

If one doesn't reach the zero point and does not ask oneself about the meaning of life at the low point of the 9th house, then everything becomes boring and lifeless, for meaning and life are connected! However, if we do step over the threshold of the identity crisis and dive into our own inner being at the zero point, then we connect with our own creative potential, which far exceeds our own expectations. The potential of the soul lying dormant within us is awakened by the consciousness.

At the 9th house low point we also talk about the so-called "Socrates Experience", which says "Wisdom only begins when I know that I know nothing", a typical ninth house experience. At the low point, we often experience a situation where we think we are lost, where all our accumulated knowledge of philosophy, esotericism or natural science can no longer help us. We reach a zero point of knowledge, where intellectual knowledge is no longer useful, where everything that has been learnt before is meaningless. We experience this zero point like Goethe's Faust, who had reached the point where he cried out in despair: "Here I sit, a poor fool, no cleverer than before."

The Self

In this zero state we must let ourself fall, consciously let go of everything we have learnt and thought before. As we fall, we are caught by an infinitely meaningful omniscience, which carries us and gives us intuitive knowledge, new life, new hope, new meaning. It is the self, that then works through us and shares its knowledge with us. The awareness of the self is vast; it is the new knowledge in this Age of Aquarius that we must acquire in the next 2000 years! It is already widely accepted that this divine spark is dormant in each of us. Assagioli calls it the Higher Self, and we call it the circle in the centre of the horoscope, which we consciously come into contact with at each low point. The low points are gateways to the innermost core of being. All low point planets are oriented inwards and this is also how we should experience them. If we experience them outwardly, absurdity is guaranteed! We only find meaning when we direct these low point planets inwards and deal with them consciously. In short: zero point (low points) give us the experience of the "I am" and allow us to find meaning.

The Great Whole

If we allow ourselves to fall into the inner core at the low point or zero point of the ninth house (or another house), we then experience the "I am" as the only reality. Nothing more exists outside the "I am". That is the great experience, where everything suddenly makes sense and we are caught by the Great Whole. We then really experience the Great Whole and the macrocosmic and religious consciousnesses. Meaning can therefore only be found in the connection with the Great Whole and the personal evolutionary process which is leading us towards it, towards that which is greater or macrocosmic.

Karma

Playing with karmic elements brings the danger of regressing to the second level. If we excuse everything because of karma and know that we have to put up with it, because this is the only way to free ourself from it, then we return to being trapped in polarity, even with one of these "higher" ideas! Because karmic thinking is based on causalities of cause and effect, everything necessarily takes place on the polarity level! Only when we understand the dharma (creative functioning) can we leave the second level. This is the third pole, which is already part of Indian philosophy, but almost nobody still speaks about it, only the "enlightened" or the "awakened". The idea of karma is so easy for us to understand because it involves the concept of guilt and atonement that we have been learning for 2000 years. It is so similar that all we need to do is apply it, and we are again trapped in dualism, swinging from pole to pole, caught up in a hopeless situation.

Dharma

Only the discovery of the third pole, the knowledge of "dharma", can set us free. When we understand that, a creative potential lies dormant within us, which by using our intelligence we can use to shape a new destiny for ourselves and extricate ourselves from polarities. When we discover inner freedom, make our own decisions and can consciously say "yes" or "no", free will emerges, with which we can begin to have a new relationship with the environment. Now we are unbiased, knowing that we have found our inner self, our creative power, with which we can change our environment and help other people! That is the stage at which we can find meaning.

Universal Conscience

But we are still all involved in the process of transformation, aren't we? Who has already managed to find meaning to the extent that he really feels completely responsible in his creativity as a part of the whole, by putting aside his personal goals in favour of the whole? Or as Karlfried Dürckheim puts it: "When the universal conscience awakens, we can no longer stand by, but have a responsibility to work together for the good of the community". This can be a difficult experience for many people, because they don't know what to do! People whose universal conscience is awakening feel called on to undertake a task for the benefit of the collective or to work for the Great Whole. They are able to make a creative contribution to evolution. They take responsibility not only just for themselves but also for the environment and everything that happens around them. Nothing else interests them any more. Working just to survive doesn't stimulate them and is no longer a driving life motivation.

Inner Mission

At this point, there should be some knowledge of inner mission. We first experience this when we have heard the inner voice, the inner call! Once it has developed, then life becomes a vocation! Then we live and experience as "representatives" of the whole and are ready to carry out tasks that serve the whole, the community.

The inner mission, the vocation are the final goals. Before we achieve them, we have to satisfy all the different demands of existence. But we should still think such lofty thoughts, for they inspire our fantasies, awaken our spiritual potential! We should be convinced that we are all capable of making a creative contribution, whatever stage of development we are at.

Ego

But those who have found their vocation must also control their ego goals. If we start to think we are fantastic, the ego easily becomes dependent on such thoughts. This can be dangerous, especially if there is a "vocational aspect", which usually involves Pluto. If, for example, Pluto is aspected to an ego planet, the awareness of vocation can even become a messianic complex. The ego inflation caused by Pluto can make a person so delusional that it can cause megalomania, when the ego comes to life and goes on a "guru trip". This should be avoided.

Those who have found their Vocation

Someone who has really found their vocation works in silence! He does good where necessary by reacting non-judgementally to events and sensitively to the needs of the environment. He finds himself in a permanent creative exchange with the environment without having to draw attention to himself. But there are also obstacles and pitfalls for those who have found their vocation, especially when they are in positions of power. Then it depends on whether they live on the first, second or third ray. Ray theory is a macrocosmic law that stands above astrology, and is relevant to this topic when we start to deal with greater connections! [See *Astrology and the Seven Rays*, B&L Huber.]

Motivation

The connection with motivation becomes important for the inner mission, vocation and meaning. Motivation is central to all of our astrological work. One must question oneself seriously and ask: "What is my life motivation, how many sub-motivations are involved on the different levels? Is there really one, pure motivation, or is getting right to the root of one's motivations not a multi-dimensional matter?" We have to ask ourselves questions like this when analysing our inner driving force. It is as though we have to shovel everything away in order to find the basic life motivation underneath. It is exactly the same process as "it can't get any worse than this", a process of abstraction with a deep effect. Here too it helps to use a three-stage structure, as described above.

There on the Moon level, you find the second stage, where we experience the discontent that we are all burdened with. Esoterically, this stage is considered to be an ancient Atlantean consciousness that we all have within us, and which determines part of our life motivation. However, the question of meaning already exists here too. In modern times, this expresses itself in the question "why". In earlier times, people were still too strongly determined, and were not yet allowed to be so awake! (Under all these dictatorial regimes.)

Young people today have more freedom of thought, many only do what suits them. They refuse to obey external authority, which constitutes a great change, and many have the courage to say "no". They do not let themselves be pressurised as people used to be. Many have already reached the third level (Sun). Of course, there are still many others, especially because in the current time of transition all levels are incarnated in the whole generation of mankind.

Consultation

People may still come to you for a reading wanting to know whether they will be lucky in their lives and win the lottery. But there should be fewer of them, because the whole concept of "astrological psychology" is on an entirely different level compared to giving prognoses like the yearly forecast, etc. If we are offering something holistic, i.e. astrology as a way to the self, where the person can ultimately free himself, then we automatically attract a different kind of person. It is always important to know that the motivation of serving and helping is something that is only really developed at the fourth level.

When we pose the meaning question and seek clarity and have also analysed our motivations to a deep, personal, inner life sense, then our motivation will be completely different to someone whose motivation is still to get rich! In the latter case, the person is definitely under pressure to be successful, possibly ruthlessly, and to take up a position as leader somewhere. Usually the person's horoscope reveals if they are ambitious and want to assert their ego or are ready to help and inclined to the You. Nevertheless, as often previously mentioned, the horoscope does not show the person's developmental stage.

However, we still need this motivation model in personal consultations. This enables us to establish whether or not the client is already a little awakened or is still sleeping. Being spiritually awakened means that the client has already addressed the question of meaning, he has already asked "why?" Or is he still so immersed in projection that he blames the environment for everything that happens to him, in which case he is on the second level. If he comes and insults his parents and teachers, the environment, etc., then he is still living on the polarity level.

We should then try to raise him to the third level by dropping into the conversation a few words about seeing things from a non-judgemental point of view. Making it clear to him that everything that takes place outside first takes place inside! That is the most important part of the meaning question because in the above-mentioned "zero experience" of the life principle, we can say "yes" or "no" to our existence.

No to Life

It is possible that a person wants to end their life, fully aware that next time he must keep going where this time he has given up. He knows that he cannot escape his developmental path; the self cannot be destroyed completely! He must be prepared to continue in his next life, to fulfil his tasks, perhaps under more difficult conditions, because he has run away before. It is fairly widely known nowadays that, even in cases of suicide, the law of evolution does not change.

However, free will does exist, where he has to say: "yes", because life in itself already makes sense – so he should not end it. Then he must also know that when he says "no" to his own existence, because he has lost his positive attitude towards life, then he quickly becomes negative. "Saying no" is also selfish, because we then concentrate one-sidedly on ourselves and cannot accept that life is a learning process and that the environment is also part of our existence.

The Environment and I

It is an astonishing phenomenon when one delves into a horoscope and suddenly realises that the environment is nothing other than the mirror of oneself. That can be a shocking experience! One sees very clearly that "inner" and "outer" are the same, suddenly experiences the Hermetic maxim: "as above, so below, as within so without" as a truth in itself. Part of this realisation is learning that we create our own bogeymen and cause our own problems with the environment; that we are responsible for luck, strokes of fate, growth and actions; that we bring everything that is outside within us. If we then go a step further, we see the point and know that everything is ultimately useful for our personal development. If we see everything in a negative way, then it is all is reflected back to us negatively. If we accept conflicts and problems as tasks, then our powers increase so that we can deal with them. Perhaps we will then realise that we possess a creative potential of strength and will power, which we can use to get our lives onto a new track and change the environment. All we have to do is to exercise our right to say "yes" or "no"!

Our inner attitude towards life and the environment changes abruptly after such a zero or turning point – suddenly the whole environment is different, we see many things in a new light. How often does an inner awakening happen at such a zero point, where in an instant one experiences oneself as part of the whole and has an experience of unity, where inner and outer flow together. One senses that there is absolutely no escape from the environment, even if one commits suicide. Our environment is always with us, even when we appear again in another environment; "environment and I" belong together, are always one and cannot actually be separated.

If, however, we no longer feel in touch with the stream of life, no longer find protection in the centre, feel cut off from the environment and people we love, and the constant exchange of life in our life experience comes to an end, it is as though we have fallen into a great darkness. Maya, illusion, the original sin of mankind! Satan in Sanskrit is called the Separated One, who is cut off from the Whole! Only selfishness, darkness and meaninglessness are experienced there.

Meaning, Love and Religion

That is why this whole subject of finding meaning is a religious process. When we recognise that we are a part of the whole, this is the same as experiencing ourselves as a child of God, because the whole is the Creation, formed by the creative powers. On the one hand, this experience is an initiation into higher laws, and on the other hand, into the power of love! When we find ourselves, "integration" is the principle in our hearts. We are able to experience synthesis, becoming whole and becoming healed in our hearts, in our self. When the cosmic principle of love is both integration and meaningful devotion to something higher, noble and beautiful, then with the help of universal astrology the circle of integration can become bigger and bigger. It encompasses more and more, extends from the partner to the family, from the family to the people, to all humanity and beyond, into the cosmic unity of which we are all a part. This is the homecoming, the mystical marriage or a religious or psychological experience.

Existential Fear

The search for meaning is often thwarted by existential fear. When we find ourself in a negative situation, e.g. working somewhere where we feel misunderstood and mistreated, and suffer because our value is not recognised, then this job eventually becomes meaningless. If our self esteem is constantly knocked at work, it is an unhealthy situation that should be changed as soon as possible to protect our mental health. But many people suffer from existential fear and do not have the necessary courage to change things. They feel weak and dependent; have no energy and no idea of how to free themselves from their predicament and therefore need help.

Opposition

A horoscope reading can be used to make the person aware of their misguided attitude and suggest new ways of solving the problem. For example, when an opposition lies on the existential axis, the existential problem needs to be addressed on all three levels. On the first level, an opposition often causes a compulsive behavioural pattern. If it is burdened with angst, it becomes hardened and is not so easy to change. It is not for nothing that Thomas Ring calls this the "blocking aspect". On the second level, the person oscillates back and forth within the polarity; he experiences the planets now on one side and then on the other. This is a tiring and often crisis-ridden phase that triggers an extraordinary learning process, leading to the third level. Only by clearly recognising the two poles and the axial nature of the situation can the opposition be used creatively. The third stage is always creative; one tries to experience the poles not as opposites, but as an antagonism and strives for synthesis. If it is a 6/12 axis, then the existential problem can be solved in a practical way, i.e. when work no longer makes sense, then one resigns, looks for a better job or starts to study a course that corresponds to one's own state of development at the time. Nowadays, there are many way of improving oneself, one just has to find them and recognise them.

Freedom

Many people can only gain wisdom through suffering and experiencing setbacks, in order to realise that they can say to themselves "I am going". Actually, everyone has this freedom, but many people are not aware of it because they have existential fear and believe that they can't find a better job and would otherwise be out on the street. Fear is the greatest enemy of inner freedom. The individual autonomy of consciousness must always be worked on, it doesn't just appear by itself. Again and again, we must overcome fear in order to grow beyond ourselves, and to gain the courage to act as an individual. Many people remain stuck in an apparently hopeless situation and continue to suffer. Some sometimes come to the insight that they themselves have to end the suffering, while others like to carry on suffering. There are so many ways of misprogramming our psyches.

Polarity tension

Every polarity tension (opposition) contains illusions, delusions, self-delusions, inconsistencies, contradictions, ambivalence and the tendency to self-punishment, everything that psychology can offer in the way of knowledge. That is why the experience of polarity on the second level is also a process of learning and discovery, where objective confrontation enables us to find out what we can do and who we really are. Also on this level, the horoscope serves as a diagnostic tool for realising strengths and weaknesses, an important experience for the evolving individual.

Mother Problems

From the horoscope it is possible, for example, to see the presence of a self-punishment mechanism, with which we actually want to punish our mother for not taking sufficient care of us and not loving us enough. If we see that we are always messing up our life due to a lack of maternal affection, and always putting ourself in situations with similar prerequisites, we should do all we can to solve this mother problem. At the end of the day, only we can free ourselves. But we first have to realise this, as it is not immediately obvious.

Once this has been understood, we should act quickly, get right to the root of the problem and try to investigate it. If we see that there is some kind of automatism involved, an unconscious compulsion that we cannot easily resist – which is unnecessary and unworthy for a self-confident person – then our will power and powers of resistance awaken and we can say "no, that isn't right". Of course, we cannot just solve the problem with a ray of light. For example, a square aspect between Saturn and the Moon is still effective, even after we have analysed it as a mother problem or a fear of exposure. Doing this does not solve the problem, but we can be transformed!

Transformation

Transforming means changing your attitude, your inner approach, expanding consciousness and moving to a higher level. Transformations always result in a changed inner attitude. The result of this is that we can accept the square aspect as part of us, not letting it make us feel sorry for ourselves or a victim, but learning to use the square to our advantage in the creative shaping of the environment. By doing this consciously again and again, our misguided attitudes will gradually change. We fall back less and less into the old structures or behavioural patterns because a sense of achievement and positive experiences enable us to learn to guide and control the energies more and more ourselves. However, if we do occasionally go back to our old ways, we should not feel guilty, but laugh at ourselves. Laughing is a healing energy because it stops us taking ourselves so seriously, no longer seeing everything in terms of our EGO and reacting negatively to every failure. This constitutes a great step forward. Solving problems in this way makes us interact positively with the environment and we become more and more involved in shaping of the environment, giving us a sense of meaningful joy.

Sacrifices

Someone who understands the meaning of transformation can use or express the Moon-Saturn square (and of course all other problematic aspects or aspect figures) in a different way. Someone who no longer uses the energy of a red aspect for their ego, thereby punishing the environment, but looks after others and cares about their well-being, is already transformed. Thomas Ring, the astrological depth psychologist, describes the Saturn-Moon square as follows: "You make sacrifices so that you can complain about them later."

Anyone who recognises this way of behaving is initially horrified and will say spontaneously "no I won't do that any more! I don't want to behave like that any longer, it is unproductive and an idiotic mechanism!" Then he gets to the stage where he can say "no" with complete conviction.

Here he has arrived at a zero point again; in the same place where he could even say "no" to life. However, he is now strong enough to reject such a mechanism. That is free will! He says: "Although I have this square, I will use it differently: as powerfully as the strength of my feelings and my physical effectiveness for a goal that serves the greatest number of people, no longer my ego!" In this way, the Saturn-Moon square becomes a fantastic maternal ability, because the square gives the power to care for others. In other words, the transformation involves taking energy away from the ego. Motivation must be converted into a transpersonal goal where there is no more room for the ego and it can wither away. Then a lot of good can be done with this aspect!

Joy instead of Sacrifice!

Another transformation that corresponds to our example also takes place in the collective. Sacrifice was an important leitmotif during the last 2000 years of the history of Christianity. Someone who was willing to make sacrifices and to exercise self-mastery was seen as good and could take their place in heaven. Nowadays, meek sacrificial lambs are no longer needed; we must be autonomous and be able to think for ourselves and make our own decisions. Everyone is involved in this transformation process in some way or another.

Roberto Assagioli said that the keynote of this new age is no longer sacrifice, but joy! That is an important change. Here the spiritual path is no longer sacrifice, but joyful collaboration in the divine plan, creative cooperation with evolution. And that is really much more satisfying for a mature adult than subordinating oneself as the sacrificial lamb of a feudalistic power. If a person is willing to make sacrifices and persistently behaves like a servant in their life, by helping here and serving there and working and doing everything that is expected, they never receive the feedback and acknowledgement they really crave! The aim of such sacrifice is usually to gain the pity or admiration of others.

Psychosynthesis

The theme of transformation belongs to astrological psychosynthesis, i.e. transformation from one state of consciousness to another. Where one is still a slave of a mechanism or a mother problem or some other trivial behaviour, the consciousness transcends to a higher level by means of a crisis mechanism, to where there is greater freedom. We must go through this process alone; no therapist can do it for us. He can perhaps bring clarity, indicate the connections, explain psychic structures — but know that we must always free ourselves. Even our way of working with the horoscope is always the way to self-liberation. One person cannot take away another's inner rigidity or structure, it is part of him and he himself must make the necessary expansion of consciousness. The aim of our work is to find the path to self-liberation and to achieve greater and greater freedom! This gives us joy and deep satisfaction — we have found meaning.

Psychical Light

Working in this way, we become psychically aware of the unity in the whole. At this point not only have we found meaning and our mission, but the ability to awaken the minds of others. Our own psychical light can awaken the spark in other people. We can also see the soul in others, and give free rein to the ordering and healing powers of the soul. Everything is really all right when the psychical vibration, the centre circle, the meaning, the integration, the love and everything beautiful are present. Another dimension of spiritual contact emerges and in this dimension everything is meaningful, because everything is ok. Then I can say "yes" to my own horoscope and to other people.

Saying Yes

We must learn to say yes to ourselves so that we can become whole, so that everything becomes meaningful. We can actually only say yes to things that we love, not to things we hate. We must therefore first acknowledge the good within us. That is yet another step in finding meaning and the liberation of the self. By suddenly accepting as positive forces aspects and planets that we had previously viewed with suspicion, we experience the whole aspect pattern as an energy field containing motivation, vital energy and joy, which has a revitalising effect. However, the source of this *joie de vivre* is only effective as a self-healing power when we discover it within ourselves and acknowledge it as something wonderful. It is love that creates this energy exchange.

When we reach these spiritual depths and understand the meaning there, we become able to accept any negative experiences (e.g. where we were humiliated, could not get things right and were criticised, and where everything was so hard for the psyche) as a way of learning and gaining awareness. The unpleasant and apparently bad becomes meaningful; values are suddenly reversed. What is good for the soul is bad for the ego and what is good for the ego is bad for the soul. We can suddenly figure things out so easily; we reach a place where we do not judge, where the soul is innocent, where everything returns to its rightful place and becomes meaningful.

◻ ◻ ◻ ◻ ◻

Searching for the Life Myth

Childhood Dreams, Chronic Physical Symptoms and the Birth Horoscope

Gabriele Gertz

First published in Astrolog Issues 149-151, January - May 2006

From the view of process-oriented psychology, childhood traumas and chronic physical symptoms should be understood as expressions of a personal life myth or as the manifestation of "life patterns" with life-long significance. I wanted to determine whether and how these "patterns" can be found in the horoscope. I thought that life-long processes must be visible in the horoscope as particular structures or positions or as the effects of contrasting motivations.

The point of my research is not to find similarities or matches between different disease patterns in the horoscope – this would require a far more extensive investigation beyond the scope of this article – instead I see my findings as a contribution to how astrological concepts can aid understanding of the individual significance these life patterns in a wider context.

Strokes of fate like serious illnesses are definitely the kind of experience that raise questions about causality and the purpose of our existence. They seem to be puzzles that people have always been trying to solve. What disease processes often so painfully reveal are society's ideas of right and wrong, healthy and ill, as well as the social exclusion that occurs in these cases.

Illness, Dreams and Levels of Reality

The connection between dreams and illness has preoccupied man for thousands of years, and there are countless examples and sources in human history.

C.G. Jung believed that a person's life myth is revealed in early childhood dreams, particularly recurring ones coming from the whole, the core of the personality and fundamental long-term life patterns.

Arnold Mindell agrees with Jung, saying that childhood dreams reveal the personal life myth, which is the expression of a deeper process:

"Jung discovered that childhood dreams are like personal myths; they determine long-term life patterns. I experimented with childhood dreams and discovered that they also reflect chronic physical symptoms; the earliest dreams

and memories can indicate a person's chronic symptoms. Both first or early childhood experiences and childhood dreams tell the same story. You could use both as descriptions of the pattern of your life." (1)

Process-Oriented Psychology, also called Process Work, was founded in the 1980s by Dr Arnold Mindell, a physicist and Jungian theory analyst, in Zürich. Mindell came to develop Process Work by researching illness as a meaningful expression of the unconscious. He observed that the experience patterns of current physical symptoms appeared in the patient's current dreams, while the experience patterns of long-term processes, e.g. as they appear in chronic physical symptoms, are found in childhood dreams or memories.

An experience with a dying patient led him to realise that the reinforcing or "amplification" of physical symptoms is actually crucial for the impact of the illness. Mindell worked in hospital with a patient directly after he was operated for stomach cancer. The client told him that the tumour in his stomach was giving him a lot of pain. Mindell suggested that he follow his perception of the pain and to increase the pain even more. The patient amplified the pain until he finally cried out that he just wanted to explode, he had never felt so much like exploding. At that point, he became aware that he had never actually been able to express himself in his life before. Shortly before his stay in hospital, the patient had dreamt that he had an incurable disease and that the cure was a bomb. His missing power of expression expressed itself in his dream as a bomb and in his body as cancer. Mindell elaborates further:

"Although he (the patient) only had a short time to live, his condition improved noticeably and he was allowed to go home from hospital. Thereafter I visited him frequently and every time he "exploded" with me. He shouted, cried, ranted and raved without any prompting on my part. His problem was clear to him, and his permanent somatic experience made him painfully aware of what he had to do. He lived for several more years and died suddenly after learning how to express himself better. I don't know what helped him. But I do know that our work alleviated his painful symptoms and helped him to develop himself." (2)

This and other observations of the emergence of the same experience patterns by the amplification of physical symptoms and of dreams, admittedly in different perceptual channels – sometimes proprioceptive, sometimes visual – led to the concept of the dream body. By "dream body", Mindell means a wholeness that influences our bodies, emotions and thoughts from behind the scenes.

The dream body represents a field that emits signals we can perceive in different channels. From the point of view of process-oriented psychology dreams, physical symptoms, relationship problems or problems in the world are therefore expressions of the same information in different perceptual channels.

The dream body concept lays the foundation stone for the development of the modern, more comprehensive model of the different ways of experiencing reality. This expanded model shows that perception and experience take place on different levels, which are not exclusive but complement and influence each other.

In analogy to the findings of quantum physics, Mindell introduced the term *"intentional field"* in order to interpret the quantum wave function. This mysterious field that functions behind matter and "moves" everything, is itself invisible, immeasurable and indescribable. It functions in a similar way to a gravitational field: we see its effect but we cannot see the field itself.

Mindell calls the next level *"the dreaming"*. On this level, we are able to perceive subtle tendencies, which we notice but cannot fully describe. These experiences are transient, like seeds, from which the experiences of the next two levels emerge. Mindell also calls this whole area of deepest trace experience the "essence" beyond polarities.

On the next level, *"dreamland"*, we experience dreams and dream-like processes such as, for example, physical symptoms and relationship conflicts. These perceptions and experiences are always subjective, but the information exists for long enough that parts and polarities can be described.

Mindell calls the upper level *"consensus reality"*. This refers to that part of perception considered by the majority of a collective as being "real" and that can be measured and described in terms of space and time. Consensus reality gives us cultural-social pointers by which we can orientate ourselves, and also means that perceptions and experiences that do not correspond to these criteria are considered to be invalid or non-existent.

Levels of Perception and Experience in the Horoscope

Here I see an analogy with astrological psychology. The clear display format of the horoscope developed by Bruno Huber allows us to see the astrological elements that belong to different interpretation levels. The horoscope is composed of different layers, and there is also a field in the centre that cannot be described with words. Another important innovation is the inclusion of the whole "aspect pattern" in the chart – previously the individual aspects were only shown in tabular form and mainly interpreted separately.

The comprehensive nature of the aspect pattern shows something that moves deep inside us and structures our life, it shows something that would otherwise be hidden, that wants to reveal itself and

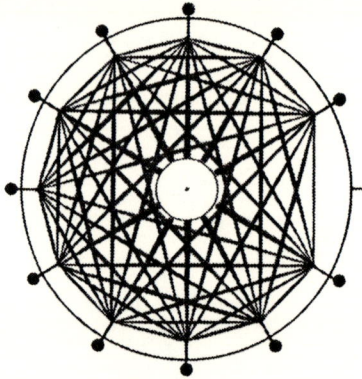

Diamond
Largest possible Aspect Figure with 10 planets and Moon Node

develop in the world. It has its own expressive value independent of the planets and their positions in the signs and houses that form it.

We cannot completely describe or define the interpretation of the aspect pattern, but, using colour and shape criteria, we can recognise and name them and so come closer to the essence. Actually, the aspect pattern shows a potential that can be expressed in different ways.

For me, these levels correspond to those Mindell called *"dreamtime"*, analogous with the cosmology of the Australian aborigines, who speak of *"the power and the pattern created by physical reality"*(3). We are not usually aware of these levels of perceived and experienced reality; however we can sense them in the form of subtle tendencies and thereby connect to the underlying essence of our lives.

Although the aspect pattern alone is already expressive, the planets and the Moon Node are also crucial, because their aspects to each other form the overall design of the aspect pattern. Their position in certain signs and houses creates a connection between the patterns within us of which we are barely aware, our hereditary physical and mental constitution and the way we experience the external reality of the environment via the process of socialisation.

We usually focus only on the level of external reality. In the horoscope this corresponds to the house level, and/or the position of each planet in the houses. Mindell calls this level *"consensus reality"*. This corresponds to our everyday reality that can be measured in terms of space and time and is defined by the majority of a collective as "real". In the horoscope the positions of the planets in certain houses and house areas show how this external world affects the individual and shapes it by suppressing certain areas to a greater or lesser extent in favour of others.

Between the levels of the aspect pattern and the houses is the zodiac level. In the horoscope, the position of the planets in the zodiac signs shows which qualities we have inherited from our ancestors and/or how we have been endowed with certain element combinations or temperaments. The genetic make-up is a challenge for us, for it gives "parts" that to do not "fit together". The questions that perhaps preoccupy us throughout our lives are: how can these parts come together, get to know each other and get along with each other? And how can something new come out of them?

For Mindell, these levels correspond to *"dreamland"*. On this perceptual level we experience our personal processes and conflicts, for instance in dreams as inner figures, ancestors, archetypes or as universal symbols, but also in oneiric processes like the experience of physical symptoms or relationship problems.

This is the field of process work, whose central concern is the deepening of individual and collective life processes, making them conscious and experiencing their pattern. As individuals, we are linked to the collective via our archetypical processes. Jung's idea of archetypes as inner figures has inspired the idea that mental processes and conflicts are experienced as inner figures. The focus of process work lies less on the interpretation of symbols and much more on direct, live experience of the developing process dynamic. This means that process workers follow their clients and work with the experience hiding behind the concepts so that each individual interpretation can be experienced and understood on the basis of the process. The interventions should help the client to perceive how the different "parts" relate to each other and how in certain moments a new identity is about to emerge.

Mapping Exercise

As I wanted to investigate whether the patterns that connect chronic physical symptoms and childhood dreams are visible in individual birth horoscopes and how they reveal themselves, I tried to collect data from people who are affected in different ways by chronic physical symptoms and carried out interviews with them. I found 16 women and men with chronic physical symptoms like poliomyelitis (1), ankylosing spondilitis (1), osteoporosis (1), slipped disc (3), knee problems (1), carcinoma (1), meningeoma (brain tumour) (1), bronchial asthma (2), neurodermatitis (1), chronic sinusitis (1), migraine (1), angina pectoris (1), strabismus (1).

I conducted the interviews in a semi-structured format and recorded them on tape. In the first interview, which lasted about one hour, I asked questions about the individual's living conditions at the time of the first appearance of the symptoms, about subjective experience and fantasies of symptoms and about changes, features and difficulties in everyday life, about their personal significance, and about what would happen if the symptoms were suddenly to disappear. My point was to capture something of the subjective experiences pertaining to the history of these people.

Eleven of my interviewees had a recollection of an impressive dream from early childhood; four had a particular memory from early childhood and remembered a strange, worrying dream that they had at about age 15 and which later preoccupied them.

Eleven people could give exact details of their birth time; four could give their birth time to the nearest hour and one person knew only the birth date.

After these first exploratory interviews, the mapping exercise was concluded and I started to study the 16 horoscopes.

Analysis

The 16 horoscopes showed a great variety of aspect patterns in terms of shape and colour, and I found it fascinating to see that there were actually aspect patterns that immediately evoked associations with the corresponding childhood dreams and chronic symptoms. Some showed the theme in the pattern itself, others in the nature of certain planetary positions.

Two examples, which I admittedly did not investigate further, may illustrate this.

One person dreamed at the age of about 5 that they were going down the street and saw that four big, frightening dogs sitting on top of each other formed a living pillar. This person suffered many problems with his spinal vertebrae, which were either broken or compressed. In the aspect pattern, the most pronounced structure was an emphasis on the vertical axis with a red tension aspect, surrounded by a big blue triangle that functioned like a soft vertebra.

Another person dreamed as a child that he swam in a seemingly infinite space full of water or turquoise liquid, quite alone, with no contact with the outside world. When he awoke, he felt completely alone. In his horoscope, the Sun and Mercury, the two instruments with which we can express ourselves as autonomous people, were in an intercepted sign, with no direct contact to the outside world. This person's chronic problem is strabismus, a squint, which became more pronounced in tense situations. Squints often happen to people who have very deep physical experiences, spiritual experiences that are almost incommunicable and very intimate.

In the first example there is a direct relationship to the form of the aspect pattern; the second example shows how a discrepancy between inner experience and outer demand is represented. In both examples, the Moon Node is in a prominent position, in the first in a large blue triangle and in the second connected to the Sun and Mercury.

My attention was first directed to the features of the aspect patterns, for example those consisting of two or more parts, their size, the emphasis on one shape or colour, detached, unaspected planets, rare planetary combinations.

I found that in the aspect patterns there were no superficially cumulative occurring features. The only significant features were indicated by the Moon Nodes and the type of aspect. Of the 16 horoscopes, 12 showed either red aspects with the Moon Node or even no aspects:

Eight had oppositions (180° aspects)
Six had exclusively or mainly red aspects
Two had no aspects at all
Two were connected with an otherwise unaspected planet.

Red aspects indicate that it is not easy for the consciousness to access the theme indicated by the Moon Node. This is particularly difficult if a planet is situated in opposition to the north Moon Node. This planet then lies at the southern Moon Node and its corresponding planetary function works as a natural talent that can be successfully implemented in life. This position initially makes it hard to get along with the theme of the opposing pole.

The situation is different when the Moon Node is unaspected. Here the effect is similar to that of detached, unaspected planets: there is no direct access to the theme. This can be expressed in different ways, for example as powerlessness or self-doubt *vis-à-vis* one's own developmental potential.

As far as the position of the planets in the houses is concerned, I had to bear in mind that five of the interviewees could not provide their exact birth time. However, this is a prerequisite for a differentiated interpretation of the planetary positions within the houses. The most important are the positions before house cusps, so-called "stress" positions, particularly before the main 1/7 and 4/10 axes, positions in intercepted signs or low point positions, particularly if there is a discrepancy between sign and house, for example if a planet in a weak position in a sign is in a strong position in a house. I found all of these in different combinations, but with no significant increase in the frequency of the occurrence of any planets.

For the case studies, I chose three people whom I wished to interview a second time. The selection criteria were firstly that they could provide an exact birth time and secondly that they had physical symptoms that impacted greatly on their professional and everyday life.

Sample Case: Poliomyelitis

C. is a woman of about 50 years old, who at the age of four came down with polio. She stayed in hospital for a whole year, until she had made a good recovery from the paralysis was able to return home to a familiar environment. As a result of the illness, she started to form a scoliosis [curvature of the spine]. That meant that during her schooling C. was excluded by many people, and also often had to miss lessons due to therapy and cures. She felt lonely in her role as outsider, and was often not able to defend herself against unfair treatment. At the time C. did not feel that things were so bad, it was only later that she realised how ignorant those around her had been of her living conditions. She had always felt herself to be "different", particularly due to her external appearance. C. was a good student, went to grammar school and on to further education. For many years she worked happily in an interesting profession and although she could never work to her full capacity, this meant a lot to her.

About 10 years ago, her health began to deteriorate so much that she eventually had to give up her job completely, which was painful for her and hard to cope with. One of the consequences of post-polio symptoms is serious breathing difficulties, because over the years the weakened respiratory muscles lead to hypoventilation, which means that the body receives too little oxygen and too much CO_2 remains in the body. For one year, C. has had to sleep with a respirator at night.

C. has very limited mobility, everyday activities require a lot of strength, everything must be planned beforehand and carefully organised. The medical description of polio is as follows: "an inflammatory disease of the central nervous system caused by a virus, which damages the stimulus-channelling structures in the plasma of the nerve cells. The mortality rate is up to 20%. The disease process involves varying degrees of paralysis. After about one to one and a half years, the paralysis recedes and permanent consequences of the disease become visible – especially skeletal and joint damage (for example, scoliosis), as well as the delaying of bone growth of some limbs" (summarised from Pschyrembel [German medical dictionary], 1977).

The symptoms C. experienced as a result of polio are comprehensive. She is quite weak; restricted mobility and associated limitations affect all areas of everyday life. She has suffered from this since childhood. She knows that she has to be economical with her strength and can never do what she wants spontaneously. The worst thing for her though is that the disability is progressing inexorably and not stabilising, which means that she must constantly adapt. Her fear is that at some point she will be only be able to move in a wheelchair or have to be on a ventilator, because otherwise she would suffocate.

Childhood Dream

At about the age of 7, C. had this dream several times: burglars enter the house, they are cannibals. She is very afraid and says to them: you must not take me, I am so small, there is not much of me!

It also occurred to her that at that time, she often had the feeling that she was followed by wild animals, lions or monsters when she walked up the steps of the dark corridors of the house where she lived as a child.

At this point, I would not like to forget to mention how amazed I was when reading Pschyrembel I came across a passage in which he mentions a certain stage of the disease, actually "the presence of infiltrators in the nervous system by numerous neurophagia". Phagocytosis is the consumption of the phagocytes, special feeding cells, which absorb and digest necrotic tissue, foreign bodies and microbes.

In the dream situation it occurred spontaneously to C. that she probably just wanted to survive and emerge from the threatening situation safely. The girl in the dream did not let herself be intimidated by the far stronger cannibals, but tried to save herself on the spot with a trick. C. said that she knew that she may have a strong will, but spontaneity is not her strength, she may often not be able to defend herself or react immediately. She remembers from childhood that her parents and other relatives just told her what to do without asking her and she did not stand up for herself. She said that she often perceived little injustices and inconsistencies, but at the time was too overwhelmed to address them. She sometimes found this irritating, however she also found it unpleasant to go back to the event afterwards and always have to explain her feelings. The chronic symptoms of the disease are powerful and existential. The poles revealed in the experience of the disease symptoms are on the one hand an inexorable, constant deterioration and on the other hand an infinite capacity to adapt. Another polarity is the lack of mobility versus being mobile and flexible. A great worry that affects C. is: will my flexibility always keep one step ahead of the progress of the symptoms or will they one day catch up with me and overcome me? Another polarity would be her physical weakness and mental alertness.

Her childhood dream features on the one hand cannibalistic burglars and on the other hand the child who is in danger and tries defuse the danger she is in with an idea, a creative spiritual act. Another polarity is the insatiability of the cannibals versus the "smallness", the lack of substance of the child.

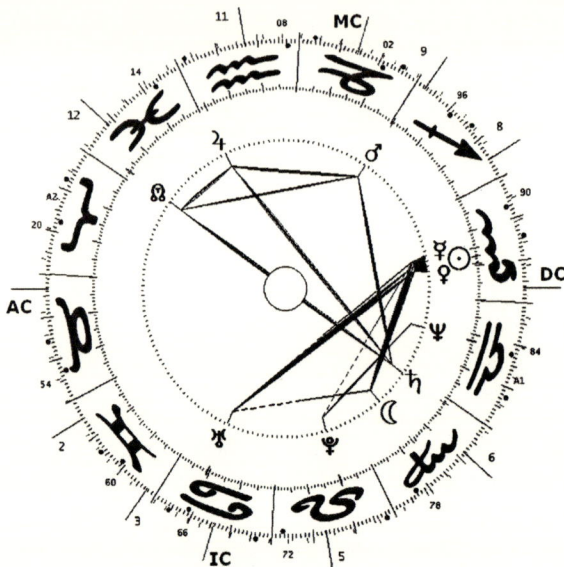

C. 05.11.1950, 16:40, Leistal, Switzerland

What does the Horoscope show?

My first impression was of something overpowering colliding with something soft.

The structure and arrangement of the aspect pattern is clear and consists of two parts, a small blue talent triangle with two lines attached to it and a three-coloured quadrilateral. That means that there are two separate "circuits" with completely different attitudes. The blue triangle works like a basket and radiates peace. Triangles represent a "both…and" attitude, indicating adaptability and flexibility. The colour blue indicates a calm, receptive, observant mood. The asymmetrical quadrilateral collides with this calmness. The dominant red-green colours have a hyperactive, restless effect, always on the go. A quadrilateral indicates a striving for security and order. The red-green colouring stimulates the willingness to actively make an effort and constantly be thinking of new solutions.

If we look at the house level, we see that there is an agglomeration of planets on the You-side, notably including the three ego planets. The talent triangle with the Sun and Moon extends from the You-side to the collective area. This part of the personality is totally oriented outwards, towards others. It would like to live in harmonious exchange with others and is able to constantly readapt according to the available possibilities. The asymmetric red-green quadrilateral has Saturn as the limiting principle on the You-side. Saturn in the 6th house on the You-side longs for a concrete physical sense of identity, so that the personality is not overwhelmed by external demands. The quadrilateral extends further with Mars and Jupiter in the individual area, and with the Moon Node in the 12th house reaches the most secret and intimate area of the I-side. This part of the personality is "private", it is not revealed on the first meeting, but only after long acquaintance. The planets forming this structure indicate alertness, an intensity of perception, the ability to perceive discrepancies and inconsistencies and recognise weak points and perhaps bring them to the light of day, and a certain striving for perfection. It is noticeable that the planets forming this structure all lie at weak points in the signs, but are strongly placed in the houses. This means that her genetic make-up is weak, but everyday life makes great demands on her. This causes conflict, which may be felt as a constant pressure, an inner threat.

Synopsis

The aspect pattern shows two completely different basic orientations that are not easily reconciled and which are subject to constant and often abrupt changes. One part is more easily visible from the outside and appears as the natural talent, the available energies that are adapted to the possibilities that arise, cleverly discriminating, flexible, open and responsive to others. The other part is not directly accessible from outside, and probably always limits itself or inwardly says "stop" if things get too much. It is dynamic, alert, has high expectations of itself and others and does not give up until all is in order. This reminds me again of the phagocytes, feeding cells that put everything "in order" by "eating" the necrotic tissue and foreign bodies.

The two opposing structures in the horoscope – on the one hand intelligent adaptability and relative openness to the outside world; and on the other a tireless, almost "voracious" dynamism, behaving or organising energetically – have their equivalents both in the experience of symptoms and in the childhood dream.

In the childhood dream, we have on the one hand cannibals that break into the house and on the other hand the child in danger and her quick-witted attempt to escape danger. My hypothesis is that C. needs the indefatigable, "voracious" energy of the burglars – which are also shown in the dynamics of the red-green quadrilateral – in order to protect the most intimate parts of herself. Her otherness forces her to work hard to limit and process the injustices to which she is

constantly subjected. Her flexible, adaptable and open side – visible in the blue triangular structure – corresponds to the child in the dream.

In the experience of the disease symptoms, we find on the one hand infinite adaptability and on the other hand a progressive degeneration process. C. finds that this process always requires more energy than she has to give. One of the life themes of C. is the relationship between the poles "inflexibility" and "flexible adaptation". On the material level, there is no solution: there is no new body. The solution is spiritual and mental freedom.

The Moon Node is included in the dynamic part of the horoscope, and stands in opposition to Saturn. This reinforces Saturn, symbolising the body – the theme of this Moon Node axis, the 6/12 axis, is "existence", with that of the 6th house being "material existence" and that of the 12th being "spiritual and mental existence". Only once we have the ability to set boundaries, to react to danger and to develop a certain immunity can we preserve our identity and therefore our existence. That is the theme of Saturn in the 6th house and also one of C.'s talents. The Moon Node in the 12th house could mean in this context that I know I am a unique being with my very own character who is also part of the great whole and it is in this knowledge that I find my absolute freedom.

During both interviews with C., I got to know her as a person. She has a cheerful and relaxed charm, does not let her considerable disabilities get her down and has become an expert at always managing to retain a certain degree of freedom.

The Personal Mythology

The idea that people are living their own personal myth is not new. It appears that an underlying process, an unconscious pattern, motivates us and pushes us in a certain direction, structures our perception and conditions our experience of the outside world. Many of us have connected with these inner forces, even though we cannot exactly put them into words. Sometimes we have fantasies or dreams that allow us to sense things and such inner images can help us to explain the mysteries of our existence or to give meaning to fragmented experiences that we would otherwise find chaotic.

David Feinstein and Stanley Krippner have dealt thoroughly with the personal myth. They talk about a "personal mythology" which they define as complex inner structures *"which explain the world to the individual, guide their development and establish a relationship with the mysteries of existence in a form which corresponds to the one in which cultural myths fulfil these tasks for society."* (4)

Their concept came about in the context of a comparative study at the Johns Hopkins University School of Medicine, in which Feinstein compared 46 different theories on the theme "Psychotherapy, personal growth and spiritual development". He used the term "personal mythology" to describe "the changing sense of reality" that appeared to be a central theme in the various clinical and spiritual areas that were presented in the study. Later, Feinstein in collaboration with Krippner developed a workshop concept and completed it by linking the "personal mythology" with the current scientific understanding of cognitive processes and indicated the possibility that this could be an important psychological perspective. In the book that they co-wrote, *Personal Mythology* (1987), they describe that in the personality the urge for perfection and unity does exist, but in the same person there are conflicting myths that are expressed at different times. These relatively autonomous subsystems are the source of possible, often unconscious, conflicts.

According to Feinstein and Krippner, the personal mythology of a person develops from different, independent sources, i.e. genetic, biological, biological, cultural and transpersonal:

"Personal myths are conditioned from within and without. Their origin lies in the body; they are formed by the environment. The organic origin of personal mythology is both biological (in the traditional sense) and biologically-based, though transpersonal. Influences from the environment are both cultural influences and the unique experiences that make up an individual's personal biography."

"The different origins of personal mythology influence each other. Innate qualities that in themselves are of minor importance can for example become very important when the myths of a culture attribute special value to them. Whether someone is born tall or short, black or white, thin or fat, man or woman, weak or strong can have a great impact on their lives. If one is born black in a predominantly white culture, the personal mythology that one develops is quite different to that of a white person. A little girl in an authoritarian, male-dominated society will develop a different personal mythology to a boy in this society. The same is true for children who either do or do not correspond to the standards of beauty of their culture and those young people who are innately equipped with particular strength and adaptability."

There is a parallel between the concepts of the "personal mythology" and astrological psychology. The birth horoscope shows how the complex inner structures are interconnected and interact with each other. In the chart we see that the different components work on different levels. These levels are mutually dependent and complementary; they are expressions of the different worlds of a person's subjective perception and experience. For example, the horoscope can show the potential for conflict between profound inner motivation, the innate personal physical and mental constitution, or the demands of the external environment. Understanding this allows the unique subjective experiences to be placed in the appropriate context and to be given meaning.

Long-Term Life Patterns

It appears that we replay our "personal mythology" over and over again in countless variations in our everyday life. This individual system of constantly changing, complementary and often contradictory "personal myths" structures our perception, thoughts and

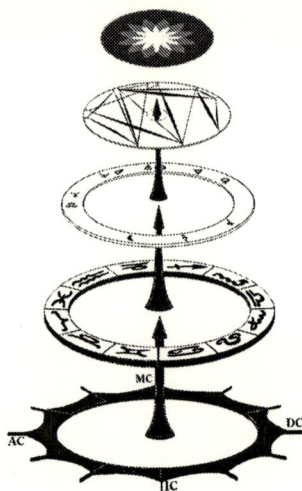

The five levels of the horoscope

actions. They are patterns and processes that work throughout our lives and determine our thought patterns and therefore our reality. They establish our role in society and, not least, also guide our development so that we find spiritual connectedness.

Some of our personal myths do not conform to current cultural myths. As we do not live in isolation, we cannot separate our destiny from the community and society in which we live. This conflict can sometimes have a threatening, iniquitous and destructive effect, or enable us to free ourselves from a one-sidedness oriented to everyday reality so that we can connect with our personal power.

In his autobiography *Memories, Dreams & Reflections*, Jung describes in detail his individuation process, which he saw as a process of maturing and development that follows an individual pattern. This individuation process, also described by Jung as a method and way of broadening the personality, consists of a gradual convergence to the centre, the centre that is the source and ultimate base of our psychic being. For Jung, this means recognising oneself as what one intrinsically is, becoming oneself and understanding one's own personal myth. Jung used the image of the medieval alchemists, who tried to heat prima materia – or raw material – until it turned into gold, to describe the developmental process of the unconscious and to recognise that its contents are revealed in dreams. According to his observation, early childhood dreams give clues about a person's long-term life pattern.

One of Jung's most important principles was the concept of teleology, which states that all events have a meaningful purpose or goal. While Jung mainly applied this principle to dreams, Mindell also used it to research into disease processes. In his work with dying people, he discovered that physical symptoms, if amplified and allowed to evolve, reflected dream images. Process-oriented psychology or process work, as developed by Mindell from analytical psychology, assumes that in the structure of what is happening, i.e. in the "process" of the client as manifested at a given point in time, a pattern appears as the perceptible expression of an inner autonomous power whose message can be decoded.

One foundation for the understanding of long-term processes, with which we sometimes have to deal over a whole life-time, we can find in the pattern of childhood dreams and in chronic physical processes. These processes only reveal themselves gradually and much love and patience is required for them to unfold. Such almost timeless processes confront us with our innermost patterns and appear to work on a deep level, on which current processes build on each other in countless variations.

The Puzzle of Perception

In an article that appeared in the *Journal of Process Oriented Psychology* in 1993, Joe Goodbread speculated among other things on how perception occurs, how experiences are structured and the challenges this presents to process oriented psychologists.

The main ideas are summarised briefly below: it appears that perception of an experience is regulated by the whole context of the experience. For example, we could perceive a certain group of people as "the family that live down the street". If we were to get to know them better, they would become separate individuals. If we were to meet one of them in the street, we could either identify them as a member of this family or as Jenny, the 12 year old girl. If we were to learn more about the family, we would know that her father was in prison or that all the children were excellent musicians or that they were all political refugees from Haiti. The more information we have about them, the more details we have about their everyday lives and background, the richer and more complex our perception becomes and the more difficult it becomes to adapt this family stereotype to the needs of our own projections.

According to Goodbread, there are no chaotic experiences. Experience is structured according to specific patterns. Experiences in new or unfamiliar areas tend to be structured according to experiences that appear similar in already-known areas. If there is really no chaotic experience, what is chaos? Chaos is a special way of experiencing a certain aspect of reality, for which we have an unclear or limited existing pattern. "Chaos" is a description that people use when they consider an already existing facet of their experience for which they do not yet have a clearly structured mental image or for which their existing imagined structure leads to something unusually unpleasant.

Truly unstructured experience is usually not perceived. There is a story told by Marshall McLuhan, in which a group of well-meaning filmmakers went to a third world country to prepare materials for hygiene education. They made a film that showed how to handle food hygienically. Eventually they showed it to the target group and asked them what they had seen. Some replied that they had seen a chicken. The film makers were taken aback, firstly because the viewers of the film had obviously not understood the message and secondly because they could not remember filming a chicken. Finally they found a sequence in which a chicken was barely visible in the corner of a frame. Why had the viewers seen the chicken but not understood the message of the film?

It appears that instead of perceiving an experience as disturbing, because it lacks coherence within a certain perceptual context, we simply ignore it. We tend to impose a structure on disturbing experiences that is based on what we already know about experiences that appear similar.

Goodbread elaborated further, that the "normal", habitual way of structuring is overruled if we are not in our "normal" state of consciousness, but in one that is slightly or very different. In the example already mentioned of Mindell's patient who had just had a tumour removed from his stomach, and directly after the operation found himself in a very different state of consciousness, the patient still felt the presence of the tumour. Normally we are encouraged to organise our personal experiences according to general standards of knowledge, which marginalizes our subjective inner experiences. The experience of Mindell's patient was structured in a different way though. It was an experience that evolved: every aspect of his experience arose from the preceding one and it was barely influenced by "accepted knowledge". However, the unfolding of this process was not completely spontaneous. It was structured by the interaction between Mindell and the patient. Certain key features of Mindell's attitude towards the patient were beneficial in that they helped the patient to evolve his experience to greater awareness and at the same time also to interpret it in such a way that it allowed him to connect present and past experiences of his life story within it.

A Map of Subjective Perception

Goodbread goes on:

"Our desire to research experience is based on an apparent impossibility, a contradiction. We wish to follow the experience of another person into

uncharted waters. However, we have now discovered that where there is no map, there is also no experience. We simply do not perceive things for which we have no existing perceptual model. Equally, that which we experience in a given situation can be dramatically affected by what we expect to experience. To help others to follow the trail of their unfolding experience means on the one hand risking imposing an arbitrary structure upon it and on the other hand there is a danger of being unable to see any structure at all and finding that experience completely chaotic. However, finding somebody else's experience chaotic harbours the danger of branding the person as mentally ill and leaving them at the mercy of the highhanded masters of psychiatry. Following other people's experience professionally is therefore a serious and delicate task, which requires a deep understanding of both the philosophical and practical problems involved on the part of the process worker." (5)

This being the case, it is definitely a great challenge for the process worker to lead a client into the unknown and to help them to follow the process that is trying to express itself at that precise moment. Following the process means exploring uncharted territories. It can be that as a process worker I have experienced similar landscapes before, but on the way there are always surprises, sudden twists, unexpected perspectives or insurmountable obstacles. A lot is happening simultaneously on many levels. Following the process means also seeing how a new experience changes the client and to what extent the client is aware of this.

Sometimes it would be helpful to have a map that the process worker could use to orient themselves and to see "how the land lies". The birth horoscope represents just such a completely individual map, and allows her to see the wider context, or the big picture. The big picture gives her clues about the subjective frame of reference, which she can use to see the layout of factors that generate a certain process dynamic at a given moment. This map of subjective reality can also help to find coherencies where she herself cannot yet see any. Last but not least, the client's horoscope shows the differences between her own frames of reference. The knowledge of different perspectives and perceptual models can promote empathy and also create awareness for possible relationship pitfalls into which she could fall.

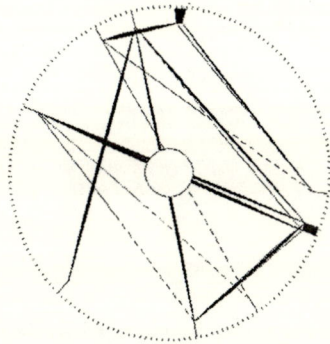

Case Study

The following example illustrates how valuable it is to include the birth horoscope as an additional source of information and orientation in a long-term process, in order to understand the subjective experience and the newly unfolding personality in a wider context.

D. is a women aged 58, who has been a client of mine for a good four years. Thirteen years ago she suffered a brain injury as a result of an operation to remove a tumour, in which the frontal lobe of the cerebrum was damaged. That is the region of the brain in which brain research tells us that the cognitive faculties are located: planning, deduction, calculating, associating, abstract thought, recognising laws and so on. Although she can live alone again thanks to an arduous rehabilitation process lasting several years, she still finds it hard to cope with everyday life.

The symptoms that D. has experienced as a result of the brain injury are altered sensory perception, such as distortions of space and time, the inability to separate or combine sensory impressions, threatening physical symptoms like the "disappearing" of the left side of the body, the lack of "presence of mind" – a kind of stepping outside the body, memory disturbances, reduced ability to concentrate, great fatigue, dizziness and other border experiences that she found hard to classify. The result of the brain injury is that, in a manner of speaking, her knowledge and skills are suddenly no longer automatically available. She can no longer rely on anything that she used to be able to know well. Above all, she can no longer classify her perceptions as she used to. She described to me her experience as beyond words – particularly painful for her, for her eloquence and love of language are important parts of her self-awareness, and, not least, are also her profession. "It feels a bit like someone blindfolds you, then turns you round and round and then lets you go again and you open your eyes and you no longer know who you are or where you are."

Her main problems are the perceptual disturbance, the sudden fatigue and the experience that every action is an enormous effort for her.

At the start of the process work, D. set two goals: she wanted to find a way to live with her brain injury and to find out what life wanted from her.

Initially we worked for a long time with the experience of fatigue. D. had a great *edge* (*) accepting the fatigue as well as an *edge*

(*) *Edge*: experience that one is not capable of doing or thinking something. It means the edge of our identity, the edge of what we like and are familiar with. *Edges* are reinforced by belief systems.

concerning physical awareness mainly, because this sensory process was so painfully linked with the symptoms that she suffered as a result of the brain injury. At the *edge*, she felt a kind of dizziness and a pull into the void, which caused her great anxiety. She was afraid that she would get lost or disappear, fall into a hole or disintegrate. Once we did an exercise where the point was to experience no longer having an identity and then to sense what was left. D. felt an empty space and a centre in her stomach. She found this to be paradoxical and incomprehensible. There were waves and particles next to each other. There was something primeval and it filled her with joy. But her intellect was not satisfied because it could not classify and explain it. Another time, she had a deep physical experience, when she just trusted her feelings. First she was afraid of disappearing, then she perceived how the right side of her head crumbled and she felt a hole in her body that became bigger and bigger. I encouraged her to concentrate on her breathing. She breathed calmly and evenly and her facial features relaxed. After a long time, she said that she was in a cloud and had a "blue feeling". In her head were ashes. She immediately wanted to analyse and question everything. At that time, I had not yet seen her horoscope and had not yet made a connection with her childhood dream. I only knew that this was an important clue.

At the age of about five, D. had a recurring nightmare. She dreamt that she was a little girl dancing on the water of a lake and wearing a little blue dress. She then found herself in a canyon with high, steeply-sloping rock faces. The walls came nearer and nearer and eventually collapsed on top of her. She then woke up screaming with fear.

When we analysed this dream, D. did not find it strange that the girl could dance on water. The rock faces were ominous. It was important that she examine them closely and thereby discovered that they were covered in ferns, "primitive" plants that she loves. She developed the dream further, in answer to my question "where are your feet?" "feet with water swilling around them" – wading down the middle of a stream in the canyon. Unexpectedly, she did not arrive in a barren rocky landscape, but into a green wood, that looked like a "cathedral-like hall". The trees only had branches right at the top and formed "a cloud". Then, still walking through the stream, she reached a lush, green meadow, where the source of the stream lay. Everything felt soft and round and her feet, up to the ankles in the water, gave her a sense of repose. She felt content and completely empty. The "sense of a repose" is confidence-giving. She does not need to do anything, take care of anything or achieve anything. At some point she will continue on her way, for sure, but now she is resting – like a great void. There is feeling and knowledge with no need for reflection. It is like dancing on the lake; as soon as one starts to think about it one sinks.

In the course of the four years, there were different phases. There were blockages and very slow changes. I will now describe a couple of important stages.

D. grew up in a world in which both personal achievement and social adaptation were required. One part of her identity longed to adapt to the norms of social behaviour. She identified herself as an intelligent, cultivated and aware woman. Her *edge* is being "emotional", losing her temper or getting angry. A limiting figure said that it is primitive, ignorant and backward to show uncultivated emotions like anger, rage and hate. She found herself to be "monstrous" if she had feelings of anger or rage. She visualised a "nagging monster" that did not stop nagging until it was listened to. It did not ask if it is intruding if it gets in the way, and expresses its frustration if someone offends it. D. has an *edge* when it comes to controlling this figure. The thought that the brain injury had left her with strong, unprovoked, uncontrolled emotional outbursts, was too painful for her. The fear of being "worthless" was too great.

Over several sittings we approached the theme of worthlessness. Once she visualised the figure of a "badly dressed and coiffed American girl". She is "common and vulgar, but confident in her own way". She doesn't care what people say about her, but just looks out for herself and makes sure that she is comfortable with herself in all aspects of her life. She is not at all refined, not very conventional, and her main concern is that she "is happy in her own way". Once D. had also tried out the girl's posture, facial expressions and movement patterns, she thought that this girl had her own way of moving and she wanted to copy that too. Another question that preoccupied D. in connection with relationship conflicts that she was experiencing at the time was the question of why she was often perceived to be arrogant. She said that she simply did not want to react emotionally, but then she was accused of being arrogant. Since the brain injury, D. suffered even more from conflicts than before, found them even more threatening and felt powerless. She did not dare to defend herself against attacks, because as a result of the brain injury, she did not know which social behaviour was appropriate when. When she gradually succeeded in consciously accepting her reproached attitude and became "conceited", "arrogant" and "a know all", an impressive figure emerged. She was powerful, autonomous and positive. "She knows what is right – she knows how it must be" – she wants to "take control" and evidently has the ability to do that. D. laughed with a deeper more powerful voice, which gave her an imposing persona. Conscious experience of this figure was an important step for D. Gradually, she was able to examine her own powerful and self-willed side. She began to define herself more clearly, without such a bad conscience, and was consequently better able to express her abilities and skills. Interestingly, the reaction from her environment was mainly positive. She herself was surprised that her expertise was so appreciated. This gave her renewed hope that there may be a place for her in society and she had more confidence in "my existence as a brain-injured person". This process seemed to her to be very long and reminded me of the collapse of the rock face in her childhood dream, which was a catastrophic event for the girl. The threatening rock wall appears both in D.'s experience of conflicts and in the absolute, powerful and self-willed figure. An important theme for D. is dissociation, not getting too emotionally involved.

Something was changing very slowly in D.'s life. Very unremarkable things became more and more important: simply "being", listening to herself, being aware of herself. Doing "trivial, banal things" like going to the market, making jam, taking a coffee with her daughter and chatting, repotting plants – without feeling insignificant or superfluous. There were more and more often moments in which she felt a deep, serene feeling of "nothing is important, everything is the same – everything is equal". However, although D. was more and more amazed at how she mastered things, which gave her the feeling that she could cope with everyday life, she "forgot" the good experiences again. She suffered from often not having reliable access to them due to memory disturbances. She also often complained that she experienced the world as chaotic, and creating order and structure required a lot of energy. Also, she always wanted to classify her experiences as universal concepts, so it was difficult for her just to trust the experiences for what they were. Something within her was always looking for more. Something was still missing. Her indefatigable searching and wrestling reminded me sometimes of modern physicists and their search for a single theory that could explain all phenomena.

A mere 6 months before the end of our work together, we started to talk about astrology. Together we studied D.'s birth horoscope. When I looked at it for the first time, I got the impression of multi-facetted cut crystal. The aspect pattern is highly structured, dominated by an absolutely symmetrical pentagon formed of all three colours, in which all three ego planets are connected. That shows a personality that confronts things, gets to the bottom of things and thereby creates its own security. A high achievement potential, adaptability and the desire for almost unattainable goals are combined here. The equilibrium of the pentagon is broken on three sides. A single green linear figure runs through the middle of the pentagon, indicating a constant searching for meaning and connections. Another striking feature is that the Moon Node is unaspected, so that it is not

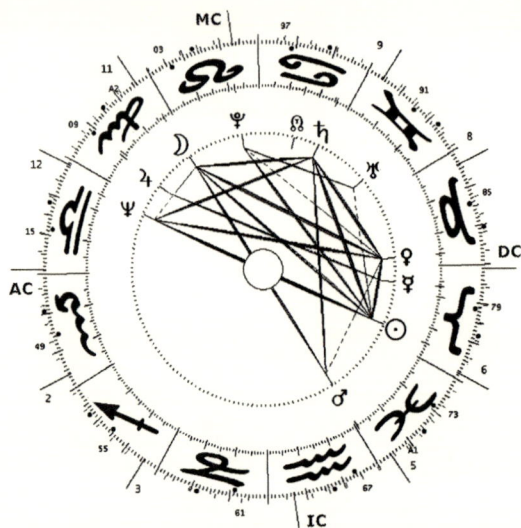

D. 25.03.1945, 20:55, Basle, Switzerland

encompassed by the inner "circuit" of the personality and therefore does not have direct access to this potential. That can lead to a feeling that one is not getting anywhere despite one's best efforts.

If we consider the outermost level, the houses, we see that the majority of the aspect pattern lies in the upper half. In cases like this, priority is given to knowledge over experience and to planning over execution. All three ego planets, Sun, Moon and Saturn, are in strong positions in the houses and are directly connected to each other, producing a natural "I am" feeling. This personality places great importance on creating something with their expertise that also means something to other people. It wants to be guided by its own perceptions and has a clear idea of decent and respectable behaviour. There is, however, a limiting factor here: Saturn, symbolising the limiting principle and physical awareness, although in a strong position in the 9th house, is situated in the intercepted water sign of Cancer. This constitutes a two-fold insecurity: firstly, planets in intercepted signs cannot be outwardly effective and receive little acknowledgment from the environment and secondly, the element of water is not optimal as an instrument responsible for setting boundaries. Along with the stable, large aspect structure, there is a separate green linear figure joining the two intelligence planets, Mercury and Jupiter: this personality has the ability to perceive and evaluate things, situations and people devoid and isolated from personal needs. This can make the person seem cold and impersonal.

The unaspected Moon Node is situated, like Saturn, in the 9th house in the water sign of Cancer. The theme of the 3/9 axis is "thinking" and "communication" in the broadest sense with both poles "public opinion, collective, standardised thinking" in the 3rd house and "autonomous thinking, personal opinion, intellectual independence" in the 9th house.

D. felt that the association with cut crystal was appropriate. A crystal is something everlasting and unchanging. The highly structured and almost symmetrical aspect pattern also appears solid and unalterable, like a mighty rock face. In the childhood dream the rock face collapses. The brain injury also caused D's life to collapse. She can no longer classify her perceptions as she used to. She has no structure and orientation, which she sometimes finds almost unbearable. Symptoms such as exhaustion or dizziness force her to surrender to chaos and "step outside" of the known world. By trusting physical perception, she first found a void, then a cloud in which she felt a "blue feeling". She experienced something similar when she developed the childhood dream. First of all, she was afraid of the rock faces, then she entered a cathedral-like vault made of high tree tops, felt great emptiness and contentment and had a "sense of repose" in her feet. As she followed her body, she had new experiences in other channels and so broadened her perception: the threatening and mighty rock face became a protective cloud.

For D. it is vital to create personal security by ceaselessly ordering and structuring. The unaspected Moon Node seems to say to her: drop out, take a break, trust your experiences – it's true that the world is changing, but you are changing with it. D. said that for her there are two kinds of chaos: one is meaningless and has a disintegrating effect, and the other makes sense. The difference stems from the means of perception: in the auditory-visual channel it is confusing – in the proprioceptive-kinaesthetic channel it is the perception of the freely moving flux of things. Everything moves easily and organically.

D's old identity needed first to create order and structure, just to do something, which is very tiring. The *edge* is to say: It doesn't matter! The expanded identity is knowing and feeling how "it" moves at each moment and wondering at it. When she analysed the childhood dream, and discovered the "sense of repose" in her feet, she said that this feeling and knowing required no reflection, it is the same as dancing on water; as soon as you start thinking about it, you sink. Both these things, the "sense of repose" in her feet and the girl dancing on the water in the childhood dream are, in my opinion, patterns that reflect the unaspected Moon Node.

The earlier work with the dream figures, starting with the nagging monster via the common American girl to the powerful, self-willed figure, seem to have prepared the terrain: they are all connected with the intercepted Saturn in the 9th house, i.e. trusting only herself, her own experiences and perceptions.

D. also gained a new perspective on her way of communicating, sometimes criticised as being impersonal, which made sense for her. Referring to her horoscope enabled D. to situate and understand her "new, other knowledge" in a wider context. Once she was able to identify more with her inner world, she no longer felt judged or forced to accomplish something in particular. Knowing about her character revealed to her a deeper "order". Perhaps the most important thing was that she felt that her behaviour was validated and acknowledged deep inside herself. She realised that she could write well, speak in public and teach people. However the deciding factor was, she said, that by trusting her experiences and finding her own truth, she could also help other people.

For me as a process worker, the inclusion of the horoscope as a frame of reference was enlightening, inspiring and complementary in the sense that it helped me to connect, interpret and place in her personal context D.'s experiences so that she was able to give them meaning.

Bibliography

(1) Arnold und Amy Mindell – *Riding the Horse Backwards*.
(2) Arnold Mindell – *Dreambody*.
(3) Arnold Mindell – *Working on Yourself Alone: Inner Dreambody Work*.
(4) Feinstein D./Krippner S. (1987) – *Personal Mythology*
(5) Goodbread J. (1993) – *Journal of Process Oriented Psychology*

Illustrations: Jac H. Riger

❑ ❑ ❑ ❑ ❑

The Trinity – Ideality, Reality, Hope

Wolfhard König

First published in 'Astrolog' Issues 124-127, October 2001 - April 2002

Ideality

I consider this subject to be very important, because I believe ideality is something uniquely human, so that when we have understood its value and role in human life, we have understood something of what it means to be human.

In this article I will use the terms ideality, reality and hope with quite specific meanings that I go into in more detail below. They are often used differently in everyday language and in other fields.

In my opinion, ideality is a uniquely human quality, which is a product of man's characteristic capacity for awareness. His ability to confront the world perceptively and with awareness and curiosity, i.e. to question the world as he finds it, enables him to relate to his ideality. For if I have a model of the world within me, an idea, an ideal, of how it could be or how it should develop, then from this inner reference point I can question or criticise what I find in the external world in which I want my ideal to be actualised. This therefore means that this inner reference point, this ideal, is what enables me to distance myself from a world, an environment that I experience as the reality of the status quo.

This ability to dissociate is something specifically human, and is not found in the animal kingdom. The animal is actually unconsciously completely identified with the environment in which it lives, to express it in our human language. In biology this fact is called the key-lock model: the animal is as adapted to its environment as a key to a lock. It can react to this environment, but cannot reflect on it, contemplate it or reach insights or perceptions.

The animal will approach its environment with certain needs and try to satisfy them; that is to say firstly the primal urge to survive and to find food, then to dominate a territory, live in a pack, find a mate, etc. In the process it will experience difficulties, resistance and restrictions from its environment. It will very probably learn to cope with these difficulties and overcome and avoid them. Very probably it can learn to adapt its vital functions and abilities optimally to its environment. But all this is just a more or less unconscious reaction to environmental conditions. What the animal is unable to do is to "step back" from the world, to contemplate it, reflect on it, understand it and in such a way become aware of it.

This is precisely what humans **are** capable of. We have the ability to dissociate, which allows us to stand back from the world, to reflect on it, to become aware of it and to confront it sensibly. Erich Neumann (1) in particular has clearly shown how important this ability to dissociate is for the emergence of human consciousness.

Instead of the ability to dissociate, I prefer to talk about being able to establish a "distance relationship" with the world. By this I mean man's ability to perceive and be aware of his environment, the reality that he encounters, and thus to remain grounded in it – but without necessarily having to react "blindly" and only according to his previous experiences and hereditary or learnt behaviour patterns. Instead, man can step inwards, go within himself, step back from and contemplate his environment, perhaps gaining new perceptions in the process that make him change his subsequent behaviour. This allows man to react to his world quite differently to the way an animal can; in a way that is unique to him, i.e. in a conscious way (2).

It can happen though that a person who lives consciously by his ideals often encounters a restricting environment that completely or partially prevents the actualisation of these ideals. Often the environment will confront him from a position of power and try to block his ideas and criticisms (e.g. the Spanish Inquisition, political persecutions, etc) or put pressure on him as regards his basic survival needs of food, clothing, somewhere to live, work, etc. In this type of situation the best he can do is try to react as well as possible to the environmental conditions, the hard challenges confronting him, to comply with and adapt to them.

This process of adaptation can be a conscious one, i.e. the individual can be aware of the adaptation; he does not therefore necessarily need to identify with the corresponding environmental conditions (unconsciously) and inwardly accept them. The adaptation can remain on a purely external level. Internally though, he must maintain and protect his relatedness to his ideal and, from the perspective of this inner reference point, continue to criticise and

1. Erich Neumann, *Krise und Erneuerung.*
2. When I talk about "animals", I am referring to averagely occurring abilities and ways of behaving. Specifically, I would like to open the question as to whether the ability to dissociate in the above sense, i.e. ideality, is not also present in a rudimentary and sporadic form in the most developed animals, the anthropoids, as demonstrated by W. Köhler, with reference to intelligence. However, the fact that ideality is something specifically human should tell us that it is of a pre-eminent and central importance in human life and for the development of human consciousness, which it does not even come close to for animals, even the anthropoids.

question the circumstances and want to work towards changing them. This is how what I mean by dissociation works. On the one hand the person concerned is completely adapted to the conditions of his environment, which he cannot immediately change and is therefore still related to; on the other hand he maintains an inner distance from them and therefore does not stop measuring them by his ideal, questioning and wanting to change them. The fact that we can do both of these things at the same time is what makes us human, what opens up our vital and most important spiritual *lebensraum*, and which has most effectively and meaningfully

Detail from Botticelli's "Primavera"

changed the face of the world and people during the course of human history. Such an inner reference point and its universe is what I call ideality.

This is what should be understood by "ideality in the broader sense"; later we will also encounter what I call "ideality in the strict sense", or "intrinsic ideality".

An inner reference point, as described above, can generally be understood as an expectation that the individual wants to actualise, with which he approaches the world, and by which he measures it (3). I now distinguish three possible sources of such expectations.

The first source we can consider to be biologically preconditioned or innate. We share this with the animal kingdom. The expectations involved here are the expression of the drive for self and the preservation of the species, i.e. the expectations of being able to survive and live in this world, of being able to acquire all that is needed to do this and to be able to reproduce.

The second, and most common, source of such expectations is the inner urges that push people to confront the world and even make demands of it. These expectations are the result of conditioning, upbringing, the influence of parents, teachers, the child's environment, which teach it to face its environment with certain expectations and overall concepts.

The third source is the essential impulses and expectations that come from our core being, our innermost selves. I will call this combination of expectations, inner impulses, inner reference points "ideality in the strict sense", or intrinsic ideality.

---

3. This definition of ideality is given e.g. by Johanna Tamm in her work *Angst und Subjecktivität*.

Impulses from the first source initially secure not much more than our survival and then, fundamentally, our physical well-being.

Impulses from the second source ensure our adaptation to the cultural values that prevailed when we were growing up. They ensure that we identify with the cultural values in force, to apply and develop them in our lives. This is admittedly generally only desired to ensure that the structure of existing values is not overstepped.

But this is often what happens when essential impulses from the third source are awakened and push for actualisation from within. This is how real, new ideals and values emerge as the expression of human culture, for these essential impulses allow us to be creative and in this creativity to overstep the limits of the status quo, indeed to go beyond it on the way to new, more advanced goals and ideals.

The individual is a product not only of his biological nature and prevailing cultural values, but also of his self, his core being, his creative source. As this is where his inner reference point is situated, this is what enables him to dissociate from the reality of the world as it currently is, so that he can contribute to its development from a perspective of detachment and overview, even if this means encountering resistance and conflict.

We can find plenty of examples of the existence of this third source, the core being, and of what can happen when it becomes active in a person in the history of our culture – from Giordano Bruno, Galileo Galilei and Johannes Kepler via Charles Darwin to Sigmund Freud and C.G. Jung.

I found an impressive example of how far people are willing to go to stand up for their ideals and how much humanity can be revealed in the process when I was given a book about World War II. Inside was a picture of a group of hostages, men, women and children about to be executed. Among them stood a German officer, carrying the gun with which he had been supposed to shoot them. He had refused to participate in the execution of these people, preferring instead to be shot himself. We can only imagine what an extreme essential impulse and what awareness and relatedness to the ideal of humanity must have been necessary for him to be able to act in this way.

Majesty and dignity, true greatness that lie within him – the Greek Apollo

At the same time, the fact that it is possible to act in this way is clear proof of the existence of this third source of individual ideality.

Here the impulse originating from the third source gives rise to actions, goals and values that contradict those coming from the first source, which are intended to ensure the survival of the individual, pretty much reducing them to absurdity when they lead to the above behaviour.

Values from the second source, however, are essentially far too much a product of cultural adaptation to lead to the above behaviour. How easily the officer in the above-depicted situation would have been able to justify his actions: "I had to obey orders, there is a war on after all." Indeed, perhaps another soldier may have been so amazed at the conduct of this officer, that he too would not have obeyed orders as usual, not have excused his actions by saying he was only following orders, preferring instead to follow his ideality!

As values of the second source are the result of conditioning, the familiar "carrot and stick" method, the same method must also be used to change them. By threatening the officer with death, the superior introduces the strongest stick and at the same time the most effective carrot, i.e. survival. Nevertheless, in this case the officer's relatedness to his ideal, a value from the third source, proved to be stronger than even this method. The same can be said for the likes of Bruno, Galilei and Freud. For each of them, certain key issues made living according to their inner reference point, their third source, their true ideal, more valuable than the demands and expectations of their biological nature, i.e. survival and inclusion in the prevailing cultural values and the solidarity of the collective ("carrot"), and being mocked, isolated or scorned ("stick") by their environment (c.f. Kepler, Darwin, Freud). Here we also come across an important paradox that is evident in every stage of cultural development.

On the one hand, the ideas and ideals of the above-mentioned creative individuals are now part of our world view and acknowledged as values upon which our culture is now based, for example the important contribution of Bruno and Galilei in the emergence of our scientific worldview, or Freud's claim that the unconscious should also be taken into account to enable us to have a holistic view of man. They managed to transform the existing worldview and cultural values, and were subsequently to be acknowledged, even admired and acclaimed.

On the other hand, when they first challenged the status quo and its prevailing cultural values, towards whose creative development they were working after all, they were perceived as a threat to the exclusive, absolute dominance of these values and therefore treated as a threat and vilified.

So it can easily be shown that the main impetus for new developments, specifically in our western culture, came from just this kind of creative individual, who, supported and encouraged by impulses from the third source, were able to push beyond the restrictions of the status quo into new territories and enable the emergence of values that would frequently become the supporting pillars of a new worldview. However these new values initially came up against resistance from the previously existing values (4).

We can now define more precisely the meaning of the term reality, as it is used here, and how it relates to ideality.

Reality

I would like to define reality as the sum of everything that exists and is established at a particular time and in a particular culture, i.e. what people are generally aware of during their lifetimes. This includes firstly all physical, material things, e.g. landscape and the climate. Then man-made material objects like houses, clothing, machines, and also man-made social values and government institutions, laws, legal forms of living together (e.g. marriage) and working together. Lastly there are the spiritual values, scientific statements and theories, philosophies, religions, etc. Reality in this sense therefore does not mean everything that can in some way (i.e. scientifically) be proven objectively or by particular, existing and acknowledged methods. It is established almost by a general consensus, by the interpersonal communication (5) of the collective.

The gods, spirits and demons that animistic, primitive peoples believe animate nature, for example by triggering thunder and lightning, are just as much the reality that they base their lives on, by which they orientate themselves and which conditions their behaviour, as for medieval man the ideas that the Sun and planets revolved around the Earth, or that the Earth was flat. In principle, all our modern values and ideas belong to the same category: they make up what for us is the established status quo: i.e. reality.

At this point I would like to emphasise once more that the definition of reality discussed here is not absolute, not definitely established, and above all not static! It is in a state of continual flux and is constantly changing. But the reality that exists at a certain time is very influential on the lives of people at that time.

This does not change the fact that reality does not mean exactly the same for everyone. Admittedly, we can assume that there is a basic reality that is valid for most people, but after that, it can be different for different cultures, nations, groups and finally for each individual.

---

4. Erich Neumann described this problem particularly clearly in *Origins and History of Consciousness*.
5. See Paul Watzlawick, *How Real is Real?*

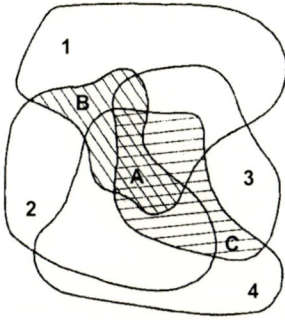 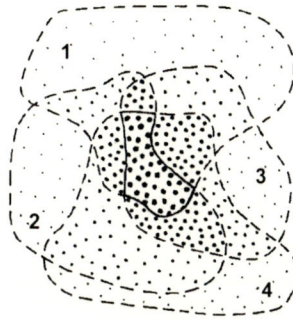

Figure 1   **Figure 2**

Let us look at figure 1 for a clearer explanation. The intersecting sets represent the conception of reality of four individuals, 1, 2, 3 and 4. The intersection A of these sets shows the basic reality that all four have in common; intersection B represents the common realities of individuals 1 and 2; intersection C of individuals 3 and 4, and so on. In figure 2, this is illustrated in another way: the more points there are in a certain area, the more individuals consider that area to be reality. We find the highest concentration of points in the centre (Set A), the area with the greatest agreement on reality, which then reduces on all sides. If we also imagine that this diagram is constantly changing, then we have a good picture of my definition of reality. This may seem disconcerting to some, but if you just think carefully about the nature of reality, I think you would come up with this model or one like it. In any case, we find such models again and again in human intellectual history, starting with Heraclitus in Ancient Greece right up to a co-creator of modern physics, Nobel Prize winner Erwin Schrödinger (6).

In any case, it is essential that we remember that ideality and reality are not fixed, unalterable factors, but are actually changing all the time!

The Interaction between Ideality and Reality

We must not forget that ideality and reality are engaged in a process of mutual transformation, and that reality does not "like" change. The components of reality, such as man-made social and spiritual values, have a certain inbuilt "inertia", and resist attempts to change them.

However, the most important factor in human life, which is geared towards changing it, is actually ideality. Above I have tried to give an idea of just how many crucial changes would have remained

---

6. See E. Schrödinger, *Was ist ein Naturgesetz? Beiträge zum naturwissenschafftlichen Weltbilt.*

unmade without this factor. Reality is therefore highly dependent on ideality for its transformation and development; ideality is essential to provide the impetus that forces reality to change. We should not forget that vital parts of what we now consider to be reality in our western culture, were originally idealities and were in conflict with the reality of the time. Consider an example: before the start of the French Revolution, the political reality of France (and in principle, also of Europe), was characterised by the dominance of Absolutism (Louis XIV said: "I am the state"). The birth of a new ideality, expressed in the principle "Liberté, Egalité, Fraternité" and in the demands for human rights, equal rights, the separation of powers, led to a confrontation with the old values in which they were overcome, and to the establishment of a new reality. Today, the above-mentioned demands are defining elements in the constitution, jurisdiction and political life of all European nations and the western world. Ideality is therefore not only a factor that forces reality to change, but also the substantiating factor for the emergence of new realities.

To summarise, it could be said that the source of every new reality is an ideality, particular social or intellectual idealities, which shows the relatedness, if not the dependence, of reality on ideality.

However, in order to better understand the complex, multi-layered interaction between ideality and reality, we must further examine how ideality is related to and dependent upon reality (7).

At first, it is easy to see that every ideality has the inherent tendency to be actualised, to become reality. The individual in whom a certain ideality is germinating wants it to be born someday, i.e. to become reality; and the same is true for groups of people or whole nations and cultures.

More important still is the reverse action, or the impact of reality on ideality. It plays a crucial part in the emergence of consciousness and development of human awareness. To understand this elementary connection between ideality, reality and the development of human consciousness, we must go back to the above-mentioned definition of ideality as an inner expectation, which is supplied by one of three described sources (or by several at the same time). At the same time, we shall see that this definition was very useful.

If an individual with a certain expectation – be it that of survival from the first source, or that of the wish to have one's own

---

7. Here we are considering the given definition of reality. The claims listed above are part of the intellectual, political and social reality of our lives. This does not mean that these social realities are never violated. The laws of our nation are social, societal reality and have an important influence in our lives. Nevertheless, they can be abused and the "underworld" of crime is also a component of our social reality.

achievements acknowledged from the second, or even an essential impulse from the third source – they will be confronted with reality and one of two things may happen.

Firstly, the expectation may be actualised; the expected really happens. For example the individual gains the recognition he desires. He will react with joy, gratitude and satisfaction to the situation in which he finds himself. As there has been a congruence of expectation (ideality in the broader sense) and reality, we can say that the individual is happy or in harmony with the world.

Secondly, reality may not meet the expectation and deny it instead. The person concerned is usually upset, if not shocked and disappointed, and starts to examine the situation in which he finds himself. He will focus his attention on it and try to understand what went wrong.

The thwarting of these wishes and expectations has had a kind of awakening or galvanising effect. Attention is initially directed to the denying reality, in an attempt to understand it, also to the personal expectation that confronted it, and finally to the discrepancy that has arisen between the two. This is the start of a process of comparison of ideality and reality (8), where the aim is to understand and eliminate the discrepancy, which is found to be rather painful. It requires examining and changing either reality or ideality or both.

So we have made the astonishing discovery that an "enabling reality" may well satisfy the individual on a certain level of awareness, but a "denying reality" encourages the development of an awareness of the problem and pushes the consciousness to confront both the expectation that wants to be met and the reality encountered, and therefore leads to an overall increase in awareness, to the further development of consciousness (9).

It is by no means the case, though, that every time a person's expectations are thwarted his consciousness is developed.

8. In these statements concerning the comparison of ideality and reality, its successes and the forms of its failure, I partially agree with the ideas of J. Tamm in her previously mentioned essay *Angst und Subjektivität*.

9. Please note that I do not claim that this is the only method of consciousness development, but only one that is important in our context.

A precondition for this is, at the very least, that an expectation, an ideality is present as a starting point or an inner benchmark.

Let us assume that a person approaches reality with an uncertain, diffuse expectation, e.g. for "pleasure". If this does not materialise, the morning after an evening of pleasure he still feels dissatisfied. He is unable to say exactly which expectations have not been met, but just has a sense of disappointment. He is then equally unable to identify which circumstances of reality are really originally responsible for this, and which he should therefore try to change. Maybe the cause of his lack of pleasure is that he lacks a partner, or that he does not get on with the one he has, or perhaps it is more a question of his dissatisfaction with a job that he doesn't like, or that he cannot find meaning in his life, or… Finally the person suffocates in such a network of imponderabilities. He can neither really understand the circumstances and realities that have denied him (or more accurately here, frustrated him), nor change his own expectations, they are even alien to him and express themselves at best in a vague feeling of uneasiness. He is therefore not really able to find starting points for change, and resigns or lapses into doing things for the sake of it. The "search for fulfilment" that follows is like looking for a needle in a haystack, but without the searcher knowing exactly what a needle actually is.

This situation fundamentally changes if an expectation or inner reference point exists, which can serve as a benchmark in the consciousness. If the expectation is then met by a "non-compliant reality", using the inner reference point he can then take a step back from this reality, as described above, and question, examine, criticise and meaningfully confront reality. Irrespective of how legitimate or not the expectation is, its presence as an inner reference point in the consciousness allows a dialectical process to begin between the expectation (i.e. ideality) and reality, with the aim of reconciling the two. Without ideality as the starting point of this process, the person concerned is grasping at straws.

This is therefore the main role of ideality, to be a starting point for this process of the development of consciousness. If we investigate ideality from this point of view, it can be paraphrased quite well and in the most general sense by the term expectation.

Nevertheless, it is primarily ideality in the strict sense, the intrinsic ideality whose source is the core being, which sets new human standards and therefore encourages the development of consciousness and cultural creativity in man.

It is important to understand that such an inner reference point or benchmark in consciousness need not necessarily exist in any particular form, e.g. formulated in language. It is precisely these essential impulses from the third source that initially appear as qualities in our consciousness, as absolutely clear and vividly experienceable powers within us. But it can still be quite difficult to put them into words and express them, which generally helps us to share them with others and encourages similar experiences.

However, the existence of a clearly experienceable characteristic in consciousness as an inner reference point is quite sufficient. Admittedly it is then more difficult to explain or justify personal behaviour to others; but in terms of inner orientation there is no difference between an ideal that can only be experienced as an ideal and an ideal that can also be expressed in words. It is important that every individual ideal, i.e. every impulse from the third source, can first be experienced internally and only later does it need to be more or less accurately expressed. If the opposite is true, when an expressible form/ line of argument can be expressed verbally but is not related to an inner quality, this is not an ideal, but an ideology. This is unfortunately an extremely common occurrence that we have yet to discuss.

What I have tried to clarify so far is the extremely complex and multi-layered interaction between ideality and reality and their purpose, which is our further development and transformation. The view of man as a being in a constant state of transformation is the real intellectual starting point for this work. Only from this starting point can the given definitions of ideality and reality really be grasped.

I would also like to clarify the most important laws governing the interaction of ideality and reality.

The Meaning of Ideality

We can now understand the crucial role that ideality plays in human life. Only if an ideal exists as an inner reference point can a person manage to successfully dissociate from reality as described above. Only when an expectation or ideal inwardly anticipates the expected encounter with reality, as it were playing it through in an inner model of reality, does a benchmark appear by which we can then measure the reality actually encountered later on. If someone encounters reality with no expectation or inner standard, they just have to take it as they find it.

Only comparison with such an inner benchmark enables us to question reality, and only if reality is questioned can an answer be expected. An answer can only be obtained by questioning reality.

Making statements about reality and having an opinion about it requires a

benchmark; only then is it possible to criticise it. For making statements
about reality is strictly speaking just comparing reality and ideality.

An important factor is also that ideality is our inner guide when
we confront and try to change reality. Our relatedness to ideality is a
pre-requisite for our ability to make statements about, criticise and
then change reality.

To the extent to which this relatedness to ideality is lacking, we
lose our ability to dissociate, distance ourselves and hence truly
criticise reality. In this extent, we are then forced (unconsciously) to
identify with reality and the well-known saying applies, that man is
just a product of his environment.

To the extent that ideality is present as a guide, the person lives
his life as a spiritually oriented being. To the extent to which this is
lacking he becomes a pawn of the world in which he lives. This clearly
expresses the incontrovertible and almost inestimable importance of
ideality in human life.

In the first case, an existing ideal can be actualised in reality, so that
ideality and reality are united. If this happens, the person concerned
reacts with deep satisfaction, fulfilment and joy, which increases the
more central, fundamental and meaningful the fulfilled ideal is for his
life. If this happens, the individual lives in harmony with the world.

In the second case, the prevailing reality prevents realisation of
an ideal. Now, with the help of the ideal as an inner reference point,
we must dissociate from reality and, enabled by our relatedness to the
ideal, adopt a questioning and critical approach to reality, with the aim
of at least realising the ideal in the long term, and in any case using it
as the starting point for an ongoing confrontation with reality.

Failure of the Interaction between Ideality and Reality

Unfortunately, successful interactions between ideality and reality
tend to be the exception. Instead of the second case above, which
represents a real and sometimes extremely difficult spiritual challenge
for the individual concerned, it is much more common to find two
other typical scenarios when this interaction fails.

The starting point for both incorrect ways of handling ideality
and reality is the second case above, where an expectation/ ideal
is denied by reality. Unlike the first case, the person now suffers
consternation and pain. The painful tension, the discrepancy between
ideality and reality must now be acknowledged and tolerated. The
more importance the ideal has for the individual, the greater this is
– the more intense the essential impulse functions lying behind it, and
the more "psychic energy" it possesses.

There is now a three-fold demand on the individual: to remain
related to the ideality, to reality and to the discrepancy between
them!

This entails dissociating from reality, on the one hand remaining attuned to the inner reference point (the ideal) and on the other hand also remaining aware of reality – and accepting the tension experienced between the two, now getting involved in the dialectical interaction and confrontation between ideality and reality, to try to reconcile them.

However, if the person finds the pain of this discrepancy overwhelming, two obvious possibilities arise: denial and abandonment of either ideality (the most common scenario) or reality.

Jupiter at the centre of the zodiac, *Rome*

Abandoning Ideality

The first incorrect way, which has now become almost commonplace, is referred to in everyday language with an appropriate word: resignation. The tension between ideality and reality is eliminated by forsaking relatedness to ideality; in other words, by repressing the ideality. We think: if I no longer have any ideals, I can no longer be frustrated or disappointed by reality. What an apparent triumph over the otherwise powerful reality! A person who decides to have no more ideals that can be thwarted by reality will no longer have to face the pain of the discrepancy between them as a result.

What is the price that must be paid for this though? Renouncing ideality means losing all those abilities that stem from being related to ideality.

Resignation and Adaptation

This involves the loss of inner reference points, inner "benchmarks" and orientation. Abandoning ideality admittedly allows us to avoid experiencing the discrepancy with reality; however the consequence is that we are left at the mercy of reality. It will now no longer be possible to dissociate from it, question it or even to criticise it from the perspective of the inner reference point. Now we must resign ourself to reality and take it as we find it with (apparent) indifference, as expressed in the saying "that's life".

The resulting relationship to reality can also be described as being engulfed by reality. From the standpoint of the preservation of reality it is a victory. However it can no longer be a potential source of criticism, creativity and transformation.

A person who has betrayed his ideality must now feel like a "leaf in the wind", at the mercy of the forces and currents of his environment, while sensing his own helplessness, for he no longer has any real inner orientation at all. By renouncing his ideals he has also given up his possibilities for conscious spiritual development, so that he will also start to find himself increasingly rigid, lifeless or "dead". Erich Fromm has very aptly termed the resulting personality state necrophilia ("joy in death") (10).

The Search for "Ersatz Ideals"

In order to avoid this unpleasant experience, people tend to search for "ersatz ideals". Examples of these are the theories and opinions of the prevailing reality, or following the teachings of a leader, an "authority". While the stability provided by these admittedly does not match the dynamic stability offered by ideals, giving instead the stubbornness and inflexible rigidity of an ideology, at least one has regained some kind of ideal and orientation. Above all, one need no longer be in the position of having to defend them single-handedly if necessary, for one has the prevailing collective opinion or an authority on one's side.

Worse still, the sensations of emptiness, dissatisfaction, even deadness experienced after the repression of ideals can lead the individual to rely purely out of desperation on ersatz ideals. They are passionately defended with a rigid fanaticism, as they are now a vital part of his personality, as were his previously-held genuine ideals, therefore even sometimes as important as his relatedness to his core being, his Self. The extent to which authoritarian states can manipulate people in this way, particularly young people, is well-known to us all. This clearly illustrates the main goal of every authoritarian upbringing, which first creates the preconditions for success of these methods: i.e. the destruction of people's genuine idealities.

There is yet another important consequence: psychoanalysis has rightly shown how serious the consequences of repressing drives can be for people's psychological equilibrium. But not until modern Self Psychology (Kohut, Wolf, Ornstein, etc.) has psychoanalysis discussed the equally serious consequences caused by the repression of ideals in the context of further development. Along with the immediate effects already discussed, we should examine another long term consequence of abandoning ideality: the usually unconscious feelings of guilt and the also mainly unconscious tendency to self-punishment they cause, due to the repression of ideals, the sources of new life possibilities and new developmental impulses. This is the main cause of a very common malaise: depression in old age. I would summarise the transforming and developing potential of the ideals that are repressed as a kind of "unlived life", which avenges itself on the person concerned in this way. It is therefore crucial to have an

---

10. See Erich Fromm, *The Anatomy of Human Destructiveness*

inner orientation, to know which ideals are important impulse sources on our individual life path, indeed, for actually finding this path in the first place. Tolerating their occasional denial by reality seems to me to be the lesser of two evils.

I would like to conclude this point by summing up: the purely instinctual, natural man is alive only as long as he remains related to nature. However, the individual who is also spiritually and consciously active is only alive as long as he remains related to his ideality.

Abandoning Reality

The second mistake is to try to "overcome" the apparently unbearable discrepancy between ideality and reality by abandoning reality, i.e. abandoning relatedness to it.

Common to both mistakes is the fact that they prevent the individual from dissociating from reality and therefore take away his ability to give his opinion, criticise and make changes. In the first case, the abandonment of ideality, the discrepancy is lost, in the second case, relatedness to reality is forsaken.

Escapism

One possible outcome of the latter is renunciation of reality or withdrawal into a personal ideality, sometimes called "inner emigration", which does preserve ideality, but causes a loss of contact with reality. Relatedness to the ideal is indeed then safeguarded, but it is usually only lived out in an "ideal dream world". However, the basic aspiration of every ideal to be realised is lost, so that the ideal is "sterilised". By giving up relatedness to reality, the person usually lacks a suitable moment to realise the ideal or take the first step towards it.

Aggression

A second manifestation of this mistake (abandoning relatedness to reality) consists not in renouncing it, but in aggression against it (11).

The discrepancy between ideality and reality is found so intolerable that the person is not able to engage in dialectical interaction between the two to overcome it. However, he definitely wants to safeguard his ideality, which leads to an intolerable and painful tension caused by the experience of the discrepancy. This is discharged in pure aggression against reality, the status quo, that has denied the ideality. The reasoning behind this is that if I destroy or even annihilate the reality that has contradicted my ideality, then my ideality has won.

This can be illustrated by many historical examples, including "angry young men", terrorists and revolutionaries. However, these are the very people who teach us that this process almost always fails, in

---

11. Erich Fromm describes this connection clearly in *The Revolution of Hope.*

the sense that it is still the ideality that must pay the price – which was the very thing that was supposed to be safeguarded or implemented in the first place.

The unresolved tension that is transferred into hate and aggression distorts the vision of reality that needs to be changed; being no longer related to it, the person is also no longer oriented by it. The resulting misjudgement of reality (e.g. regarding the power of government bodies) then leads to the failure of the attack and ends in extradition, prison or death, which do not really help the ideals to be actualised.

However, if such an attack, e.g. a revolution, is successful, we very often find (one could even say, in nearly every case), that the ideals that are to be implemented after the successful struggle of the revolutionaries are not implemented at all but actually attacked by them. How many revolutions have been fought for the ideal of liberty against a totalitarian-authoritarian regime and admittedly end with the prevailing regime being deposed, but then the victorious revolutionaries go on to found a no less totalitarian regime.

If the unresolved tension caused by the discrepancy between ideality and reality turns into hate and aggression, the resulting struggle against reality nearly always corrupts the ideals that were initially intended to be implemented. (This does not include revolutions that from the start have nothing to do with ideality, but only the acquisition of power.) The whole tragedy of this process is reflected clearly and realistically, if also crudely, in the phrase written by American students at the end of the 1960s on their university walls: "Fighting for peace is like fucking for virginity".

We must not forget though that there are also revolutions that have led to a successful implementation of their ideals. One example is the American War of Independence of 1775, after which a new regime was established, not according to the authoritarian model as was usual at the time in Europe, but a democracy, which at the time was unique.

In the first case, after their victory, the revolutionaries are suddenly confronted with the "harsh realities" of maintaining power and resort to just those methods of authoritarian-totalitarian repression, which (in our example) they had criticised in their predecessors. The conflict caused by hate and wild aggression has brought them face to face with reality, in the process of which their ideals have been more or less lost, almost without them noticing. In the end, they find themselves in the same position as those who chose resignation. Their ideals have fallen victim to the fight for these ideals, so at the end of the struggle they have no more ideals left to which they can be related: they also find themselves in a state of being trapped by reality, and must now pay the price.

It is all the more tragic when this happens to people with genuine ideals. At the beginning, they are still convinced that they can serve their ideals in this way, but as time goes on, they find themselves forced to act in ways that gradually corrupt these very ideals. Indeed, they may still talk of their initial ideals, but are betrayed by their actions. As the saying goes: "By their fruits ye shall know them".

In the second case however, the relatedness to ideality and reality was strong enough to result in implementation of the ideality, surviving the struggle, which is why it led to the creation of something genuinely new and creative.

This brings to an end our discussion of the main types of failed interactions between ideality and reality. We now return to the successful interaction.

The case where ideality and reality coincide needs no further discussion, as happiness has been found. Where there is a discrepancy, the ground first needs to be prepared for happiness, the seeds sown and then harvested. This represents a real spiritual challenge and therefore deserves further consideration.

Hope – a Third Pole as a Possible Solution

Where there is a pronounced discrepancy between ideality and the reality encountered and an important life-enhancing ideal is involved, the painful inner tension caused is extremely high. Coping with it in the right way is the real problem. If there is a chance that the ideal concerned can be actualised in the short or long term, the tension becomes more bearable.

However, what if no timeframe can be given within which this important ideal can be expected to happen, indeed what if it becomes impossible for it to be realised in one's lifetime?

What if reality is so cruel that it never gives this ideal a meaningful chance to be actualised, therefore preventing the above-mentioned dialectical interaction between ideality and reality?

In such an extreme case, it is quite understandable if the attitude of the person concerned is "corrupted" by the excessive pain. Nevertheless, let us be very clear that neither resignation nor aggression is very helpful in this case either. Despite an apparent release of pressure (particularly in the case of resignation), they create problems in the long term. Even in such an extreme case, one is at the mercy of the reality that is so hard to bear. After resigning, one is even more at its mercy. What is more, one no longer has the repressed ideal as a psychological force with which to fight it. The hate or aggression arising from such excessive tension can be catastrophic, or, as described above, lead to the corruption of the ideal.

**The duality of the Sun and the Moon and their intermingling and
interpenetration lead to a third "tria principia".
Together they form the "philosopher's stone".**

Since ideality and reality are now irreconcilably opposed, the
"victorious" reality also hinders the open confrontation of ideality
and reality; in addition, for the foreseeable future no change can
be expected. The individual experiences a mental block, which can
only be meaningfully resolved by the inclusion of a third pole that
supplements ideality and reality.

It is one of the theories fundamental to the context of this article
that a strong polarisation between two positions can only be resolved
by the addition of an appropriate third position, indeed that there
actually are no real polarities. Behind apparent polarities there are
always trinities, in which the involvement of a third pole transforms a
rigid polarity into an active, balanced interaction of the three poles.

The best name for the third pole that complements ideality and
reality seems to me to be the word "hope". Erich Fromm gave an
outstanding definition of the nature of hope, from which I quote:

*"Hope is a paradox. It is neither a state of passive waiting nor an unrealistic
force of circumstance that cannot occur. It is like a crouching tiger, which only
pounces when the right moment comes. Neither a weak attempt at reformation
nor a seemingly radical spirit of adventure can be considered as expressions
of hope. Hope means being ready at each moment for that which has not yet
happened – and in spite of this, not to despair if it does not happen at all
during our lifetime." (E. Fromm, Revolution of Hope)*

*"Hope is a state of being. It is an inner readiness, a state of intense potential
activity."*

*"...someone who is very hopeful recognises and embraces every sign of new life
and is always prepared to help to deliver what is ready to be born."*

To further clarify the nature and effect of hope, let us consider again an extreme case, i.e. what happens if, to quote Fromm, the ideal *"will not be born at all in our lifetime"*, i.e. will never be actualised. What good is hope then? Wouldn't resignation be more appropriate in this case?

Hope as the Best Basis for the Search for Actualisation
We have already dealt with one reason for the value of hope even in this extreme case. Real hope now shifts us into a state of the "tiger that is ready to pounce", in a state of "potential activity" that allows us to remain related to ideality and also to reality, in which we are poised to do the right thing at the right time, instead of being resignedly half-asleep or attacking prematurely out of aggression. The state of hope is therefore the best starting point for the actualisation of our ideality.

Equally important though is a second argument, which emphasises the value of hope for the well-being of the individual concerned.

Hope for Mental and Emotional Well-Being
As hope allows people to remain related to ideality, even when there is a discouraging discrepancy with reality, ideality can still be the source of new energy and creative impulses. That enables people to confront ideality at least one more time, thereby allowing them to treat the ideality with greater perception and penetration and more developed lucidity. This may lead them to a new, previously overlooked solution, or a new way of achieving actualisation.

Moreover, the negative consequences of the repression of ideality are avoided: the shutting down of the energy sources that are our true ideals. The impoverishment and increasing rigidity of the personality this causes are avoided, which would otherwise take their toll in the form of resignation and depression in old age. Hope allows people to remain intellectually alive and is therefore also a prerequisite for mental and emotional well-being.

The essence of hope lies in preserving the basic aspiration of ideality to be actualised in a kind of seed of activity, which absorbs the tension between ideality and reality, making it fruitful by transforming it into an "inner gestation". Thereby is created the willingness and ability to contribute at the right moment to the actualisation of the ideal, the birth of a new reality.

Origin and Further Development of Ideality
The Birth of new Ideality
We have hitherto only discussed which processes can occur when the already existing conscious ideality that aspires to be actualised meets the prevailing reality. We have also described three different sources of ideality, in particular the source of intrinsic ideality, the

core being. We have not yet examined in more detail what can happen when a new ideality impulse emerges from a person's core being and enters his consciousness, how he may experience this event and which misunderstandings and subsequent dangers can occur in the process.

Very often, this "birth of new ideality" happens in such a way that the new ideality impulse initially remains unconscious after its release from the source. It then starts to take effect and only slowly enters the person's consciousness, so that they begin to clearly experience and understand it.

The problem with this is that an extremely unstable intermediary or transitional situation can arise on this path to awareness of the ideality impulses.

On the one hand, the ideality impulse can still not be clearly experienced, otherwise it could already be used as an inner reference point and the confrontation with the demands of reality could begin. On the other hand, this impulse already exists in the whole personality and has an influence, even if still unconscious. The person can be affected by no longer being able, as before, to fulfil certain demands of the status quo (e.g. for adaptation or a certain type of behaviour), as this impulse is already providing a strong unconscious resistance. He can be completely blocked and incapable of fulfilling demands placed on him by reality that he possibly takes for granted.

However, and herein lies the tragedy of this phase, he is also not in a position to know why he is behaving in this way. Indeed, he cannot clearly experience the impulse causing his behaviour as a quality at all, so that even if he could not express it in words, at least he would have some idea of the causes of his behaviour. To put it another way: the ideality impulse has not yet "arrived" in consciousness, but is already effective as a kind of "unconscious gestation" and already declares its desire to be born, as it were already claiming its future place in consciousness, "demanding" the place is kept free for it and that its availability is protected.

Angst as a Precursor of a New Reality

In a situation like this, when the old reality is no longer acceptable and can no longer provide stability, but the new ideality is not yet tangible enough to enable it to confront reality, we experience something very particular: angst. It is in a way the expression of the new ideality's desire to be born, as if it were holding the place that the ideality impulse wants to occupy in the future and keeps it free. It is this angst that stops the person in this situation from complying with the pressure to adapt to reality and create 'facts on the ground' which could seriously hinder or even prevent if not the nascence of the new ideality, certainly its subsequent actualisation.

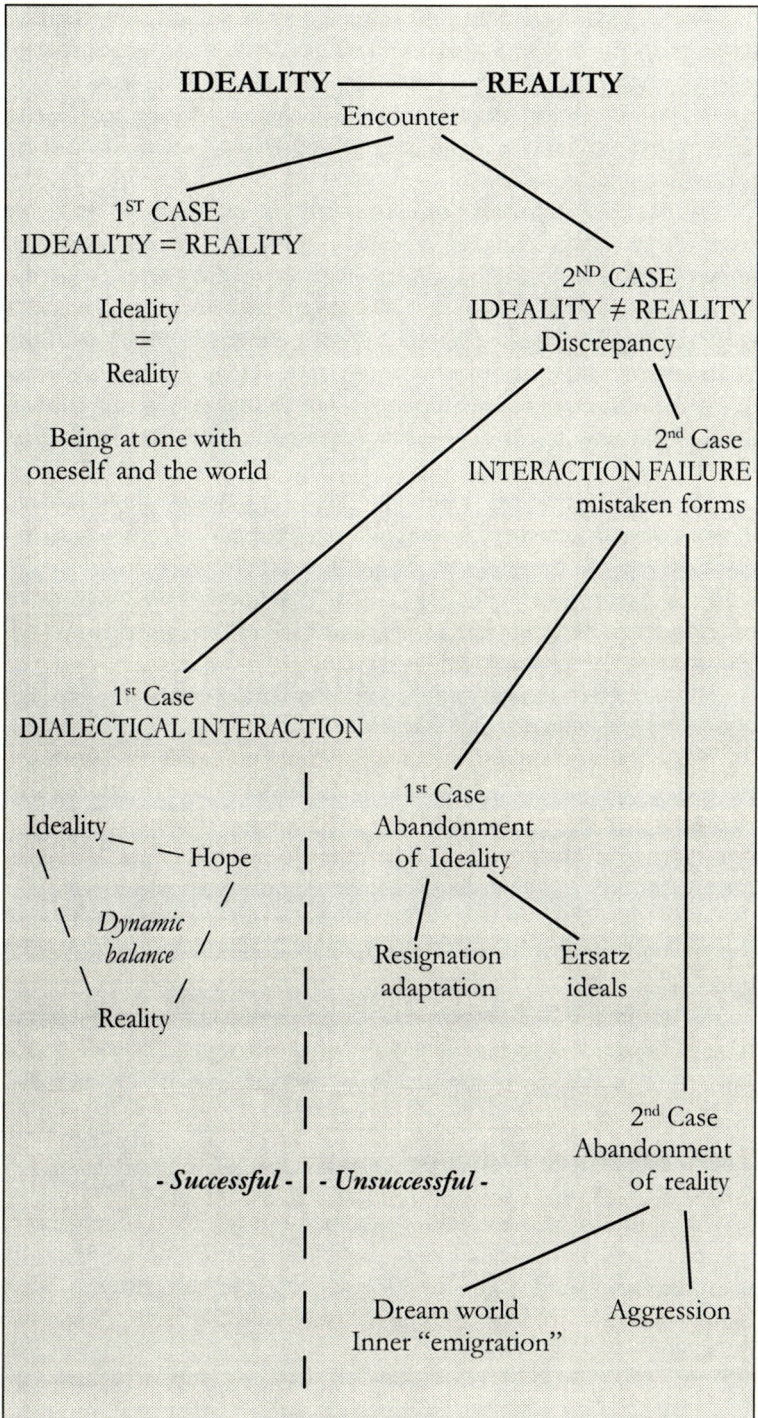

IDEALITY ——————— REALITY

Encounter

1ST CASE
IDEALITY = REALITY

Ideality
=
Reality

2ND CASE
IDEALITY ≠ REALITY
Discrepancy

Being at one with
oneself and the world

2nd Case
INTERACTION FAILURE
mistaken forms

1st Case
DIALECTICAL INTERACTION

Ideality
Hope
*Dynamic
balance*
Reality

1st Case
Abandonment
of Ideality

Resignation
adaptation

Ersatz
ideals

2nd Case
Abandonment
of reality

- Successful - | - Unsuccessful -

Dream world
Inner "emigration"

Aggression

Although the experience of angst is a worrying one, it would be wrong only to see it in a negative light and overlook the constructive role it can play and its value, indeed its necessity in this phase.

A basic need for ideality is revealed in the courage to tolerate the angst of this phase, to remain related to it as a clue or hint of something new to come.

At the same time this angst contains an equally basic need for truth. It prevents taking of the easy option of pushing aside the uncomfortable fear and repressing it. Instead the person uses the angst, questions it, scrutinises it, tries to define which space it wants to be kept open, therefore what it opposes, either vicariously or as the precursor of a new ideality [this is a warning function]. This gives rise to a pull in the consciousness that is totally supportive of the coming birth and an awareness of the new essential impulse and, ultimately, the new truth.

These increasingly frequent and apparently unavoidable intermediary phases of "no longer" and "not yet" clearly reveal the value of angst as the signpost for spiritual development.

To avoid misunderstandings, I will now explore in more detail the difference between fear and angst, which is also emphasised by J. Tamm after Kierkegaard and Jaspers.

Fear is object-related; it refers to something concrete. One can fear a person, a situation, a task, etc.

Angst does not relate to anything. It is intended, as described above, to cause a place to be held open for something not yet determined. It means that the person falls into a void, into emptiness, but does not yet provide him with a clear inner orientation point. This can only be found when the angst is accepted and treated as a meaningful phenomenon, when it is examined until the demand for ideality and truth lying behind it is met, by becoming aware of the new essential impulses.

As angst and fear apparently function according to the same biological pattern, our experience of them is often practically identical. Nevertheless, the above spiritual interpretation applies only to angst, and not to fear.

The Clarification of Ideality

Earlier I emphasised that the value of an existing ideality is that it provides an inner orientation point, without which no meaningful confrontation with reality can take place, and indeed, initially irrespective of how "right" or "wrong" the ideal concerned is. This confrontation should bring about a change in either reality or ideality or both.

What is it that determines whether or not an ideal that confronts a conflicting reality is preserved or changed?

CONSCIOUS

UNCONSCIOUS

distortion

core   essential impulse   "complexes"

being

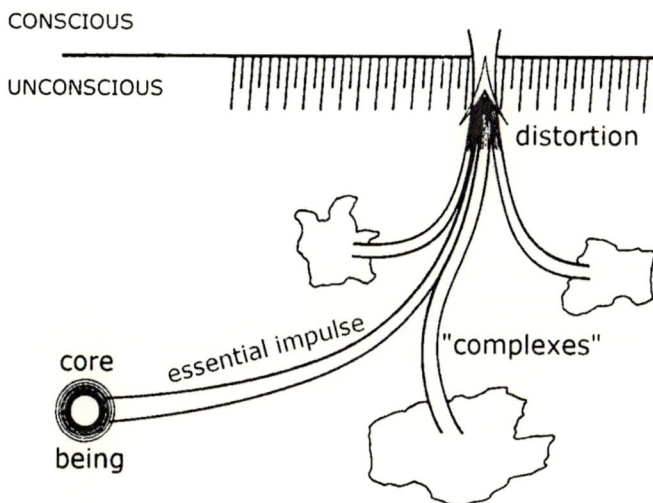

On no account can it be the case that a genuine ideal, an essential impulse, is only changed because reality persistently or forcibly opposes it. That would be a lazy compromise! If something really new and genuine is to be actualised, in the context of the developmental and evolutionary thought process it is already justified that the old, the status quo, must give way.

The question must therefore be: how can we know what is "genuine"? This is where the real problem lies.

An essential impulse has a "long" way to go from its source in the core being to the consciousness, which means that there is a substantial danger of it being contaminated, diminished and corrupted along the way. As a large part of this process takes place in the unconscious, unprocessed and unconscious repressed personality impulses can distort the essential impulse, thereby changing its original character in varying degrees.

This must of course seriously jeopardise the confrontation with reality. On the one hand, the strength of the essential impulse is reduced, and on the other hand, it gives reality not only the opportunity to identify this "weakness" in the ideal, which would be only right but, as so often happens, the whole ideal is unceremoniously rejected for this reason.

Symptoms of such contamination of ideality can be: very hasty resignation or escapism, willingness to make "lazy compromises", aggression and excessive action for action's sake, and also angst, which wants to "place-hold" and whose existence points to inconsistencies in the ideal.

Self Reflection

I now introduce two ways of clarifying ideals. One consists of self reflection, diving deep into ourselves, dissociating from our own ideal in order to confront it. If our own ideal symptoms appear to be similar to those described above, we should dissociate ourself from our own ideal, that is to say the demand for truth, in order to question it and see if new insights and perceptions can be discovered behind the old form of the ideal. This old form of the ideal has become a piece of reality that has to be changed. This self reflection has to be be carried out with the greatest possible lucidity.

However, can we really hope to achieve a definite, comprehensive clarification of the degree of "purity" or "distortion or contamination" of our ideal, and of whether and how it should be changed, by self reflection or meditation alone? This is a key issue of the utmost importance. To discuss this carefully and thoroughly would go way beyond the scope of this paper. I will therefore limit myself to giving my personal point of view.

The Need for Dialogue

I believe that diving deep into oneself by self reflection and meditation alone cannot determine whether or not an ideal is distorted. This is because the unconscious, distorting impulse can be strong enough to make the self-reflection fruitless, and influence the process in its favour.

If this were otherwise, I could achieve a kind of "total insight" all by myself. My relationships with my fellow men would be reduced to convincing them of my "truth" and gaining supporters, or they would confront me with resistance as "reality". In principle, I would not need discussion, dialogue and exchange with them. I could even manage to gain clarity by myself. The most difficult thing would still be "convincing" others. My relationship to my fellow men would then become an object!

I therefore think that self reflection can only lead to a qualified (very broad) clarification of an ideal. After this, dialogue and exchange with other people as subjects, as equal "supporters of a core being", are vital for further clarification – in the encounter of a subject with a countersubject (12).

Such a real encounter or dialogue involves mutual questioning of ideality, of the ideality aspirations of the other, challenging of apparently distorted ideality aspirations, and addressing the impulses and demands for ideality of my dialogue partner. This process of clarification and inspiration, combined with the self reflection, can

---

12. Erich Fromm coined this term in *The Revolution of Hope*.

provide an effective examination and further development of the ideality. For only by the "mutual demands of ideality, which determine the real encounter, and stimulate and engross the parties concerned" (J. Tamm, *Angst and Subjectivity*) can that field of relatedness (13), indeed of real love, be created, which in reality touches the core being of each one of us and triggers essential impulses.

The Connection with Astrological Psychology

I will now try to establish relationships between the ideas and processes described particularly in the earlier part of this article and the theories of astrological psychology.

The source of actual ideality, the core being, is represented in the horoscope by the inner circle. It is the source of new essential and life ideality impulses.

The tri-polar process involving ideality, reality and hope is clearly and accurately reflected in every house, more precisely in the three different points of every house recognised by astrological psychology, the Low Point (LP), the cusp (C) and the Balance Point (BP), as shown in the illustration.

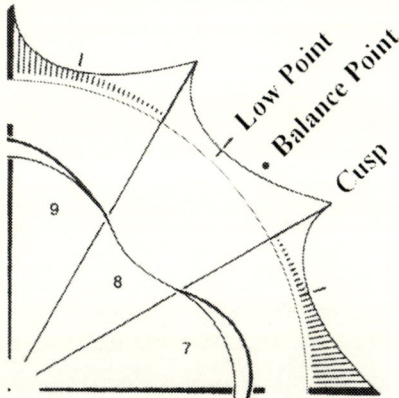

Low point: finding ideality
Cusp: actualising ideality
Balance point: preserving ideality

We can analyse this diagram in two ways. We can consider it chronologically, in the sense of the passage of the Age Point (see *LifeClock*); starting from the low point, via the cusp to the balance point, we can compare the process that takes place with what has been written above about ideality, reality and hope. Or we can consider the diagram spatially, in terms of the significance of the location of the

---

13. Martin Buber used the terms "encounter" and "I-Thou" for this.

planets in a house and the tasks that are conferred on them as a result of the interaction of ideality, reality and hope.

With both approaches, chronological and spatial, we must also consider the other approach and the horoscope as a whole.

The Task of the Low Point: Finding Ideality

In the illustration, the LP is listed with the concept of "finding ideality". In fact, for example during the age point transit through a LP, or for a planet that lies at the LP of a house in the basic horoscope, it is a question of turning inwards to the innermost circle, to the core being, and capturing the impulses released from there for new ideas, for ideality, for new life – and to form an inner benchmark or guide for one's own actions, or inner orientation points. We quote for comparison from *The Astrological Houses*:

> *"The low point always has an inner, introspective quality. Here one can gain access to one's innermost core being, to one's own spiritual realm and one's own inner life as directly relevant to the self. Self observation and self perception can be experienced experimentally."*

> *"One should listen to oneself, heed the will of the core being, go inside oneself, comply with the inner voice, let everything go and make room for the new life that wants to come into being. This will not only set free completely new, fresh energy from the inexhaustible spiritual source, but will also establish a rootedness in the innermost being."*

It is easy to see the connection here between the ideality described earlier as the source of new life and further development against reality, the status quo.

The Task of the House Cusp: Actualising Ideality

In the illustration, we find the house cusp listed alongside the concept of "actualising ideality". Let us compare how the house cusp is described in *The Astrological Houses*: "

> *"All properties of the planets that lie at the house cusps or their vicinity can be fully implemented in life and used effectively."*

> *"All planetary forces at house cusps flow outwards, they are always usable in the environment, are externally visible and yield immediate results."*

Here it is therefore a question of actualising the ideality found at the low point: asserting its demand to be actualised, converting it into action and confronting the prevailing reality with it. Here we find the described process of the encounter and confrontation of ideality and reality again. Here ideality can either be actualised or rejected, as described earlier.

If the ideality can assert itself in this confrontation, overcoming the old, the status quo, the new idea must be realised into a viable, stable, functional form and take the place of the old form. (Let us assume for example that here it is a question of the assertion of a new state or form of government, e.g. the French Revolution.)

The Task of the Balance Point: Preserving Ideality

The actualisation of just such a new, viable form, which now has to be able to preserve itself, is the task of planets at the BP and/or the Age Point transit through it. Compare again with statements about the balance/ invert point from *The Astrological Houses*:

> *"The "invert point" indicates an accumulation of forces generated by the "energy differential" from the cusp of the house and the "energy stop" of the low point. Psychologically, this "oscillation of forces" forces increased concentration of remaining energies on actualisable goals with long term effects."*

> *"The idea, the vision, the impulse, can be harmonised with reality, allowing the appropriate, viable form to be found and created, which expresses that which is intended and desired. That is a real creative process, which is undergone with intelligence and insightfully controlled will."*

We must therefore say instead that an actualised ideal in a viable form, i.e. a piece of reality, is preserved. If the Age Point then moves on to the next low point, criticism and suggestions can further develop ideals of which we are just becoming conscious.

However, if the attempt to actualise the ideality rejects the process of direct, offensive confrontation at the cusp, it can happen that the ideality is not brought to bear, in which case at the balance point it is a question of accumulating the forces remaining at the cusp and directing them towards the inner preservation of the ideality. It is then therefore a question of finding an inner form of the ideal, in which it remains as an inner orientation point, even if it cannot be actualised for a long time.

Here the issue is therefore whether the individual concerned is capable of preserving his ideality in a state of hope.

The "Quadrant Diagram" and the Tasks of the Planets

We can now examine our whole horoscope according to this theme. Particularly suited to this are the "quadrant diagram" and the dynamic quadrant in which we can plot all the planets.

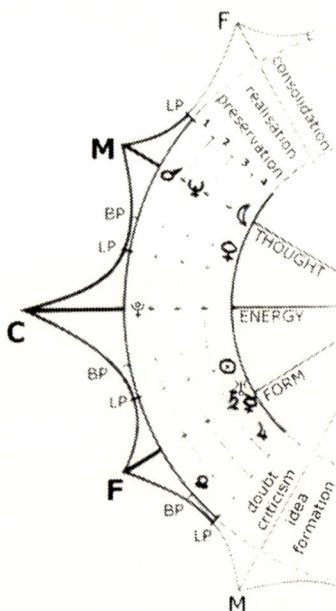

This diagram combines all four cardinal, fixed and mutable houses into a single quadrant. The planets are plotted according to their respective positions in a cardinal, fixed or mutable house. We can quickly see from this which planets lie at a low point and consequently are mainly suited to the task of finding ideality; the planet concerned indicates the theme of the search for ideality. Neptune at the LP will search in the area of love; Uranus will favour the field of scientific research, but the position in the sign and aspect pattern should also be taken into consideration.

I space:	LP11 – LP2
Collective space:	LP2 – LP5
You space:	LP5 – LP8
Individual space:	LP8 – LP11

We can also see which planets are on the cusp, so most suited to pushing themselves forward for actualisation, and which planets are at the balance point and can best work and preserve for the long term.

At the same time, this diagram shows something else very clearly: that ideality must be found before it is actualised.

As obvious as this may appear, it is not at all obvious in our achievement-oriented society, because in the modern world it is still the person who can deploy strength, create effects and accomplish externally visible achievements who gets the most recognition, irrespective of how meaningful they are.

The extreme example of a person for whom all planets lie right on the axes, and who therefore is best equipped to fulfil the above demands, must then be a kind of "model" person. Now this person would indeed definitely assert himself throughout his life, that is, "be successful". Even if his enormous potential is admired, it is possible that at the end of his life, he would have to admit to himself that his life was just a great odyssey; that he had been constantly chasing goals, however successfully, which were mainly set for him by his environment; that perhaps he never really found his own path, what suited his own nature, and what his own personal goals looked like. Perhaps he would then realise how difficult it is for him to achieve this vital inner orientation without planets at the low points.

Every creative process, every attempt at actualisation must therefore be a preceded by a process of introspection that should clarify the goal, purpose and meaning that the creative process then has to serve. The low point planets must therefore first find the values that are to be actualised. Finding and asserting the ideality involves creating that inner stability and inner orientation that then acts as the inner guide to allow a meaningful, meaning-oriented external effect.

The Low Point as a Conscious Method of Insight and Change

There is a further important low point task. Consider the house "energy intensity curve" illustrated in the diagram on page 143 (see also *The Astrological Houses*). This illustrates the "energy distribution" in the house, showing the relative amount of energy with which planets function at the cusp, LP, and points in between, or which the person concerned experiences when the age point passes through the house. Imagine that our AP is transiting a house. We start at the cusp, full of momentum with which to address the life theme that this house confronts us with. (Imagine that it is the 6th house: the mastery of existence, particularly in terms of career). Let us start from the ideal scenario, that already at the preceding low point we familiarised ourselves with the values that are now to be actualised.

In our efforts to assert them, such as building up a career, our expectations will partly succeed and partly be rejected. Efforts initiated after the cusp, when energy levels are highest, will now as it were separate the wheat from the chaff as far as the current actualisation possibilities in reality are concerned.

The closer we get to the BP, always assuming the ideal scenario, the more we focus our energies on the one hand on the goals that can be implemented, which should now be realised, and on the other hand prepare ourselves for long-term effort and the other goals, and for remaining related to them in a state of hope. We are now able to be considerate enough to listen to others, which is not often the case in the highly active phase after the cusp, but the introversion of the balance point has not yet occurred, making this also the best point at which to start the real dialogue for clarification of the rejected values with our fellow men. For this reason we could also call the balance point the dialogue point. We eventually then move to the low point, to the point of self-reflection, new beginnings and reorientation.

What we are driving at is that this point of new consciousness comes not right at the end of the house, after we have finished dealing with the relevant life theme, but about two thirds of the way through it at the LP.

This is a requirement to turn around, as it were looking back at the path travelled, the results achieved and the behaviour shown. It is a requirement to reconnect with the values from which one started at the previous LP, the place nearest to the core being, which have perhaps faded into the background and been partially forgotten in the momentum and problems involved in the confrontation with reality. Now, with the stimulation and impetus from the dialogue in the BP area, is the time to examine and further develop the ideals and open oneself up to new ideals that will lead to new horizons.

The important thing is that after this new awareness, there is still a third of the house left to travel through, so that in the life theme concerned we still have the chance to do good where we had got it wrong before. We can still compensate for something that we had previously not done, and that, newly oriented by and in touch with ideality, our guide, we can make the best possible use of the rest of the way. We have therefore had the opportunity to learn from our experiences with this life theme and to benefit from it before the task comes to an end in the chronological passage through the house, i.e. not only in retrospect after confrontation with this theme has finished.

Therefore, reflected in the passage of the intensity curve through the house, we see the fact that man is a conscious being who is capable of learning, that he is capable of insight and cognition and that the house system takes into account these specific human qualities and abilities.

The Ethical Claim of the Low Point

This is why the low point also proves to be the "ethical point". A person's ethical standard should, like the requirement of the LP, immediately focus his actions and functioning, even at the energy peak after the cusp, on meeting a new LP further along the way and then, at the nearest point to his inner core, being able to tolerate the confrontation with his own ideality. He should then be able to deal openly with himself, with his Self; or even better, able to look himself in the eye. The ethical standards that arise in this way are therefore not the result of adaptation to environmental influences, as described by psychoanalysis for the development of the superego, for their source is the core being. They therefore form what Erich Fromm calls the "humanistic conscience", to differentiate it from the superego.

They then give rise to an individual, essence-oriented ethic, what Neumann calls "new ethic", which is so urgently necessary for mankind now.

Every low point is therefore a new requirement and opportunity to reconnect with one's essence, the source of real ideality, to re-orientate oneself and to live according to the standards found there.

Horoscope Examples

If we now want to know which themes we need to follow up in more depth and deal with at our deepest level, and which ideals are unavoidably part of our journey, the ideality we must understand more clearly, we should look at the planets that lie at low points in our horoscope.

For in the context of the search for ideals, it is the planets situated at the LP that have the strongest effect. But planets in the vicinity of the LP also have similar effects. By vicinity, I mean from the LP half way back to the BP in one direction, and half way to the cusp in the other direction. Planets outside this area are no longer directly or indirectly concerned with the search for ideals.

However, it should be noted that a strong planetary presence in the mutable signs and houses (even if they are not situated directly at the LP) can have a similar effect, because the mutable cross itself is concerned with reflection and the search for meaning. However, the search for meaning will then take the form of an active search in the outside world, rather than of the introversion and inner reflection typical of the LP.

The search for ideality is primarily conditioned by the theme of the planets. The Sun at the LP reflects on the questions "What is self-actualisation? What is self assertion? What is success?, etc." and is not easily satisfied by the answers given by the outside world and the *zeitgeist*. It tends to be rather contemplative and looks for its own answers. The influence of the sign temperament is only of secondary importance. A fire sign, for example, will tend to limit the introversion and push for a quick transfer of the values found into dialogue with the outside world. A water sign will deepen the introversion, particularly due to the emotional need for wanting to find good values. The inward reflection tends to be preserved for too long, and is perhaps even repressed. There are advantages and disadvantages to both.

However, it is the aspects to other planets that are crucial. For example, if an LP planet has a strong aspect to a planet at the cusp, this planet can be used in the transfer of the ideal concerned, which makes it likely that it will be successful. A planet used at the IP works in the same way, although admittedly the actualisation of the ideal is a slower and therefore more long-term process.

This also affects the interpretation of the planets right on the axes: if the Sun on the MC is trine to the Moon at the LP of the 1st house and sextile to Venus at the LP of the 7th house, this Sun will be considerably more gentle, emotionally receptive and sociable and less prone to "ego trips" than would be expected of a Sun at the MC. It will instead be more concerned with taking the ideals of the Moon and Venus seriously and involving itself in their activities. If it does not do this, LP planets often have a disastrous effect on such cuspal planets: in spite of all external success, the LP planets can create an inner feeling of emptiness and lack of meaning. The enjoyment of purely external success, which has nothing to do with inner values, is then greatly reduced.

The final important thing to bear in mind is where an LP planet lies in the Moon Node horoscope (MNH). If the Sun lies e.g. in the Radix at LP 5, but in the MNH at cusp 8 (see example horoscope of WHK), the intended evolutionary step from the MNH to the Radix demands that the old pattern – being successful, taking acknowledgement seriously – is put into perspective in favour of reflective values: what is inwardly essential for my I? The LP is then found to be more painful, more like a stopping point, because the old, activity-oriented pattern is still working in the background.

However, if the Sun lies at LP 9 in the Radix, but comes from LP5 of the MNH, the requirement to reflect is followed through in more depth (only the house theme varies). The requirement of the old Sun and the new Sun work in the same direction, which is often found to be a relief (see example BH.).

Let us briefly consider two examples, i.e. the horoscopes of Bruno Huber (BH) and Wolfhard König (WHK).

In both horoscopes, the Sun lies at the LP, for BH at LP 9 (in MNH at LP 5), for WHK at LP 5 (in MNH at cusp 8). In both horoscopes Mars influences the LP: for BH it lies in the vicinity of LP 6 (in MNH from cusp 9), for WHK at LP 6 (in MNH also from LP 6).

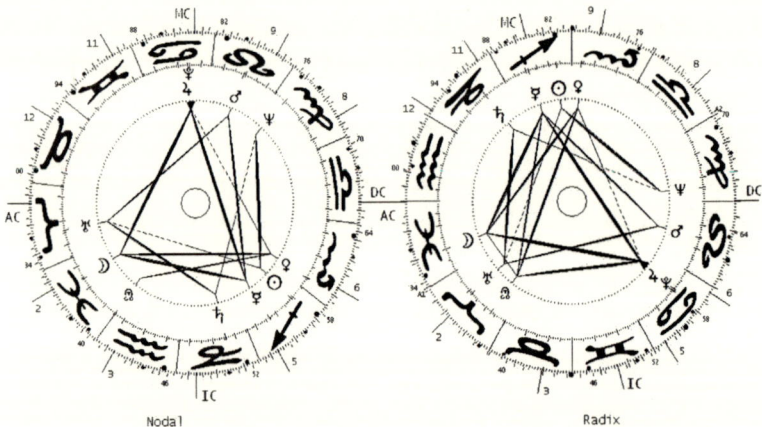

Nodal   Radix

Bruno Huber 29.11.1930, 12:55. Zürich, Switzerland

We have had heated arguments on the themes of self actualisation, self assertion, concepts of success and the rewards of success, fighting, war, fighting in the spiritual sense, fighting for convictions or good values (e.g. astrology) in the course of the last three decades.

Rembrandt's
Philosopher with an open Book

Particularly as far as the theme of the Sun was concerned, we agreed closely on the criteria for hedonistic or capitalist success, but not always about the new, more ideal values. Bruno was much more radical than I, which I link to the two LP Suns in the Radix and the MNH.

I will recount a short anecdote about Mars by way of example. The outbreak of the Gulf War in spring of 1991 between Saddam Hussein's Iraq and the USA-led coalition led to heated debates between us (especially in July in Achberg, where we always had time for such things).

We agreed that it is totally unacceptable for a neighbouring state (Kuwait) to be attacked and annexed and the local population then annihilated. However, the question of when and how which measures would be justified led to heated discussions and intense struggles. If a war was justified, which borders would it be limited to and who would monitor this, the UN?

The old Jesuitical saying: "The means justifies the ends" was brought up, and I argued quoting Martin Buber: "Not every end

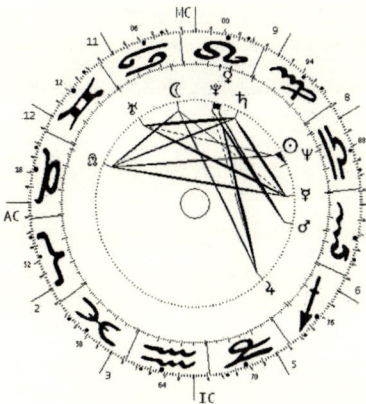

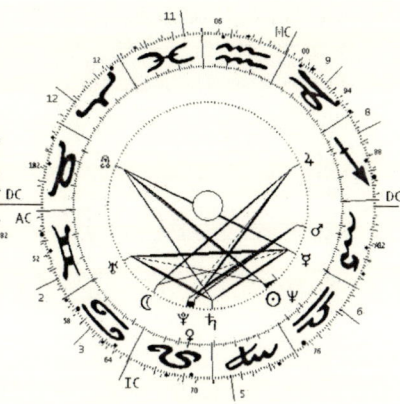

Nodal

Radix

Wolfhard König 27.09.1948, 21:00 Oberau, Germany

justifies the means. But some means corrupt perfectly good ends". Bruno then wrote a manifesto outlining seven demands as to how such a "just war" should be conducted, if at all possible.

Two Sun-Mars reactions were deeply influenced by the low point, by doubt and the search for the right ideals and the right way.

However, it may also be of interest that other, earlier patterns often lie behind the LP requirement for introversion and reflection. For example, in rare moments, Bruno recounted that he liked to sing old foot soldiers' songs and even did so, thus showing a quite different, older experience that lay behind the LP requirement to search for new ways.

Likewise, I wondered why between the ages of 10 and 14 I spent almost all my time drawing maps, hanging them on walls and covering them with drawing pins, red for aeroplanes, blue for tanks, yellow for steelworks, etc. Actually, at this time I wanted to be an army general. Five years later, I became an active member of the peace movement, participating for years in every Vietnam demo and Easter March.

Perhaps both of us under the challenge of the Gulf War had found a synthesis between the necessity not just to stand by and watch in the case of genocide and a very critical assessment of what measures should be taken.

Some such experiences argue that perhaps in principle behind every low point planet lie old, karmic patterns and influences, which must now be questioned and improved and that a little evolutionary step is leading to new values and ideals.

Bibliography

Huber Bruno and Louise, *The Astrological Houses* and *LifeClock*
Kohut Heinz, *Analysis of the Self*
Neumann Erich, *Depth Psychology and a New Ethic*
Wolf Ernest, *Theorie und Praxis der psychoanalytischen Selbstpsychologie.*

❑ ❑ ❑ ❑ ❑

Moon Node – Ascendant

The Line of Development in the Horoscope

Ruth Schmidhauser

First published in 'Astrolog' Issue 149, January 2006

To be able to accurately understand and interpret the Moon Node as a correction point, we need to know the three developmental stages of each house, as the Moon Node does not represent the visible outward form but the potential present in the house. Following repeated requests at the API counsellor training course, I have written this article describing the essence of the three stages of each house, which can be used in Moon Node interpretation. I have also summarised the factors involved in interpreting the Moon Node, with an example.

Stages in the Houses

1st House
1st stage: drawing attention to oneself, wanting to assert oneself, to struggle.
2nd stage: meeting resistance, experiencing setbacks leading to conflicts with oneself or the environment
3rd stage: self-perception, becoming aware of one's own needs and standing up for them.

2nd House
1st stage: striving for possessions, collecting, wanting to keep everything for oneself, even ideas, knowledge and people, "the more I have the more I am worth."
2nd stage: losses, having to let go. Crises and therefore conflict with oneself and/ or the environment
3rd stage: trusting oneself, daring to do things by oneself, doing things alone, being true to oneself.

3rd House
1st stage: following trends, wanting to be in on everything, being a member of groups, going with fashion, trying to get the best possible education
2nd stage: realising the impersonality of the relationships in the collective and the pressure to adapt, but being afraid of being expelled, leading to conflicts with oneself and/ or the environment
3rd stage: willingness to learn from every person, every situation and from everything because one assumes that people, animals, plants, stones, objects and situations all have something to teach us.

4th House

1st stage: depending on the family, being domesticated/homely, rejecting outsiders.

2nd stage: feeling dependent, not being able to live one's own life, leading to conflicts with oneself and/ or the family as one often feels guilty and is afraid of no longer belonging.

3rd stage: letting one's own roots grow within the family, standing on one's own two feet, treasuring the family but still going one's own way.

5th House

1st stage: adventure, eroticism, play, having to prove oneself and seeking approval, bossiness

2nd stage: weariness due to missing deeper meaning, combined with the fear that life could become boring, leading to conflict with oneself and/or the environment

3rd stage: being active, getting involved in life in order to find oneself and to gain self-awareness.

6th House

1st stage: looking out for others, serving, working hard and not delegating, "the more I do, the more I am worth"

2nd stage: feeling the pressure to work, feeling overloaded, perhaps even used, leading to conflict with oneself and/ or the environment as one is afraid of no longer being needed.

3rd stage: serving the soul and thereby being true to oneself, having a real task, not just doing one's duty.

7th House

1st stage: putting oneself out for others and thereby being successful, having influence over other people

2nd stage: feeling that one gives a lot and receives little in return, fear of losing importance or success, leading to conflict with oneself and/ or with the environment

3rd stage: proving oneself to be honest and letting oneself be touched by others, finding a balance of giving and taking

8th House

1st stage: loyalty, striving for status, good conduct, taking laws seriously and adhering strictly to them

2nd stage: feeling restricted and realising that others interpret laws more loosely and being less committed, leading to conflict with oneself and/ or the environment as one is afraid of being punished

3rd stage: finding one's own way within the structure of society and being true to oneself, recognising and using possible freedoms

9th House

1st stage: urge for freedom, need for independence, longing for the far-away/ *wanderlust*, one often knows better than others
2nd stage: missing out on belonging but being afraid of losing freedom, leading to conflicts with the self and/ or the environment
3rd stage: independent and responsible thought, feelings and substance, real freedom

10th House

1st stage: leading, taking responsibility for others, exercising power and/ or control, being in the spotlight.
2nd stage: taking on too much, feeling isolated but also afraid of losing influence leading to conflict with oneself and/ or the environment
3rd stage: living one's own vocation and being fulfilled by it, the ego is satisfied and contented.

11th House

1st stage: elitist and therefore intolerant, critical and judgemental; one knows how everything should be and fights for a better world, which often lead to perfectionism, keeping the trust of long-standing friends
2nd stage: suffering from hostility in which one has first-hand experience of cruelty/ hardship, fear of losing principles leading to conflict with oneself and/ or the environment
3rd stage: realising what one really needs and also letting oneself have it, at all levels when it corresponds to one's own ideals, serving the plan.

12th House

1st stage: wanting or having to be alone, escapism or loneliness or withdrawing to regenerate
2nd stage: feeling loneliness or feeling like an alien on earth and simultaneously being afraid to really get involved leading to conflicts with oneself and/ or the environment
3rd stage: feeling part of the whole cosmos and therefore guided and supported, experiencing the quality of oneness, leading to the freedom to do or to be, to get involved or not.

Now that we are equipped with these pre-requisites for interpretation, we turn to the actual interpretation of the Moon Node.

Interpretation of the Moon Node

1. Interpretation in the Aspect Pattern

a) according to the shape of the aspect figures:

Depending on whether the Moon Node is in a quadrangular/ polygonal, triangular or linear figure, it requires the appropriate basic motivation (fixed, mutable or cardinal) to really be able to develop:

Quadrangular: this is all about allowing enough time for everything and proceeding according to a certain order or system. Stability and peace can be gained by going slowly and steadily.

Triangular: here flexibility must be developed. As the saying goes: "the path is the goal". The priority should be to search for insight and communication between people. The more relaxed the better.

Linear: This is all about developing the ability to want something and to be able to reach a goal. Clarity, goal-directedness and dynamism are the keywords.

If the Moon Node is situated in several figures of different qualities, then all these qualities must be developed and combined.

Incoherent horoscope:
In addition to the above, you should also pay attention to which figure the Moon Node is located in, for the Moon Node is only accessible in it, making this figure particularly important for the purposes of development.

Conjunctions with the Moon Node:
This emphasises the planet concerned, giving it a key role in the growth theme.

Unaspected Moon Node:
In the case of a unaspected Moon Node, there is no aspect pattern to consider. It is dependent on outside directions, which it also receives. It is interpreted in the house and sign.

b) Interpretation of the aspect colours:

If [aspects to] the Moon Node are tri-coloured, it has all the qualities. If they are two-coloured, the two colours are combined.

Blue aspect: we are automatically led to the Moon Node theme, even if this is due to a crisis and an emergency.
    As the Moon Node is a kind of correction point, it is not easy for us to follow it, even with a blue aspect.

Red aspect: either the planet is in opposition to the Moon Node and therefore in conjunction with the rising Moon Node, or the square

Stonehenge – a stone-age lunar calendar

Astrology was born out of the rapt admiration for and careful observation of the Moon and its amazing movements and changes of shape in the night sky. Proof of this is provided by the earliest evidence of human culture in the different parts of the world; like the Old Stone Age cave paintings or the megalithic burial sites, monoliths and stone circles.

causes it to be in a state of tension with the whole axis. Either way, the red aspect indicates resistance to the theme of the Mood Node, which must be overcome by the power of awareness due to the lack of blue, as we are masters at finding arguments against the Moon Node theme.

If **red is combined with blue**, we are torn in two directions. If **red is combined with green**, we find particularly clever arguments against the theme of the Moon Node.

Green aspect: the green aspect makes one a seeker. We inform ourselves and look for new possibilities.

In **combination with blue**, it lets the Moon Node seek and find us, in **combination with red**, green is not asserted and joins forces against the Moon Node.

2. Interpretation in the House

We always interpret the Moon Node in the house in which it is located, by using the 3 house stages described above.

The Moon Node is interpreted in the static house system, not the dynamic one.

As it is a point of intersection and an instruction, it cannot be stressed.

If it is located just before the cusp of the next house it has two themes: firstly the theme of the house in which it is located, and when this is fulfilled it can work on the theme of the next house.

3. Interpretation in the Sign

The house states the task that is set by the Moon Node; the sign indicates how this task can be fulfilled.

Aries: by understanding ourselves and imposing our will
(esoteric ruler: Mercury)

Taurus: by communing with nature and allowing ourselves to have substance
(esoteric ruler: Vulcan)

Gemini: by looking for a great deal of information and then deciding what is suitable and what is not
(esoteric ruler: Venus)

Cancer: by being true to our feelings and accepting them, by daring to be soft
(esoteric ruler: Neptune)

Leo: by following our heart, taking the path of our heart
(esoteric ruler: Sun)

Virgo: by working on self-healing and eventually developing healing qualities
(esoteric ruler: Moon)

Libra: by being guided by what is beautiful, and making the right amount of effort
(esoteric ruler: Uranus)

Scorpio: by plumbing the depths of our psyche and allowing fundamental transformations to take place
(esoteric ruler: Mars)

Sagittarius: by using our external and internal senses, and looking for ever greater truths
(esoteric ruler: Earth)

Capricorn: by pursuing our goals and never giving up no matter what obstacles stand in our way
(esoteric ruler: Saturn)

Aquarius: we should take both the physical/ practical and the subtle realities seriously, and always be slightly ahead of time
(esoteric ruler: Jupiter)

Pisces: by opening channels and letting the forces of light work in us and through us, we can have a healing influence
(esoteric ruler: Pluto)

4. Goal: Ascendant

The ascendant represents a sort of archway in which the threads of our life can converge.

We cannot aim directly at the ascendant; the path always leads via the Moon Nodes.

Whenever we are at a loss in life, the best thing to do is to consult our Moon Node. It will always guide us to the ascendant.

The ascendant, along with the three stages of its zodiac sign, represents our life vision, which the seed thoughts of Alice A. Bailey can also help us to find. Louise Huber included these seed thoughts in Astrological Psychology (see *Reflections and Meditations on the Signs of the Zodiac*).

Interpretation Example: George W. Bush

1. Moon Node in Aspect Pattern by Shape

The Moon Node lies in a triangle in conjunction with Uranus. The triangle (mutable) wants to be relaxed and flexible and to seek insights and to be interested in people.

The conjunction with Uranus calls for intuition to be followed, for one to place oneself at the service of evolution by striving for wholeness and interconnectedness.

George W. Bush, 6.7.1946, 07:26, New Haven/USA

The Moon Node lies in a pattern containing the Sun and Moon, emphasising that development takes place from this pattern and not from the unaspected Saturn.

2. Moon Node in Aspect Pattern by Colour

The Moon Node is only blue, guaranteeing that George W. Bush will come into contact with his theme, however it happens.

3. Moon Node in House

The 11th house is all about being clear about one's own needs. One should have only what one needs. As most people have more than they need, be this in material, emotional or spiritual terms, some should be given away.

Therefore the ideal is to make everything that is superfluous available to others.

4. Moon Node in Sign

Gemini wants to be well informed about everything and to select the correct information by itself.

5. Leo Ascendant

(esoteric ruler: Sun)
"I am that and that am I"

The Leo ascendant provides charisma as a life vision.

Living according to the heart and not according to ideas brings ever greater fulfillment and satisfaction, and it is this state of plenty that produces the charisma.

The Leo ascendant then becomes a pinpoint of light or a source of warmth for others.

Let us remember that the pre-requisite for this quality is perpetual orientation to the Moon Node.

I have deliberately chosen the horoscope of a very famous personality, but I would not like to judge the result.

◻ ◻ ◻ ◻ ◻

Sagittarius Sun and AC Signs

Bruno Huber

Edited by Rita Keller

First published in 'Astrolog' Issues 124-126, October 2001 - February 2002

The Interpretation of the Ascendant Sign

A great deal has been written about the zodiac sign at the ascendant, much of which is contradictory. The fact is that the ascendant, or rising, sign has always been considered particularly significant since the earliest days of astrology, and we can now take it for granted that astrology began with the observation of "what happens at the ascendant". Observations were made not only of the rising times of the Sun and Moon (which were important in the development of the calendar), but also of the signs and planets that were ascended at the time of important events such as the birth of a king. The event was then "interpreted" according to what was at the ascendant. This is a historically interesting fact, which also explains the misunderstandings that still exist in astrology today.

Which characteristics does the ascendant sign have? What is its significance in the horoscope? This is where opinions sometimes diverge. It is very probably true that it has a certain goal-setting function. We assume that the AC sign represents the quality that one consciously or unconsciously aims for in life, which is usually distinctive in older people. It is less pronounced in younger people. It also indicates how the person can develop during their lifetime.

In the early days of the astrological observation of signs and stars that were rising at the time of a particular event, the terms birth star and birth sign were used. This rising star and the quality of the sign were understood to be lodestars in the sense of "the person who rises to their individual evolution".

Now, careful observation and research has shown that in middle-age, some people show a distinct influence of their AC sign quality, but in other people this characteristic is either barely noticeable or completely absent. Some people appear to have no characteristics at all of their AC sign. So what can we make of all this?

If there is a pronounced influence in middle age, the AC sign contains one or more planets. It is these planets that give the sign a particular characteristic, which is obvious in the character right from birth. If the AC sign contains no planets, this quality develops only slowly, usually subliminally and often unnoticed by the person concerned during the course of their lives. It will only really become noticeable in the person's later years, but can then be seen clearly in the person's facial features.

The view that the AC sign is fundamental and always significant can therefore not be justified. It does have an interesting history however.

For every sign at the AC there is also a certain Sun position. In this case, let us consider the example of the Sun in Sagittarius. The ascendant sign changes depending on what time of day the Sagittarius child is born, and the position of Sagittarius in the horoscope therefore also changes. For example, if Aries is at the AC, the Sagittarius Sun is in the 8th or 9th house, but if Libra is at the AC, Sagittarius is not at the top of the horoscope but at the bottom, in the 3rd or 4th house. If we see a horoscope with an Aries ascendant, we know that this person was born at lunchtime or in the early afternoon; in the case of a Libra AC, he was born after midnight.

The Sun in the House System

The position of the Sun in the house system is particularly important for interpretation purposes. However, in vulgar and newspaper astrology it is usually ignored. Newspaper astrology does refer to the rising sign though, and publishes so-called ascendant or rising sign tables, where the rising sign may be discovered if the birth date and time are known.

Another point regarding the rising sign and the Sun's position in the house system is that the AC in the house system shows how the person sees themselves, but also how they try to present themselves in order to make an impression on those around them. It is also the way in which the "I" says this is who I am and this is how I'd like to be seen.

If there is one or more planets in the rising sign in someone's horoscope, we can assume that this person wants to present his own personality with a certain awareness and tries to find out who he really is. If the rising sign contains no planets, this tendency is reduced or completely absent.

Nevertheless, every person has a basic need to present themselves in some way. If a person's rising sign contains no planets, he will not draw attention to himself, but will instead try express his abilities, aptitudes and character properties in his family life and/or career. He therefore tends to communicate through those around him. In this type of case it is particularly important to observe the position of the Sun in the house system.

Sagittarius Sun in the Houses

A Sagittarius native, for example, will express himself very differently depending on which house their Sun is in. Every person grows up in a certain environment and is brought up in a different way, so for this reason, all Sagittarius natives should not just be lumped together indiscriminately. Every Sagittarian of course has qualities common to all Sagittarius natives, but due to his upbringing and the environment in which he grew up, these qualities are always expressed in different ways. The influence that the background and educating adults have had on a young Sagittarian, and the way in which he experiences and expresses himself, are indicated by the position of the Sun in a certain house. This is due to the simple fact that the environmental influences of the background, education and upbringing of a growing person are revealed in the house system of the horoscope.

When we go into detail about the rising sign in the case of Sagittarius Sun position, we shall therefore also give a detailed description of the houses of the Sagittarius Sun and take these into consideration.

Yet another basic observation is that if the rising sign is empty of planets, it is like a symbol which represents other qualities in the horoscope as a goal. If for example a Sagittarius Sun is in the eighth house, then Taurus is at the AC. The Sagittarius Sun would like to experience freedom, search for knowledge and gain awareness. However, in the eighth house it is bound by social responsibilities and the searching spirit, the expansive principle of Sagittarius, must be devoted to a career.

A phenomenon is visible here which is not typical of Sagittarius, i.e. possessiveness, which in the Taurus AC can be summarised as spiritual quest, striving for form, status and possessiveness.

The position of the Sun in the sky relative to the birth position is of fundamental importance. The cause cannot be traced back to the rising sign but to the Sun position in the house system, i.e. in the location system: top, bottom, left, right. This is summed up in one unified concept, represented by the rising sign. That is why we can only consider the rising sign as a symbol not as an effective force.

If the rising sign does contain planets, they influence the character. Each planet represents a typical force, while the AC at the start of the house system is a force that actually works on people from the outside, and therefore does not form the character at birth, but only during the course of the lifetime. This is why the characteristic of the rising sign becomes more and more noticeable as conditioning during the person's life. The self is affected again and again and plays a certain role, which can change substantially from youth to old age. The quality is visible in the rising sign.

Sagittarius with Consecutive Rising Signs

Below, we differentiate between two or three types of Sagittarius, either by separating the Sagittarius month into two halves (21.11. – 6.12 and 7.12 – 22.12) or three thirds (21.11 – 30.11, 1.12 – 10.12 and 11.12 – 22.12). This is necessary to be able to give an accurate position of the Sun in the house system, and also in order to determine the AC. These values are calculated for 42 degrees latitude, i.e. the northern latitude of Rome.

Aries Ascendant

Sagittarius natives with this ascendant are born between midday and early afternoon. People with AC in the first half of Aries have their Sun in the 9th house, at the top of the horoscope, while those with the AC in the second half of Aries have their Sun in the 8th house.

When the Sun is in the 9th house, the Sagittarius native is really typical of the sign. The quality of the ninth house is similar to that of the sign of Sagittarius. It does not usually have a great interest in worldly matters. It is not really interested in material possessions and career, but mainly in the meaning question. The person is therefore to a greater or lesser extent a born philosopher. He wants to understand everything and his interest in the world is focussed on understanding contexts.

He will find it a little difficult to cope with this world. His limited interest in worldly matters creates problems for him. He is looking for meaningful explanations that give him a better understanding of the world, and is not particularly interested in action.

Depending on the structure of the individual horoscope and the positions and aspects of the planets, he can try to communicate his wisdom in a domineering leadership role, possibly as an advisor for influential people, by going into politics himself or by seeking a high rank in the clergy. This corresponds to the upper position of the

Sun in the horoscope. When the Sun is in the 9th or 10th house, there is usually a basic need for a high individual aspiration, which must manifest itself somehow sooner or later.

Sagittarius Sun in the 9th House

A ruler or politician with Sagittarius Sun in the 9th house will surely want to become a wise statesman and not just a politician or power holder. Exercising power for its own sake does not interest this Sagittarius.

These qualities, particularly the aptitude for leadership, are also characteristic of the rising sign Aries. This type of Sagittarius can seem quite egocentric, particularly if the character qualities are not strongly formed. This is again linked to the high position of the Sun in the horoscope and is influenced by Aries, known to be a selfish sign. Self-confidence is therefore strong, even if it has been damaged by upbringing and environment, although it may not appear to be so.

Professional aptitudes are therefore basically either scientific and philosophical or the chosen professions requires wise leadership, be it in the ethical religious sense or in the worldly sense, in politics. Leadership roles are aspired to sooner or later. Various areas of the legal profession are also found here, e.g. judges and lawyers.

Sagittarius Sun in the 8th House

With the AC in the second half of Aries, Sagittarius comes closer and closer to the 8th house, particularly for those born in the first half of the sign. In the 8th house, the original quality of Sagittarius comes

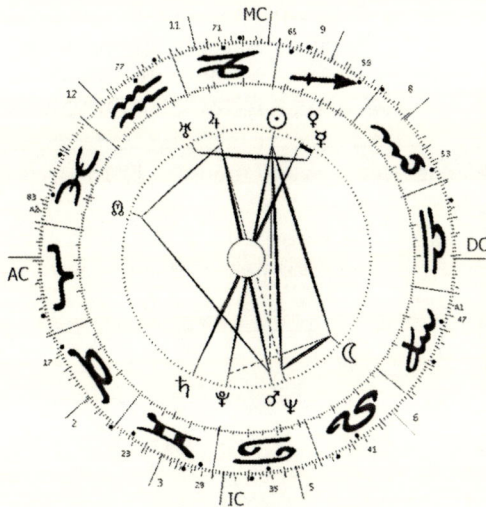

Willy Brandt
German Chancellor
1969-74

Willy Brandt
18.12.1913, 12:45, Lübeck/Germany

under great social pressure. The requirement to do one's duty and also the striving for status of the 8th house indicate that these were the values that the Sagittarius child was brought up with.

The consequence is that aspirations are much more focused on the worldly, social sphere. The main interest is no longer the philosophy that is so typical for Sagittarius, although philosophy is not completely absent here. It is just that there is a clearer desire for status and possessions. If the aptitudes in the scientific or philosophical areas remain, they will indicate a socio-critical attitude, an interest in history and very often in work for charity. Such Sagittarius natives can frequently be found in aid organisations where they want to play a certain, usually leading role.

Many Sagittarius natives with Sun in the 8th house are forced by the circumstances of their lives and/or by their social background to take on a leadership role. They are usually not completely happy in this function, because it greatly limits their freedom.

The self-confidence of the Sagittarian is here very strongly dependent on approval by the environment and on the success of the aspiration to status. This is not nearly as pronounced as with the 9th house Sun. It is much more dependent on external circumstances and on social recognition.

Taurus Ascendant   ♉

Those born in the late afternoon until sunset will have a Taurus ascendant. When the AC is in the first 20° of Taurus, Sagittarius is in the 8th house, and in the last 10° in the 7th house, with the exception of those born in late December. The difference between the two types with the Sun in the 8th and 7th houses is less pronounced than the difference between the two possibilities mentioned above.

With the Taurus ascendant there is a careful, cautious but distinct and interested attachment to the environment. Sagittarius is by nature interested in the environment, but in the 9th house it observes the world from a distance. In the 7th and 8th houses, it is more sociable, wants to participate in life and, particularly in the 7th house, wants a rich and stimulating social life, even relationships with individuals. In the 8th house, there is a stronger interest in position in society and social structures, so it tends to be more aloof.

Sagittarius Sun in the 7th House

We have already mentioned the professional aptitudes of the 8th house and the degree of self-confidence. In the 7th house, as mentioned above, the person is very sociable, has an interest in personal relationships and also tries to form close and committed relationships, often with a very small number of people.

Whereas self-confidence of the 8th house Sagittarius is strongly oriented towards successfully achieving social status, in the 7th house, self-confidence is quite clearly measured by how popular he is with individual people. Sagittarius in the 7th house would like to be seen as a brilliant entertainer and to be well regarded. He also has what is not so typical of Sagittarius: a distinct diplomatic aptitude and ability. He therefore tries to create harmony in his environment and tends to look for what is good and beautiful in life. Here he may even develop the tendency to compromise by becoming economical with the truth due to his need for harmony.

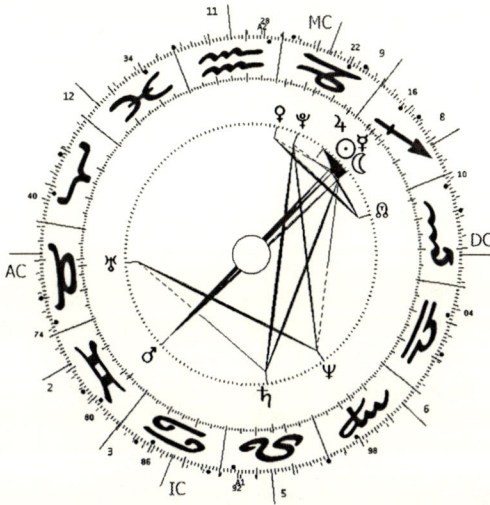

Ludwig van Beethoven, 16.12.1770, 13:30 Bonn, Germany

There is a quite distinct tendency for 7th and 8th house Sun positions, i.e. for all Taurus ascendants, to form stable, ordered and committed relationships. Terms like loyalty and trust are important.

Career possibilities are quite wide-ranging here, from top diplomat to socialite. In extreme cases with certain constellations, there is even a leaning towards con artistry. The more intellectually and scientifically inclined Sagittarius who has a certain amount of education will also show an interest in psychology, especially if the AC is in the middle of Taurus. An interest in psychology born from a strong liking for the people encountered need not necessarily lead to the academic study of psychology or sociology. It can quite simply be developed in personal life and there is often a good understanding of human nature, in any case an intense psychological interest in people that is far from superficial.

Sagittarius would also be suited to an acting career, also indicated by a few individual planetary positions in the horoscope. His acting talents are proven here, as a Sagittarius often takes on a few Aquarian traits. All in all, he will aspire to be a successful and popular human being. In order to achieve this, if he has any problems, which a Sagittarius ultimately cannot cope with, he will either turn more intensively to psychology or tend to repress his own psychological problems.

Self-confidence is highly dependent on the success of relationships with individuals. The affirmation of compassion they give is very important. In the 8th house, one is still interested in social status and appearances. However, in the 7th house, the individual is important, especially a potential life partner, who should provide the Sagittarius with constant, plentiful approval.

It is rightly said of the Sagittarius native with Taurus AC that he displays a certain stability and reliability. This stability has two dimensions: on the one hand the degree of personal ownership and on the other hand the amount of affection, sympathy and approval coming from the environment.

Gemini Ascendant   ♊

Gemini is the opposite sign to Sagittarius, so that the Sagittarius Sun now lies on the horizon. Births with a Gemini ascendant take place in the evening, before or after sunset.

Here we have an extreme form of Sagittarius with great affection for the environment. If the DC, opposite the AC, lies in Sagittarius, no matter where in the sign the Sun is situated, our Sagittarius is very active. It is very occupied with the people around, and ends up knowing a lot about them. On the one hand the person wants to be Gemini, i.e. someone interested in exchange, networking and information, and on the other hand they also want to be a teacher, which gives rise to a certain duality.

He is mainly interested in the environment, and individuals are not that important to him. He is always on the lookout for positive encounters and, alongside an intense relationship, which may also have an element of commitment, he may have a large number of frequently-changing casual relationships. There is a constant supply of new acquaintances and so-called friends. Here he is a little like a bloodhound that tracks all the clues that it scents. He has great curiosity and usually impresses with the extent of his knowledge.

He is well-informed and sees things that other people miss. This is therefore a wide-awake, busy, constantly active Sagittarius, who admittedly loses something of his profundity and occasionally evokes a restless superficiality. This can lead to a certain cynicism in philosophical and above all religious matters. There may also be insecurity and the question of the meaning of life can cause repeated crises.

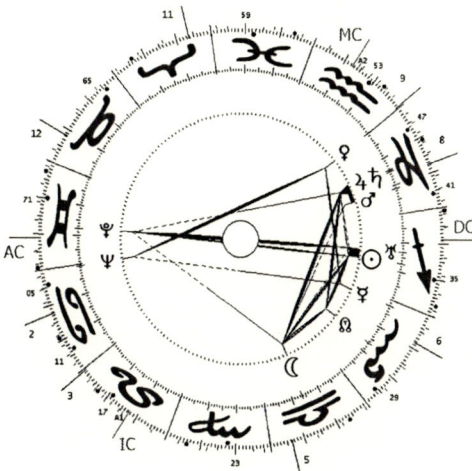

Werner Heisenberg
Atomic Physicist/
Philosopher

Werner Heisenberg,
5.12.1901, 15:45, Würzburg/Germany

This is particularly true when the Gemini ascendant is in the second half of the sign, where the Sun is in the 6th house. Here there is definite existential angst, and self-confidence is dependent on the compassion of the environment and on professional success.

Sagittarius Sun in the 6th House

Typical professions here are acting, writing and teaching. When the Sun is in the 6th house, below the horizon, Sagittarius's pedagogical aptitudes come to the fore, as in the 9th house. The ability to communicate knowledge, associated with Gemini, is all the more emphasised with the Sun in Sagittarius, so that the person becomes an educator, which in the 7th house reduces his popularity, as the environment does not want to be taught.

The Sagittarian with the Sun in the 7th house knows that. However, Sagittarius in the 6th house wants to find ways of sharing his rich wisdom with others, and particularly enjoys teaching children. He will therefore probably become a teacher, a pedagogue who is usually dissatisfied with his status though, so that he will want to undergo professional development to better himself. This can actually lead to many career changes for the Sun in the mutable 6th house. It is very common for someone with this Sun position to initially choose a profession to which he is not suited and in which he cannot express his typical Sagittarian qualities. In youth he may not have had enough educational opportunities, or his self-confidence was crushed during childhood. This means that sometimes he is unable to assert himself adequately and falls into life situations that do not really correspond to his essential qualities. He is therefore a Sagittarius with a tendency to be driven by his financial, existential situation and different experiences cause him to redefine his goals throughout life. The important thing is that he eventually finds a career that really suits his character.

A Sagittarius Sun in the 6th house may indicate a susceptibility to a whole range of psychosomatic illnesses, to which the person can easily succumb whenever situations in life do not go as he would wish and he feels frustrated as a result.

Professional aptitudes clearly lie in the area of pedagogy, and all branches of the healing or helping professions. The teacher would be the prototype. He must not be a primary school teacher though. He could be a specialist tutor, although such a Sagittarius would prefer to be a professor in higher education. This is reinforced by the Gemini ascendant, as Gemini and Sagittarius both strive for academic success. This Sagittarius is constantly setting himself higher and better goals.

The psychosomatic illnesses someone with a Gemini AC is susceptible to tend to be caused by nervous over-stimulation, so that they are not serious illnesses, and are relatively easy to cure.

Cancer Ascendant   ♋

With a Cancer ascendant, the Sagittarius Sun lies in the 5th or 6th house. In the first half of Cancer this the 6th house and in the second half the 5th house. In any case, with this AC there is always a part of the Sagittarius sign in the 6th house.

What has been said above about the 6th house also applies for the first half of the Cancer AC, where psychosomatic processes are common. Here the states of nervous irritation mainly affect the stomach, and there is a possible tendency to depression and a certain melancholy that is typical of the 6th house and also of Cancer due to a distinctly low self-esteem and a certain diffidence. Feelings of low self-esteem or even inferiority complexes or failure complexes are very common here and are a real handicap for Sagittarius. They can cause long periods of frustration and the feeling that one is not making progress.

A pronounced self-pity is nearly always evident here. This Sagittarius has the feeling of being misunderstood, or of being cheated by destiny. He feels confused and that he must clarify and justify his self-pity. He may periodically become depressed and also tends to be pessimistic, which is quite untypical for Sagittarius, which is by nature a great optimist. Even in this position, optimism often breaks through, but only between long periods of pessimism.

The 5th house is still not fully active in the case of the Cancer AC. Sagittarius must wait for the boost that it could receive in the 5th house. This is the cause of the rather depressive or at most rather

Thomas Ring, 28.11.1892, Nürnberg, Germany

melancholic mindset, connected to the fact that the sign of Sagittarius does not manage to reach the cusp of the 5th house. It may even be intercepted in the 5th house, i.e. the Sun in Sagittarius lacks a house cusp, which symbolises connection with the environment. This greatly affects self-confidence, for the Leo house expects a great deal of affirmation from the environment. One would like to be better than others, and is very disappointed if this is not the case, as it may be if Sagittarius is intercepted.

When the AC lies at the end of Cancer, Sagittarius is intercepted in the 5th house. This gives rise to an unpleasant duality; one has high standards for oneself and also expects a lot from fate, yet there is always the feeling that one is nowhere near good enough. One may therefore swing between being up one minute and down the next. Occasional successes alternate with longer failures, which can knock self-confidence as approval is then not forthcoming.

Professional aptitudes tend to be sporting and also spiritual. There may also be a pedagogical aptitude and a great love of children. Sagittarius with the Sun in the 5th house can be almost fanatical about teaching. If the person is mature and educated he can easily work successfully with children.

The love of children is typical here, and working with children in some way would be desirable. This need not necessarily be as a teacher, as this quality can also be used in other helping professions.

We should not forget to mention the philosophical mindset that always characterises Sagittarius. In both positions of Sagittarius, in the 6th or 5th house, with Cancer AC there is often the typical appearance of a person who knows something about everything and who conveys this knowledge in a matter-of-fact and platitudinous manner.

He measures himself by collective norms and knows that he lacks the courage of his convictions. That is why he can concentrate on interpreting the works of others or on providing instructive synopses of complex subjects.

Leo Ascendant   ♌

The birth time is approximately between 21:00 and 23:00.

When Leo is at the ascendant, the 5th house cusp lies in Sagittarius. Here the Leo qualities are strongly expressed, as this house has similar qualities to the sign of Leo. The sign at the AC therefore has an affinity with the house containing the Sagittarius Sun. This phenomenon is clearly discernable in people born in December. For those born in November, the Sun is usually in the 4th house, so that this influence is somewhat mitigated. From a normal human point of view, here we have a glorious Sagittarius. He is an achiever, James Bond personified! There is boundless self-confidence to the point of arrogance. This Sagittarius can crave success and in particular need the support and encouragement of enthusiastic followers.

Sagittarius in the 5th house must have supporters; he must be king in a kingdom of knowledge, philosophy, ethics or intellect. He will want to be intellectually superior to his entourage and actually has to be. However, as with all kings, this makes him dependent on his subjects; on their approval, encouragement and blind adoration. If this is ever lacking, either due to the person's own horoscope or a phase that they are going through, the self-confidence of this Sagittarius is greatly reduced.

This type of Sagittarius is strongly inclined to repression. If

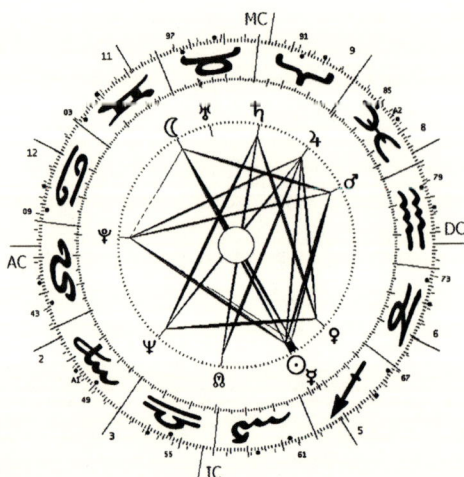

Tina Turner, 26.11.1939, 22:10 CST, Brownsville TN/USA

something is going badly, it is never his fault, always somebody else's, a phenomenon that could be considered untypical for Sagittarius.

Here the decidedly experimental, risk-friendly and adventurous characteristics of Sagittarius come into play. There is a tendency to do unusual things, seek out unusual experiences and work in unusual professions. Here we find the pioneer, looking for unfamiliar climes, the expedition leader and — due to Sagittarius's characteristic desire to serve and help — working overseas as a development aid volunteer in large aid organisations. They are best suited to trouble-shooting roles in catastrophes and for large-scale projects, possibly in a managerial capacity. In extreme cases though we also find the gambler who dedicates his time, mental powers and resources to gambling. This Sagittarius is quite openly trying to reach his limits in order to see how far he can actually go. He is also prepared to take great risks and pay the price if necessary. He often tends to aim too high. This is really a combination of Leo and Sagittarius, which in many cases, particularly when it comes to overreaching himself, makes him almost "Arian".

The charismatic socialite who is noticed by all when he moves in polite society, who is popular and always has people hanging on his every word, can be found here.

However, this is also a Sagittarius who does not really know what he actually wants from life. He is therefore searching for the meaning of life and, although not quite sure where to find it, he is prepared to risk a great deal in the process.

The Leo AC makes him very generous. He puts himself out for others and can go through hell and high water for them. He even accepts material losses in his generosity and desire to help others through hard times. The philanthropic side of Sagittarius is certainly not lacking here either.

As mentioned above, these influences are more pronounced in those born in December than in November. The latter admittedly also have high-flying plans and delusions of grandeur, but they are significantly more modest, probably due to childhood experiences where things did not go as well as they would have liked. There can be feelings of inferiority, especially for Sagittarius with the Sun in the 4th house.

With a Leo ascendant, Sagittarius is gloriously confident and ambitious, although his goals may not be as realistic as he thinks.

Virgo Ascendant ♍

With a Virgo ascendant, many typical Sagittarius features are not usually present, as Virgo is characterised by its modesty. This Sagittarius is easily influenced by collective pressure from the environment. The Sun here lies in the 4th house, where Sagittarius can also be intercepted.

Queen Christina of Sweden, 8.12.1626, 23:55, Stockholm, Sweden

The time of birth is between 22.00 and 02.00.

The development of the Sagittarius native with Virgo AC is already challenged in childhood. Adaptation to the environment is required and he cannot do "what is not done". However, that is exactly what Sagittarius wants to do! He wants to be an individualist but is unable to be one here, it is not allowed. He feels guilty for wanting to follow his not quite hidden instinct for individuality.

He reproaches himself for wanting to do anything unconventional. An example is provided by the premature abdication of Queen Christina of Sweden. Either due to family tradition or generally-held opinions of the collective, Sagittarius is influenced by and adapts to prevailing political, religious, artistic and cultural opinions of the majority. His upbringing has required him to view these collective norms as the only valid ones, and this is where his individualistic tendencies repeatedly clash with his personal barriers.

If the AC is in the first half of Virgo, the Sun is in the 4th house. This makes him very dependent on family, roots, tradition and the ethic that this tradition has created. There is also an interest in history that can be quite strong and develop into a professional activity.

Judges are also found here, for this Sagittarius accepts the validity of prevailing collective norms and acts individually in the name of the people in a judgmental and critical capacity.

Another possible field is social work in all its guises and charitable activities – like in the 6th house – i.e. social work in the widest sense. If there is academic ability, areas like history and sociology will be favoured. Self-confidence is extremely dependent on the collective environment here, on being popular and accepted by the environment, and on the ability to adapt and thus on belonging.

This Sagittarius often develops a strong sense of family. He will be devoted to his own family and really put himself out for them. Some horoscopes show a strong upward pressure, bringing Sagittarius back to its own territory. In such cases there is a strong interest in politics and leadership roles. This can be in the civil service, particularly in the area of government law; it can also be in the religious hierarchy of the clergy.

Sagittarius is in the 3rd house when AC is in the second half of Virgo. Typical characteristics here are a distinct intellectualism, a liking for information activities and sometimes a certain spiritual fanaticism or a demagogic inclination, typically in the area of party ideology. Dogmatic tendencies can be strongly pronounced, as the truth-seeking typical of Sagittarius is combined with the 3rd house tendency to view the opinions of the collective as valid and the only possible authority. This means that Sagittarius's ability to reason and to think creatively can be paralysed here. He needs to be guided by the conventional mindset of the collective and, despite the Sagittarius quality, is inclined towards a certain fanaticism or dogmatism.

Here too, a career can be in the clergy, but in a theological capacity. It is more usual to find theologists here than when the Sagittarius Sun is in the 4th house.

Intellectual activity has a slightly creative quality here, if not actually artistic. This can be positively exploited in a scientific capacity, as a researcher in some field where human concerns should be a priority. There is an interest in philosophy, psychology, sociology and history, but this tends to be expressed in a meticulous, nit-picking fashion verging on pedantry, known typical qualities of Virgo.

As often with the 4th house, there is potential for the person concerned to become a "domestic tyrant"; there may be great tensions in the individual horoscope and a strong desire for public approval.

Self-confidence is also dependent on public affirmation in the 4th house, but here in the 3rd house, the person is more intellectually-inclined, so that affirmation is sought from the exercising of intellectual power, and may be derived from a feeling of intellectual superiority. A certain type of socialite who is a leading light in cultural circles may also be found here.

Libra Ascendant ♎

The sign of Libra has the longest transit time over the horizon, taking more than 3 hours, approximately from midnight to 3am. Sagittarius Sun with Libra AC is therefore more common than with the other AC signs. This balances out the fact that there are fewer Sagittarius than other signs (Sagittarius is one of the least frequent signs).

With AC at the start of Libra, the Sagittarius Sun is in the 3rd house. Here it can be intercepted, which again can mean that self-confidence is significantly reduced. The same applies as for AC in the second half of Virgo. For a significant number, especially those born in November, the Sun is already in the 2nd house, with the AC towards the end of Libra for nearly all Sagittarius natives.

In the 2nd house, Sagittarius tends to be a worrier. This anxiety can be caused by the strong influence of the collective, and also by the upbringing, which is intended to turn the child into a good citizen; the person allows himself to be influenced by those around in terms of behaviour and goals, and above all is forced to be in harmony with those around him. The individualistic Sagittarius is therefore under pressure from two sides here: from collective norms and from the acquired fear of causing offence.

Particularly when the Sun is in the 2nd house, Sagittarius can develop the instinct of possessiveness, which is alien to its nature and can only really exist in this position. It tends to be expressed as the desire to possess those around, rather than to possess material things. This is due to the influence of the Libra ascendant. He wants to possess one or more people. Another inclination found here which is untypical of Sagittarius is that of clinging to others. Sagittarius is normally a free spirit. Here though, he has a distinct tendency to loyalty, sometimes even blind loyalty towards those with whom he has become intensively and deeply involved. He can take this to an extent that can be amusing for others to observe, at which point he no longer knows why he is being loyal; he just feels that this is the way it has to be.

Another typical feature of this Sagittarius is that he does not really know what the meaning of his life is. He tends to allow some authority to decide this for him. That is why people are found here who let others give them the answers to religious and political questions and who work for these authorities. Typical examples would be a priest and a diplomat.

This type of Sagittarian tends to have a strong attachment to others in the general sense of the word; they have an interest in the You that is contradictory. For this Sagittarius is, quite untypically, also motivated by the strong need for a clear, ordered and secure situation in life, due to the demands of the 2nd house Sun. This leads to an internal conflict, whether to come out of his shell and turn towards others or to keep himself to himself.

Hence the desire to pursue a profession that provides the above-mentioned qualities, i.e. find a secure job enjoying the protection of an employer. This Sagittarius would like to work for a big organisation, preferably one that is spiritually-oriented, where he has the possibility of an intense and varied social life.

This Sagittarius can be very sociable, but can become superficial. He has a clear aptitude for dogmatic thought and can display an often superficial aestheticism.

In this position, the Sagittarius Sun can develop a sense of beauty that can lead him to pursue an artistic career. There are two main possibilities: the representative, plastic arts on the one hand and music on the other. The literary talents are less developed, unless the Sagittarius Sun is near the 3rd house cusp. If the Sun is in the 3rd house, and has a literary bent, he will tend to be interested in history, social criticism or psychology, not literature or poetry.

This is a rather unassertive Sagittarius. He is actually not quite sure exactly what self-confidence is. His self-confidence depends on whether his need for security is being met. He cannot give up existing security easily, even when his ideology or his own creative thinking consistently force him to do this, possibly because his employer may no longer be sympathetic. He is afraid to give it up because it has a kind of comforting, maternal function. This Sagittarius is scared of being unprotected and alone. He can easily accept being unpopular with a few individuals he works with, but to lose the support of his whole environment, the source of his security in life, is very hard to handle. That means that he must stop thinking for himself.

The Libra AC causes his priority to be the desire for harmony with the environment. He is therefore less interested in getting on with individuals, and more in having a good relationship with the environment as a whole. If this is lacking, he becomes insecure, as mentioned above, i.e. actually for egocentric reasons. One could say

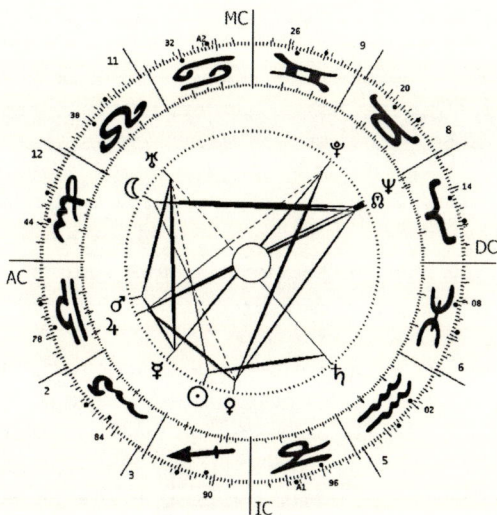

Winston S. Churchill, 30.11.1874, 01:35, Blenheim Palace, UK

that this type of Sagittarius suffers a subconscious existential anxiety, like that of the 6th house Sagittarius, where it is more on a conscious level though.

Scorpio Ascendant   ♏

When the AC is in the first part of Scorpio, i.e. up to about 20°, the Sagittarius Sun is in the 2nd house as before. Here it is all about ownership. A characteristic example of this type of Sagittarius is the patriarchal big landowner, who looks after his flock and treats them like a benevolent father. This is very pronounced. He is the owner and therefore rules over everyone who is subordinate to him, treating them as though they were his property and looking after them as if they were his children.

The pedagogue that is always present in Sagittarius is now expressed, as he looks after the spiritual well-being of his protégés through their ups and downs. The socially aware and active pastor may also be found here, but he always acts from a position of ownership. He probably does not renounce material possessions, because for him, possessions and economics are the basis of his more spiritual interests.

There is spiritual activity here, but he is forced to compromise it with a more worldly mentality, which makes him existentially highly dependent on circumstances, and this can interfere with his need to find the truth. Compromise may therefore be required due to the desire for security, which is clearly based on ownership. Everything depends on his financial situation.

Such a Sagittarius can get into financial difficulties because Sagittarius is aware that ownership ultimately has nothing to do with philosophy. Our personal financial situation should ultimately not be more important than the search for truth. This can lead to a lifestyle that jeopardises existential security, causing real temporary or permanent problems.

The professional aptitudes of this Sagittarius depend on the extent to which he is able to assert his own ideals when faced with the harsh realities of life. If he cannot do this, then he suffers and self-confidence is affected. The polarisation of spirit and matter that these people experience so strongly leads to ethical, philosophical or religious crises; even to identity crises.

An extraordinary amount of self-denial is required here in order to eventually be able to rise above material needs in favour of a discerned truth. Superficially, criticism is directed against the structures of those holding worldly power. However, this is how this Sagittarius attempts to justify his own lack of power, and explains how these people can become tyrants and dictators.

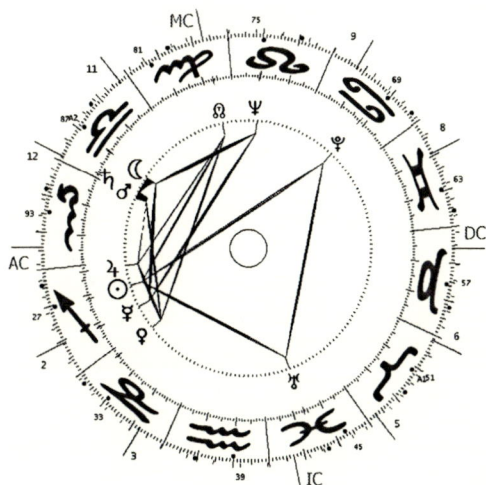

Maria Callas, 4.12.1923, 05:42, New York, USA

This type is relatively hard to understand. He is deep but can be unfathomable. This Sagittarius tends to always want to get to the nitty-gritty, to get to the bottom of things and may become involved with the "dregs" of society. This is one possible cause of his artistic activities. In his art, he tries to give a form to the inner distress, to become aware of it and communicate it to the world. He is therefore always somehow a slightly tragic figure.

If we compare the Sun position in Sagittarius with the Scorpio ascendant, the former is a great optimist and the latter a great pessimist. These two qualities oppose each other and whatever these people do, they can never escape this problem. He can never be truly happy because one part of him will always be either unsatisfied or must be denied.

Sagittarius Ascendant ✒

Birth time: approximately 5am to 7am.

One could say that a Sagittarius Sun around the AC is a good match with Sagittarius. It indicates an optimist, an individualist but definitely also an egocentric. These people want to assert their individuality and typically also want to save and help others, improve them and teach them. In the process though, they try to place themselves above others, which can put some people off and make them more than just friends. They are troubled when their truth is doubted because they then feel that their whole self is being called into question. They are extremely dependent on their truths being approved of and acknowledged by others. If this does not happen, and their self-confidence is threatened, they become bossy and can use their sharp intellect to hurt others. They are the centre of their universe and want to teach others, but show little inclination to learn from others in return.

When criticised, he takes an intellectually superior stance. He assumes that others have not understood his truth, which makes him feel isolated and unhappy. This particularly affects those born in November and at the beginning of December, due to the position of the Sun in the 12ᵗʰ house. They feel like misunderstood geniuses, for a certain brilliance, based on their capabilities, cannot be denied. This a good prerequisite for his self characterisation and the clear expression of his individual qualities, which are important to this Sagittarius.

He therefore becomes a truth fanatic, in the good and bad senses of the word. He will always be keen to find the truth and use it to help others. These qualities do not make him self-critical, but make him critical of everything that happens to him and which he is able to discern. He has a sharp intellect with which to develop his genius. Only when strong tensions appear does it tend not be developed in the intellectual sense. In that case, Sagittarius nearly always turns to art as a way of expressing his genius, corresponding to the typical idea of an artist who is misunderstood in his own time and only becomes famous after death. Perhaps because he is sometimes too much of a maverick; his art is too different, too offbeat, or because he is really ahead of his time.

When the Sagittarius Sun is clearly in the 12ᵗʰ house, he may also be a hermit; the type who withdraws from the world or keeps it at a distance, leads an offbeat independent life, or even a double life.

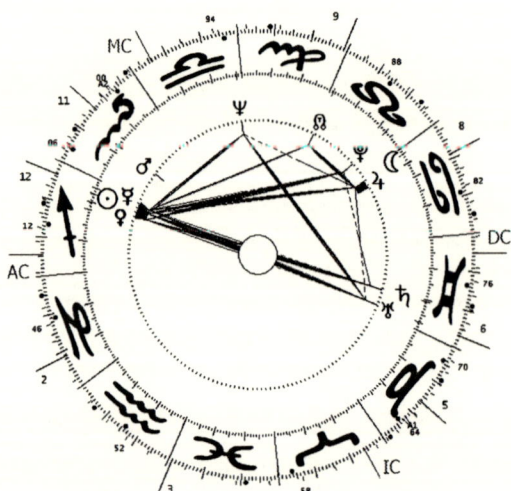

Jimi Hendrix, 27.11.1942, 10:15, Seattle, USA

The latter may occur when his horoscope indicates a strong need for affirmation by those around him.

The hermit or recluse is naturally a fundamentally philosophical figure, with a philosophy generally involving being detached from the world in the sense of human drives, but not from nature. He usually has a great love of nature, so that the need to give love, so typical of Sagittarius, can be satisfied by looking after the natural world. He has a profound love to give, often to an extreme degree, and would be a very good vet. A profession where he could respect and love the great outdoors, such as forester or farmer, would also be suitable, as would that of the hermit who dreamily wanders around the countryside, feeding birds and observing plants. This would allow him to indulge in his inner philosophical thoughts, which are philosophical in an emotional or intuitive sense rather than a sharply intellectual one.

In any case, this Sagittarian has a tendency to solitude that, depending on the overall situation of his horoscope, makes him rather unhappy. A certain unworldliness and other-worldliness or even loneliness may cause him frustration. Then, particularly when the Sun is in the 12th house, pessimism can set in, which is very untypical of Sagittarius. However, a Sun in the 1st house indicates a quite definite, often overpowering optimism. This pronounced self-confidence can sometimes even be unpleasant for the environment, and is then the reason for his loneliness.

In the 12th house, self-confidence is more profound and comes more from within, making it less dependent on the environment. This Sagittarius is modest, a real lover of people and animals. He is interested in nature and looks after animals with infinite care and patience, asking little or nothing for himself. Here self-confidence in the worldly sense is not developed – as though it did not exist.

In any case, this is an individualistic Sagittarius who unconditionally asks fate to take him as he is.

Capricorn Ascendant ♑

Birth time: about 7am to 11am. The Sun can be in the 12th, 11th or 10th house, and each house produces a different character.

In the 12th house, Sagittarius is withdrawn and rather detached. In the 11th house, there is a certain aloofness, and Sagittarius is definitely not worldly but is extremely interested in the world, albeit from an ethical, philosophical, moral or dogmatic perspective. He is interested in developing solutions for the world to give it a universal, if possible a utopian order. This Sagittarius is an eccentric figure firmly believing in a perfect world: all that is needed is the right recipe for it.

The lively intellect of Sagittarius, which is most strongly developed in the 9th house, now seeks out fixed thought structures. He invents intellectual systems and wants to stick to them, making him dogmatic. We often find this type of Sagittarius in large corporations with an idealistic political or religious leaning.

This also includes charities and philosophical groups, even secret societies. He tends to join smaller, closed groups where he can show off his own intellectual status.

Intellectual status is his way of measuring his self-confidence. He has a tendency to have exclusive ideas and solutions and thinks at a rarefied level, where a sense of reality may be somewhat lacking. This is despite his almost obsessive tendency to arrange everything into systems and to want to be able to explain everything. Here the versatile intellect of Sagittarius is combined with the dogmatism of the 11th house, which wants to order everything systematically. This can lead to mental rigidity, which is not alleviated by the Capricorn ascendant.

When AC is near the end of Capricorn, November natives' Sagittarius Sun is already in the latter part of the 10th house. This indicates a desire to enter politics or to take on some other kind of position of power or leadership. This Sagittarius is not suited to the acting profession, although some acting may be required. He then tends to behave like a typical Capricorn and becomes a puller of strings, an *éminence grise*, or power behind the throne. This quality is most clearly expressed with a Sagittarius Sun and Capricorn AC.

This type can develop a decidedly shady quality that the environment finds unsettling; unknown forces seem to be at work here. They make others afraid that they are being controlled by an unidentified higher power.

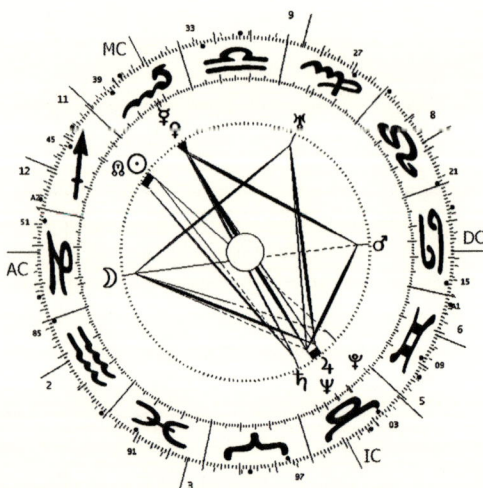

Pope John 23rd, 25.11.1881, 10:15, Bergamo, Italy

In both these positions, 10th and 11th house, Sagittarius is at its most austere. Intellectually, they are hard and intransigent, uncompromising and disinclined to accept other points of view.

Their self-confidence appears to be completely unassailable, at least from the outside. Their attitude is imperturbable, but merciless. He never wants to lose face, never wants to be soft, but he can also never shed tears.

He must have a place somewhere in the corridors of power and have the feeling that he is pulling strings and influencing the world. This is the source of the *éminence grise* in politics, business, religion or philosophy, and can also be found in secret societies. He must be able to exercise power over ideas. If there is no danger of him being criticised, particularly in the 11th house he can be generous, but here too he will also ruthlessly assert his opinions if necessary.

If the Sagittarian is mature enough to behave with responsible authority, he has the ability to organise or mechanise processes that involve people, or to invent systems of classification that can improve human lives.

Aquarius Ascendant   ≈

Birth time: 09.30am to 1pm. When the AC is in Aquarius, the Sun is in the 11th, 10th or just inside the 9th house. All three types share a striving for leadership roles, power and influence in as many places and contexts as possible. This is another very strong personality, who has an unconditional desire to be intellectually dominating.

There is also a highly-developed individual awareness, which can be startled by the slightest thing. Those born in November, whose AC is right at the end of Aquarius, are different though. There the Sun is already in the 9th house, where self-confidence is reduced, which could hardly be said to be the case when the Sun is in the 10th or 11th houses.

These people always view their situation according to their own abilities. They keep an eye on everything and don't miss a thing; they are in absolute control of their circumstances. They are able to have a far-reaching overview. Particularly in the 10th house, they are good organisers, relatively wise leaders and are progressive and go-ahead. They are receptive to new methods. However, they can appear impersonal. They can be kind and responsive to individuals' circumstances, but tend to keep other people at arm's length.

Such a person will find it hard to cope if circumstances, especially at an early age, prevent him from taking a leading role. He needs breadth and living space in which to truly actualise himself. He needs space to think, even if his intellectual education is relatively limited.

This Sagittarius aims for fixed goals and always sticks to his principles. He can act rigidly, is incorruptible and does not let himself be pressurised.

He has a distinct dislike of manipulation, for example in politics, which he considers to be unfair and cruel.

He is a seeker of truth and a philanthropist by nature, which makes his path to power a slow one. His motivation can easily be misunderstood. He could be reproached for being incompetent because of his occasional inconsistent behaviour caused by his humanity or idealism.

This Sagittarius has ideas for world improvement. If for example he is running a business, he will want to be progressive in this area.

Suitable professions for this person are personnel consultant or human resources manager, where he can exercise power and help people at the same time. He has the motivation to enter these professions, anyway.

If this Sagittarius is an entrepreneur, which is often the case, he will follow his own original ideas. In business he will do his own thing instead of following convention. He has ideas that nobody else has and special "trouble-shooting" skills that always emerge when everything has gone wrong and nobody else knows what to do next. Then he is able to gain an overview of the situation and provide the original ideas that will get the business going again. He is creative and confidence is the key to his success. He is not afraid to think completely outside the box in his search for solutions. It might be hard for him to doubt his self-confidence, unless the AC is at the end

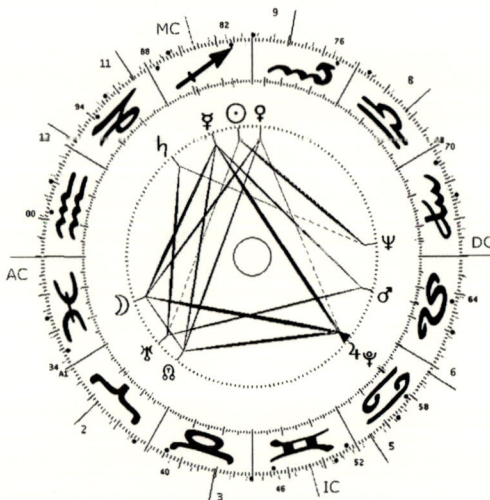

Bruno Huber, 29.11.1930, 12:55, Zürich, Switzerland

of Aquarius, when he tends to undermine his own self-confidence by philosophising.

Pisces Ascendant ♓

Birth time: between 11am and 2pm.

When Pisces is at the AC, the Sagittarius Sun is in the 10th or 9th house. December natives with AC at the start of Pisces have their Sun in the 10th house, and for the others it is at different stages of the 9th house.

The 10th house description above also applies here. Even with Sun in the 10th house, there is a combination of qualities that peaks when Sagittarius is found "at home" in the 9th house, when the humanitarian and philanthropic tendencies are emphasised much more strongly.

The Jovian qualities attributed to both Sagittarius and Pisces now come to the fore. Even when the Sun is in the 10th house, there is more interest in a philanthropic or humanitarian profession than in a career in politics, business or in the civil service. Even with a civil servant there will be an emphasis on humanitarian and philanthropic activities.

These people's motivation is to make a contribution to the improvement of the human condition, particularly on an individual level. To what extent they succeed depends on the individual horoscope. If they do manage to attain the higher ranks of the civil service, it is not impossible that they will retire again. It may be that they are too idealistic and that it is not possible to put their ideas into practice. He tends to pay too little attention to reality and to demand too much of the present. That is held against him and he is misunderstood. He is either described as too good-natured or a fantasist.

The field of politics, in particular, is ultimately not very satisfying because a politician must exercise the art of the possible and Sagittarius in the 10th house is more interested in exercising the art of the impossible. He can easily lose touch with reality here, even if he aspires to public office. He will not lose touch with reality though if he pursues non-worldly activities, which is usually the case when the Sun is in the 9th house. Instead he should focus on doing what Sagittarius does best, i.e. understanding the world and then making his knowledge available to the world as and when it is required.

With a Pisces ascendant, Sagittarius has little need for a worldly echo. He prefers to find approval by coming up with an intellectually outstanding idea that he would like to use to help others, i.e. his motives are truly altruistic. He then identifies himself with his idea and is not understood by those around him.

He is usually quite self-confident, but does not show it. He often appears shy, particularly when the Sun is in the 9th house, and responds well to human need and his attempts to do something about it can even fail due to his own sadness. His empathy for suffering people can distract him, as the pain of the world can be too much for him. This is a strong feature of the Pisces ascendant, particularly if the Sun is in the 9th house, although the sign of Pisces as such is not worldly.

There is a strong interest in psychology here. His great sympathy for human need makes him want to know the reason for it, and he finds the answers either in religion or in psychology.

If the person has an intuitive nature, which is more likely, he will tend to look for answers in religion. However, if he is more intellectual by nature, he would tend to be more scientific and deal with principles, so that he would be more likely to be interested in psychology as a way of understanding others. This Sagittarian is definitely a sensitive therapist and counsellor, who can really get to know people. He could, for example, also be a travel agent and recommend the right holiday for each customer, and always want to find out exactly what each customer needs.

This type is also known to be a great traveller, a wanderlust that can stimulate him to travel endlessly, another feature of Pisces. They want to find out what is over the horizon, and have a longing for the faraway and a curiosity about the unknown.

He may want to work in the world of travel, particularly when the Sun is in the 9th house. When the Sun is in the 10th house, he has a need to travel in order to seek the extraordinary and the unusual.

Sagittarius with 9th house Sun is rather susceptible to illness, mainly provoked by stress. This type hates any kind of routine.

The self-confidence is characterised by altruism, with a great interest in people. This person is likely suffer if he gets on badly with someone and they do not understand him or misjudge him. This makes him react like a typical Pisces; he withdraws into himself, cuts himself off, disappears from the scene and feels terrible.

□ □ □ □ □

Part 3: Age Progression

In this third part of the book we have grouped five articles related to age progression, the approach developed by Bruno and Louise Huber that enables understanding of key psychological events and phases in our lives.

The Journey through the Zodiac in the Age Point, **by Rita Keller**
Archetypal themes experienced as we make the age point journey through the signs of the zodiac.

Age Point Biography, **by Michael A. Huber**
Bruno and Louise's son discusses factors involved in the creation of an age point biography and its interpretation in the natal and Moon Node charts.

The Zero Point of the Zodiac - The Pisces/Aries Border,
by Louise Huber
The significance in the horoscope and age progression of the border area between Pisces and Aries, a gateway to the spiritual and herald of new beginnings.

The Cosmic Fissure, **by Dr Hans-Martin Domke**
Gives real life examples of the significance of the Zero Point in four example charts, and points the way to further research.

Transits of the Spiritual Planets, **by Birgit Braun**
On the significance of transits of the three transpersonal planets and their relationship with age progression.

The subject of Age Progression is covered in the following original Huber books:

LifeClock, by Bruno & Louise Huber
The essential basic reference.

Astrology and the Spiritual Path, by Bruno & Louise Huber
Subtitled *The Spiritual Significance of Age Progression.*

Moon Node Astrology, by Bruno & Louise Huber
Covers age progression in the Moon Node chart.

The Journey through the Zodiac In the Age Point

Rita Keller

First published in Astrolog Issues 111,112 August - October 1999

Working with the Age Point allows us to recognise a temporal dimension in the horoscope, or an inner clock. At some point in the zodiac, we start our journey at the ascendant that will take us through our whole horoscope in 72 years. The radix chart reveals on the one hand our genetic make-up, and on the other hand the environment and the ways of thinking and behaving that we learn from it as we are growing up. The genetic component is indicated by the zodiac signs and planets, while the houses show the environmental situation (influence of upbringing and background).

If we now assume that each one of us "runs through" the entire horoscope during a 72-year period, we all have the opportunity to find ourselves, get to know ourselves and gain self-awareness. We all have our "own time" that is distinct and different from other people's. For in every horoscope the ascendant is in a different position at the moment of birth, the time when the life of a child begins and his life motivation towards others is formed, influenced by the sign at the AC.

Our assumption is that we have to deal in a different way with twelve different life themes during the course of our lives, corresponding to the twelve houses. How we relate to these themes is indicated by the zodiac signs, which symbolise certain qualities.

Every sign contains a cross quality and shows our inner motivation towards an area of life. The temperament of the sign shows the way in which it is expressed. This combination of cross, temperament and planetary sign ruler gives each life theme a particular behaviour pattern.

If we now take a look at the zodiac sign in which a person's age point starts, we can draw certain conclusions about a theme in the family situation at the time of birth. A certain sign is often repeated over different generations within a family. This frequently happens on the mother's side, when the mother tries to bring up her children in the same way that she was brought up. However, this is only really a question of an acquired attitude to the environment, which can be overcome despite the sign being the same. The awareness of the individual is a deciding factor in this process. The sign at the AC by itself gives no information about the personality, but rather about the mask that we wear to protect ourselves or to show ourselves in the best possible light.

Every zodiac sign is followed by another sign. Every sign contains certain life experiences in the archetypical human mind, the collective unconscious (C.G. Jung), which are available to us as resources. With this in mind, from the point of view of the age point dynamic, during our lives we get to know the contents of the sign and can use this to deal to the best of our abilities with the demands of the environment.

Sign changes in the age point are often perceived as problematic, especially by people who do not accept that life is flux and who are proud of the fact that they want to things to stay as they are.

Nature shows us that changes are completely natural, but such people find changes threatening; they are afraid of what is different, as it cannot be classified, it does not fit into our established, familiar system and we cannot control it. People often come for a consultation after a sign change because they sense a purportedly unwanted change within themselves. However, knowledge of the dynamics and the learning process during the journey through the zodiac signs teaches us that this is not threatening at all, but exciting and fascinating. It then feels rather as though one could dip into the unconscious, in order to benefit from it by becoming aware of, learning from and understanding its characteristics.

It is worth getting to know the 12 archetypes so that you can travel as awarely as possible through the zodiac. There is nothing threatening about them; one sign conditions the next, and they develop quite organically one from the other.

Aries   ♈

Let us begin the journey with Aries, the sign of new beginnings, symbolised by spring, the time when nature reawakens. This is a cardinal fire sign that likes to give momentum. The emphasis is on the I. It wants to impose itself with fiery power, and is impatient, enthusiastic, impulsive and entrepreneurial. In this period, we can participate very actively in life; we feel an inner force, a forward-driving fire. We know no limits and when we find them we push them aside. We can use the passage through Aries to reinforce the I, cast obstacles aside and to approach new goals with courage.

However, if we want to understand what this power means for the individual in the truest sense of the word, it naturally makes sense to consider the whole horoscope. We can only really understand the primeval force of Aries in the context of the whole horoscope. I can assume that the theme of the house in which the Pisces/Aries cusp lies says much about which environment offers us possibilities for self-renewal and self-assertion. For the house whose cusp lies in Pisces shows that our upbringing has taught us to be passive and to adapt completely, out of "love", and to do all that we can for others. This is self-sacrificing behaviour. However, if we recognise our own ability to learn, this is also the house of wisdom. In the sign of Pisces, we therefore see the end of an intensive learning process, and realise that everything has a meaning, and that we can let go of everything, because we understand and because we can accept love.

Taurus ♉

Our journey then leads to the next sign and a fundamental change in inner motivation. Taurus is a fixed earth sign, characterised by tenacity, perseverance and a highly urge-driven and indulgent nature. Everything must be doable, everything takes its time, we must exercise patience and have sufficient resources to achieve our goals. It is the time to become clear which possessions are essential, and which talents are present and usable. If we compare these characteristics with those of Aries, the problem of the change of sign becomes clear. People experience an extreme braking effect, and time acquires another dimension. If we take a look back into the time of the cardinal, masculine fire energy, we had big ideas and felt capable of anything. Have most of these not been realised? Have we not often had problems with other people because we wanted to charge ahead without thinking?

The feminine energy of Taurus helps us to come back down to earth, to remind ourselves of what we are actually capable of, and what our talents really are. We can enjoy this; even rejoice in it when we see results. Everyone has a lot to give, without having to be afraid of losing everything. It corresponds to the season of blossoming, and we know that blossoms turn into fruit that we can harvest. In this time, we want to be needed, in order to acknowledge and reinforce our self-worth.

On the other hand, this period can be linked to fear of loss. This gives us the chance to deal with this fear. Confidence in oneself can be the reward, the knowledge that we have the ability to protect ourselves and set boundaries for ourselves should this be necessary for our own security. If our expectations of others are too fixed during this period, and we think that they should make our lives as comfortable as possible, we can meet with resistance, which shows that we should be capable of doing this for ourselves.

Gemini ♊

On the next stage of our journey, we meet the mutable air sign Gemini, which is motivated by love, and is where relationships and communication with others begin. We are interested in all kinds of information and are open and eager to learn. However, we have previously learnt that when we do what suits us without considering other people, or when we isolate ourselves or cut ourselves off out of fear, we are alone. The developmental process pushes on and shows us that we feel the need to actively approach people to understand why we are alone. We learn to listen to others, to communicate and to think about everything. We want to understand and to be understood. We want to love and be loved. We are open to change and feel that the world offers countless possibilities. There is such a lot on offer that we often find it hard to know what is right for us. We therefore remain spontaneous and open and just learn in this way, without being able to decide for ourselves. Everything we come across is worth looking at and thinking about. This phase is often rather superficial, but it is all about making a subjective choice out of the variety of possibilities available.

Cancer ♋

This brings us to the cardinal water sign of Cancer, where differentiation begins. We have experienced the three prototypes, Aries, Taurus and Gemini, corresponding to the cardinal, fixed and mutable crosses, and learned from them. We have now moved on to the first phase of our emotional world, in which we get worked up if the people that we love are not close to us and the love and understanding that we think we need unconditionally are lacking. We do so much for others though, and think we are right in expecting something in return. We are active, as befits the cardinal cross, but this time on an emotional level, and experience ineffable desires, for who can really put feelings into words?. However, we have found that we were laughed at if we tried to express our feelings, and were misunderstood if we ever had the courage to declare our secret desires in the hope that they would be requited by an object of our affections.

This experience teaches us that it would be better to invest our energies in learning to take our feelings seriously. We recognise that we can fulfil our desires ourselves, but also that we can be there for other people who are suffering from loneliness. We can only understand this if we have personal experience of it, if we ourselves have suffered and know how painful such an experience can be. This is how we learn to treat others more considerately and become more independent.

In the air sign Gemini, it was still possible to find solutions by talking about everything. If we are confronted with our own feelings, talking is often no longer helpful, as it is hard to understand the feelings of others when we are not exactly sure about our own feelings, or about our unconscious expectations of others.

Cancer corresponds to the fourth house, the lowest point of the horoscope, the place we come from, our roots, and the place where we belonged emotionally when we were still dependent. We were willing to do a lot for other people because we thought this would make them love us. We were disappointed because we deluded ourselves and because we didn't know exactly what others expected of us. We were hurt and did not fulfil others' expectations of us. Out of these experiences comes the urge for independence.

Leo ♌

The next step leads out into the big wide world, into the fixed fire sign of Leo, where we start to relate to the environment. We want to conquer this world, impress others and show how strong we are. We want to increase our living space, expand our means of expression and be the focus of this self-created world. If we do this without consideration for others and strive ambitiously for power and influence, we will be brought up against our limitations. As in Leo we also want to experience relationships with our loved ones, the experience of isolation is all the more hard to bear. However, there is the chance to grow, to open our hearts, to stabilise our ego, and to express ourselves honestly.

Photos: Rita Keller

This is how Leo helps us to learn a lot about ourselves, due to the increasingly differentiated perception of ourselves and the reactions of the environment. Being honest with oneself, being able to perceive and test oneself lead to inner strength and to real self-awareness. It makes one truly able to structure one's own world, enjoy life and to meet other people with an open heart.

Virgo   ♍

A strong ego that is sure of itself, a personality that knows what it wants, now has to deal with the next theme. Change, an aptitude for learning, adaptability and (if possible) subordination are now required. The transition from a fire sign to the mutable earth sign of Virgo may make it clear that reality shows us what is feasible. Reality is often not very exciting, so that much of what happens does not coincide with our ideas and expectations. However, we have to manage, show character, and prove ourselves in order to find our place. This can make us highly critical of our environment, for it is always possible to find shortcomings, situations that we don't like or cannot adapt to.

It can seem that after flying high in Leo, the "landing" in Virgo feels rather as though we have not achieved our goals, even though we were convinced that we were finally going to be able to actualise ourselves. We often forget in times of trouble that in Leo we had created our own particular reality, which at the time had manifested itself rather negatively in our consciousness. For we must now deal with details, serve, order, understand and help where help is needed. We do all this out of love and in order to be loved. However, we find that all this devotion and helpfulness is not appreciated, that people often do not notice what others do for them. This makes us critical of other people, or we criticise ourselves and believe that that we cannot cope with the demands of life. We withdraw, close ourselves off or take refuge in illness.

Psychosomatic illnesses can also be a chance to reflect on our own attitude, to focus love and understanding on ourselves and look after ourselves. We can learn to pay attention to our own needs and find time for them in our daily schedule.

We should not forget that in the feminine mutable sign of Virgo we want to be needed, are motivated by love and have an aptitude for learning. It is important to find the right balance between inside and the outside. It is often easier for us in this You sign to help others than to help ourselves. However, it is definitely worth learning to help ourselves for the sake of our own well-being, so that we relate well to ourselves and to our environment.

Libra   ♎

With the age point in Libra the "ascent" to the conscious part of the zodiac begins. What we have learnt from our experiences in the first six signs constitutes a valuable resource that we take with us on our journey through the You signs and helps us to cope with their demands. We are sure that we do not want to subordinate ourselves any longer, but in Libra we must learn how to be in harmony with the You. We meet all kinds of people in the process. Every relationship is a new challenge; we realise that people think, act and live very differently. If we assume that we finally want to have a say, we must accept that other people exercise this freedom for themselves as well. What should we do when we know that everyone wants to find and advocate their own way of living? On the one hand, we are looking for harmonious relationships, and on the other we want to assert our own way of thinking, because we are convinced that it is right. Conflicts often arise when we try to manipulate others to get our own way. We must therefore try to strike the right balance, so that we can live in harmony and equilibrium with the environment. We find that every You is also an I with its own ideas. If we respect this, relationships become valuable learning experiences and our dealings with others become more and more differentiated. In the process we learn a lot about ourselves, for we also see a part of ourselves in others. This realisation shows the intelligence associated with Libra.

The better we know our own needs and perceive and meet them, the easier it is for us to accept that others want to claim the same rights for themselves. These preconditions lead to awareness in our dealings with others and it becomes possible to live in peace with others without self-sacrifice.

So-called conflicts occur in Libra, because the undifferentiated power of the opposite sign Aries ensures that we do not escape into an ideal world and avoid conflict out of convenience and an exaggerated desire for harmony. In Libra we seek the You so that we can get to know ourselves and how we react in a variety of different situations. As long as we tend to understand our world in terms of the polarities of good and bad, and to judge these by our own standards, we will become involved in conflict and have problems making decisions. Libra therefore offers us the opportunity to cultivate our decision-making abilities. When we know that harmony and conflict are wrestling within us, we realise that the environment serves as our mirror and conflictive situations in the environment disappear.

Decision-making ability on this level means being honest with oneself and others so that we can make decisions from our core. As Uranus is the esoteric ruler of Libra, we are required to strive for solutions that are a developmental step forwards for all concerned, so we must be able to take the risk of opening ourselves up to the unknown. Creative intelligence is the willingness to get involved in new adventures and to write new discoveries on a "blank page".

Scorpio   ~♏

When we move from the air sign of Libra to the water sign of Scorpio, there is again a change of attitude and motivation. Still we find ourselves in a You sign. However we now experience this theme passively and on the emotional level. Feelings are always subjective and the result of our own mindset. Depending on the awareness of the individual, these feelings can be extremely varied. We experience ourselves as more or less combative, possessive, vindictive or aggressive. We encounter negative feelings in this sign and are confronted with fears and urges that allow us to discover the intensity of our emotional world. In this phase we fight and triumph, lose and win, vindicate ourselves and eventually want to let go.

On the Libra/Scorpio level, we are dealing with two signs with Mars-Venus characteristics. Scorpio has an affinity with Mars, while opposite Libra is the Venus sign of Taurus. This makes us tend to think that everything that we acquired in the past, everything that we own is good, because we have invested a lot of time and energy into them. We needed them for our security and well-being and believed that without these things, these resources, we could not survive. That is why we defend our "precious" possessions without realising that we are carrying a lot of ballast around with us, which restricts and burdens us and hinders our further development. Being intensely affected by our emotions is essential to make us willing to let go.

Water always has a purifying effect, but Scorpio is a fixed sign. Imagine a reservoir that is full to the brim with water. This is a calm state, revealing nothing of the concentrated and destructive power that can be triggered by sudden, unforeseen changes in the "secure" retaining wall. This can actually be tested for security, just as we are always trying to control our feelings within the framework of the norms of society. But we also know that emotions can break through in certain circumstances, just as the retaining wall can crack, causing death and destruction. If correctly regulated though, this power can be made available to others in the form of energy. The motivation, awareness and decision-making ability of the individual determine how he will use his power.

If in Libra one of the reasons we needed the You was because we wanted to take advantage of him, in Scorpio we may realise that this can also lead to obligations and restrictions. That is why in Scorpio questions are always popping up whose answers can only be found in our own emotional depths. We realise that the external things of life cannot bring lasting satisfaction, and this insight makes us want to try to restructure our lives, this time based on our own inner values. This is the start of the process of death and rebirth. The realisation that we are not losing anything, but winning something instead, leads to spiritual freedom.

Sagittarius

Freedom is the key that leads us to the sign of Sagittarius. We have been longing for this freedom all our lives, and it is such a worthwhile goal. The question now is: what does freedom mean to the individual? There are possibly as many answers as there are people. In this mutable fire sign, we will get the opportunity to ask ourselves what this theme means to us personally. On our journey, we have seen that life has offered us many opportunities to gather experiences in order to be able to choose our goals for ourselves. Whether or not we succeed reveals much about our mindset and our previous life experience. If we have dealt with polarities in our life and have tried to find our own centre in the face of love and hate, war and peace, guilt and atonement, inner and outer, the Jupiter principle will help us to choose freely. The house in which Sagittarius is situated indicates the life theme in which we need freedom and want to use it in order to realise our goals.

In this mutable fire sign we have an aptitude for learning and the goal that we are aiming for is as individual as we are. In Sagittarius, we want to experience ourselves as an individualised personality, strive for meaningful goals, achieve them and aim for new goals based on what we have learned. Enthusiasm is an important companion in our search for the right path. The right path is the path to ourselves, so that in this life phase we learn to listen to ourselves.

If we want to achieve something, in order to impress other people or because the collective attitude thinks that something is good, we will not be able to enjoy the success we had hoped for. For what matters is what we think, not other people's opinions.

We will find that it requires courage to stand by our own ideas of what freedom means. "Other people" do not always approve, but we should dare to take the step towards ourselves based on our own life experiences. Only we know what our next goal can be and why this is necessary for the development of our personality. Now it is evident how our I (Aries) has developed and been formed by experimentation (Leo).

Capricorn ♑

The transition to the cardinal earth sign of Capricorn may bring us back down to earth, if in Sagittarius we had set our sights high but were not successful. We always find out why it was not to be and are confronted by our own limits. We must realise that we alone are responsible for everything that happens to us. Limit experiences are never pleasant, but only by acknowledging our own limitations can we redefine them.

The character of Capricorn can help us to activate our willpower and not to give up when the going gets tough. On the contrary, we want to overcome anything that challenges us and our ambition is awakened. We want to prove to ourselves that we are capable of carrying out apparently hopeless tasks in the face of all resistance. It may well be that the fact that others doubt us can motivate us to achieve great things. If we have enough resources available to draw on, we are ready to learn new things and we will reach the "peak" that we are striving for.

For this we need the qualities of the other two earth signs; from Taurus, time, patience and perseverance and from Virgo, the love of detail and the aptitude for learning, possibly even the criticism of the status quo. All of this helps us on our way, full of conviction that this is exactly the right thing for us. We are required to deal with all the consequences and only if we do not give up can we achieve our goal. Whatever happens to us in the process encourages our individual development and makes us aware that each one of us has the freedom to choose and to act with autonomy. In the process we must be prepared for the possibility that we have to travel alone without the support of others. However, if we live for our vision alone, the experience of loneliness can become painful. Because in Capricorn we want to rely only on ourselves, we can lose touch with the people that we love.

Aquarius ♒

If on our journey we have reached the lofty goals we have set for ourselves, in which we have invested all our time and energy, we realise that we have missed out on an important part of life. This experience causes us to seek out relationships with other people again, people who mean something to us. In Aquarius, we gain the opportunity to find our friends, people on the same material and spiritual level as us with whom we have an affinity. We are looking for an exchange with these people, and want to discuss God and the universe. The group we choose to associate with reveals much about our own way of thinking and living. In this phase of our journey, we are required to be tolerant on the one hand, but on the other there is a danger of an elitist attitude and of rejecting those who think differently to ourselves.

Aquarius offers us the opportunity to question our way of thinking, for with our thoughts we manifest reality. In this fixed air sign, we also encounter entrenched ideas, which can limit our relationships with others and the world in which we live. Or we use this character to try to explore great spiritual connections in order to find solutions for the world's problems. We can participate in some form of humanitarian projects, or work for a more humane world.

The choice of theme depends on the awareness of the individual. The symbol for Aquarius consists of two lines on top of each other. The bottom line symbolises the material level and the top one the spiritual level. Saturn and Uranus are associated with Aquarius. These two planetary qualities are another indication of the duality of the sign; we can and must dare to take a mental leap into the unknown to discover the cause of the problems. Again and again we will push to the limits and must test whether our visions of a perfect world can be converted into reality. Or we may cling to the old, and let ourselves be discouraged because we feel misunderstood by the world.

Sundial, Church tower in Wangen/Allgäu

We are once again required to learn to discriminate, to activate our creative intelligence and when necessary, to rebel, be it against our own stale thoughts or against hidebound structures and forms that restrict life. The group consciousness of Aquarius shows that the most different types of people can support each other if they work together on a project. Each person is aware of themselves and their own abilities and can make their own individual contribution. The group structure allows us to relate to each other, exchange ideas and realise visions together. That requires tolerance, but we find that a group of individuals of different types and talents can be very enriching. People who place themselves above others, who assume that they are better than others, who are not ready to open themselves up to the new and the unknown, are not tolerant, close themselves up and shut others out.

When at this point of our journey we enjoy a little peace and quiet, and let images, experiences and people we have met roll by us, we will notice that we undertook this journey in order to gain wisdom. Everyone will have to reflect once in their lives on what life means to them. We will ask ourselves what the highest meaning of our life could be. We will be alone with big questions and only we can provide the answers. We have lived our lives in our own way, were given the possibility to set goals, and chose every step ourselves. From this position, who still wants to judge which decisions were right and which were wrong. The I still has learning processes to go through that it must deal with by itself. These experiences take place within us, when we are alone with our infinite emotions. At this point, we must close the circle and relate everything that we have learned to our self. We have become whole and wise as a result of all those experiences. Nothing was bad enough that we couldn't learn something from it; nothing was good enough to retain us on our life's journey.

Pisces ♓

It is the mutable water sign of Pisces that enables such experiences. It contains passive, feminine qualities that lead us to ourselves. This does not refer to the real exterior world, but to the inner life, to heeding the message of our emotions. To find answers deep within ourselves we need peace and quiet and distance from the hectic world. Withdrawing into ourselves enables us to recognise connections and realise that everything has a meaning. This also means loving ourselves, for in this sign we are confronted with loneliness. Not because we have been abandoned by the environment, but so that we can be at peace and learn to trust our feelings.

If we run through the journey through the zodiac again, we see the unlimited possibilities that life offers us. We recognise the dynamics of the crosses and the temperaments of the zodiac. We are constantly required to adapt to new combinations and to refine our self-expression.

◻ ◻ ◻ ◻ ◻

Age-Point Biography

Michael A. Huber

First published in Astrolog Issues 106,107, October - December 1998

"A personal biography is a natural and effective path to the self"

Life Course Analysis using the Age Point

The chronological description of a personal life course is an extremely individual thing, for no two biographies are the same. The knowledge we can gain from them is therefore precisely adapted to our own personality and contains no generalisations. We are more than used to reading the generalised psychological rules contained in most interpretation books and are often forced to say: "this statement is just as true for another person who does not have the same planetary positions!"

So, if we are able to associate individual life experiences with the planets in the horoscope, this gives us a direct description of the planetary forces as they are to be interpreted only in this particular horoscope. Generalisations disappear and the individual essence is revealed. This allows us to learn to get right to the heart of problems and deal with them with awareness and consistency.

We are all aware that a problem can only be dealt with by finding the root of the matter. This almost always means regaining the qualities of each individual planet, which involves leaving aside external issues in order to enter more deeply into our personalities.

The facts of the situations experienced are of secondary importance and merely serve to give clues as to what lies behind or beneath them, for different underlying problems may lead to the same or similar experiences.

For example, many people can miss the train, but they could all have different reasons for missing it. Mercury caused one person to mix up the departure time, Saturn caused another to forget the time, or Venus caused yet another person to sit eating in the restaurant for too long. Such external events just give us clues and stimulate our consciousness to look within ourselves again to find the inner causes. The repetition of problems in similar situations gives us the opportunity to better get to the root of the problem, until one day the problem stops happening. In this way, everyone can gain a better understanding of their own personality.

This developmental process is called "the integration of the personality", which should be regarded as an ongoing process that takes place on all levels and in all areas of the personality.

The processes even run parallel to each other in different time rhythms, and throughout our lifetimes new facets of the personality that require integration are always emerging.

We should indeed all aim to understand our own personalities. However, this requires daily mindfulness of our internal processes and images. The inner life is rich and complicated, and our consciousness is only aware of about 15% of our total potential, hence the need for the biography, which focuses on different facets of the potential of the personality one by one. A lifetime is quite long enough to become aware of all of our abilities, qualities and potential, and if a new facet appears, there is plenty of time to understand it.

The Age Point has proved to be a reliable and chronologically accurate method of correlating individual experiences with planetary forces. That opens up unimagined possibilities to the person who is working on themselves to be able to live a freer, more aware and less stressful life.

It should be pointed out in advance that the benefits of this very deep method can only truly be recognised and understood if one is convinced of the basic principle of self-responsibility:

"What I experience, what happens to me from the outside and what is done to me is a reflection of my inner imaginary world, which is what really determines my destiny".

Possibilities and Effects of Biography Analysis

1. More distance from ourselves: studying our own biography gives us the ability to see ourself from the outside. It is as though a sort of manager grows within our consciousness, who enables us to evaluate situations and ourselves at any time from an overall perspective, which greatly helps in decision-making. We can also forgive others more easily when we understand why things must happen.

2. More success: the more perspective we can gain, the more we learn quite automatically to live by the principle of focusing our energy and attention on our strengths, on that which we are given and that we can do well. This leads to much greater success than spending energy on our weaknesses. This is in line with the principle of psychosynthesis for integration of the personality: emphasise your strengths and only work on the obstacles that are really in your way.

3. Increase our own potential: new ways of developing our own abilities become apparent, that we do not normally perceive in the heat of the moment. Furthermore, we can use a comprehensive and accurate study of our earlier life to learn how each planetary ability works quite individually, without needing the traditional

planetary interpretations. This can allow us to find a practical, personally tailored solution and developmental path.

4. Awareness training and self-control: by learning to differentiate our experiences, we get rid of illusions and projections. In a new situation, we can know from the outset where it will lead. If it is a familiar repetition, we can nip it in the bud to make better use of our time.

5. Joie de vivre: the study of the Age Point can teach us how to reactivate and fully benefit from the energies and hidden qualities suppressed in childhood. If we know exactly when certain childhood experiences become active again, we can prepare ourselves optimally for future experiences in order to draw more on the joie de vivre of childhood.

6. Intensifying development: it is not a question of preventing certain experiences because we are afraid of them. If we do that, they just become too charged and turn up at a later date as strokes of fate. Although we are able to put off experiences, it is better to intensify them with the willpower, thereby accelerating them! The list of experiences that we still have to undergo in the future is just as long as that of the ones we have already undergone, i.e. infinite, so why should we put these things off?

7. The end of fear of the future: a person who deals deliberately and precisely with the processes in their life supports the processes of experience, thereby accelerating development and influencing more and more the course of their destiny. With one provision: if we know what is going to happen to us and can accept it, situations are no longer automatically presented by fate or even forced. They can even not happen at all, if we mentally go through the experience first. However, the pressure of experience can still arise and in many cases raise development to a higher level.

The Age Point and the Course of Time

Our genes determine our appearance, organ functions, basic needs and a great deal of mental information (behaviour). The genes are influenced by three factors: the mother and father (and their parents and ancestors) and the incarnating individual. This third source is the unknown factor for biologists and in the future a connection should be proven between this and the horoscope. This probably influences the genetic information that comes from the mother and father.

The genetic structure is a complex multi-stranded spiral along which information is stored. These strands also contain the experiences of our ancestors as well our experiences from earlier lives. A particular feature is that information is changed during the course of our lives and gradually, conditioned by the aging process, permanent electrical connections are established between individual links. These are very stable and can no longer be changed. These are fixed life experiences that only death can release from the tissue in the form of energy and take with it to the "other side".

The AP is the power that makes these connections permanent

The above-mentioned, as yet uninvestigated chemical-electrical vibrations contain our experiences and all that we have learned during our lifetimes. However, we could also say that these had to happen, due to inherited experiences from former lives and parental choices. The behaviour and attitude of our parents and of those around us condition a part of our destiny. Much of what we must live and experience was established by the influence of our parents, for example the first choice of partner, place of residence and profession. Even later on, things can happen that parallel our parents' lives, like separations, bankruptcy or other strokes of fate.

The AP determines the course of time and how we experience it

If we know at a given moment why a situation has come about, then at the same time we also know where it will lead. Each person knows their own chains of cause and effect well, but cannot consciously access them as they are in the subconscious.

If the subconscious pursues a certain goal, it will try to influence decisions in line with this goal in every situation. For example, it knows that a friend goes away when I say or do a particular thing. If my subconscious wants to undergo the experience of being abandoned again, all it needs to do is to make me say something stupid, apparently without realising it, so that the other person feels offended and leaves. But it is up to me whether or not I say those words at that moment, thereby activating the predetermined future. A few minutes later the familiar feelings of sorrow and self-reproach set in. It is an old, recurring pattern that emerges from the subconscious.

A couple of years later, however, this does not emerge automatically, and other old patterns take its place, which are based on certain inner images. The transformation of inner images can be seen in our dreams, or better still in imagination exercises. Over time, our inner nature reveals all possible inner images so that we can process them.

The AP gives rhythm to the coming and going of the inner images

Time is a great wheel around which we can arrange our spiritual qualities. It is a long chain of cause and effect that can only be altered by growing awareness, love or one's own decision-making and perceptual abilities. These three energies are timeless, which is precisely why they enable us to influence the here and now.

Our soul resides in the so-called causal body, which is responsible for our present life. Vast amounts of different experiences and wisdom are stored in the causal body, which, in astrology, is shown in the aspect pattern. If we assume that the causal body places a selected number of qualities in the personality that must be actualised during a lifetime, there will always be many necessary experiences that we have to get through in our 72 years. The course of time forces us to get to know, complete and classify these experiences one by one.

"The Age Point shows the current pressure of experience, which forces the consciousness to undergo the necessary experience"

Event – experience – learning

In the following we will discuss in detail the experiences we have, repeat and even bring with us. We must therefore first define more precisely what we mean by experiences and how they come about. The difference between experiences and events has often been discussed, but the direct connection between them has rarely been recognised, for there is actually a link between events and how we live them, and hence our experience. These three things therefore belong together, giving rise to the mental leap of associating them with the three crosses:

C = cardinal, M = mutable, F = fixed

This sentence summarises the order:

Every **event** is also an **experience** and a **learning situation**.

C: events are happenings that take place outside the personality, which trigger certain mental reactions. The nature of the reaction depends on what has already been learnt and changes with time, as new experiences come along.

M: experience means the impressions and inner effect within our personality, which is dependent on our perceptual and interpretative abilities. The more alert and receptive the consciousness, the more intensively everything is experienced and stored in the form of learning.

F: learning is the result of experiences and lasts longer. It is often formed of lessons or findings that have been reworked many times, and which are needed for the successful guidance of the personality. The more a person has learnt, the more confidently and responsibly they can live and the fewer errors they will make.

Now, the whole is just a cycle that is not so easy for us to understand if we don't know that everything that happens to us is a reflection of our inner imagery. The lessons that we have learned are mainly stored in our subconscious. They have a gravitational pull, like matter, which is the real cause of unforeseeable events. Consequently, another cycle begins with an apparently new event. A newly-converted horoscope in the Huber method is presented below in an attempt to find and better understand the deeper causes in our subconscious.

The Moon Node Horoscope and the Second Age Point

If the Moon Node signifies the first step into something new, then it can be compared to the first step in this life, which takes place at the AC. Furthermore, we can also say that just as the Sun rises at the ascendant, the Moon travels upwards at the ascending Moon Node, and as the Sun sets, the descending Moon Node lies where the Moon starts its downward path. From this we can deduce that the AC-DC axis has the same qualities as the Moon Node axis if we turn it towards the AC. However, because the Moon Node axis itself is

retrograde, the house divisions also run backwards. This gives rise to a mirrored horoscope, the Moon Node horoscope that turns on the axis of symmetry that lies about half-way between the AC and the Moon Nodes.

A good definition of the Moon Node horoscope is that it shows the totality of all experiences as completely stored potential going back in time to the most ancient past starting from today.

From a psychological point of view, the Moon Node horoscope is a representation of the shadow personality. This contains both unconscious and repressed qualities from childhood and also the ancient learning that we bring with us, whose exact origin is hard to determine. Certain beliefs call it karma, but to us that seems too narrow a view. We prefer to say that it shows the sum of all experiences from former lives, which contain much positive and useful know-how. Each time we ask ourselves why is this happening to me, or why have I been so lucky to have so many good things in this life, the answer can be found in the Moon Node horoscope.

In a crisis, we are usually afraid of a known pain that we must experience many times. After the crisis, we realise that it actually involved the same experience that we had to go through the last time and many more times before that. It runs through life like a chain, always with the same links, right back into the earliest days of

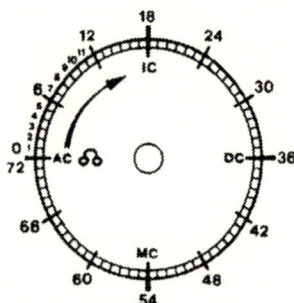

childhood. There we had the "necessary" experiences for the first time, which naturally made a great impression. However, if we could follow our incarnations back even further, we would notice that the same themes, the same pain or the same experiences were also present then.

It is a natural function of the human psyche that old problems and memories from childhood usually reappear automatically. On our life's journey, these reminiscences from the subconscious seem to be unpredictable, as though they occur sporadically with leaps in time and time stretching. However, this is not the case; we are actually able to predict them accurately. We use the AP to establish when certain childhood experiences and problems will emerge again later in life. It is only possible to do this accurately, though, if we take into account two counter-running time mechanisms: that of the consciousness and that of the subconscious, the shadow.

We can find the second Age Point in the Moon Node horoscope, where we can also calculate time divisions in 6-yearly intervals starting from the AC. The AC in the Moon Node horoscope is the same as the Moon Node position in the radix. It is also plotted in an anticlockwise direction, due to the mirror-imaging effect, so that the houses and the AP run in the same anticlockwise direction. The discovery of this second Age Point not only results in many chronologically accurate event correlations with the Radix AP, but also offers our consciousness a greater insight into the connections of human destiny per se. [See *Moon Node Astrology* for more on the Moon Node horoscope.]

We will use the abbreviation MN-AP for the Age Point in the Moon Node horoscope and the abbreviation AP for the normal Age Point in the basic horoscope.

Differences between the AP and the MN-AP

The AP enables us to consciously recognise and interpret our current life situation. The AP shows the interest and the way of interpreting the consciousness. It allows experiences to be identified and combines these with certain lessons we have learnt, and qualities and abilities of the personality. As a function of the will, the AP initiates actions, and in the process we learn and try to find out why we have to experience certain things.

The MN-AP releases old lessons from the subconscious and activates related qualities in the area of life so that they emerge like backdrops, create parameters and appear to be real matter and people. Although that may sound like magic, it is just like what happens when light falls in the darkness outside a spotlight. What happens is that we notice people or things that have been there for a while, but we just had not spotted them before.

208 Part 3 – Age Progression

The Interaction of both Age Points

The AP aspects contain the current contents of the consciousness and store them in the degree of the zodiac in which the AP lies. They remain stored as fixed learnt matter until the MN-AP reactivates them the next time it transits them. It should be borne in mind that all archetypes and therefore also previous life experiences are also stored in the zodiac. These are activated in the first life phase, when the MN-AP first runs through certain zodiac degrees in which the AP has not yet made learning situations.

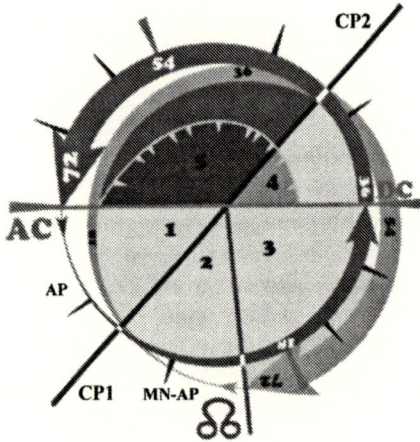

Constructing a complete Biography

The ability to remember depends on various things: on the strength and accuracy of the memory at the time of the event and on our situation and emotional state at the time when we are trying to remember what was happening.

It is possible that we are now able to remember events from childhood that we had no recollection of at all a couple of years ago. There are also memories that are only accessible at certain times, and that is the first problem that we are faced with when trying to construct a complete biography.

The logical order of the passage of time in the horoscope is helpful here. Using AP aspects, we can both search for certain occasions that we have no memory of, using "important aspects" and specifically enquire about them, and we can also use the planetary qualities to formulate statements and questions that lead to the memories.

The second problem is the accuracy with which we can remember experiences. We often get the seasons wrong, or even the year. But that is not good enough; we need reliable information, if possible accurate to the month. The following elaborations, imagination exercises and lists of characteristics will help you do this.

Experiences that we can no longer pin down accurately are however included, just as variable data in an extra column. It often happens that later on, when the lists slowly fill up, these data can be made more accurate or corrected. We can also try to use the AP to determine the month in which something happened.

The third problem is that of different typical psychological patterns. When something bad happens, related to fear, emotion or sexuality, memories are sometimes subsequently and deliberately changed; partly by the subconscious out of self-protection or by adults in charge who are trying to cover something up. Memories can also be inaccurate, usually in the following instances:

1. A shock can almost completely erase the memory. Or other external influences like violence, suggestion or even hypnosis that are not apparent in the horoscope, or indicated only by a corresponding character.

2. In the case of emotional pain and injury, the psyche uses its repression mechanism, which with time we can familiarise ourselves with and learn to see through more successfully.

3. A common repression trick is projection: when I think that the other person has a problem that I actually have myself. I have cheated myself: by repeatedly projecting my unconscious memories of pain onto other people, I am sure that I don't have this problem myself. This allows it to disappear from my memory.

Incidentally, the three problems described above correspond to the three cross qualities: the first is a cardinal problem that can be addressed with the will; the second is a fixed problem that can be solved in a systematic way, and the third problem is mutable, i.e. it always functions differently and can be solved by communicating to find the right information. The same three types of energy are also available in the case of our search for our memories.

There are three paths into the past:

C: Our soul prefers chronological order; it goes purposely forwards in time from birth onwards. The emphasis is on listing visible, external events and the most important decisions, which are also required in our official curriculum vitae.

F: The path automatically selected by our psyche goes slowly back in time from the now into the past. In the process, we view our life in images, more emotionally, almost from within, and can also gain access to the subconscious.

M: The thematic connection of momentary and past events helps the integration or reparation of certain experiences. For example, an argument with a partner can cause us to relive a similar childhood situation and we are then able to forgive the partner more easily.

The Four Chains of Memory

1. **List of Events, AC**
   (Fire, impulsive)
2. **External Biography, MC**
   (Earth, real)
3. **List of People, DC**
   (Air, communicative)
4. **Experience Book, IC**
   (Water, emotional)

The terms are based on the context of the chain from the standpoint or perspective of the memory in the horoscope, and the brackets contain the perceptual style of the respective ruling elements.

The first step is to totally "ransack" the memory and sift through all our previous experiences. This can be done by writing down clearly and concisely the four types of memories, which naturally often overlap and intermingle. The memories should be consistently written in all four lists in the following order:

Date
AP position
Key word
Brief description
Other information

It is almost impossible to complete all four lists at the first attempt. In the first half of the life, there should be about 180 items, i.e. on average one per degree of the zodiac. Time and patience are of the essence. It is necessary to go over it a few times and try each time to activate the memory from a completely different perspective and using a different method. We should also keep on flexibly swapping around the four memory chains, each time taking all three paths into the past.

Someone who has kept a diary has a good base from which to start this process. If you have ever written a curriculum vitae for a job application, you can use this at least for the first memory chain, but bring it up to date though and extend it right back to your birth.

The table on the next page presents an overview of the four memory chains with a few comments. This will give you an idea of what kind of research is required and what to look out for.

The New Age Progression Chart

The newly developed accurate Age Point chart is still not available. Inspired by the diploma work of Hansueli Wild, this chart shows accurate data for the triggering, course and repetition of certain events.

List of Events	Node Points	Short-term

Accidents, strokes of luck and deaths, winnings, inheritance, large fines, normal holidays, failures or setbacks, all kinds of sudden losses, births, illnesses, accidents or operations also affecting loved ones.

External Biography	Structure	Characteristic

Change and examinations on the educational and professional paths, awards, diplomas, professional changes of location, all house moves, marriage, separation, catastrophes, political or religious change.

List of People	Changes	Life phases

Short descriptions and dates of the relationship. People who have made a particular impression (role models, authorities) or who have somehow influenced our developmental path. Often, the first meeting and the start of the relationship are different, especially in the case of people we have known for a long time.

Experience Book	Completion	Longer term

Larger acquisitions, car and house purchases, stays at home, in prison, or convalescence, long study or adventure trips, strange events and perceptions, driving licence confiscation, important cognitive and decision-making processes, times of confusion or clarity. Achieving long-term goals, periods of separation, strange encounters, good and bad experiences with people and, last but not least, lovers and erotic adventures.

For the time being, only those participating in the "AP Biography Seminars" can receive their own AP charts directly from me.

They contain a whole page featuring all the AP and MN-AP aspects for each house (6 years), where every aspect is drawn with different ascending curves for each planet. Hansueli Wild discovered that, especially in the case of intersecting aspects, the location of the trigger is clearly visible at the apex of the curves. The cusps are clearly visible, and the degree distribution is adapted to the size of the houses, so that every event that is included in the monthly range can be read to the exact degree.

The most interesting part is the retrospective time scale, which shows when the MN-AP has the same aspects as the AP currently does, and vice versa; when the AP had the same aspects as the current MN-AP. There are periods of life in which this scale is empty, because they would show prenatal aspects. However, those occasions when previously experienced aspects are repeated will be very illuminating for anyone studying and researching the chart. For the repetitions vary so much from person to person and from situation to situation that it is difficult to recognise them as such.

The newly developed chart also takes into account the difference in strength of the effect of the Age Progression according to the following table:

Table of the Effectiveness of the Age-Point Aspects:

1. **Primary Aspect:** conjunctions and oppositions

2. **Tipping Point:** can work very suddenly and therefore be destabilising. Half-way between two adjacent planets. The closer they are, the more abrupt the change in theme. (Not very effective if a conjunction!)

3. **New Aspects:** Secondary aspects, which the planet concerned does not already itself have in the radix.

4. **Cusp:** The new orientations are strongest during the change from water to fire.

5. **General Effects of the Houses:** Weak point and low point transits, crossing points, etc.

6. **Known aspects already available to the planet:** tend to have a supporting or dull effect.

Over 72 years, all the planets and the Moon Node are aspected 12 times, making a total of 132, plus 11 tipping points and 12 cusps, or a total of 155 AP dates, plus the same number again going backwards from the MN-AP.

That means there are over 300 possible events of differing strengths that are repeated in differing rhythms.

□ □ □ □ □

The Zero Point of the Zodiac – the Pisces/Aries Border

Louise Huber

First published in 'Astrolog' Issue 36, February 1987.

Many years of observation have shown that a certain place in the zodiac has something special about it – the border area between Pisces and Aries, corresponding to the AC in the house system. The zodiac starts and finishes at 0° Aries, and the AC is the start of life. Life begins in a kind of darkness. Out of the nothing a person emerges and begins their life's journey. We could easily imagine that at the Pisces/Aries cusp, there is a *seam* where the two ends of the circle meet. With a little imagination, it can be seen as a gap through which life can enter and exit. The soul descends from its spiritual realm to the human realm through this gap, like a gateway to incarnation. It is the place where a new cycle of manifestation begins, and at the end it goes back through this gap to the spiritual realm. There is a mysterious contact between life and death here.

Opening to Transcendence

From another point of view, this *zero point* of the zodiac corresponds to an opening to the transcendent, a gap extending from 29° Pisces to 0° Aries. Here there is a *zero sphere*, a *cosmic fissure*, linking us to cosmic influences and transcendental worlds.

Purple

It is interesting to note that if we place a colour circle around the zodiac, this place corresponds to the colour purple, which has a particular affiliation with the spiritual, unrevealed world. Purple is a combination of 50% red and 50% blue. Purple is a special colour worn by high-ranking clerics, kings and emperors, those who stand above or apart from others. A king or cardinal is untouchable, removed from everyday life. He wears purple because he stands outside normal human standards.

Purple and violet (which corresponds to the 12ᵗʰ house) are concerned with nothingness in colour psychology; violet in paintings or pictures signifies nothingness. Something that does not exist, or is so transparent that it cannot be perceived from the earthly dimension. Purple is an unreal colour which does not produce light. Illusions are a more worldly, more understandable effect of purple. It is often found in paintings of the mentally ill, as they live in an illusory world. In terms of colour psychology, purple therefore represents an unreal mental state, indicating that the person lives with at least part of his being in a world *different to this one*, perhaps a fantasy world. A planet on the *zero point* has something of this quality; it is not completely incarnated, part is still stuck in the other side.

Sun at the Zero Point

In research studies and consultations, we have noticed that people with Sun at the *zero point* are often unable to react directly to the realities of life. Vital Sun energy appears not to get through, as if not completely incarnated, or as it were hanging halfway through the gap. Reactions to normal situations are often delayed or postponed; they either react rashly or at the wrong time. We know such people who often react at the wrong time and say the wrong thing, or want something at the most inconvenient moment or share personal opinions with no relevance to the actual situation. Others always arrive late and have forgotten something important. It is as if there is no close contact with reality; the consciousness seems to hover above the ground.

Artistic Talent

We know of others with Moon and Venus in this gap who have special artistic abilities. They bring something of the transcendence of other spheres into their paintings or music. One paints enchantingly tender angel figures of fascinating beauty, which are not kitsch but reveal something of the vibration of spiritual spheres.

Age Point at the Zero Point

The AP of many API students has already passed through the *zero point*. We have already received interesting reports, assembled in [the book translated as] *Astrology and the Spiritual Path*. We quote:

The zodiac ends in Pisces, and begins in Aries. At this juncture, the circle is closed: alpha and omega, death and rebirth mysteriously meet. As AP enters Aries, you pass through the so-called *zero point* of the zodiac. Here you usually feel a strange connection with transcendental realms. Consciously or unconsciously, you will be touched by something that may appear strange and yet somehow familiar – an experience of subtle energies acting on you through this *gap*. Some people are strongly affected, others not at all, depending on their spiritual receptivity. Many feel troubled and do not know what is wrong, especially if they are trapped in the material world and know nothing of their self's real home. There can be death and rebirth processes and profound transformation crises. Some feel helplessly at the mercy of some power. Others wait consciously for connection with spiritual worlds, open themselves up to subtle healing forces through prayer, meditation, spiritual withdrawal or search for mystical knowledge of God. Many whose AP has crossed this point report a *pull*, a longing to return to the spiritual home. This often brings an inner conversion, a change in life motivation, a decisive climacteric. In any case, a new cycle begins with the entrance into Aries, for which you should be well prepared.

◻ ◻ ◻ ◻ ◻

The Cosmic Fissure –
Zero Point Experiences

Dr. Hans-Martin Domke

First published in 'Astrolog' Issue 89, December 1995

The Zero Point in Age Progression

In astrological psychology consultations it is always helpful to use the client's current life situation as a starting point. Age Progression and the Age Point (AP) method are useful sources of information for this. AP moves around our individual house system like a hand on our life clock, zooming in on our current life theme as it passes. Its interpretation is dependent, among other factors, on its location in the zodiac. The character of the zodiac sign and its position in this sign reveal that energetic quality that has a key influence on the inner experience of the life phase concerned. Inner changes frequently cause visible external events.

The following comments concern a particular place in the zodiac, which is especially important as far as the AP is concerned; the transition from Pisces to Aries. The point of 0° Aries is called the *zero point* – or more descriptively the *cosmic fissure* (the area from 29° Pisces to 1° Aries is relevant for interpretative purposes). What does a person experience, what happens to him, which developments does he undergo, when his AP reaches this place during his life? Clues to answering these questions should be provided by the analysis of the four sample horoscopes below.

Beforehand, though, here are a few basic reflections about the *cosmic fissure*. Entering Aries represents the most abrupt change within the cosmic energy cycle. There is a kind of quantum leap from a mutable water sign into a cardinal fire sign. After a phase of calm searching and yearning, dynamic, visible action is now required in order to take a major step forwards in personal development. The vernal equinox or the start of spring represents just such a new beginning in the natural world. The energy that had in a Neptunian way turned in on itself and gone back to its roots now turns outwards again with the impulse of Mars, literally causing plants to bloom again! What a fundamental transformation! A transformation that follows the cosmic plan and represents the start of a new cycle!

We have an ongoing relationship with our inner worlds, even if we are not always aware of them. Certain events can trigger significant inner changes related to spiritual influences. Some people feel helplessly at the mercy of such "springing charges", while others try to make an inner link with transcendental or spiritual worlds, to deliberately make contact and in this way overcome a dramatic life situation. The *zero point* represents the opportunity to undergo such transformation crises, or even *zero point* experiences.

Such transformation crises are vital for developing an awareness of our own identity. They enable us to change our attitude towards ourselves and life in general, as clearly expressed in the seed thought for Aries "I come forth and from the plane of mind I rule." This kind of rebirth reminds us of the comparable point on the house level. At the ascendant we see the start of a new life cycle, a life that emerges from transcendence and is incarnated.

In the psychological colour circle, purple characterises the *zero point*. It symbolises the connection to an invisible spiritual world. Paradigmatically, such connections stand for death and (re)birth. It is therefore not surprising that experiences linked to the *cosmic fissure* are reported in a few cases of serious illness or even near death experiences.

Experiences of the *cosmic fissure* by means of four real example horoscopes are presented below.

Consideration of practical Example Horoscopes

Horoscope 1

A young man aged 28 underwent his major AP transit over the *zero point* in February 1981. The possibly more long-lasting effect of the transit of the minor age point in the 5th house was still to come. As it appeared in hindsight, that time involved the longest-lasting upheaval in both his inner and outer life until now.

The phase of upheaval had begun 2 years before the transit of the Moon Node age point across the exact opposition to the zero point at 0° Libra in July 1979. He had just passed his university economics exams. In June, he began his professional life in a bank. This entailed moving house, leaving the student residence and renting an apartment. More or less right in the middle between both age point transits, in May 1980, the client met his future wife. A relationship developed that strongly influenced the changes that took place the following year. Also in May/June 1980, he started to find his job less and less enjoyable: tension with superiors and the feeling that he had chosen the wrong profession led to severe depression (semi-sextile AP to the Moon in an achievement triangle). This situation was apparently caused by old patterns and attitudes, with good reason, for it culminated in a transformation crisis that peaked in the first three months of 1981, around the exact time of the AP transit on 26th February. He was made redundant and took a scientific job involving research and teaching. He got married and set up home with his wife.

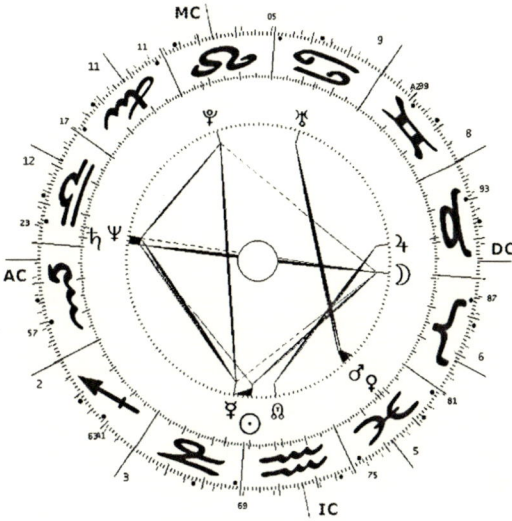

Horoscope 1 22.01.1953, 01:40, Unna, Germany

However, the crucial process was the transformation of his attitude towards his exterior and particularly his interior world, towards the question of the meaning of life and finally towards himself. His father was an evangelical priest, and in his family a correspondingly dogmatic religious worldview prevailed, rejecting astrology and similar consciousness-expanding systems, branding them as superstitions. An acquaintance with a doctor of anthroposophy since February 1980 led to deep conversations about the work of Rudolph Steiner and about astrology (prepared for by the quincunx AP – Neptune conjunction Saturn). The charisma of this man encouraged him to overcome inner barriers and ask new questions. Anthroposophical literature and books about positive thinking were devoured avidly, in contrast to his attitude towards his job. His partner had been interested in esoteric matters for a long time, and their many conversations supported this transformation process (Mars conjunct Venus in the 5th house trine Uranus in the 9th house).

Eventually out of this came a rebirth, a job that he enjoyed, the deep desire to learn more about the spiritual world, preferably having personal experience of it, the start of long-term work on himself that led to new self-awareness and a new attitude towards life (sextile Sun). He undertook the search for reconnection with himself with Arian energy, wallowing in books, attending seminars and lectures and joining self-awareness groups. Here the qualities of the 5th house and the mutable area in which the *zero point* lies are expressed. The whole transformation process is unthinkable without the desire to learn as much as possible and with a certain spirit of adventure to try things out, while in the process being open to other people, to the YOU. A key theme, but not a new one, for the relationship axis is not abandoned as the *zero point* of the Moon Node horoscope is in the 11th house. A deep-seated tendency to deal with questions about transcendence or rather meaning questions in a restricted group, perhaps in a monastery, or at a certain distance from other people, had to be overcome.

As this example shows, the *cosmic fissure* can have an important effect on life, even if there is no planet in conjunction or opposition. This transformation process enables the Aquarius energy to strengthen the weakly positioned Sun and flow over it in the life area of the 3rd house, as the nearby Moon Node recommends.

Horoscope 2

The second horoscope belongs to this man's wife. Here too, the *cosmic fissure* lies in the mutable area of the 5th house of the radix, but in the 10th house of the Moon Node horoscope. As the AP transited the cusp in September 1983, she felt the strong desire for a child, which was however unfulfilled both then and during the following year (*zero point*-AP square Mars and quincunx Sun conjunct Mercury/ Pluto). The birth would have allowed reinforcement of the personality elements represented by the Sun. Another chance about six years later (AP semi-sextile *zero point*) resulted in a miscarriage.

Also during the AP transition, the client's morale was very low at work. In a work place to which she had previously had to move for operational reasons, she found it hard to cope with the bad atmosphere that prevailed due to continual disagreements among her colleagues. The employment market at the time did not allow a rapid

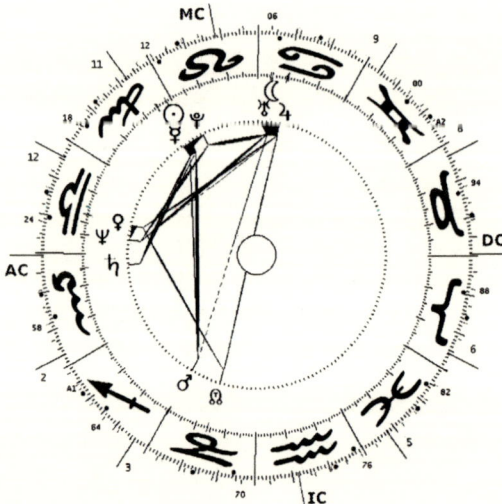

Horoscope 2 25.08.1954, 10:50:10, Berlin, Germany

exit from this disagreeable situation. The accumulated Aries energy was then released three months after the AP transit in the form of a bout of pneumonia. Only once AP had reached the 6th house was she liberated by a change of job.

This shows another interesting aspect: the marriage of the two example horoscope owners had remained childless, despite their intense desire for children.

Both partners have their *cosmic fissure* in the 5th house, in that area which is known to be related to one's own children. Even if the fear suggests that the longed for offspring could remain "trapped" in the *cosmic fissure*, this does not necessarily mean that a couple with a *zero point* in the 5th house must always remain childless. In particular, this constellation is all about nurturing an intensive love relationship and opening up spiritual worlds together. This creates strength and confidence (5th house cusp in Pisces), without losing touch with the physical world.

Horoscope 3

In the third horoscope, a young woman had led a withdrawn life since childhood, in which in hindsight she realised that most people had found her unapproachable.

In March 1963, her AP reached the *cosmic fissure*. A few days before, she had celebrated her 16th birthday (in the presence of her completely uncomprehending mother) in a state of serious mental agitation: "I don't want to grow up, I don't want to!" That same month she suffered a painful accident. A medicine ball hit her in the head during a gymnastics lesson, giving her severe concussion which meant she had to spend the next two weeks in bedrest.

The symbolism is interesting: a "medicine" ball is "thrown at" her from a great height, literally shaking her out of her previous mental attitude. It brought her out of her strictly controlled behaviour, which she used to keep others at a distance. The accident was the result of the inner, unconscious tension (having to grow up but not wanting to), which arises when trying with all one's power to stop the maturing process. Here the *zero point* resulted in a real turnaround and a new start in life: a month later she was elected head girl, 6 months later she started dance classes, and towards the end of that year met her future husband.

It was time for her solitary life to end. The 3rd house, in which her *cosmic fissure* is situated, indicates that the new life should take place in public. The woman needed to open herself up to other people and the environment, to gain maturity by joining them and learning how they think. This psychological theme of coming of age is also underlined by the intersection of the radix and moon node age points, which also takes place in the 3rd house (21° Pisces). This intersection and the *zero*

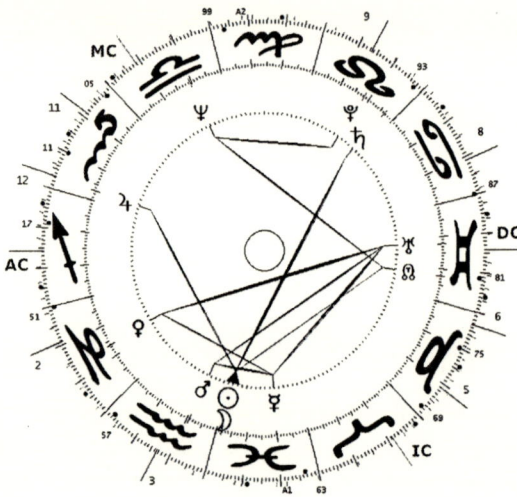

Horoscope 3   21.02.1947, 03:35, Lübeck, Germany

point go either side of the low point of the 3rd house. As on top of that only four planets are located in this symbolically emphasised life area, the elementary significance of the 3rd house and the entire axis theme cannot be underlined more clearly.

Horoscope 4:

The last horoscope belongs to the husband of the young woman in example 3. His *zero point* transit took place in February 1974 in the 6th house, only 1° away from the intersection of both age points at 29° Pisces! Furthermore, the Mars/Neptune conjunction stands out, although in a weak position with the Sun near the 12th house cusp, in almost exact opposition to the *cosmic fissure*. What happened at the age point transit?

The horoscope owner could not hide for much longer that he wanted to escape responsibility towards his partner and in a broader sense, towards the YOU. He surrounded himself with dubious characters who were no good for him, liked to drink and slipped more and more into alcoholism. At the end of a period of excessive, uncontrolled alcohol consumption, he suffered delirium tremens then a six-month rehabilitation program. The fact that the search for himself had been conducted not in a relationship but under the influence of alcohol, (possibly an obvious "old story" with the ascending Moon Node in Pisces) enabled Neptune in the 12th house at the *zero point* to have such a dramatic effect in its destructive form. The cosmic fissure had become a kind of crevasse.

Comparison of the two horoscopes, easiest to do on the "click horoscope" of both partners, reveals a striking sign layout. Both

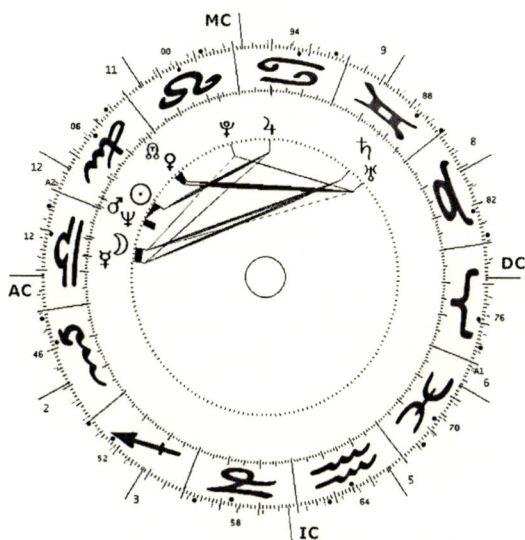

Horoscope 4 12.09.1942, 09:49, Sulzbach-Rosenberg, Germany

charts have, opposite the axis on which the *cosmic fissure* is located and near (less than 6° gap) the exact opposition point, a conjunction of their own Neptune with the other person's Jupiter. The search for the meaning of life and personal transcendence becomes extremely effective when its theme is charged by the AP opposite, on the *cosmic fissure*, generating a voltage just like a battery. The nature of the new beginning determines the life path that follows. In this case, both partners have a lot of work to do together.

Conclusion

The example horoscopes provide enlightening evidence about the significance of the *cosmic fissure*, which is most noticeable when the AP passes over it. This naturally applies to the astrological psychology consultation. Sensitive exploration of inner and outer experiences during the AP transit can unearth valuable material with which to work with the client on the meaning and direction of their life.

The following factors should be borne in mind in interpreting the meeting of AP and the *cosmic fissure*:

Which planets, particularly ego planets, are aspected and how?

In which house and where in house is the *cosmic fissure* located?

How are the location and alignment of the *cosmic fissure* different to those in the Moon Node horoscope?

The whole horoscope with its planetary positions and aspects should naturally be consulted during this process, just as in the interpretation of the *cosmic fissure* the connection with aspected planets (from the perspective of AP) and the position in house and on the house axis should be considered! For example, it is conceivable that someone with the Sun directly above the *zero point* always has the feeling that they are living in two worlds, with the result that they do not have both feet on the ground in this life. This means that they are not always able to understand life situations straight away, with all the disadvantages that this can bring in everyday life.

Let me repeat that the above study can only provide clues for ways of interpreting the cosmic fissure. The sample of horoscopes analysed is small and therefore insufficient for the requirements of statistical methodology. Also I have focused on the AP transit. Also interesting would be a general consideration of the *zero point* in the horoscope, involving finding out in which house it is located and how its transformation powers affect the theme areas concerned during the person's lifetime.

As far as the *cosmic fissure* is concerned, there are several features that could be interesting for interpretation purposes, for example:

The *cosmic fissure* in conjunction or opposition to ego planets

AP in opposition to the *cosmic fissure*

Influence of the *cosmic fissure* when at a low point or house cusp

What happens when it meets the Moon Node age point?

The *zero point* in the three crosses

The *zero point* in the four (dynamic) quadrants

The *zero point* on the main axes, particularly the AC

Regarding the zodiac colour circle, which starts at the zero point, and the house circle that starts at the AC: which combination of colours or compound colour occurs at the *zero point?*

An interpretation inspired by the psychological colour theory can be carried out at this point.

The contact with the Moon Node axis.

The contact with the Moon Node crossing axis.

These features are starting points for further astrological research.

Bibliography:

Bruno and Louise Huber, *LifeClock*

Louise Huber, *Reflections and Meditations on the Signs of the Zodiac*

□ □ □ □ □

Transits of the Spiritual Planets

Birgit Braun

First published in 'Astrolog' Issue 116, June 2000

Age progression is used in astrological psychology consultations to gain an overview of which themes are particularly stimulated in the consciousness of the client at the time of the consultation. In many cases, the transits of the slow moving planets to planets of the birth horoscope can be a rich source of information about the client's current experience/ situation.

The transits of Saturn, Uranus, Neptune and Pluto combined with current Age Point (AP) aspects can give the astrological psychology consultant a comprehensive and deep insight into the client's current circumstances as well as indications of future developmental and transformation processes.

Distinction between Age Progression and Transits

The Age Point symbolises the focus of our consciousness, which moves through time and space and looks at different aspects of our character from ever-changing perspectives in our consciousness. It indicates how we can gradually achieve an expanded awareness of ourselves. Seen in this way, the AP corresponds to an inner clock that shows us the prevailing theme at any given time, and is therefore a quite subjective perception of the development of our personal awareness.

Transits of the moving planets through the heavens symbolise how my being and consciousness relate to the Great Whole, which time quality is generally prevalent there and how this affects me and stimulates my further development. According to the hermetic law of analogy "as above, so below", not only does the position of the planets at the time of my birth affect me here on earth, but the change in the position of the planets relative to my birth horoscope is also significant. We could say that transits correspond to a more objective view of the development of our awareness.

It is important not to make the mistake of thinking that the transiting planets produce or cause anything. They just reveal something that is happening, or that should be happening, within one, because the time is right for it in the here and now.

Example horoscope 1

Horoscope Example

A woman (example horoscope 1) asks for a consultation on the subject of relationships. At the time of the consultation, her AP lies at the DC at 16° Gemini, in opposition to Mercury. It had previously passed through the 6th house with aspects to the linear figure Uranus, Saturn, Moon, Jupiter, Venus and Pluto plus the unaspected Neptune. The AP now enters the sphere of influence of the linear Sun/Mars/ Mercury figure trine the Moon node with a primary aspect. This indicates a turning point for the consciousness: themes of autonomy, personal independence, self-assertion and learning now come to the fore. The basic horoscope points in this direction, with conjunct Sun/Mars/Mercury directly on the AC in Sagittarius and the Moon Node on the 9th house cusp in Leo, meaning that the development of spiritual autonomy and independence is stimulated and that other people cannot determine one's life path.

In the consultation, the client reports that after a six year relationship, her partner has suddenly and unexpectedly left her. She is very upset, sad and also angry. She is still suffering from the shock of the separation. She does not want the relationship to end and is seeking reassurance. During the consultation, we concentrate initially on the theme of the conjunction of Saturn/Moon/Jupiter at the Low Point of the 2nd house, which is related to the theme of separation and the separation anxiety of the client. She herself acknowledges that her relationship with her partner was sometimes very symbiotic and that she could not imagine living without him.

A glance at the Ephemerides confirms this connection by current transits (example horoscope 2 transits):

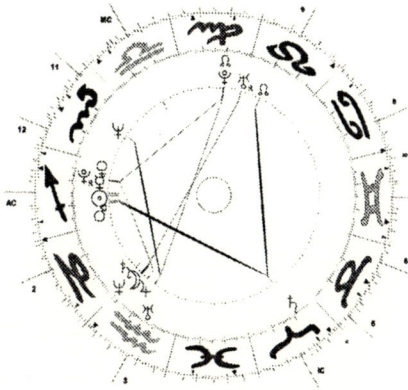

Example horoscope 2: Transits

The transiting Neptune stands in conjunction with the Moon at the start (1½°) of Aquarius; the transit across the radix Saturn happened a while ago. The emotions are wide open, extremely sensitive and therefore also very vulnerable. This is the experience of true love, which is closely linked to her self-worth in the 2nd house. Neptune often brings with it the possibility of a distorted perception of reality, which can lead to disappointment and disillusionment, but which always underlies deception and illusion.

The transiting Uranus at 11° Aquarius a few months previously was conjunct Saturn/Moon/Jupiter and is now square birth Neptune. It vigorously unsettles romantic ideals that may tend to solidify (Neptune in the radix is unaspected in a fixed house and sign). Uranus also opens up new dimensions and allows the previously high ideals of love and friendship (11th house) to appear in a new light.

Transiting Uranus and Neptune both form quincunx aspects to the spiritual radix planets Pluto and Uranus in the 9th house, indicating a long-term learning process in the consciousness (the long thinking step) relating to autonomy and independence.

The transiting Pluto (8° Sagittarius) forms an exact conjunction to the radix Venus in Sagittarius and in this area promotes metamorphosis and reorientation. This offers the client the opportunity to redefine herself as a woman and to examine in depth whether the choices she makes in her life are really right for her. The sextile to radix Jupiter allows for consciousness expanding experiences and perceptions in these areas.

The current Saturn is located at 20° Aries, trine Sun/Mars and Moon Node, and points to existing talents in this area (it forms a large talent triangle with Sun/Mars and Moon Node). Here there are hidden resources upon which she could build.

The rising Moon Node current at the time of the consultation lies at 10° Virgo in exact conjunction with radix Pluto, and here again the theme of metamorphosis and the 9th house themes of autonomy, individual thought and personal life philosophy are emphasised.

In this horoscope example, the AP gives a clue as to where the current life phase is going from an internal point of view, i.e. when the client thinks more about herself, her ego and her goals and plans (Mercury/Sun/Mars in Sagittarius at the AC). The rising Moon Node is also a part of this linear figure, indicating an opportunity to take a major step forward in the spiritual development process towards autonomy (9th house). In fact, the client plans to become self-employed in the near future.

The transits of the spiritual planets, though, show where the client still needs to undergo metamorphoses and adaptation processes in order to be able to really follow the mandate of the AP and the radix horoscope. The transits emphasise the aspect figure Uranus, Pluto, Venus, Jupiter, Saturn and Moon and in the process the themes of self-worth and emotions that the client with the Moon/Saturn at low point 2 perceives to be sensitive points. She will be made totally aware of any obstructive ideas and ways of behaving, thus enabling a more active confrontation.

Transits of Uranus, Neptune and Pluto

The main use of the transits of the spiritual planets Uranus, Neptune and Pluto is to aid understanding of the current time quality in the radix. They always indicate the need for metamorphosis and reorientation. In addition, aspects of the transiting Saturn to the planets of the birth horoscope can give meaningful clues as to the client's current circumstances.

The more unaware we are and the more superficial or externally-based our existence, the more afraid we usually are of changes and the more we tend to attract external events that force us to change or adapt during transits. We then feel helplessly at the mercy of a destiny that we cannot understand. However, the more our consciousness is centred in our innermost core being, the more we are able to deal productively and with awareness with transits and use the changes they provoke in us as a springboard into a meaningful future.

Transits of the three spiritual planets therefore appear like messengers from another dimension. They constitute a push from spiritual realms to reflect upon our life to date and to establish whether or not we are actualising our inner potential in line with our basic horoscope, or if our previous development has been too one-sided in some way and now the time is ripe for a change, reorientation or correction.

Times when Uranus, Neptune or Pluto aspect important constellations of our radix chart, e.g. one of the ego planets or a tension ruler, are painful for us if we cling to old structures and leave no room for further development and change. In this case, their energies initially have a destructive and metamorphosing effect on solidified forms, be it in our consciousness, in relationships or at work, in order to create space for the new and the different that is necessary from a higher perspective for the rounding and further development of our personality.

We can therefore experience transits of the spiritual planets as springboards for expanding our consciousness. In the process, we can use them to actualise our true inner nature. The question is only whether we want to jump of our own free will or whether we must first be pushed.

Transit Aspects

Empirical evidence shows that conjunctions, oppositions and squares, i.e. the **red action aspects** of the transiting planets, have a very distinctive effect. Perhaps because we are then least able to avoid the themes concerned, their appearance often appears dramatic to us, especially the transits of Uranus and Pluto. They urge an active confrontation with the theme concerned, and stimulate our total commitment, as well as changes where they appear necessary.

The **blue transit aspects** show apparently smooth changes in our personality, things run automatically and do not necessarily require our active intervention. We change in a more unobtrusive and organic way, a "natural" metamorphosis is triggered, and a kind of inner redeployment of resources takes place. It is also possible that we feel powerless and inactive during the changing process.

Green transit aspects indicate processes that occur in our consciousness. We deal intellectually with the theme and experience it in a new way. Or we are left hanging, are dissatisfied, experience the theme in projections and turn in circles until we manage to reach a decision. These transits do not generally present themselves as forcibly as conjunctions and oppositions.

The **duration and intensity of a transit's effect** vary, perhaps depending upon the person's level of awareness. Usually effects can be felt from 1° before the exact aspect up to around 15 – 30° after the exact transition. Due to retrograde action the transit can be repeated several times. Some people are able to sense the process of inner change that is stimulated even 2° or 4° before the exact transit. It can happen though, that transits appear to pass us by without affecting us at all.

Saturn

Transits of Saturn across birth planets often indicate a kind of reality check of the planetary ability involved. Saturn is the keeper of the threshold, and vets everything from a point of view of its feasibility, utility and safety. Powers and energies concentrate and solidify to minimal levels, anything superfluous is eliminated and any inadequacy is compensated. To us this may feel like reduction, constriction or even depression, but we also sense a naturally emerging awareness of responsibility and reality that provides us with inner security, stability and structure.

The aspects of the transiting Saturn to the radix Saturn are interesting, as is the return of Saturn to its radix position in the zodiac that occurs approximately every 29 years (the so-called Saturn cycle).

Uranus

In astrological psychology, Uranus symbolises our capacity for creative intelligence. It enables us to have sudden insights and intuitions that can change our whole worldview in a matter of seconds. This often means a sudden intrusion of the new or alien into our everyday lives. In periods of Uranus transits, everything is in upheaval, events are precipitated, things suddenly happen that were unthinkable even a short time beforehand.

We may tear down barriers ourselves and break through the walls that have hitherto confined us and impeded further development. We gain access to a new and "better" world; to a new more perfect order. We can free ourselves from old habits and behaviour patterns in a flash.

However, the more we cling to old structures and oppose new ones, the more painful we find the experiences of such transits. We may lose our job or our lover. What mattered to us yesterday is now meaningless. We must naturally take into account the radix planets to which the moving Uranus is aspected. Masculine planets like the Sun and Mars or even [neutral] Jupiter may be better at implementing and using the newly emerging spiritual energies than sensitive planets such as our feeling self Moon or our protective Saturn, which can be badly destabilised by a Uranus transit.

Uranus Transits to Personality Planets

☉ Uranus lights the creative spark in our mental self, a light whose beam enables us to radically change our world in a short space of time. We may recognise we are no longer happy with our current career, partner or self, and want to heed the call for change. We strive for pastures new in the future, work for an ideal world and are impatient to put our new plans into action. We come into contact with new spiritual theories that change our life, broaden our spiritual horizons and develop new worlds and areas of existence.

☽ Our feeling self is stimulated by the spiritual quality of Uranus, and emotional blocks may dissolve. The emotions, including childhood experiences, are examined from a higher dimension and also stimulate change. Our feelings and emotions, our contact self, are now in a state of high tension. We may initially react in an appropriately sensitive way, for example if a close symbiotic relationship is threatened by separation. However, we may want to free ourselves and our feelings from one-sidedness, and are now ready to take a step into new areas of existence.

♄ The new order encounters the old order and may question it. Do traditional ways fit into our concept of an ideal world? Where do changes need to be made? Where are we too rigid, too anxious, too in need of security? Solidified structures now start to flow again. Matter [♄] and spirit [♅] collide.

Neptune

The higher love ideal causes our personality to change and readapt in a quite different way. The experiences are not abrupt and destructive as with Uranus, but more subtle, subliminal and insidious. Neptune above all stimulates the emotional and astral bodies; it arouses longings and desires and provokes dreams and fantasies.

We yearn for and look for the ideal love, the ideal relationship, the dream partner, the dream world, the dream job. We dream of peace, protection and redemption. It is therefore natural that we succumb to a few illusions and delusions in the process.

Neptune often imperceptibly and very subtly dissolves hardened boundaries and walls and in this way also destroys obsolete structures that are no longer necessary in our consciousness, which oppose a more ideal communication between the creatures and things of the cosmos. This liberates new ways within us of approaching the ideal of love so that we become more and more aware of the fact that we are at one with everyone around us.

Here too we can get an idea of the difference between how the Sun, as autonomous self awareness, or the Moon, as a personal desire for love, transform these transit energies.

Neptune Transits to Personality Planets:

☉ When the transiting Neptune touches our mental self, it can evoke a strong need to escape everyday life in order to devote oneself more fully to the subtle, mystical, esoteric or occult things in life. Our self awareness opens itself smoothly to the spiritual worlds. We may also feel a certain self alienation; we are no longer quite sure who we really are. On the search for more love and understanding, we may also react uncritically, develop and pursue longings and desires that are unrealistic or irrational. We may want to escape from reality, search for a spiritual leader, for the saviour of mankind or for an intergalactic solution for our problems here on earth.

☽ This transit sees the most direct stimulation of the developmental step from the egocentric Moon-love to the transpersonal, ego-transcending Neptunian love. Depending how we have fared on this journey, we may think we have found the great love of our lives, only to find later that we were deceiving or deluding ourselves. Or we feel within us the connection with all living beings, at one with the cosmos, the mystical union. However, this identification with the highest love ideal may also lead to a dissolution of the I. We lose ourselves in other people, in social work, in a spiritual ideal (helper syndrome).

♄ Under a Neptune transit to Saturn, our ability to set boundaries is "undermined". Neptune as a sensitive planet actually wants to transcend boundaries, open up to the greater meaning, be at one with and merge with everything. This contradicts Saturn's goals which are to set boundaries and forms. Consequently, angst can arise at these times; our defence mechanisms can fail, (perhaps even in the literal sense), we react with doubt, insecurity and defensiveness.

Neptune encourages our physical awareness to test the need for and extent of our boundaries, and to realign or readjust ourselves to the spiritual world. This transit may also offer us the opportunity to manifest and act on the level of reality of the principles of Neptune, i.e. with social commitment and empathy.

Pluto

Pluto is a cosmic messenger of the spiritual will. Everything it comes into contact with is intensified and exceeded by its spiritual will energy. It sets in motion a process of metamorphosis, in which all that is not in agreement with the divine will and which hinders its activities is destroyed and eliminated

Pluto brings us a vision of the spiritual will regarding the purpose of our existence, the evolutionary plan. In a manner of speaking, it guides us to our core being, the circle in the centre of the horoscope. It symbolises the ideal of the perfect, superior being. Everything that stands in the way of this is eliminated during a transit, transformed and razed to the ground so that new things can emerge and grow which correspond more to the nature of the core being.

Pluto transits can therefore indicate rigorous death and rebirth processes, which our personality would all too often like to oppose. The metamorphoses and changes are usually total, sometimes even affecting the physical body. There can be a great fear of the dissolution of the self, of the relentless energies that Pluto can bring into our consciousness.

However, if we do manage to use the Pluto transit in a way that benefits our development, we have come a step nearer to our evolutionary goal, despite all the suffering.

Pluto Transits to Personality Planets

⊙ If the transformative power of Pluto affects the mental self, our self-awareness is transformed. "Become what you are" is the motto. Often we must cast aside the false, outdated parts of our nature and undergo a metamorphosis. At this time, we may realise how powerful, autonomous and independent we really are, and to what extent we can use these abilities for the good of the Whole, also in a spiritual sense. If we do not manage to do this, we will come into conflict with authorities and the powers that be.

Sometimes the personal will is also required to conform or align itself with the spiritual or divine will. The period when Pluto transits the Sun may offer us opportunities to do this that are worth taking up.

On the way to finding the meaning and purpose of our lives, Pluto transits can also develop new dimensions and areas of experience related to our self awareness; we discover hitherto hidden realms within our being (Pluto/Hades as ruler of the treasures of the underworld).

☽ Pluto transits to the Moon intensify and exaggerate our emotional life. Often Pluto brings to the surface deeply hidden emotions that may even reach back to our earliest childhood. We may now be confronted with intense feelings of sympathy or antipathy. Sometimes Pluto acts like a finger that is placed on our deepest emotional wounds so that they are brought to the attention of our consciousness, where they can be confronted with more awareness and accessibility.

♄ Here again the issue is that of the "actively developing shaped form". In order to correct possible hardening and undesirable developments or even to initiate any necessary spiritual "reforming", the Pluto transit to Saturn can at times have a destructive effect on this form, so that something new can emerge from it that is more in line with our inner nature. Initially, Saturn understandably finds it difficult to cooperate with this almost alchemical process of metamorphosis – it braces itself against it and tries with all its might to cling to and preserve the old and oppose the changes, leading to angst and sometimes dramatic "release" conflicts. However, what is actually happening is that the manifested form is realigning with the inner, spiritual nature.

Our reactions to transits of the spiritual planets – if this is how we want to term these events – are always individual and dependent on past decisions and developmental steps. That is why it seems rather meaningless to follow future transits in a prescriptive way and want to use them to forecast our future. This should not be the purpose of astrological psychology, which offers us a wonderful support that enables us to deal with constant challenges and to get to know ourselves better so that we can become what we really are.

Bibliography/Literature on Transits:

Howard Sasportas: *The Gods of Change*
Alexander Ruperti: *Cycles of Becoming*
Stephen Arroyo: *Astrology, Karma and Transformation*

□ □ □ □ □

Part 4: Growth and Transformation

In this fourth part of the book we have grouped together five articles related to growth and transformation.

Astrological Transactional Analysis, by **Detlef Hover**
Psychologist and astrologer Detlef Hover summarises the essentials of Transactional Analysis, relating them to the three ego planets.

Learning to Let Go – Becoming Authentic, Developing Yourself
by **Reinhard Müller**
Takes inspiration from Dane Rudhyar's work on the 'karmic New Moon' preceding the birth date, which indicates the start of the solar/lunar cycle in which we were born, and gives an unconscious spiritual influence to our personality. Its relationship with Age Progression is explored, with real examples.

Light and Shade in Astrology, by **Detlef Hover**
Considers the psychological concept of the shadow and its relationship with the polarities found in the horoscope.

Our Lady's Child, by **Christian U Vogel**
An astrological-psychological interpretation of the fairy tale of *Our Lady's Child*.

Pluto in the Twelve Houses, by **Bruno Huber**
Bruno's consolidated understanding of the significance of Pluto, the archetypal planet of transformation. Includes the significance of Pluto's position in each of the twelve houses.

Astrological Transactional Analysis

Detlef Hover

First published in 'Astrolog' Issues 152-3, July - September 2006

The Founding of Transactional Analysis

Psychiatrist Eric Berne (1910-1970) is acknowledged as the founder of Transactional Analysis, which he developed in the USA in the 1950s. Since then, Transactional Analysis (TA) has gone on to become one of the best known procedures in Humanistic Psychology.

About Eric Berne

Eric Lennard Bernstein was born on 10th May 1910 in Montreal, Canada. As a young man, he moved to the USA where he developed Transactional Analysis as a psychotherapeutic procedure. In 1935, after his medical doctorate, he came to New York to work as a psychiatrist. After training for 15 years, in 1956 he gave up the attempt to become recognised as a psychoanalyst. His attempt to become a member of the San Francisco Psychoanalytic Institute had been rejected. Although he separated – in his own words – "on good terms" the rejection was very painful for him. Berne did not talk about the reasons for his rejection, but one could guess that he was not sufficiently prepared to conform to the orthodox concept of psychoanalysis. One of his main criticisms of the psychoanalysis at that time was that he believed that a therapist should take a more active role in the therapy process than was customary. When he published his book *Transactional Psychoanalysis in Psychotherapy* in 1961, his own approach was already obvious. His book *Games People Play* (1964) became a bestseller, and is still one today. The founding of the *Transactional Analysis Journal* and the International Transactional Analysis Association can be traced back to him. Berne died on 15th July 1970. He is considered one of the most important psychiatrists of the 20th century. Since the 1970s, Thomas A. Harris has contributed greatly to his popularisation.

The Roots of Transactional Analysis

Transactional Analysis has its roots in Psychoanalysis (Freud, Adler) and in Humanist Psychology (Maslow), but also integrates elements of behaviour therapy.

In TA, the image of man used is that of humanistic psychology: each person is unique and is viewed holistically, as an essentially positive being. For Berne, self esteem and responsibility are crucial.

The central goals of the therapy are therefore self actualisation and growth. The close relationship between psychoanalysis and individual psychology is based on the fact that Berne selected from different psychoanalytical and individual psychological ideas. For example, he used the Freudian energy and libido concept and its structural model, which he later modified. From Adler, he borrowed the emphasis on social expectation patterns, the "family constellation" and the "life plan". A key point is Erik Erikson's idea of basic trust in the newborn baby.

In addition, different systems and communication theory ideas have influenced TA, without it becoming a jumbled hotpotch. That is why TA can best be understood as an integrative procedure.

The presentation of TA below requires some prior explanation of the following important key terms:

1.   structure of the personality (ego-state)
2.   communication (transactional and game analysis)
3.   biographical levels (script analysis)

Propositions of the Human Image in Transactional Analysis

1.   All people are ok – Every person has a fundamental core that is positive and loveable, and which cannot be destroyed even by negative behaviour. Every person therefore has an inalienable right to life and to the protection of his dignity. This also includes his right to develop his potential, which is unique.

2.   Every person is a whole. He is a combination of thoughts, feelings and actions, of inside and outside. Therefore, he must always be considered as a whole and all aspects of his lifeworld considered.

3.   The person is a social being. As a social being, he needs contact, affection and attention. He is dependent on mutual support. In particular, he is involved in the formative order of his original family. For him, this represents a system that has an inherent tendency to order and equilibrium.

4.   The person is a needy, vulnerable being. In addition to the needs for affection, activity and security, Transactional Analysis emphasises the need for meaning (life script).

5.   The person possesses the potential for freedom of choice. He is not the victim of his circumstances, which are determined by external influences. He is much more an active architect of his life and can take responsibility for it.

6.   The person has the possibility for self-actualisation. As a responsible being, he can control his actions, thoughts and feelings, and as an adult, can revise and correct decisions that he made as a child when not yet mature.

The Structural Model of Transactional Analysis

According to the structural model of Transactional Analysis, the human personality is divided into three "ego-states", which condition the intra-individual processes (perception, feeling and thinking, including the "inner dialogues") and external activities.

The Three Ego-States

Berne developed his approach of the three ego-states from Freud's structural model of the psyche. Analogous to their division of the psyche into Id – Ego – Superego, the structural model of TA considers that the levels Child-ego, Adult-ego and Parent-ego make up the human personality (henceforth *parent*, *adult* and *child*).

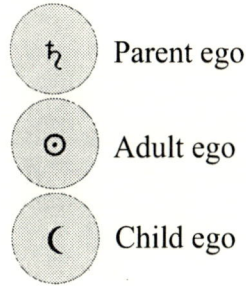

ħ Parent ego

☉ Adult ego

☾ Child ego

**Structural Model of
Transactional Analysis**
(the three ego states)

Parent [Ego]

The *parent* is the level of the psyche that houses the memories of behavioural patterns and parental rules, as they are adopted by the child in the first five or six years of life. This also includes "recordings" of unexamined, accepted and forced external events, the rules, norms, conventions and behavioural instructions of our psychological parents.

Child [Ego]

The *child* represents the emotional part of the life concept, i.e. emotions, wishes, dreams, fantasies and illusions. Stored here are "inner events" as they happened during influential experiences in the first years of our lives, usually associated with our parents. According to TA, there are five basic feelings: love, joy, sadness, fear and anger.

Adult [Ego]

The *adult* represents the ego in the narrow sense of the word and is the integrator of the different ego states, as it perceives impulses from the *parent* and *child* and can identify them as such. As it is more rationally oriented than the *child* (sense of reality), it also has the ability to compromise and solve problems. It processes consciously caused experiences.

Ego State Forms

Traditional Transactional Analysis assumes that the *parent* has two
forms, the *critical parent* and the *nurturing parent*, the *child* has three
forms *conforming child*, *contrary child*, and *natural child*. The table below
presents three forms for each of the three ego states. Analogous to
the three astrological crosses – and the Indian Gunas – every ego
state can occur in an inhibited (fixed), over-compensative (cardinal)
or free (mutable) form.

	Inhibited	Free	Over-compensative
Parent	Overprotective *parent*	Supporting *parent*	Critical *parent*
Adult	Inferior ego	Autonomous ego	Inspired ego
Child	Conforming *child*	Natural *child*	Rebellious *child*

Critical, Supporting and Overprotective Parent
We differentiate between the critical and supporting *parent*, which is
also a feature of traditional TA.

Typical of the *critical parent* is the supply of mainly negative
feedback, where the *child* is called into question. The *supporting parent*
is predominantly encouraging and nurturing, which provides the
child with a high degree of confidence in life overall and in their own
potential, and a great willingness to adopt the parents' values. There
is also an *overprotective parent*, which tends to encourage a lack of
autonomy and doubt in one's own abilities. But this is not discussed
in traditional TA.

Natural, Conforming, and Rebellious Child
In the case of the *child*, we may differentiate between a *conforming child*
and a *rebellious child*. Common to both is the experience of too little
of the right kind of attention. The *conforming child* has learned that
by behaving well he will receive more attention, which is why he is
particularly mindful of the needs of others and respects them. The
rebellious child has learned that rebellious behaviour at least attracts
negative attention. The *natural child* is neither over-adapted nor
rebellious, but in touch with its own feelings and needs. These are
accepted and expressed as natural and intrinsic. The *natural child* is
therefore emotionally free and spontaneous and can enjoy itself, play
and deal openly with other people.

Problems in the Structure of the three Ego States

For a person to be happy and psychologically sound, all three ego states must function well both separately and together.

As different and opposing needs must be integrated, the issue is one of optimisation. Given the complexity of this task, diverse problems can arise, of which two, exclusion and contamination are particularly important.

Exclusion and Contamination of the Ego State

According to the concept of TA, the normal state is where the three ego levels touch but neither overlap nor are separated from each other. If the personality is healthy, the three ego states are clearly delimited one from the other, but interact with each other. Two problems can be caused by defective boundaries between the ego states:

- exclusion: the boundaries are too rigid
- contamination: the boundaries are too permeable.

The *adult* has the difficult task of reconciling the differing demands of the *child* and the *parent*. If this task and the tension it causes overwhelm the *adult*, one "solution" can be to repress one of the two sides. Exclusion happens when the *parent* or *child* is separated from experience and therefore tends not to be experienced.

It is quite obvious that exclusion is not a real solution, and instead causes several negative consequences. If the *child* is dissociated, the person represses their vital needs for contact, joy and drive satisfaction, leading to depressive tendencies. However, if the *parent* is dissociated, the person will not pay sufficient attention to rules and social norms. This easily leads to significant conflict when dealing with other people.

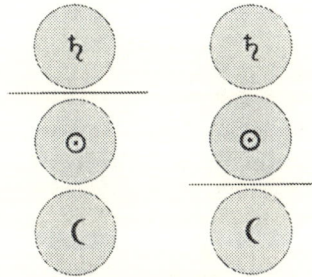

Exclusion

Contamination is characterised by an unclear separation between the different ego states; they actually partially overlap. This significantly hinders the *adult's* ability to make intelligent decisions appropriate to a situation; judgement and decision making abilities tend to be contaminated by impulses that are not appropriate to the occasion.

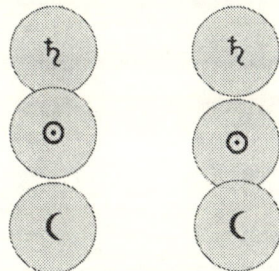

Contamination

If the *parent* and *adult* merge, this leads to the formation of prejudices, as valuations and norms are accepted without checking them against reality. Overlapping of the *adult* and *child* leads to wishful thinking, illusions and the contamination of the sense of reality by delusions. If all the ego states are blurred, then the ego boundaries of this person are not clearly defined, causing several prejudices and delusions.

Where there is simultaneous contamination and exclusion, the psychological interpretation of the combined form is the same as that of the individual forms. It is clear that significant exclusion and contamination are very stressful and debilitating, which can lead to clinically relevant disturbances. Contamination is considered to be the cause of neuroses and exclusion of psychoses.

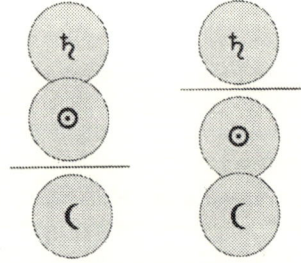

**Combination of
Contamination and Exclusion**

Biography and Approach to Life

A person's attitude towards themselves and towards their life is mainly a result of how their basic needs have been satisfied.

Basic Needs

According to the concept of TA, our behaviour is conditioned by three basic needs, which according to Berne are innate and which he also calls "hunger". These mental basic needs are the "hunger for attention", the "hunger for stimulation" (activity) and the "hunger for time structure" (procedure, rituals, pastimes). The following connections can easily be made between these innate psychic basic needs and the main planets:

- hunger for attention   Moon
- hunger for stimulation   Sun
- hunger for time structure   Saturn

The Need for Attention

The most important human psychic need is the "hunger for attention". This is satisfied by "stroking", initially physical, and later also by praise and recognition. The term attention is widely used in TA and does not just mean the experience of being liked. There is a clear distinction between positive and negative attention. Furthermore, attention can also be conditional or unconditional, so that we can distinguish between the following forms of attention:

Unconditional, positive attention is characterised by the fact that the *child* feels loved and cared for by the psychological *parent*, allowing basic trust to be formed and the *child* to feel they are ok. This is the best form of attention, as it is also not withdrawn from the *child* if they do something wrong.

Conditional positive attention is the second-best form of attention, as unlike unconditional positive attention, it is only given to the *child* in the case of certain types of behaviour, e.g. in the case of achievement or adaptation.

Due to its one-sided emphasis and reinforcement, the significance of this behaviour increases over time, and can lead to an imbalance (e.g. excessive ambition, over-adapted behaviour).

Conditional, negative attention is a form of rejection, which is dependent on certain behaviour on the part of the *child*. This is problematic in so far as it establishes the basic pattern that they are not ok.

Unconditional, negative attention represents the greatest form of rejection that a person can experience. Irrespective of what the *child* does and how hard he tries, he is rejected. It is obvious that a positive self-image cannot be developed under these circumstances.

	Positive	Negative
Unconditional	Unconditional, positive attention	Unconditional, negative attention
Conditional	Conditional, positive attention	Conditional, negative attention

Forms of Attention

The Four Attitudes to Life

The way in which the child's basic needs are satisfied with time leads it to develop a certain basic attitude towards life. Transactional analysis distinguishes between "I" and "You" and a positive and negative attitude. Four basic attitudes can therefore be established, which can be developed and reinforced in different phases of life.

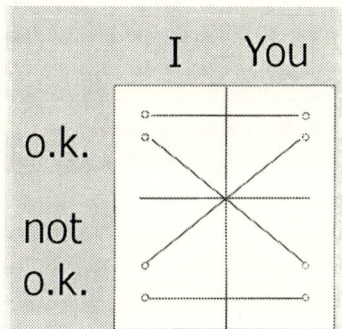

I You

o.k.

not

o.k.

I'm ok, you're ok   (pre-postnatal)

This is the best attitude to life, the reaction of a mature individual who is at peace with himself and his environment. The child comes into the world with basic trust (Erikson), as the security and protection experienced during pregnancy are initially preserved after the baby's birth. The child is the most important person to himself, a basic attitude that however must lead to disappointment as time goes on.

I'm not ok, you're ok   (first year of life)

Soon after birth, the child realises that it is small and helpless, and therefore needs the support of the environment and is dependent on its attention. It experiences itself as not ok. As the environment possesses what the child needs ("strokes"), this is experienced as ok. This attitude to life leads to feelings of inferiority, which are the typical attitude of the fearful child (worm's eye view). If the person maintains this attitude in later life, the result can be a lack of self-esteem, depression and a tendency to suicide or addiction.

I'm not ok – you're not ok   (approx. 2nd year of life)

If the strokes become less frequent and the child is also punished, he becomes convinced that the environment is no longer ok either. If this state persists, the development of the adult ego stops here, resulting in a basic attitude of desperation and resignation, leading to diffidence and even schizophrenia.

I'm ok - you're not ok   (poss. from 2nd year of life)

Unlike the three other basic attitudes, this does not correspond to any stage of normal child development. It is much more the consequence of persistent cruelty or even abuse, which means that others are seen as not ok. As a result of "self-stroking", one perceives oneself as ok. With this basic attitude, one thinks one is better than others and above the law. An arrogant attitude is developed, which can be found in criminals, sociopaths and terrorists. If the disturbance is only mild, a so-called "saviour" syndrome can develop.

I'm ok - you're ok   (realistic)

The four previous basic attitudes are formed unconsciously in early childhood. However, this fifth basic attitude is the result of a conscious decision. It is based on the person's thoughts and beliefs and is the goal of Transactional Analysis therapy.

Life Attitudes and Developmental Phases
I'm ok – you're ok Pre-postnatal
I'm not ok – you're ok 1st year of life
I'm not ok – you're not ok Approx. 2nd year of life
I'm ok – you're not ok Poss. From 2nd year of life
I'm ok – you're ok Realistic

Script Analysis

A main concept of TA is that of the life script. It expresses the basic assumption that at the start of their life, the person constructs a kind of script, or life script. This life script is like that of a film or a play, and it influences the whole course of our lives; whether we are in a comedy or a tragedy or a crime thriller, which kind of people we meet and which we don't (casting). TA even assumes that the life script determines how long we will live and how we will die. The type of life script we construct depends on our childhood experiences and how we interpret them. However, we can also change our script by recognising the key script assumptions and deciding to change them. The script can therefore be considered to be a "fixed life story". The more fixed it is, the more unconsciously and automatically the script functions, and the more the consequences of the script are interpreted as being caused by external destiny and not by ourselves.

Destructive Basic Commands (Injunctions)

If the life script contains ideas that go against the self, other people or life in general, they are called destructive basic commands. These are acquired by internalisation during childhood. Good examples of this are: Don't be there! – Don't be you! – Don't be in touch with your body! – Don't be in touch with your feelings! – Don't be important! – Grow up quickly! – Don't grow up! – Don't be healthy! – Don't be normal! – Don't be successful! – Don't think too much! From an astrological point of view, this is primarily associated with the planets Saturn and Pluto.

Drivers

As well as the destructive basic commands, the script can also contain several drivers, which can also lead to significant psychological conflict. This conflict is also caused by the basic assumptions which give the person great confidence. They are almost seen as recipes for success, and are then readily passed on as pieces of advice: Be perfect! – Be quick! – Make an effort! – Lead the way! – Be strong! – Meet other peoples' expectations and make them happy!

These psychological drivers assume that we must first behave in such and such a way before we are ok. There is also a simultaneous subliminal message that we will not be able to do it. From an astrological point of view, this is primarily associated with the planets Sun and Mars.

Frames of Reference

As man is a cognitive being, he asks himself fundamental questions about his existence and about life itself. Who am I? Who are other people? What is the world? How can I structure my life and my coexistence with other people? Although none of these questions is easy to answer, the answers we do give ourselves have significant consequences as they create a global thought structure which in TA is called the frame of reference. Once the frame of reference has been constructed it becomes a kind of filter through which we see the world and ourselves. Only that which corresponds to the assumptions of the frame of reference is allowed through the filter. Experiences that are not compatible with our frame of reference are not allowed through and assimilated. In other words, scripts tend to be self-confirming and to be immune to change.

Script

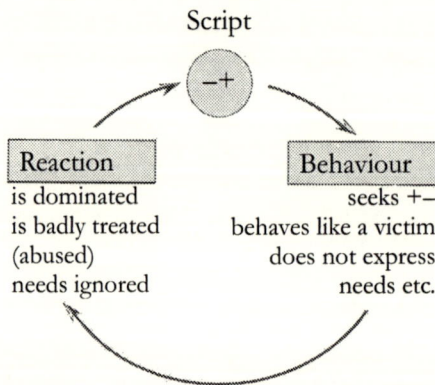

Reaction	Behaviour
is dominated	seeks +–
is badly treated	behaves like a victim
(abused)	does not express
needs ignored	needs etc.

Interaction of script, behaviour and reaction from the environment

This can be illustrated by the offender-victim script. The victim's life attitude is: "I am not ok, you are ok". (–+). She therefore tends to look for a partner with the life attitude "I am ok, you are not ok" (+–). As she believes that she is not ok, she does not express her needs and is afraid to assert herself. She will be treated badly by her partner, in line with their pattern, and her needs will be ignored, so that the victim ultimately finds that her script is confirmed.

Passivity

It can often be noticed that people do not use their energies to solve psychological problems, but instead tend to cling to them to stop them from being solved. In TA, this behavioural pattern is called passivity. The basics of passivity are also acquired in childhood, with two processes being particularly important. It can be that at one time the independent action and thought of the child was externally blocked, and even in later life the person still cannot rid themselves of this attitude. Or the child can have found that somebody else took care of their own tasks, if they just waited for long enough. In both cases, passivity encourages the formation of symbiotic relationships.

Often, passive behaviour is initially not recognised as such. TA should allow the client to develop the ability to see their own passivity for what it is and to stimulate their ability to solve their own problems, which will make it much easier for them to structure their own lives.

Important forms of passivity are complaining and nagging. These processes waste psychological energy and hinder problem solving. If we find ourselves in a difficult situation that we think we are unable to solve by ourselves, we may complain about it, thereby maintaining a passive attitude that does nothing to solve the problem. However, this pattern may be reinforced if our complaining brings us attention (strokes), e.g. from "co-complainers" or people with a strong motivation to help. From an astrological point of view, this is primarily associated with the planets Venus and the Moon.

By nagging, I assume that someone else has the solution to my problem. By delegating the responsibility to others, I have the impression that I cannot solve my own problem. Instead, I want the other person to change themselves or change something. To make them do this, I put pressure on them and try to put them down, i.e. adopt the attitude of the *critical parent* and want to force others to take the role of the *conforming child*. Even if this pattern works, the other will sooner or later get fed up, which can lead to future problems. If the other also has the same style, energy is wasted in the mutual shifting of responsibility (ping-pong), which does nothing to solve the problem either. From an astrological point of view, this is primarily associated with the planets Saturn and Jupiter.

Both with complainers and naggers, the person's ability to solve problems is denied and responsibility is transferred to other people. Both patterns are also characterised by the transaction pattern "*parent and child*". As complainers also nag and naggers also complain, the two behaviours can be seen as complementary and caused by the same basic attitude, i.e. passivity.

Transactional Analysis   (Communication model)

The smallest unit of a social interaction is one where one person's behaviour causes a reaction from someone else. This form of social interaction is called transaction and is the source of the term Transactional Analaysis. Analysing people's transactions, gives important diagnostic information about them. TA distinguishes between three types of transaction:

- parallel (complementary) transactions
- crossed transactions
- covert transactions

Parallel Transactions

Transactions can take place on different levels according to the structural model. The most common type of transaction in adults takes place on the *parent* level, but can also take place from *adult* to *adult*, or from *child* to *child*. Such interactions are called parallel or complementary transactions. Parallel transactions are stable, i.e. they have a tendency to be self-perpetuating.

A parallel transaction can also exist if the *parent* of one of the partners addresses the *child* of the other person and the latter then responds with his *child* to the partner's *parent*. This hierarchical form of transaction is very common and corresponds e.g. to the traditional relationship between the sexes. The "transference relationship" of psychoanalysis can also be represented in this way, as

Parallel Transactions

can conventional (astrological) consultations in which the consultant adopts the superior role of the expert, to which the consulter "subordinates" himself.

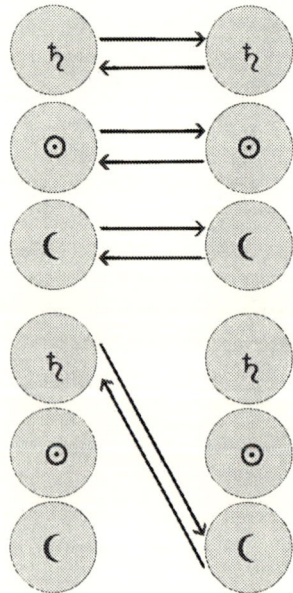

Crossed Transactions

Crossed transactions are different in that sooner or later they lead to a rupture or change in communication. They are therefore considered unstable. They exist if the ego state of the reaction does not correspond to that of the stimulus and is also not addressed to it.

There are two particular patterns here: firstly a person with a *parent* addresses the *child* of another person, but the latter does not reply in a parallel transaction but in turn responds with the *parent* to the *child* of the other person. Conflict is inevitable as now both want to dominate. Either both parties compromise and change their transaction pattern, or they go their separate ways; in any case, the pattern is unstable.

The other crossed transaction, is important in counselling and therapy. By talking to the counsellor from their *child*, the client hands over responsibility to him. The counsellor now "frustrates" the client by crossing the transaction and addressing him as an *adult*, thereby encouraging him to be independent. This pattern is also unstable as the client now either lets his *adult* reply or turns away in disappointment.

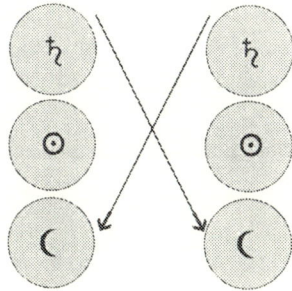

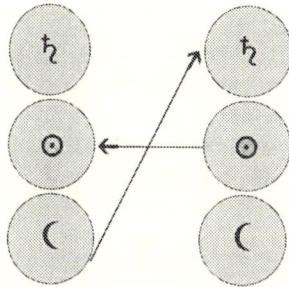

Crossed Transaction

Covert Transactions

It is not uncommon that when we communicate there is a difference between what is said and what is meant. TA deals with this by differentiating between the social message and the psychological message. If these two messages diverge, it is called a covert transaction. Facial expressions, gestures and turns of phrase, etc, make it clear that what is said is different from what is meant. In such covert transactions it is the covert level, not the apparent one, that determines how the transaction will continue.

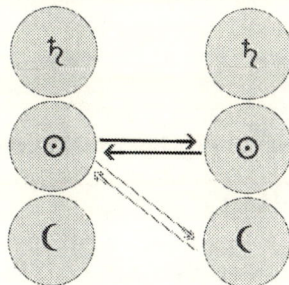

Covert Transaction

Such covert transactions play an important role in all manipulative situations. For example, a car dealer says to a client: "of course, this car is the best one for you, but it is probably too expensive." On the open level, he seems to be advising the customer objectively. However, the hidden message that he is giving the customer is: "you are not old enough to have this yet." If the customer answers: "yes, I can easily afford it", the *rebellious child* has replied: "no, I am not too young." Covert transactions are also important in all psychological games, as we shall see below.

Game Analysis

Games People Play

In TA, importance is given to the exploration of psychological games. The wording for the *Games People Play* can be traced back to Eric Berne. By a game, Berne understands a complex communication between two partners that always runs according to the same pattern, and which neither participant enjoys. This communication pattern can be defined as the consequence of covert transactions, which lead to a predictable result. This result is connected to negative feelings for both parties. When considered from outside, a game can appear to be plausible and rational, but it is actually conditioned by unconscious motives. Berne himself described a game like this: "a game consists of an ongoing series of covert complementary transactions, which lead to a quite specific, predictable result. It can also be described as a periodically recurring series of frequently repeated transactions that are externally plausible but are however governed by hidden motives; colloquially they can also be termed a series of individual actions that are part of a trap or a deceitful trick." (Eric Berne, *Games People Play*). Every person prefers certain games, those that he has learnt in childhood. Berne analysed and described a whole series of these games, including the "yes, but game" or the "if you were not there game". There are also life games, marriage games, party games, sex games, robber games, doctor games, "good games", etc.

The "yes but game"

She: I think I'm getting headache

He: We should definitely do something about that. The last time, a hot bath helped you.

She: Yes, you're right, but that's why it got worse, because I got my hair wet.

He: Then go and lie down for a while

She: Yes, that sometimes helps. But today I still have things to do.

He: Then go for a walk

She: Yes, that is a good idea. But today it is too windy and it will make my headache worse.

He: I could massage your shoulders

She: Yes, perhaps, but sometimes you are too rough, which makes my headache worse.

He: (annoyed) Then do what you want

She: You see, even if I am ill, you don't do anything to help me!

The use of the term "game" should not be understood in terms of having anything to do with fun and pleasure. TA uses the term more broadly, to cover basically all covert, parallel transactions. If one of the actors leads the game from the position of *adult*, then we call it an angular transaction; these are important in manipulation and deception. In a therapeutic context, however, duplex transactions are more important, which are unconscious on the part of both actors.

By game analysis, Berne understood the examination of the communication pattern of a relationship with regard to a couple's favourite games. It is basically the case that for every game there are specific exit strategies that enable one to avoid being drawn into the game. One of these can be giving special attention and positive affirmation to the other person.

From an astrological point of view, this is associated with the planets Moon and Saturn, or Neptune and Mars.

The Games People Play (schematic sequence)

Trick: Someone who wants to start a game lays a hook, which is the trigger for the game. For example, the trick can consist of misunderstanding, ignoring or one-sidedly quoting the other person.

Gimmick: The trick targets a weak point that he knows the other possesses. By managing to hook the other person with it, he makes them enter the game.

Covert transaction: As a result, a situation arises that is characterised by different covert transactions. For example, by switching ego state one person can confuse the other. If he recognises the switch, he often reacts angrily, which leads to the end of the communication and therefore to the end of the game.

Pay-off: The goal of the game is to provoke negative feelings, with which the game ends. Berne assumes that this is the unconscious agenda underlying the game, and considers the negative feelings to be a form of attention.

The Aims of Transactional Analysis

An analysis of the four life attitudes shows that there is no meaningful alternative to the attitude "I'm ok, you're ok". A primary goal of TA is therefore to make the client aware of and encourage this process of accepting the self and others. It is difficult to find myself ok if I am confronted by my weak points. It is difficult to find the other person ok if they do not fulfil my expectations. Both usually require a change in my habitual and often unquestioned attitudes.

This requires that I see through automated scripts, emotional masks and mind games, make new decisions and repeatedly confirm this reorientation in my everyday behaviour. The clarity I gain towards my thoughts and feelings also helps me to be more tolerant of other people, and last but not least improves my communication skills.

(Astrological) transactional analysis can therefore be used in a wide range of possible ways. It is not just a psychotherapeutic procedure; it also represents a comprehensive theory of the human personality and how people communicate. It can therefore be beneficial in many different areas of interpersonal contact and personal growth.

The author

Detlef Hover is a psychologist and psychotherapist in independent practice. He heads the *DAV-Ausbildungszentrum* (German Astrological Society Training Centre) in Stuttgart, is long-time President of the DAV, and president of the "Union of German-speaking Astrology Organisations."

❑ ❑ ❑ ❑ ❑

Learning to Let Go

– Becoming Authentic, Developing Yourself

Age Point and Prenatal New Moon

Dr. Reinhard Müller

First published in 'Astrolog' Issue 153, September 2006

The Creation of Sun and Moon, by Raphael

Why are people with the Sun in Aries sometimes so emotionally sensitive and have such a strong urge for symbiosis and unity with others? And why are people with a Virgo Sun so self centred or, if they are self actualised, able to spontaneously, dynamically and freely implement their creativity and creative potential? Why are a few people generally more strongly influenced by the zodiac sign that follows the one in which their Sun is situated? Why is what is profoundly spiritual within us revealed at quite specific points in our lives, and exactly at these points are we offered the opportunities to express even more profound spiritual aspirations? And how is it that sometimes old conditioning breaks through almost compulsively and we have the feeling that it is hard to break free from it?

The Sun and Moon are both important points in our horoscopes as they are so easily visible in the sky. They symbolise important parts of our personalities: aware self expression and development of our own creative potential (Sun) and unconscious emotional reactions especially with regard to protection, feelings of acceptance and rejection and, in the developed stages, cognition and understanding of one's own feelings and active capacity for love (Moon). (1)

The Sun symbolises the inner core of the personality, our inner self as well as that spiritual principle that develops from our core life concerns. It describes our inner identity and how we as individuals feel about it. It indicates how we express the essence of our personality, and gain and radiate strength, self-confidence and power in the process. The Sun is our spiritual basic concern, and our self-awareness: the more we are aware of what and who we really are, the freer we are in our actions and the more freedom of choice we have with respect to our behaviour. We gain self-confidence by becoming aware of ourselves. "Real self-confidence is revealed... in that the person is aware of his innermost power, his own creative potential, knows the purpose of his life and that he has a self-directed life goal, a developed and decisive life plan." (2)

The Moon stands for our emotional world, our emotional needs and our unconscious reactions in every day life. It reflects those influences, conditionings and script patterns from earliest childhood, which process the child's need for love, devotion, acceptance, protection and sensitive understanding. It is shown – as the store and emotional memory of our past experiences – in our particularly sensitive and sentimental reactions to experiences that profoundly damaged our basic feelings of protection and security, and in how we repetitively try to avoid negative and painful experiences and for this reason always experience the same pain. The learning process of the Moon's qualities involves understanding our own emotional world and that of our fellow men, and the active giving of love. It is all about developing inner trust of life that naturally develops from the flow of love in give and take.

The integration of the qualities of the Sun and Moon also develops: "The transition from the level of the Moon to that of the Sun takes place when the will awakens and the person realises that he no longer wants to suffer and can make his own decisions. This transition can happen relatively quickly, if one has overcome the ordeals of the level of the Moon." (3)

What exactly is it that makes up the deeper spiritual structures in our personality, which are emotionally so profound that we almost have the feeling that we cannot control them? How does a sometimes almost stubborn compulsion to repeat certain behavioural and emotional patterns occur, in the hope that we may avoid the recurring negative reactions (which are a mirror of our inner themes)? Why do we have the feeling that the injuries they cause are so firmly part of us? And, what is the origin of the deep spiritual inner compulsion to actualise quite specific issues (which are sometimes quite different from the Sun position in our horoscope) and how can we explain them astrologically?

In the horoscope, there is a series of karmically relevant points that point up deeper spiritual structures. Many of them are connected with the Sun and the Moon, e.g. the Moon Node axis or also planets and aspect figures, which are affected by a current solar eclipse. One of these points is the karmic or prenatal New Moon.

Back in the 1940s, Dane Rudyhar started researching the solar and lunar cycles. He worked out that the Moon phase at the time of birth is an important key to the understanding of the personality and its emotional expression. At the same time, he assumed that the start of a cycle was the germ and seed for what would unfold during the cycle itself.

This also led to his chapter on the prenatal New Moon. The prenatal or karmic New Moon is the New Moon that lies immediately (in the last four weeks) before our birthdate. We can find it in the Ephemerides under the heading Moon Phases, by searching for the New Moon that precedes our date of birth. The karmic New Moon indicates the start of the solar/lunar cycle in which we were born, which gives an unconscious spiritual influence to our personality.

New Moon positions are always connected with the start of something new, with the unconscious germination of a vision that will only become evident and really take effect and make sense during the cycle that follows. It is therefore still unclear as to how it will develop; we only see contours of experiences that are yet to develop emotionally. However, as every cycle is an extension of the preceding one, New Moon positions are always connected with the "result", i.e. with the inner learning process of the previous cycle: what do I want to say goodbye to? To what extent have I consciously realised that changes to my inner attitude and awareness and external approach are needed? What new things am I aiming for? Which areas would I like to learn more about? The New Moon represents the "potential answer to the need" for a "new cycle of growth and development" (4)… "In the unification of the Sun and Moon, a "ray" of solar potential, a new growth impulse, symbolic of the Sun passes to the Moon… The concrete forms that the impulse takes on can be ways of behaving, ways of thinking and feeling, interpersonal relationships, …certain undertakings in life like a career or a project. However, the new cycle does not usually begin with a loud bang. It is much more likely to start gradually and experiences a kind of childhood, for what it is trying to develop is still not yet fact, but just potential that must be concentrated and nurtured until it bears fruit during the course of the cycle." (5) Unresolved themes from the past must also be successively overcome, changed and integrated into the new development.

The karmic New Moon is – like every relationship between the Sun and the Moon – an intersection between emotionally-stored impressions, conditioning and experiences from the past (related to the themes of protection, rejection, authenticity, emotional expression, self-confidence) and the influence of a spiritual idea in the future. It is all about transforming old patterns by unfolding our creative power and restructuring ourselves. The karmic New Moon therefore expresses deeper spiritual aspirations and their characteristics on the one hand, and enables deep, unconscious spiritual levels that are rooted in the past to be expressed on the other. It therefore denotes the continued influence of karmic patterns. Occasionally, it can also have a compulsive character, so that we find it difficult to let go of old karmic conditionings, but it is essential that we recognise and transform these patterns. This is the only way we can prepare to be able to really express our own spiritual concerns. A karmic New Moon in Scorpio in the 2nd house at worst leads to a constant reactualisation of old patterns, fears and traumata with regard to the theme of self esteem, producing inner security – and externally leads to frequent experiences of personal debasement, insecurity and (sometimes apparently without success) having to fight for self esteem and self affirmation. If we do not initially accept this theme and cannot trust the flow of life and the possibilities of inner change/ transformation, we will continue to cling stubbornly to the patterns as we deal with this theme, carry it into the outside world and react to its reaction.

We will repeatedly experience the same reactions to the external reflection. If we embark on a process of inner change, at the end of this occasionally emotionally very painful and distressing phase we will be able to "stop banging our head against the wall and get on with our lives. We will never be the same again, for we have liberated ourselves from behavioural patterns and emotions that have hindered us all our lives." (6) The processes of letting go and transforming therefore allow a profound spiritual unfolding. In our example this would entail inwardly secure and confident behaviour, building on the spiritual and emotional foundation of the experiences, in particular changing the inner attitude to ourselves and to our own worth: recognising our own worth, being independent in our approach to new experiences and confident in our own potential and in life. Above all it means being able to actively choose experiences that are essential for our own spiritual growth. Changing our inner values (and in the process our emotional judgements) always creates a new inner attitude and also a new external personality. (7)

The development of the qualities latent in the position of the karmic New Moon can be on the scale of a flowing continuum, which ranges from the untransformed, rather compulsive repetition of old patterns that we cling to with a certain stubborn resistance, to the complete, confident and self-conscious exhaustion of these latent qualities – with all the intermediate stages and differentiations. This is a constant process of inner development, which can sometimes be structured very inconsistently.

The most important thing about the karmic New Moon is that it is sometimes located in a different sign and/or house (usually the former) than the one in which the birth Sun is situated. "If both the prenatal New Moon and the birth Sun are in the same sign, the characteristics of this sign profoundly penetrate the whole nature of this person, but if the birth Sun and the prenatal New Moon are in different signs, the personality will display a deep duality to some degree. If both the signs and houses of the New Moon and the birth Sun are different, this psychosomatic duality is reinforced; the personality tends to work on two clearly different fields of influence and activity." (8)

Aspects between the karmic New Moon and the planets of the birth horoscope are fundamental: "then we really see which themes and positions of the New Moon horoscope we have sought individually, in order to fill them with energy."(9)

Below, I would like to show how the transit of the Age Point across the karmic New Moon (not only in the conjunction but also in other 30° aspects, i.e. opposition, quincunx, trine, square, sextile and semi-sextile) reflects inner developments, which are both connected to the personal development and spiritual growth of deeper qualities and deeply rooted spiritual concerns and with the potentially stronger emergence of old patterns. There are therefore times and periods in our lives when the theme of the karmic New Moon in all its facets (from compulsive clinging to old patterns to profound, spiritual self-expression) comes to the fore and brings us a step closer to the possibility of developing profound, latent spiritual potential. These times offer the opportunity of dealing with them on a more emotional level and experiencing a profound inner process of change that enables us to transcend ourselves and to know ourselves in more depth.

It is vital that the Age Point relates to emotional development in certain periods of time and "that its significance extends to the regions of deeper cognition. It enables us to understand a person's life process, including all of their experiences." (10)

Let us now consider the lives of a few examples of famous personalities and the relevant biographical intersection points:

C.G.Jung

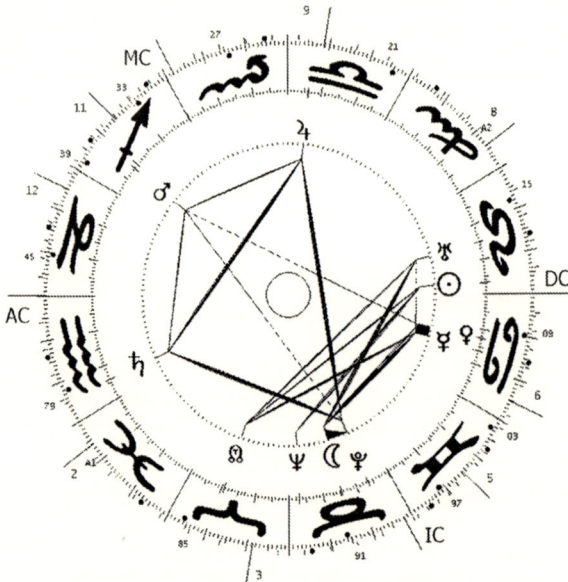

C.G.Jung 26.07.1875, 19:27, Kesswil, CH

The psychoanalyst Carl Gustav Jung's prenatal New Moon was at 10°49′ Cancer in the 6th house. It was in conjunction to Mercury and square to the Moon Node axis. This position is concerned with spiritual matters, and indicates his great sensitivity and intuitive powers for the concerns, needs and expectations of other people, to research the imagery of the soul in more depth. At the same time, the ascending Moon Node in Aries, [in the shadow of] house 3, denotes the inner development process, pioneering work in the area of spiritual conscious development, in a dynamic, energetic and experimental way. The Sun in Leo, house 7, [close to] Uranus points to the liberal, independent and creative development of his ideas in his encounters with other people.

Subsequent transits of the Age Point (AP) across the karmic New Moon (KM) can be located in Jung's biography (11):

Conjunction of the AP with the KM in 1905: in this period, Jung was working on a psychodiagnostic study after gaining increasing recognition for his research work during his work as ward doctor. There he came across the theme of "emotional complexes" by chance, a preliminary stage of his theory of the personal unconscious and his theory of archetypes. Shortly afterwards (1906), he began his exchange of ideas contact with Sigmund Freud.

During the semi-sextile of AP to KM in 1912, he not only published his book *Transformations and Symbols of the Libido*, he also parted company with Freud and developed his own theories. He gave lectures at Universities in New York and London and championed his "analytical psychology" there. Shortly after that, he gave up his teaching work in Zürich and left the Psychoanalytical Society.

Around 1917 (AP sextile KM) he continued to develop the activities he had previously undertaken, and above all developed his theory of dream symbols and human archetypes. Already in 1916, he had founded his own society, the Psychological Club, in Zürich.

In 1922 AP was square KM, and this period saw the production of his work on the psychological theory of types.

During the period of AP trine KM (1926), Jung devoted himself to extensive travelling to research his theories, especially among the Pueblo Indians in North America and also to East Africa.

At the transit of AP over KM as a quincunx in 1933, he became chairman of the *General Medical Society for Psychotherapy*, but was immediately confronted with National Socialism. He founded the *International Society for Medical Psychotherapy* and gave more and more lectures on the subject of *The Archetypes of the Collective Unconscious*. At the same time, he started teaching at the ETH in Zürich, which he stopped in 1942 at the time of the AP opposition to KM. He subsequently devoted himself wholeheartedly to his theory of the Collective Unconscious. He was also interested in Mythology and Alchemy.

Erich Fromm

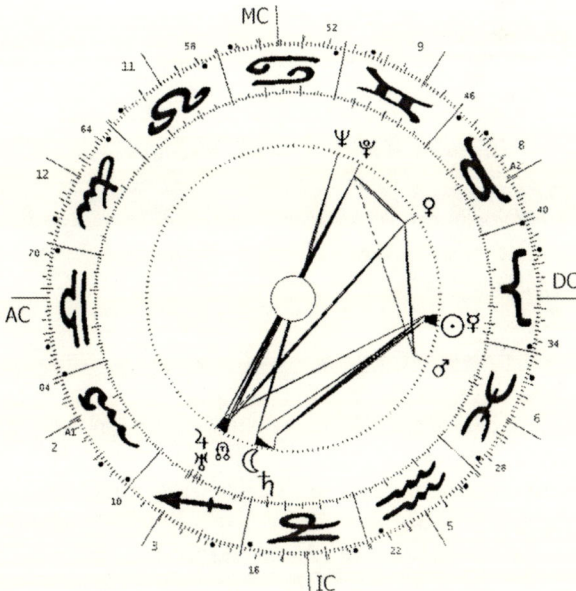

Erich Fromm, 23.3.1900, 19:30, Frankfurt a.M., Germany

Erich Fromm's karmic New Moon was at 10°49′ Pisces in the 6th house square to Jupiter/Uranus in Sagittarius, 3rd house, the Moon Node axis and in semi-sextile to the DC in Aries. His Sun was in Aries, the same sign as the DC. His deep spiritual concern was to empathise with the profound levels of the soul and to understand, differentiate and analyse the emotional universe. At the same time, he was concerned with connecting different areas of knowledge to a meaningful theory, to make his own synthesis of worldviews, in the process providing intellectual stimuli to the expansion of his consciousness (conjunction Jupiter, Uranus, ascending Moon Node in Sagittarius, 3rd house). At the same time, he has a combative, energetic, dynamic approach to things (Sun and DC in Aries).

At the time of the waning semi-sextile of AP to KM in 1923, Fromm had already finished his dissertation on the subject of *The Jewish Law*. At this time, he also came into contact with psychoanalysis and started training as analyst.

At the time of the conjunction of AP to KM in 1929, along with the end of his studies (12) and his education at the Psychoanalytical Institute in Berlin, he also co-founded the South German Institute for Psychoanalysis in Frankfurt (Main).

At the time of AP semi-sextile KM (end of 1935), Fromm restructured his life in New York after emigrating to the USA and in 1936 he started work on his first book.

With AP sextile KM in 1942, he published his book *Fear of Freedom* and took up a professorship in Vermont (USA). He founded his own Psychoanalytical Institute after collaboration on a joint institute with American colleagues had ended in separation.

At the time of AP square KM in 1948, Fromm published his book *Psychoanalysis and Ethics* and subsequently settled in Mexico City. However, he continued to give lectures in numerous American universities.

With the opposition of AP to KM in 1965, he achieved emeritus status and together with Herbert Marcuse, Ernst Blochung and others published the compilation *Humanist Socialism*.

Richard von Weizsäcker

Richard von Weizsäcker's KM was at 29°33′ Pisces in the 6th house, in conjunction with Mercury. His Sun was in Aries in the 7th house. Here too there was a concern for the deep feeling, intuitive understanding and empathising of other people's innermost motivations and expectations. The key was to integrate and express this understanding in his way of thinking and communicating with other people. These qualities help him to be personally authentic

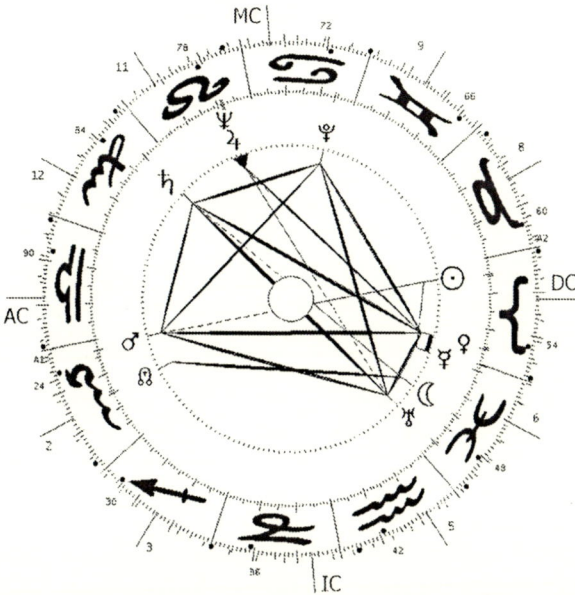

Richard von Weizsäcker, 15.4.1920, 18.30, Stuttgart, Germany

in the areas of vocation and self-actualisation and to have a caring, understanding and protective influence. The Sun in Aries, 7th house indicates a pioneering spirit as well as directness and openness in his dealings with others.

The conjunction of AP to KM in 1952 (13) coincided with Weizsäcker's legal training, especially his time as a junior lawyer. Shortly afterwards, he started his first job in the legal department of the firm Mannesmann. He very quickly rose through the ranks.

With the waxing semi-sextile of AP to KM in 1958/59, Weizsäcker became manager of a private banking house, which he took on for family reasons.

At the time of AP sextile to KM (1964), his basic understanding changed substantially in regard to authenticity: Weiszäscker became President of the German Evangelical Church Congress, and his social, humanitarian and moral side came to the fore.

During the AP square to KM (1970), he took on more positions of social responsibility: member of the German Bundestag, member of the Synod and the Council of the Evangelical Church in Germany (EKD) and Leader of the Commission of the Christian Democratic Union for the elaboration of a new basic programme.

During the quincunx aspect of AP to KM in 1981, he became the reigning Mayor of Berlin. He subsequently became Federal President, and demonstrated the required morals, ethics and values.

The opposition of AP to KM in 1988 took place just before the reunification of Germany, in which he became a moral leader. As AP formed an increasing quincunx to KM (1994), Weizsäcker ended his activity as Federal President and withdrew from public life.

Transits of the Age Point over the karmic New Moon often express important periods of change in our lives, which are characterised by learning to let go of old influences and patterns. At the same time, there may be great opportunities for psychological and spiritual growth, especially for a more authentic expression of our deep spiritual concerns. They are often connected with a step into new experiences, which are associated with a change of the structure in the external world that we have created for ourselves and the expression of our psychological inner life. This profound involvement in new areas of life simultaneously stimulates us to change our approach to things, and this is often associated with an unfolding of our unconscious potential, which can now be more strongly expressed. The acknowledgement of these opportunities helps us to gain deeper access to our own potential.

References

(1) *The Planets and their Psychological Meaning*, Bruno & Louise Huber

(2) *Reflections and Meditations on the Signs of the Zodiac*, Louise Huber

(3) *The Planets and their Psychological Meaning*, Bruno & Louise Huber

(4) *The Lunation Process in Astrological Guidance*, Leyla Rael Rudhyar

(5) *ibid*

(6) *Healing Pluto Problems*, Donna Cunningham

(7) *Esoterische Astrologie*, Dane Rudhyar

(8) *The Lunation Cycle: A Key to the Understanding of Personality*, Dane Rudhyar

(9) *Karmische Horoskopanalyse*, Vol 2, Claude Weiss

(10) *LifeClock*, Bruno & Louise Huber

(11) *Jung*, Gerhard Wehr

(12) *Erich Fromm*, Rainer Funk

(13) *Richard von Weizsächer*, Harald Steffahn

◻ ◻ ◻ ◻ ◻

Light and Shade in Astrology

The Dark Side of Human Nature in the Horoscope

Detlef Hover

First published in 'Astrolog' Issue 126-7, February - April 2002

The Shadow Side of Life

In the many film versions of the novel *Dr Jekyll and Mr Hyde* by Robert Louis Stevenson, a virtuous doctor called Dr. Jekyll performs various medical experiments on himself in his search for a new elixir. Something goes wrong during one of them and he is accidentally transformed into a real monster in human form, Mr Hyde.

This topic of the "two souls in one body" has been dealt with in different ways in art, particularly in literature and filmic art, we think for example of the werewolf theme or of Oscar Wilde's novel *The Picture of Dorian Gray*, in which the shadow is represented as a mirror image: the traces of the eponymous hero's debauched and corrupt lifestyle are shown in his portrait, where he appears more and more abject and ugly. He himself, on the other hand, remains young and handsome, while the painting of him deteriorates more and more. Finally, Dorian Gray cannot stand this any more and he slashes the portrait with a knife, as a result of which he himself dies too.

It seems to be the case that an individual consciously or unconsciously contains all psychic possibilities of human nature within himself. This thought is also expressed when we say that we have both an "angel" and a "devil" within us.

In a somewhat modified form, this shadow theme also crops up in the archetype of the enemy brother, e.g. in the biblical presentation of Cain and Abel or Jacob and Esau or in the tale of Romulus and Remus. They fell out over who should oversee the building of Rome, and therefore who would be the founder of the city. The fight escalated and Romulus killed his brother yet wept bitterly. In Schiller's play *The Robbers*, Franx Moor disinherits his brother Karl, who as a result sets up a band of robbers to fight against injustice. One part of the band of robbers becomes addicted to evil though, and starts to plunder and kill. In Dostoyevsky's novel *The Brothers Karamazov* both brothers must atone for the murder of their father, which one brother has however only committed in his mind.

We can list many similar examples (e.g. Jacob's struggle against the dark angel, Musil's novel *The Man without a Shadow* or Dostoyevsky's *Crime and Punishment*), showing how relevant the topic is.

What is the Shadow?

The term shadow was coined by C.G. Jung in modern psychology. Within his image of man the shadow has an important place, which is immediately obvious when we consider his graphic representation of the so-called "whole psyche".

Outside World

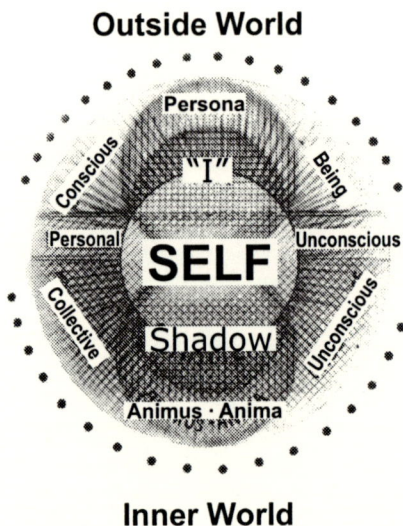

Inner World

Whole Psyche according to Jung
(from: Jolande Jacobi, *Psychology of C.G. Jung*)

The similarity between Jung's model and the astrological horoscope circle is evident: the totality of the psyche is symbolised by a circle, and the conscious and unconscious are differentiated, as on the AC-DC axis. In the centre of the circle is the self. Into the light of our consciousness (upper half), only a part of our spiritual life rises. The central structure of this illuminated field of consciousness is formed by the human self/ego, and further outwards is the persona, i.e. the image of ourselves that we want to show to the world. In a mirror image of this is the other side, in the unconscious, the shadow. In this shadow are those rooted thoughts, feelings and images that are not conscious, the undeveloped side with its unconsciously experienced possibilities and aims.

> *"By shadow I understand the "negative" part of the personality, i.e. the sum of the hidden, unfavourable attributes, which are poorly developed functions and contents of the personal unconscious."*
>
> *(C.G. Jung, On the Psychology of the Unconscious, 1917.)*

Elsewhere, Jung also defines the shadow as everything that the person does not want to be and connects the shadow side of the psyche with "unacknowledged desires" and "repressed parts of the personality". Accordingly, the shadow is therefore "the other within us", our inferior side that we are embarrassed about. There are yet more names for the shadow, e.g. the denied self, lower self, dark twin, repressed self, alter ego, brother self or even "dark brother".

Our modern understanding of the shadow is usually the part of the unconscious psyche that is nearest to the consciousness, but which is not completely accepted by it. The shadow contradicts the behaviour we have consciously decided to adopt, which is why we try to stop it from being expressed. The parts of our self that we are unable to accept as belonging to us fall into this shadow area. That which is alien to me becomes shadow; that which is not alien to me becomes part of me. According to Jungian theory, the shadow is always the same gender as the self. It is our *doppelganger*, which other people always see better than we do. Being confronted by one's own shadow is unpleasant and inconvenient, but we usually find other people's shadows interesting.

It is also possible that a person's "better half" lives in their shadow, not in their conscious self. We then say: "Deep down he is a better person than he seems." Our shadow can often contain our most important powers. The depth psychologist Verena Kast also calls this the "subversive vital force". In painting, shadowing gives plasticity and richness. People would therefore be only superficial and two-dimensional without shadows, and they are not like this, although there are people who are not aware of their shadows.

The appearance of the Shadow

To explain the appearance of the shadow, Richard Ideman says it is useful to distinguish between linear and circular thinking. Unlike Eastern, circular thinking, the Western way of thinking can be termed linear. This can be symbolically represented by a line or cross, which can considered as the main symbol for all of Western culture. The end poles of the lines correspond to the opposites of "right" and "wrong", "good" and "evil", "positive" and "negative", etc., which are seemingly incompatible. Connected with this polarity is either-or thinking, which astrologically is symbolised e.g. by the oppositions or axes (signs and houses).

The Yin-Yang symbol is used as a common symbol for circular thinking. This represents the universe in a circular form, in which all forces, i.e. also all polarities, are included in the whole. The halves are composed of opposite pairs "Yin" and "Yang". The relationship between these two

Yin-Yang

poles is not static though. It is shown as a wavy line where one side runs into the other and the two are in an ongoing exchange. Another important feature of this symbol is that each half contains a part of the other in the form of a small circle, so that the light contains darkness and the darkness contains light.

Human reality is often more complex than the linear model would allow, and is actually more like a circle: for example, we must sometimes go west in order to find the east (c.f. Columbus). The more we distance ourselves from a point on the earth's surface, the more the direct connection changes from being a straight line to being a circle. This leads to a paradox: sometimes we find that what seems good on first sight is not so good after all...

For Jung too, polarity (the problem of opposites) is vitally important, as it represents an inherent law of human nature:

"There is no balance and no system of self-regulation without opposites. The psyche is a system with self-regulation."

(C.G. Jung, *Psychology of the Unconscious.*)

In Western philosophy, the principle of polarity has a long tradition. Already Heraclitus accepted the regulatory function of the opposites, which he called Enantiodromia. By this he meant that everything runs into its opposite. Jung said the following on this subject:

"the transition from morning to afternoon is a reassessment of previous values. The necessity imposes itself, to realise the value of the opposite of our earlier ideals, to perceive the error in our previous conviction... But it is naturally a basic mistake to believe that if we see worthlessness in a value or falseness in a truth, then the value or the truth are cancelled out. They are just relativised... Everything human is relative, because everything is based on inner oppositeness, for everything is an energetic phenomenon. Energy is necessarily based on preexisting laws, without which there can be no energy... High and low, hot and cold, etc. must always come first, so that the balancing process, which energy is, can take place... Every living thing is energy and is therefore based on oppositeness. Not a conversion into the opposite, but maintaining previous values together with a recognition of their opposites (is the goal we must strive for)."

C.G. Jung, *Psychology of the Unconscious.*)

In linear thought, an opposition is created between the two ends of a polar axis. We are either one thing or the other. However, by one-sidedly identifying with only one pole, this becomes a stereotype, whereas the opposite pole sinks into the shadows. This process of one-sided identification with certain values, which leads to the creation of shadows, is already taking place in our childhood:

"The personal shadow is formed quite naturally in every small child. We identify ourselves with ideal personality features, which are encouraged and reinforced by our environment, like politeness and generosity, so leading to what W. Brugh Joy calls the "New Year's Resolution Self". At the same time, we submerge into the shadows everything that does not suit the image we have of ourselves, for example, rudeness and selfishness. The self and the shadow therefore develop together, they are produced by the same life experience."

(Connie Zweig and Jeremiah Abrams, Meeting the Shadow.)

In the personal shadow are located the unloved and unredeemed parts of the soul that are opposite to the conscious self and denied by it. Both poles, self and shadow, mutually condition each other: "Where there is much light, there is also much shadow" (Goethe) and Paul states: "The good I want to do I do not do and the evil I do not want to do, I do." (Paul, Romans, 7.19)

Collective Shadow

Devil and Scapegoats

However, the shadow is not just a problem for individuals, but also for a whole group or society, in which case it is referred to as a collective shadow. This is formed in the same way as an individual shadow by the one-sided identification and simultaneous rejection of the opposite.

Basically, in both the individual and the collective case, it is true that by denying the shadow it becomes particularly strong and virulent.

"Everyone is followed by a shadow, but the less this is embodied in the person's conscious life, the stronger and more concentrated it is."

(C.G. Jung, Psychology and Religion.)

If we are not aware of our own shadow, it is also impossible for us to "redeem" it. Instead, this leads to a certain independent existence, pushing for recognition from the conscious self, which is necessary for the purposes of balancing/ equilibrium. In the process, the shadow can be experienced in two different ways:

"One can encounter one's shadow in an inner symbolic way or in an external, concrete figure. In the first case, it will appear in the subconscious e.g. as a dream figure that represents the personification of one or maybe more spiritual qualities of the dreamer; in the second case, it is someone from our environment, who for certain structural reasons we project with the qualities that are hidden within our unconscious."

(Jolande Jacobi, The Psychology of C.G. Jung.)

In the two forms given by Jung, the shadow is therefore expressed by projecting it onto others, which is also called "scapegoat thinking". The term arose because in Biblical times, a living goat was selected that was then laden with all evils and sins. The goat was then damned and literally "sent into the desert".

Scapegoat thinking, usually in a reproachful way, and often combined with the desire to punish, usually involves criticising others for things that are much more likely to be found in one's own shadow. If the shadow is therefore projected in such a way, one experiences one's dark side as "the evil in the world out there". Here is should be noted that the shadow theme is particularly noticeable in the Christian cultural area, and the people of this area are perhaps particularly strongly covered by the shadow, which is expressed for example in the symbolism of the devil.

"The devil is an archetypal figure, whose direct and indirect ancestry can be traced back to antiquity. There he usually appears as a bestial demon, powerful and quite inhuman as per his illustration on tarot cards. As Seth, the Egyptian god of Evil, he frequently took the form of a snake or crocodile. In ancient Mesopotamia, Pazazu (the malaria carrying demon of the South West wind, King of the evil air spirit), incarnated a few of the traits that are now attributed to Satan. Certain attributes could also have been inherited by our devil from Tiamat, the Babylonian Goddess of Chaos, which appears in the form of a horned and clawed bird. Only when Satan appeared in the Judeo-Christian culture did he began to acquire human traits and in his dark urges to behave in a way that people could understand."

(Sally Nichols, The Devil in Tarot.)

**The Devil in Tarot
(Marseille-Tarot)**

Represented in a simplified form, Christian theory assumes that God is good. The Devil, his adversary, stands for Evil. God wants men to do good. This however is a particularly crass form of linear thinking and polarisation, which entails the formation of a shadow.

Seen in this way, the demonising of people and groups is a form of scapegoat thinking and is therefore connected to one's own shadow. Forms of collective scapegoat thinking are characterised by massive allocation of blame to a particular group, which then stand for "Evil". This attitude is usually combined with heightened hostility and the desire for punishment. Examples are easy to find; particularly crass are the persecution of witches or Jews, or modern xenophobia.

The Shadow in Astrology

Following these general explanations of the shadow, the question arises as to how this theme can be conceived in astrology. It is fundamentally true that all components of the horoscope can fall in the shadow. For example, let us consider the elements; here according to the Jungian functions, Air (thinking) and water (feeling) form a pair of opposites. Now, if a person identifies strongly with the element of air, the element of water could become part of the shadow; perhaps one would then look down on water-influenced people as "emotional fools" and "softies". Also the identification with a planet (e.g. Saturn or Mars) could favour the formation of a shadow (e.g. the Moon or Venus). However, the idea is particularly well illustrated by the signs and houses; due to the axis polarity, dissociation is naturally easier to accomplish here.

Aries – Libra

The starting point of Aries is the self, whereas that of Libra is the You. This inspired Richard Ideman to the basic ideas. "Aries: I want what I want when I want. Libra: I want what you want me to want when you want."

The natural condition of the small child means that Libra becomes part of the shadow. The small child is known to be selfish, there is no environment, and no You in this state.

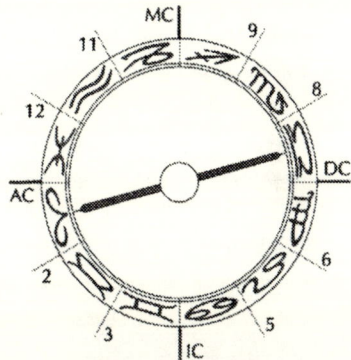

**Encounter Axis
(Aries – Libra)**

In order to balance out the Aries quality of self-assertion and to build up the Libra quality of social equilibrium, we control the young Aries with the Libra word "nice", telling him for example, "that was not very nice of you."

The Libra vocabulary is sometimes so well-learnt that a nice, well-adjusted individual appears more oriented to the norms of society than to his own needs, anxiously avoiding conflict. Now Aries has become part of the shadow. A Libra-emphasised individual once expressed it thus: "Everyone is happy with my life except me!" If adults remain on the Aries side and their Libra side remains in the shadow, it can lead to sociopathic behaviour, so such people are often found in prisons or psychiatric hospitals. This is quite rare though, as the archetype of Libra is the social norm, within which society functions. These norms naturally vary from culture to culture. Below is an example of someone with Aries in the shadow.

> *"A woman came to see me for counselling – she had Mars in the 7th house. She suffered from bad migraines. When I find out that a certain part of the body is affected by illness, I know that there must also be a corresponding problem on the psychic level. I asked her what she did with her anger, how she asserted her own needs and she answered that she did not believe that anger was spiritual and that she had been brought up to be nice, and nice girls did not get angry. So what happened to her anger? She married him. I imagined that as soon as I saw her chart and I said: "tell me about your husband" and she said "Oh, he can get very angry". During their ten or twelve years of marriage he had hit her about ten times. I asked how she could stay with a man who treated her like this, and she said "Aren't all men like that?" For her Mars or Aries was her shadow and her husband had become the dragon. During the course of counselling, we tried to work out how she could kill her dragon. She eventually decided never again to allow herself to be hit. I asked what this meant for her, and she said: "If I draw the line here, it may be that he will leave me." And I asked what this would mean for her. "It could be that I would then be alone." And that was the dragon: being alone. She decided to take the risk. The next time he wanted to get violent, she said, "If you hit me one more time, I will leave you." Suddenly, she reversed the polarity and he became the Libra. So it turned out that her dragon went up in smoke. It could also have happened that he could have hit her anyway and then she would have decided whether she was really going to leave him." (Liz Greene, The Shadow in Astrology.)*

In order to illuminate the shadow, it is however important to build a bridge between the two signs. Then Aries and Libra are no longer opposites but two sides of the same coin. From an astrological point of view this is expressed by the relationship theme that connects Aries and Libra. For a relationship, both sides – I and You – are equally important.

Richard Ideman also formulated ideas that are very incisive due to the similarity between these signs: "Aries is the iron fist and Libra is the iron fist inside the velvet glove."

Taurus – Scorpio

The sign of Taurus represents security, possession and stability, here we would like to cling to what we trust. As an ideal, we can imagine Adam and Eve in Paradise, whose every need is catered for. The shadow of Taurus is therefore indicated by terms like risk and temptation.

The sign of Scorpio instead represents the unknown. Scorpio follows Libra, which is concerned with the laws and rules of society. This theme also plays an important role in Scorpio, i.e. as the dark and hidden side of society's rules, which we know as social norms and taboos.

In Scorpio, the person is allowed to choose to leave the security and comfort of home

**Possession Axis
(Taurus – Scorpio)**

(Paradise). He gives in to the snake's temptation, breaking a taboo. By eating from the tree of knowledge, the person loses his paradisical innocence and can now distinguish between good and evil. This also gives the idea of the shadow. In this sense, Scorpio can be seen as the shadow sign *par excellence.*

Taurus identifies with pleasure, sensuality and sexuality, which are often more important to him than possessions. This leads to a certain addiction and greed. Scorpio develops considerable anxiety about these passions and obsessions, which are nevertheless also strongly expressed in this sign. In particular the power of eroticism is one of them, which is why Scorpio is often the sign of fanatical asceticism.

While Taurus strives for harmony and peace (Venus is its ruler), in Scorpio the disruption of existing forms is a key impulse (Mars and Pluto are rulers). It is often called "One thing I am not is nice!" Anything peaceful, harmonious, nice and easy must be disrupted. The integration here takes place on the thematic of the possession axis, in which the polarity is between stability and change.

Gemini – Sagittarius

This pair is probably easiest for Westerners to deal with and to keep in balance, as in our culture we are more intellectually oriented and are ruled by this quality.

The archetype of Gemini is based on a permanent quest for knowledge, information and innovation. In the process he is led by an attitude of doubt and questioning. This useful function can naturally become criticism and scepticism, an attitude that calls everything into question – except for one's own doubt. Socrates tried to solve this dilemma with humour, which is expressed in the famous paradox "I know that I know nothing!"

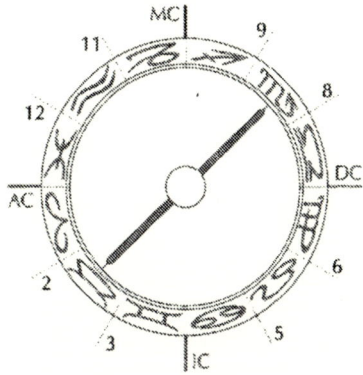

Sagittarius tries to form the available information into a philosophy, or an ethical system. Such a system naturally contains subjective evaluations and represents an individual point of view. In extreme cases, Sagittarius can be stubborn about the rightness of his position.

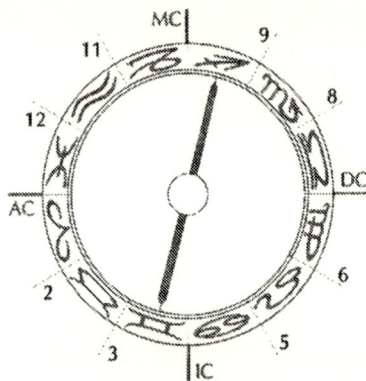

**Thinking Axis
(Gemini-Sagittarius)**

The Gemini-Sagittarius theme can be summarised in a nutshell as the teacher-pupil relationship, in which the pupil says "I know nothing" and the teacher says "I know everything".

A good example is provided by Richard Ideman:

"when I was teaching in a prison in California, I learnt that Timothy Leary was one of the inmates. Once he attended one of my courses, but I didn't have a chance to talk to him. But he wrote me a couple of lines in which he said he would like to talk to me in person sometime. I found him to be an interesting personality whom I would like to get to know. I therefore arranged an appointment and we met up. He said "Ah, astrology is very interesting, but what do you know about the I Ching?" I said that once I had studied it thoroughly. He just said "oh!" and after a short pause: "do you know anything about Kaballah?" And I answered that I had just read an interesting book about it. Then he said "Well", and hinted that he didn't have much time. Suddenly I remembered that he had a Sagittarius ascendant, and it became clear to me that he was split along this shadow line and that if I wanted him to talk to me, I had to play the role of the pupil (= Gemini). Then he asked "Do you know anything about Numerology?" and I said that I didn't know anything about it. Here he had found something to talk about and he gave me a wonderful hour-long lecture. Later he told one of his friends that he thought I was an extremely intelligent young man, who was however unable to retain anything."

(R. Idemon, Astrological Archetypes and their Shadows.)

From this example, I draw another interesting lesson: when someone has fallen in the shadow, sometimes the only way other people can connect with them is to play the complementary role. Of course, then there is not much room for manoeuvre for both sides. The example is incidentally also revealing as to how a person can be manipulated by his own shadow when one can see it.

Cancer – Capricorn

If we represent the Individuality Axis graphically as a tree, then Cancer corresponds to the roots buried deep in the earth, whereas Capricorn represents the crown of the tree that stretches up to the sky.

Cancer is the archetype of the family, ancestry and tradition. Here we feel comfortable and secure, we feel the warmth of the nest. In this nest, mother and child are still united.

**Individuality Axis
(Cancer-Capricorn)**

Capricorn is the sign of individualisation and perfection. So as Capricorn wants to reach the summit of the mountain, we must develop "upwards". In the process, Capricorn puts up with the effort and hardship that await us in the cold of a stony terrain. To get this far, we have to leave the warmth of the nest behind.

Starting from the Cancer theme, parents say to the child: "you will always be our little child. We love you most when you stay as you are." But when inspired by Capricorn, they say "Now we love you most if you achieve something in life, if you make something of yourself."

If there is excessive identification with Cancer, Capricorn will remain in the shadow. The person will then prefer to remain a child, which in women is often expressed in subordination into the role of housewife and mother. Where there is one-sided identification with Capricorn, with Cancer in the shadow, the striving for success will dominate, which is often equated with material success. Anything human and emotional is often left by the wayside; the person has no home and protection and experiences a lack of love in life.

Due to prevailing social structures, frequently the pattern is found where the man adopts the Capricorn role and the Cancer shadow role is taken by his wife. There are of course other variations.

This example of a woman for whom Cancer was the shadow, comes from Liz Greene:

"I once drew up a horoscope for an Aquarian woman with a Capricorn ascendant. She had quite a number of strong Saturn contacts in her horoscope, usually in trine or sextile aspects, and it was important for her to manage by herself. She was proud of her ability and strength. In a loveless marriage with a weak husband who offered no support, she raise two children and also had a career. She had never shown signs of helplessness, need or dependence to

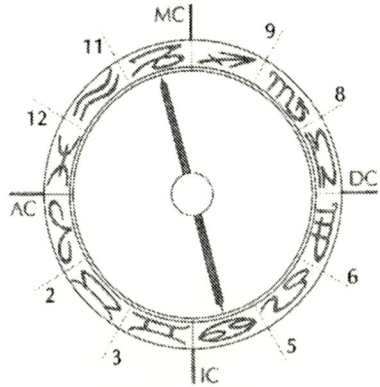

anyone. She preferred to keep quiet rather than admit to having needs that would have put her at the mercy of others. She needed this man who offered no support for he had forced her to be his shadow.

When we started to talk about these things, she told me about a dream that she'd had two or three times that she had found deeply unsettling. In the office where she worked there was a woman she could not stand. She'd dreamt that she was at home and this woman had knocked at her door and asked to come inside. She was very angry and shut the door in the woman's face. I asked her to tell me about this other woman. My client said "Oh, she is unbearable, I find her simply awful." I asked "why do you hate her so much?" She told me that this woman was about 20 years younger than herself, and was "one of these stupid receptionists." This younger woman, it appeared, was easily hurt and quick to cry and liked to act helplessly in front of the men in the office. She was always asking for help and pretended not to know what she was doing, which didn't always ring true. My client used a lot of strong language when she was talking about this woman: she was creepy, false, horrible, disgusting… My client ran down her colleague in this way for quite a while. She couldn't just say "I don't approve of this woman's behaviour." Finally I said: "Could you imagine that this woman's behaviour had anything to do with you?" She replied indignantly: "Of course not!" Here she repeated exactly what she'd done in her dream: slammed the door and shut her shadow out. After a while, I changed the subject. This is what a shadow figure and the typical reaction to a shadow figure look like." (Liz Greene, The Shadow in Astrology.)

In this example, the woman used various rude words to characterise the other person, which express a personal judgement and snideness. Generally speaking, when adjectives are used that overshoot the mark, it is usually a sure sign that a shadow projection is in process.

Leo – Aquarius

In the Relationship Axis Leo-Aquarius (5-11), elementary questions of social life are expressed, which is why it is also rightly called the "political axis". In the process, both signs assume a different model of the structure of society.

Leo stands for the archetype of the master and the strong man, who acts out of his own power and authority. It is not for nothing that the lion is called the king of the jungle. His task is the awakening of his own creative energy and mastery so that he can be a "hero of the pure heart" (Ideman). On the other hand, Leo is also a conformist, because he can only operate within the existing social system. As a king is nothing without his people, he needs the acknowledgement and love of his environment.

For Aquarius, the archetype of the group dominates as the nucleus of the social system. The group of Aquarius is however not the family of Cancer but the community of friends. One can only be part of this if one is able to bring one's ego into the community. Unlike Leo, Aquarius strives to liberate the world, he is a known rebel and iconoclast who does not care what others say.

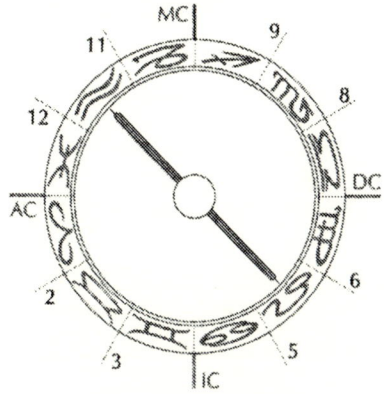

Relationship Axis (Leo-Aquarius)

In the case of identification with Leo (Aquarius in shadow), it is easy for the model of a "person of genius", a tyrannical king, who under massive deployment of his own elbows gets rid of anything that does not acknowledge his dominance or even questions it.

In the case of identification with Aquarius (Leo shadow), the group impulse dominates so strongly that the ego must subordinate unconditionally to it. Here we recognise the dogmatic and authoritarian parties (fascism, communism), that view every individual aspiration as suspicious, as it is seen as a threat to their domination. Also religious sects and terrorist groups are found here, circles in which individual lives count for nothing.

Virgo – Pisces

Virgo and Pisces together form the Existence Axis (6-12). Here the person is confronted with the suffering of life and sets himself the task of finding a solution for it. This subject is very difficult and can easily go wrong, which illustrates why this is also called the "psychosomatic axis". Illness is then in the broadest sense the result of painful living conditions and unsuccessful attempts at inner mastery.

Virgo is the sign of the helper and server, which is symbolically expressed in the activity of a nurse, who tries by work and service to alleviate the suffering of the world. This is also important to them because this is how order and structure can be brought into an apparently chaotic world.

In Pisces, the person often feels suffering and helplessness. This is particularly expressed if he finds himself in elementary situations of failure and exclusion (hospital, prison), which can also be called the "limit experiences of existence".

In the case of identification with Virgo (Pisces shadow) there is considerable fear of sinking into the suffering and chaos of the world. This leads to an excessive helping and redeeming attitude that necessarily requires victims. There can also be rituals that serve to reduce the fear of chaos, manifesting as compulsive behaviour.

In the case of identification with Pisces (Virgo shadow), the person often finds a form of retreat and escapism, which they hope will allow them to

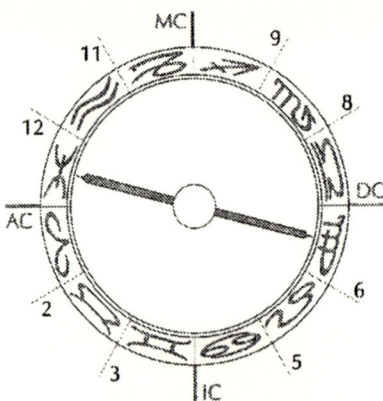

**Existence Axis
(Virgo-Pisces)**

escape from the suffering of the world; however they also often stay suffering and sulky in exile from life.

Shadow Work

The shadow and its effects always show us the "dark side" of our lives, which necessarily also must come to light if the person wants to walk the path of redemption (enlightenment). The tasks connected with this are also known as "shadow work". This process of shadow work proceeds according to the following three stages:

- Encountering the shadow (know theyself!)
- Accept the shadow (integration)
- Transformation of the shadow (illumination and transformation)

The encounter (confrontation) with one's own shadow has several different names: facing our demons, wrestling with the devil, going down into the underworld, the dark night of the soul, bringing the shadow side of the soul into the light. It is the first, important prerequisite for overcoming the shadow. The basic rule is: the more we acknowledge our shadow, the less we are victims of it. Of course, the striving for knowledge is possibly opposed by a massive tendency to repression.

"A simple repression of the shadow is however as ineffective a cure as beheading for a headache." (C.G. Jung, Psychology and Religion.)

The development of our own personality is much more about confronting our own shadow. However, the first question that arises is, how do we get to know our own shadow? The following ideas can be helpful:

- Considering our own secret interests can give us some idea of our shadow.
- Things about which we are particularly vulnerable and easily offended are part of our shadows.
- If we want to know what belongs to our shadow, we can also ask ourself the question: "What do I most hate and reject in other people."
- From an astrological point of view, we could for example think of the sign and its properties that we reject most strongly, as well as that which we idealise most.

In the second phase of shadow work it is time to integrate the shadow. An important part of our path towards awareness consists of actualising wholeness, i.e. also the hidden and not just those parts where we are strong and which we know. Everything that we deny will come back to us in some way so that it can be integrated into our wholeness. As the saying goes: "Nothing human is alien to me!" (Michel de Montaigne.)

Consider the example of an actor, who has to play the role of an "evil contemporary". So that he can do this well, he must empathise with the role, ideally feeling these elements within himself. That this is basically possible when one digs deeply enough, Goethe expresses in the following idea: "I have found the predisposition to all the crimes in human history within myself."

The process of integration of the shadow is formulated by Aeppli in the following words:

"We have to make peace with it, to accept it as part of us and to transform it as much as we are able. We cannot do it all, and often all too little. What remains dark, what cannot be transformed, must be borne as "strains of mortality". We should not identify with our shadow though. In the encounter with the shadow, we will learn to be fair with ourselves and other people, to recognise the role of the dark side in the world and not to ignore the call for illumination." (Hans Aeppli, Psychologie des Bewussten und Unbewussten.)

The advice that the process of integration is not comparable to identification is important here. If we were to identify with our shadow, it would be the same as becoming fixated with it and would not be a step towards overcoming it.

It can often be observed that, in shadow work, people want to go too far too soon, i.e. they want to proceed with the transformation as soon as they have researched their own shadow, thus almost skipping the second stage of integration. Although this may be understandable, it is not practical as we would be trying to get rid of something before we have even accepted it. As the corrector of the self, the shadow has an important role to play and is needed until this task is fulfilled. If we are impatient about it, the following ideas may help. The act of looking already starts the process of redemption, as we shine light into the darkness and the integration it brings overrides the separation.

Dragons and Dragon Slayers

The dragon is a well-known symbol also present in Christian thinking. In mythology it was overcome by the dragon slayer.

Dragon Slayer (Johfra-Karte)

In the myth the hero must slay or stab the dragon. It can also be that the hero cuts the dragon's head off and three more grow in its place and the hero is eventually killed by the dragon. These are different possibilities, but in any case the hero must face up to the dragon, i.e. come clean with it. By changing our perception, our opinion of the shadow also changes. If we want to slay the dragon or catch our shadow, this requires courage. In order to be able to catch our shadow, we must be prepared to have to give up a certain goal sometimes so that we don't get too involved with it and can be more flexible. We must also run the risk of possible failure: if the hero only attacks the dragon when guaranteed victory, he will never attack the dragon.

> *"If we imagine a person brave enough to withdraw his projections, this is someone who is aware of a substantial shadow. Such a person admittedly has brought upon himself new problems and conflicts. He has become a serious task for himself, as he can no longer say that others do this or that, that they are wrong and and that he must fight against them. He lives in the "house of taking stock of oneself", the inner focusing. Such a person knows that whatever is wrong in the world is also wrong in himself, and if he just learns to deal with his own shadow he has done something authentic for the world. He has then succeeded in answering at least a tiny part of the unresolved, gigantic questions of our times." (C.G. Jung, Psychology and Religion.)*

❑ ❑ ❑ ❑ ❑

Our Lady's Child

An Interpretation of the Fairy Tale according to Astrological Psychology

Christian U. Vogel

First published in 'Astrolog' Issues 146-7, July – September 2005

"Based on this experience of the self and the original unus mundus (one world), world and psyche no longer appear to be two parallel and mutually independent worlds, each with a self-contained legality. Both parts of the whole complement each other; …they form a coherent, complementary whole. This becomes clear in many theories of astrology, mysticism and alchemy, e.g. the Tabula Smaragdina, which emphasise identity and unity of above and below, inner and outer. In astrology, the external heavenly bodies with their regular motions are identical to the stars within us and we do not have to decide which of the two heavens, the outer or the inner, shapes our destiny, as in actual fact, they point to the existence of a unified, so-called "third" heaven. We have chosen the example of astrology, because the experience of the unus mundus is always also associated with that of synchronicity and meaningful destiny, unlike the randomness of event causality, in which there is no connection between the outer world and the inner one." (5)

Introduction

There was universal indignation during a seminar on "heroines and heroes in fairy tales" (0) when we came to the end of the story of Our Lady's Child (1). A story that so obviously deals with the resistance, growth and development of the main character should not end with her complete subordination and the breakdown of her personality. It was obvious to us that individuation, the conscious evolution of the self and the natural aim of a successful life, had been trampled underfoot. In its place appeared the naked claim to power of a religious morality, a collective norm, which deprived the individual of what all of us believed to be inalienable rights in favour of a highly inspiring miraculous salvation. In addition, this wedge of presumptuous morality was literally painfully forced between the apparently older original elements of the fairy tale, which allude if not to individuation, at least to development, and to our modern emphasis on the rights of the individual as opposed to the claims of society.

It was therefore clear straight away that a wonderful old original version had been forced to wear an extremely ill-fitting Christian coat, and those who were receptive to it were very affected not only by the old structure that shone through the coat, but also the tension between the two stories. Here two world views appear to collide, producing something that works in its own right due to their very incompatibility, although the story as we find it in the Brothers Grimm is completely unrealistic and unacceptable, despite all the reworking. The violence of its origin should not be overlooked, nor should its malicious intent. That is why the suspicion that it is a work of the counter-reformation for the purposes of converting the "stupid masses" seems quite plausible (2). However, the fact that the fairy tale was retold for centuries in this format indicates these people's willingness to internalise the repressive rules of the authorities and themselves to treat others who were somehow "different" with complete brutality. This willingness also provided the background for the great wave of witchhunts, of which the fairy tale is reminiscent and which still today guarantees it the high circulation of the media that use it.

Therefore, as it was the ending of the fairy tale that caused such consternation among seminar participants, it must also be this ending that contains the key to the puzzle. What is the aim of the story and what is the purpose of the numerous harsh trials to which Our Lady's child is subjected? Is there only one "correct" version of the fairy tale or are there several? From the footnotes of the Brothers Grimm we know that there is at least one other version of the story in which the child is not Maria's but was taken and brought up by a "black lady". Although this variant was at least as well-known as the one with Maria, it was not included in the collection of fairy tales.

It may be assumed that this unknown dark lady on her black chariot with a black horse wanted to teach the little girl different things to the Christian Queen of Heaven. In the many variations where the dark lady reigns there are those with a quite different approach: namely that in her last and hardest trial, Our Lady's child is saved and rewarded not for bowing down and confessing, but for standing firm and remaining silent! That the heroine by her unbreakable silence saves herself and the enchanted and bewitched that she discovered.

While reading a book by Wolfgang Giegerich about the Jungian concept of neurosis I became aware that the fairy tale with a practically unchanged "official" ending can also lead to a very interesting "correct" ending: namely to the transfer of a neurosis into a new state of consciousness. In this article, as well as considering object and subject levels, I would like to follow these two different developmental paths in particular.

In astrological psychology, we have the fascinating possibility of using the Age Point to experience the progress through the twelve houses as a description of an individuation process. Because when we interpret a fairy tale, we are operating on the archetypal level, we are not forced to stick to the fixed timeframe that the Age Point would otherwise dictate. We can therefore simply use the sequence of the houses with their cusps and low points in order to better understand the meaning of the events in the story of our fairytale heroine and to incorporate them into the progress of her development.

Our Lady's Child

Summary

Out of need, a very poor married couple give their only child to Maria, the Queen of Heaven, who takes the girl home with her to heaven. During one of Maria's absences, despite being strictly forbidden from doing so, the girl opens the last of the thirteen rooms to which Maria had given her the key and there glimpses the divine trinity. Confronted by Maria, she denies everything, but is betrayed by her finger which has turned to gold. She then loses her power of speech and is banished to Earth. After a long time, she is found by the King of the country, who falls in love with the beautiful, dumb girl and marries her. She becomes a mother three times; three times Maria comes, demands that she confess her misdemeanour and, as she refuses, takes the child away. Finally, under the pressure of public opinion and against the King's will, she is condemned to be burnt at the stake for child murder. On the stake, she finally prays to Maria, repents and confesses. Thereupon she is saved and gets her children back.

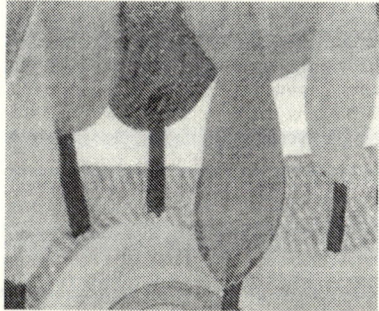

Our Lady's Child's Birth Horoscope

If we want to follow the life journey and ordeal of Our Lady's child from an astrological perspective, it is obvious that we need to think about the astrological conditions with which this person starts their life. As we have no information at all about the place and time of birth, we can draw up her horoscope exactly as we like. It is true that we find ourselves in fairyland and in dreamtime, in the archetypal unified region of heaven where inner and outer are indistinguishable and may only cause a vaguely discernable sense of order.

The **Sun** is that which Jung calls the "centre of the field of consciousness" (9), the body with which we identify ourselves, with which we say; "that is what I want and that is what I don't want." Its position in sign and house indicates the life's basic theme, which other elements of the horoscope describe in more detail in their respective ways. To the silent but stubborn heroine of our story, who goes her own way, undeterred by admonishment, threat, punishment and hardship, only one zodiac sign is appropriate: Capricorn. Saturnine in her solitude and tenacity, this creature fights her way right up to the mountain peak she has set as her goal. As the dweller of the tenth house, Capricorn is the symbol of the light towards which it strives, the cruel, clear awareness, the liberation from the mother's womb of the fourth house in which Cancer watches over the maternal unconscious, offering security and protection at the expense of growth and individuation.

As the Capricorn Sun of Our Lady's child is not noticed for so long, others repeatedly order this person about, as if she had no individuality of her own. It must be a very hidden Sun that has had to go through such a long process of self-discovery until it is noticed and acknowledged. This is why we place it at the most hidden place in the horoscope, at the low point of the twelfth house. This also seems to be an appropriate place for the representation of Our Lady's child's father, who indeed does not know how to assert himself in the hard everyday world, but has "inner eyes" that are necessary to see the Queen of Heaven. And there the Sun is also a good possible image for the second father, the legendary, invisible Godfather.

Saturn, together with Uranus, forms the mother archetype, in which Saturn has the role of the physical mother, while Uranus stands for the grandmother and beyond this for the Great Mother in the family. A transit of the age point over Saturn in the first house often indicates a very drastic change in the life circumstances of a person, a possible uprooting at a very young age. As Our Lady's Child experiences this trauma at the age of four, we therefore place Saturn at the low point of the first house. There it definitely also accurately describes the careworn mother who doubts herself and God. This situates Saturn in the sign of Aquarius, a suitable symbol for the ambivalence of both mothers: the physical mother, embittered by need, emotionally impoverished and self-suffering and the completely inward-turned, highly spiritualised Maria, who nevertheless reacts with such unbelievable cruelty when her order is disobeyed.

The **Moon** denotes the childlike ego in the family model, whose lodestars the Sun and Saturn are projected onto the father and mother, on whose guidance and protection it depends. We place it in the 6th house, which calls for devotion, service and subordination to the needs of others. From here it is connected by a long, green quincunx aspect to Saturn, representing the mother, symbol for the hopeless longing of the child for its mother, who is inaccessible for quite different reasons. It indicates the great distance this child must travel until it can accept and live out her own motherhood. This capacity for maternal love is indeed associated with the sign of Cancer, in which the Moon is situated. But it is not a gift that is there from the outset, but a potential that must be developed. At first, this Cancer Moon only shows its tendency to react touchily by sulking stubbornly when required to do something that does not correspond to its aims and beliefs.

Venus and **Mars** primarily stand for human sexual energy, largely corresponding to the Jungian concepts of *anima* and *animus*, whereby Saturn and Uranus complement the respective picture for Venus/*anima* and Sun and Pluto for Mars/*animus*. We place Our Lady's child's Venus, which plays a significant role in this fairy tale, in the eleventh house as it cannot be too far from the Sun. There she will indeed be bound by high ethical demands, however as Sagittarius-Venus she can easily touch the King and set him on fire due to her flexible fieriness that strives to evolve, a totally appropriate goal for the upward aspirations of the sign and house.

The associated **Mars** we could imagine in the stress area before the ninth house cusp. There it is in the tension field between the eighth house of social forms, the burden of inheritance, the claims of the family, court and courtly society, and the ninth house which requires independence, the desire for autonomy, for liberation from the shackles of sophisticated society, towards individuation. Anyhow, it is no mean feat to bring a dumb, naked savage out of the forest and also – undoubtedly to the consternation of the family – to marry her. This woman with her unhideable otherworldly knowledge – the golden finger! – must have corresponded perfectly to the image of the witch that prevailed at the time! Whether she had obtained this knowledge from the Queen of Heaven or the Dark Lady, is not really important here, she has already bewitched the King anyway! In addition, this Mars position shows that this woman has decided to marry "up". Whether this "up" then simply refers to the social status of the eighth house or whether it is a step into the ninth house of self-discovery, the liberation from preset norms, is initially not clear.

The joining of the opposites Venus and Mars occurs through the two different planets **Jupiter** and **Mercury**. Mercury operates on the level of the mind, of intellectual cognition and understanding, which form the core of the changes to be made. Mercury is also Hermes, the protean son of Zeus, an image for the archetype of the divine child in which masculine and feminine on a highest level find each other and produce something new and different. As he too cannot distance himself too far from the Sun, he joins Venus in Sagittarius in the eleventh house. There he represents curiosity and the thirst for knowledge, which drives Our Lady's child to break the rules she was given. As a mutable planet exiled in a mutable sign in the fixed house of Aquarius (the sign in which Saturn, the mother is situated and rules), he must break this taboo, he does not want to deny his nature. That is why the voice that belongs to Mercury must "die" as a punishment, in order to be reborn after a long night.

In the godfather **Jupiter** we encounter the archetype of the senses, the wise old man, who not only understands opposites like Mercury, but also experiences them on a kind of superior level. It is the planet of growth and development, of sensuality and meaning. Jupiter shows through its position how and where a person can look for and find the highest development and fulfilment. We place it in the ninth house, the house of external and internal travel and of the individual search for meaning, in which, as ruler of Sagittarius, it is at home. It is also placed in Libra, where it feels comfortable with its task of balancing and uniting. At the same time, here it is the nearest planet to the highest point of the horoscope. This topmost planet gives an idea of the goal of individuation towards which the horoscope owner can consciously aspire. This Jupiter position also gives Our Lady's child the clear life task of finding her own way and her own goals. As befits Libra, she strives for this goal in her encounters with other people and through conscious work on the transformation of opposing tensions. Significant pre-conditions for this work exist, as Our Lady's child is confronted with radically different ways of life at a very young age.

Four participants are still missing from Our Lady's child's horoscope. They include the three trans-Saturnine planets: **Uranus, Neptune and Pluto**, the representatives of the three spiritual principles of wisdom, love and power. We do not want to burden her any further with these spiritual forces, symbolised by the three new planets, as she already has enough problems to deal with on the journey to herself. Furthermore these three planets had not yet been discovered at that time. The other missing element is the ascending Moon Node. One could easily imagine that this Moon Node lies right up in the tenth house in Scorpio. The tenth house is the home of Capricorn, the house of individuation, in which full and unconditional development of the personality is required, the deliberate, gradual disentangling from the maternal domain of Cancer right at the bottom of the horoscope. And the way in which Our Lady's child must find her way through the most difficult and life-threatening trials would be very appropriate for Scorpio, whose journey is always a painful one, passing through limit experiences and death and rebirth processes.

Our Lady's Child's Journey

From the cusp to the low point of the first house, "In front of a great forest", on the boundary between civilisation and wilderness, between consciousness and unconsciousness, Our Lady's child is the only child of a couple who are otherwise not particularly fortunate. The father, a woodcutter, dives daily into the forest of the unconscious, but whatever he finds there, he cannot transfer into anything that could help him and his family to escape from poverty. There is no sign of happiness despite all their poverty, but of hunger, misery and worry. That is the harsh, saturnine climate in which the child spends the first three or four years of life, characterised by material, emotional and mental deprivation and the inkling of a greater, mysterious and dangerous and – for the child – forbidden world on the other side of the boundary separating the civilised world from the wilderness.

Then this strange miracle occurs: the Queen of Heaven or the Dark Lady appears to the father and offers to take his daughter from him and look after her.

At first we are shocked, for this "taking" could mean the child's death, and as far as the parents are concerned, the child is as good as dead. They disappear from the story as though they had never existed. Astrologically this is a real low point experience; one world perishes so that another can be born. But a person does not come out of such an experience unscathed. The virtual death of one mother in favour of another is a traumatic uprooting; the unquestioned security of the world has been lost forever. That is why Saturn also lies at this low point: it indicates a "constriction of the ego powers" (6), in Jungian terms, a blocking of the libido out of fear, a fundamental pessimism that makes it hard to be open to life. A "needy self" (Neumann) arises, whose aim is to ensure its own survival in a predominantly cold and unstable world. One could imagine that the later refusal of

Our Lady's Child to confide in Maria has its roots in this early loss of trust.

First House Low Point to Fourth House Cusp

We do not learn a lot about Our Lady's child in heaven. We imagine that she luxuriates in all imaginable material, emotional and mental comforts, and is nourished and cherished by the mother of God herself, surrounded by angels and saints. From the adversity and deprivation of her former life, she is transported into a situation offering all she could wish for in terms of age-appropriate development. A life like a dream, were it not for the preceding traumatisation, and she quite definitely learns things that belong to a quite different world from that which she has come from. This is also true when she lands not in heaven but in the kingdom of the Dark Lady, who will impart her knowledge and the rules of her world to her, while in a slow process of inner maturing, she prepares for the trials that lie ahead. Especially in the period from the low point of the second to the low point of the fourth houses, she learns the thought norms and dogma that are compulsory in the society in which she finds herself. Here people practice the rules that allow them to adapt to and survive in their social environment without complaining. Here we lay the foundations for our career and construct and refine our persona. But at the same time we put our thoughts (3rd house) and feelings (4th house) in the chains that society requires, so that we can be part of the group and are not excluded for being an outsider. During all this learning process, simultaneously in the hidden, archetypal depths of the personality runs another process of maturing and growth. This process prepares the person to leave the nest, the protective structure (in particular the family, but also social norms), in order to take another step forwards on her developmental path.

Fourth House

According to the fairy tale, Our Lady's child is now fourteen years old, i.e. right in the middle of puberty. She has twice passed the magical figure of seven years, and stands exactly half-way through a Saturn transit, according to the old calculations. Here, Our Lady's child's life journey reaches the lowest point of the horoscope circle, the so-called depths of heaven. (In the "normal time" of the age point, it would not come until the age of 18, at the cusp of the fourth house.) She has assimilated and interiorised the knowledge and rules of her environment; she demonstrates this knowledge outwardly and immediately comes into conflict with it. The two learning processes, inner and outer, collide, and at the same time the climax brings catastrophe. And the catastrophe, the inevitable and unpardonable breaking of the taboo, is brought about by the protector of the taboos herself. Maria herself gives her foster daughter the key to the forbidden room and by her emphatic prohibition makes the child even more curious, as people usually are at this age. God too once did this, by showing the forbidden fruit on the tree to the first couple, to be sure that they would succumb to the temptation of the forbidden.

> *"One's own path is revealed by a prohibition, yet it is the mother who has indicated this prohibition, this possibility; treading one's own path always means leaving the mother... The child should go its own way, and yet it should also not... We also have intra-psychic knowledge of the conflict between having to go forwards and wanting to stay." (7)*

Our Lady's child wanders through the twelve rooms into which Maria's – or the Dark Lady's – kingdom is divided. She marvels at the riches she finds there, which she has learnt to recognise and value. They are the twelve rooms of the socially sanctioned order, the traditional worldview, in which everything has its established place and function. The twelve hours of night and day, the twelve months, the twelve apostles – with twelve, the circle that the Sun orbits is closed. Outside this lies what is unknown, dangerous and forbidden, and the person who has been successfully socialised remains in the circle of twelve without being consciously aware of the desire to leave this structure. But Our Lady's child is wounded, she is not "normal" and in addition she knows from early childhood the attraction of the great, silent forest right behind her house. She carries within her the knowledge that she must leave her mother's kingdom in order to find her own kingdom, somewhere in the unknown and unconscious darkness – in the forbidden thirteenth room.

What she actually finds in this room is cause for all types of speculation. That a pubertal girl uncovers the entire Holy Trinity "in fire and splendour", the "official" version of the fairy tale, is rather improbable. This is an image for a holistic experience though. A whole, in any case, that is completely determined by men and the Church and from which the wholemaking fourth, here the woman, is lacking. Also, other strongly Christian versions of the taboo are not convincing: that God should not be seen when reflecting, when walking or when deciding on human destiny, nor should Jesus, Peter and Mary be disturbed at mass, etc. However, the taboo that

Our Lady's child should not overhear a private conversation between the godfather and Mary in the garden of heaven makes for an exciting story. As this still healthy old man with a white beard is on the one hand the father of the illegitimate son of Maria, but she on the other hand is the highest representative of the masculine and feminine, a wider field of associations opens up, from the heavenly lover's tryst to Hierosgamos. In each case, it would be an encounter of Our Lady's child with the theme of Man and Woman, of sexuality, with her own identity as a woman. But it is also only ever a glimpse through the keyhole, an inkling or a promise, even if it turns her finger (a phallic symbol?) permanently gold.

The Christian versions allude to the fact that it could also be a look into the dark, painful areas of human life or even at the mystery of life and rebirth, in which the girl sees Mary with the body of Christ, mourning him, washing his feet, sitting on the throne, healing his wounds. In the kingdom of the Dark Lady there are suffering figures in need of redemption such as black or green damsels, hybrids, half fish, animals, skeletons and spirits to which Our Lady's child should bring salvation by her constant and unconditional silence about the salvation she has witnessed.

The fourth house (or more accurately, the space between the low point of the third and the low point of the fourth houses) is on the one hand the place where in the course of life's journey one must confront the family and convention, the often very still quite unconscious decision about adaptation or resistance. On the other hand, it is also the place of the descent into the individual and collective unconscious, which from Cancer, the dweller of the deep, protects, and is moved and shaken by the Moon, its ruling planet. Conscious contact with these dimensions changes people, however and wherever it takes place. It is the bite of the forbidden fruit and the loss of innocence cannot be reversed. What we see and decide in these depths is not really communicable. It belongs to another world, to the world of monism (5), and the everyday world can only access it by means of images and symbols. In talking about these experiences there is always a danger of profanation, even of betraying what is new and great to the old world, which brings everything new and unknown into its power and would like to order everything according to its own classifications.

However, in accessing these depths, one always runs the risk of becoming too self-involved, for the victorious return of the hero/heroine is not guaranteed. The wrong word in the wrong place and the powers of the deep hold people forever in their grasp. And these powers can be manifested both by a loving mother and the family structure she rules over, or by experiences in the archetypal underground of our world, which cannot be integrated if the ego is not sufficiently stable and therefore destroy it. This can also be why one cannot talk about these experiences, as a defence against an uninvocable, otherwise overwhelming incipiency.

There is yet another quite different "modern" possible reason for Our Lady's child's silence, which can link the interpretation of our fairy tale to a different understanding of the key: the admission of deliberately having taken the forbidden step, having seen the forbidden, entails having to take responsibility for the newly acquired knowledge. Anyone who wants to grow up must behave accordingly; she must take responsibility for her own life in a new way. Wanting to remain outside in a childlike paradise once she has been awakened will start a process of dissociation and neurosis (3). But the childlike paradise cannot be maintained even by paying the price of neurosis; the person is awakened and paradise is lost. Our Lady's child therefore is limited to either choosing to leave heaven herself with her head held high or being banished.

Low Point Fourth House to Fifth House Cusp

Our Lady's child is silent and is thrown out of heaven to earth. For the second time she is expelled and once more it is a highly ambivalent experience. Just as in the first expulsion, the advantage of gaining an unimaginably rich new world was offset by the loss of everything ancestral and maternal, so now the gain of the unconsciously longed for liberation from the constraints of heaven is offset by the sudden fall into hard, cold loneliness. While Our Lady's child experienced the first expulsion passively and helplessly, this second time – even if not quite consciously – she contributes a good deal to it. And this knowledge of growing autonomy and authority goes with her.

However, Our Lady's child is apparently not ready to really enter the new world, for there is a massive thorn hedge all around her. (In the case of Sleeping Beauty, this is the revenge of the overlooked thirteenth(!) fairy.) This could be an alien environment that she still does not want to enter, but equally also the prickliness that young women like to build around themselves as a protective wall. However, we can also see it as the alchemical vessel in whose protection the new being must mature. If Our Lady's child has experienced the holistic trinity, the missing fourth part must now grow. Initially though, she still wears the slowly disintegrating clothes that befit her status. "The "wilderness" is not a geographical place on earth, but a mental state that resembles an attitude, in which all the theoretical and technical baggage one has brought along is left behind in order to let oneself fall into the situation without holding back, as though into the place of the source, the decision, the boundary between "Being and Not-Being", a situation whose inner truth should be experienced (but may naturally also be missed)" (3). But first Our Lady's child must find this attitude and this place. She is like a young warrior searching for her vision, like a shaman who must be initiated, thrown out into the wilderness. But she has no preset ritual to carry and support her. What she has is her experience of surviving and she has her inner guide, the pull of herself, which has its own symbolism in fairy tales: the growing of Our Lady's child's hair.

Our Lady's child cannot just remain passively suffering at the "crash site" (low point 4). Her inner process continues, even though she may consciously want to oppose it. Her age point now moves on to the cusp of the fifth house, whose themes are self-awareness, self-testing, self-development, and quite specifically also sexuality. The growing of her hair is therefore not just a symbol of the passing years. The more the clothes she has brought with her from childhood and early youth become ragged, the more her hair becomes her new clothing. And this time it is her own clothing, the clothing of the woman she is now becoming. From time immemorial, hair has been the bearer and expression of people's power. For a man, it stands for their physical strength and (also sexual) power. Like in the story of the Israelite hero Samson, who had no rival until his unfaithful lover cut off his long hair thus delivering him up to his enemies, the Philistines. That even a warrior who was unassailable for other men becomes weak in the hands of a beautiful-haired woman was one reason for the taboo that led to men dictating that women's hair must always be covered. In all three monotheistic religions, the woman must keep her hair covered, and Christian (and also Buddhist) nuns have to cut all their hair off altogether. It is therefore no accident that Our Lady's child wrapped in hair in the illustrated edition of the Brothers Grimm *Fairy Tales* (1) is very reminiscent of the image of Rusalka, the female ghost who, clothed only in her long hair, sits at the side of the road and casts spells on men and then kills them (10).

Cusp and Cuspal Area of the Fifth House

When age point reaches the fifth house cusp, the time has come to conquer another piece of the world. The King of the Land breaks through the thorny hedge and finds the fully-blossomed Our Lady's child, cloaked from head to toe in her femininity. The hunt he is engaged in, the wounded deer that he is hunting, are ancient sexual symbols, as is the white sword held in his hand. It is therefore not very likely that in this encounter he really paces back and forth as primly, even reservedly, as in the version by the Brothers Grimm. But all the same, there we read: "The King took her in his arms, carried her onto his horse and rode home with her", and as we do not know how far that was or how much of a hurry the King was in, this journey could just as easily have taken years as days or weeks.

The King of the Land is certainly a symbol of the self and the event is therefore an inner call to the passively waiting Our Lady's child to now deliver herself up to the world. The nature of his entrance also makes the King an *animus* figure though. Astrologically, this could mean e.g. an aspect of the age point to Mars (in our fictitious horoscope it would be a trine, i.e. a gentle encounter by Martian standards), linked to Venus, which itself only acts reluctantly, and leads her out of her semi-aware state into the union with nature in the different enchantment of the world of conscious and experienced opposites. But from the eleventh house that now lies exactly opposite, Venus too naturally influences the event. For it is her *"anima* effect" that attracts the man and "tempts the man and woman into life", as Jung puts it. However, Our Lady's child will only experience the whole, universal reality of her *anima* when her age point has completed the journey through the other six houses and in the conjunction with Venus is completely immersed in her experience.

Fifth House Low Point to Sixth House Low Point

Although Our Lady's child has now indeed entered into the world and has acquired quite a decent piece of it, a king with an entire kingdom no less, we still do not see her as a proactive personality; but rather that of an outwardly-manifesting pawn who is unconsciously pushed around. She still has not found her own voice; her inner self is still not expressed consciously. Throughout her external success, she maintains her distressed silence, as though she were carried inside the alchemist's retort, separated from the world by the glass wall that surrounds her invisibly. The encounter with the masculine has only superficially liberated her. It does not help her to overcome the split between outside and inside, and her dissociation remains. It is therefore not surprising that now the King commands her, dresses her in new clothes, teaches her new rules and marries her. For the low point of the fifth house brings the end of the wild years and free love; society, which will condition events from the sixth house onwards, now stakes its claims.

That the King commands her can be an expression of these societal claims. It can mean that this man indeed loves her Venusian beauty, but cannot discern her true character and the latent knowledge within her. It can also mean though, that instead of taking personal sensitivities into consideration, the self drives forward the process of development and maturing and the passion this requires and psychological stress slowly but surely increase.

The sixth house is the house of work, service and being there for others. With the eyes of the world upon her, Our Lady's child arrives at the cusp of this house with her first child. She fulfils her function as wife and mother, and as the first child is also a son, the desired son and heir, everyone's happiness is complete. Our Lady's child is not, however. She can still not grasp the developmental opportunity and as we cannot remain at a house cusp, with the climax comes also catastrophe: the child, her future and the future of her country, is taken away from her. She brings another son and then a daughter into the world, but neither stays with her. The power of being a mother and her inner struggle with this power rob her of child after child. As the psychological strain grows within her, the pressure of the collective also grows, until the King himself can no longer protect her and delivers her up, allowing her to be condemned to being burnt at the stake.

Our Lady's Child's Arrival

According to the fairy tale, Our Lady's child was saved and her children returned to her. Due to the inner lawfulness of this story – as we see it today – that cannot be seen as an act of subordination to an external power. That is why, and in order to fulfil the claim set out in the introduction, we must now let Our Lady's child find her own way out of the catastrophe. We will therefore indicate two possibilities, one "modern" and one "traditional". In the "modern" version, Maria is the ruler, and in the "traditional" version, it is the Dark Lady. From an evolutionary point of view, this can be the reason why Maria is the more modern figure as an integral part of a patriarchal system. The Dark Lady, however, only exists in patriarchal times as the dark opposite pole; she refers back to a matriarchal distant past in which people – from a patriarchal point of view – were still unconscious and whole.

Sixth House Low Point to Seventh House Cusp

This is the third expulsion of her life and this time it is not a change from one world to another; now it is a matter of life or death. She has reached the outermost edge; her last support, the King, has abandoned her, and she stands naked and lost in the wilderness as before. Her tongue is still paralysed; no explanation is forthcoming. And yet, if we have followed the story up to this point, we have the feeling that this is a different woman that is now tied to the stake. She is not just a symbol of isolation and lostness. She is also a person who, having lost all external security and hope, has been completely thrown back onto herself. Our Lady's child has gone through the trial of loneliness behind the thorny hedge, she has gone through the trial of loving her husband and her children and now she is facing her last trial, death. She stands as in the above-mentioned quote: "at the boundary of existence and non-existence", she has reached "the place of the source, the decision". And only here, in this extreme state of abandonment, appears – or rather, is found – her own inner truth. Here inner and outer, unconscious and conscious coincide in an autonomous act of truth and creativity.

The axis of houses six and twelve asks questions about external existence and the inner right to exist. In Our Lady's child's fictitious horoscope we have placed the Moon in the sixth house and the Sun in the twelfth. The Moon, which in the sixth house has always been confronted by the problem of survival, is now more than ever. And the Sun, which in its hidden place must repeatedly doubt its right to exist, is now definitely in danger. Therefore her age point at this moment lies in the sign and in the vicinity of her Moon, her inner child, which despite all the painful experiences and existential fears does not stop believing and loving. And it lies in exact opposition to her Sun, repeatedly passed by and overlooked, which nevertheless knows and wants and whose strength and power Our Lady's child now experiences for the first time. At this moment, on the burning stake, at the low point of the sixth house, the questions of existence and the right to exist coincide.

The king, the symbol of the self, has withdrawn from her, and her ego feels "abandoned by God and man". Just as no external help is forthcoming, there is also no comforting dream coming from within, no pioneering vision. "It sometimes appears as though the self wants that the ego makes a free choice – or perhaps the self also depends for its actualisation on human consciousness and its decisions", writes Marie-Louise von Franz. As Our Lady's child's ego finds her own right answer (still without guessing that it is completely inseparable from the self), not according to external opportunity but by coming as close as possible to her inner truth, she understands her neurosis, the split that makes her dumb, and she understands her self and gives herself the right to live. She understands her silence as a refusal to be stuck with what she has experienced, the steps she has taken, and therefore can go forwards on her way to herself in the attempt to escape from the inexorable process of coming into the world. Our Lady's child's confession is therefore not a confession of sin, but an acknowledgment of herself, her own knowledge, the light of her own Sun that lights the way to her Self. Our Lady's child stands by her actions and takes responsibility for their consequences, her here and now. She does not confess in order to stop her old life from ending, but for the sake of her own inner truth. In the process she finds her own voice, her own thoughts, her own awareness. Her children, who symbolise her potential for growth, come back to her and a new, mature attitude towards the king, her *animus* and her self-symbol, is possible. (One might question on the object level, what happens to a relationship in which one person is betrayed and abandoned by the other to such an extent. And whether such an individuated person would still want to be part of such a scenario.)

With this truly death-defying leap from the low point of the sixth house to the cusp of the seventh house, with this inner liberation, the result of a long and difficult process of maturing, Our Lady's child switches from social conformity to the active seventh house, in which the Self turns to the You and refinds itself in the You. In her own, fictitious horoscope, she changes from Cancer to Leo, into the sign of the Sun and the King, and from a terrifying and devouring mother, Maria changes into a liberating, feminine symbol of the self.

Our Lady's child has traversed the night sea in her Moon boat and at the moment of her demise has reached her Sun. And this experience of the Sun as the radiant centre of the field of consciousness must be made before the person can really make their journey to their Self. For the first half of the life (not counted in years) is devoted to the extraverted development of the personality, and only the second half is concerned with introversion, with the depths of the Self.

The "modern" psychological happy ending described here is naturally not really admissible, as the fairy tale was not intended by its authors to be like this. At that time, people were stubborn, obsessed with the devil or some such other-worldly being, they could be cursed, damned or have spells cast on them, but they were not neurotic. Their curse or their suffering was elevated into a collective belief system, a prescribed set of explanations, which also indicated the ways and means necessary for healing. For a Mediaeval person, repression was a completely passable route – in fact the most passable! – in order to become whole and therefore part of the collective again, and outside of this collective, there was no salvation and no survival.

At that time, in any case, as we believe that the dramatic change to the fairy tale happened under the influence of the Counter Reformation, people were no longer the unquestioning particles of an unquestioned worldview. With his search for his personal merciful God, Luther had split the Church and people's consciousness. He had demonstrated the invalidity of the old ritual methods of the Church for the modern man that was now emerging. The fairy tale in its modern form was the conservative answer of the Church, of its ruling collective, to this epochal change. Through our modern interpretation, we have, contrary to the intention of the fairy tale, made Our Lady's child into a supporter of this new spirit. In this way, she has become quite unexpectedly a "great individual", a revolutionary and a modern heroine.

What if we now proceed from the other assumption, that it is actually not the patriarchally-influenced Queen of Heaven Maria, but the Dark Lady, who belongs to the deeper, more ancient matriarchal sphere, who took away, brought up and then sent away Our Lady's child, only to save her later on, when Our Lady's child makes up her mind to comply with her role only when faced with a terrible death? The path and trials up to this real clash of heroes are the same, even if the signs are different. Here her silence right up to the imminent danger of death is not a sign of defiance or a neurotic split, but the expression of self-preservation. Through her deliberate silence, her non-submission, Our Lady's child delivers herself up to the dark, fearful and suffering inhabitants of her unconscious and lets light fall into her darkness. She keeps her secret to herself when faced with the aggressive attack of the piercing and dissolving perception of the patriarchal spirit and therefore remains in the sphere of influence of the Great Mother. Despite this, a development also takes place here. For through her refusal to surrender the power over her soul to the darkness – which is also manifested in the unconscious collective's hatred of Otherness, she capitulates and integrates herself. That means that by not projecting, by not allowing herself to be made the victim and the others as the perpetrators, she delivers herself up to the dragon within her, her shadow, and makes it conscious.

Most of the fairy tale variations mentioned above are not just concerned with the salvation of the self from the curse of the mother on the one hand and that of the collective father on the other. Much more important is the fact that Our Lady's child receives the order by her silence, i.e. by her completely passive attitude, to liberate others from their captivity. An attitude that is very appropriate for a Cancer Moon, who in such a discrete and secretive way likes to achieve her merged goals in which it is hard to separate her compassion and her own intentions. A great part of Our Lady's child strength is created not just out of the will to assert herself, but out of her empathy and compassion for the cast aside and the damned. Our Lady's child quite clearly does not represent the developing Father Principle of the Sun in Capricorn. She stands much more for her Cancer Moon that develops from the childlike to the maternal, which does not achieve her goal of self development single-handedly like Capricorn, but only by being part of a whole that is connected and motivated by love, belonging and identity. In this way she also integrates her Saturn in Aquarius. Saturn, her maternal guiding principle is in her positive form of being rooted in the maternal ultimate ground, and her sign, Aquarius, represents the ideal of the maturing of the individual as part of a greater, collective whole. In this way, the Moon in the house of Virgo connects with the Saturn to a feminine holistic figure; the Dark Lady changes from being cruelly threatening to a compassionate mother.

Our Lady's child's dramatic appearance as a victim on the stake is not in itself a demonstration of power of the self-emancipating individual. She remains still and passive and prevails due to her non-action. We do not know whether she looks into the lapping flames with great fear or great faith. But we do know that her decision is made and can no longer be influenced by external circumstances, for only this decision can bring her salvation. In this way she has fulfilled her mission and one could imagine that she simply disappears from the stake, and, like Jesus, moves unseen and unrecognised among the outstretched hands of her accusers and persecutors and goes home.

Bibliography

(0) Madeleine Rose Vögelin, C.G.Jung Institute, Winter term 04/05

(1) Grimm's *Fairy Tales*

(2) *Enzyklopädie des Märchens*, Berlin 1990

(3) Wolfgand Giegerich, *The Neurosis of Psychology*

(4) Bruno & Louise Huber, *LifeClock*

(5) Erich Neumann, *Die Psyche und die Wandlung der Wirklichleitsebenen, in Die Psyche als Ort der Gestaltung*, Frankfurt/Main 1992.

(6) Bruno & Louise Huber, *The Planets and their Psychological Meaning*

(7) Verena Kast, *Folktales as Therapy*

(8) Marie-Louise von Franz, *The Problem of the Puer Aeternus*

(9) C.G.Jung, *Psychology of the Unconscious*

(10) C.G.Jung, *Man and His Symbols*

❑ ❑ ❑ ❑ ❑

Pluto in the Twelve Houses

Bruno Huber

First published in 'Astrolog' Issues 110 –112, June – October 1999

The Three new Planets Uranus, Neptune, Pluto

Pluto was discovered in 1930. It is the slowest moving of the three new planets, and orbits the Sun in 246 years, as established using previously observed orbit sections. Since its discovery, Pluto has transited the signs of Cancer, Leo, Virgo, Libra and Scorpio and is currently in Sagittarius. Its speed is not regular, for example it takes 30 years to transit Cancer, but only 13 years to transit Libra. As such, Pluto's influence spans entire generations and eras. It gives the people born at these times a common spiritual background motivation that gives a connection between them but makes intergenerational understanding more difficult.

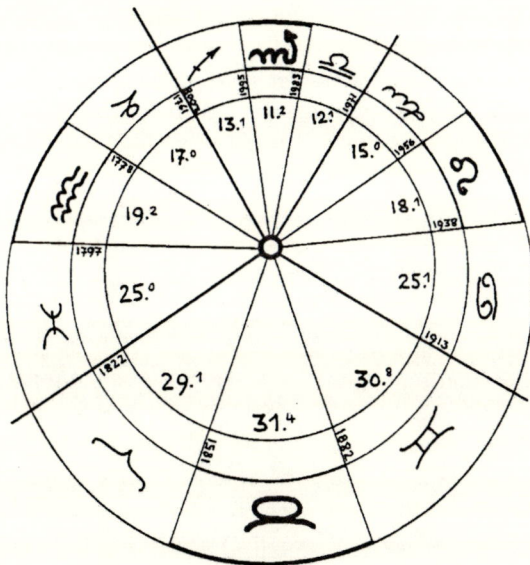

Pluto through the Zodiac Signs

The three new planets are all spiritual planets, which means that they function on a transpersonal level and affect matters of the spirit, or more specifically come from the spiritual dimension. Their definition is suitably abstract and a little out of touch with reality. However, this does not mean that they cannot produce physical effects. Pluto physically influences individuals to a lesser extent than it influences collectives, or large groups of people who have been brought together by fate. The individual can only be affected via the collective, and then only in the way indicated by the Pluto position in the person's horoscope.

For a long time, Pluto in particular had a bad reputation; it was called the Great Destroyer, and was purported to have unfortunate, even catastrophic effects. It was particularly implicated wherever suffering, instinctive power and aggression were found. We now know more and more about the spiritual dimension behind this rather one-sided point of view.

Pluto is always concerned with force or power, and its effect can best be understood according to Lao Tzu: "Power stops where force begins." Force is external and mechanical and its motivation is always selfish. Like the other spiritual planets, Pluto does not tolerate selfish motivations. It is not about me or other people, but about understanding, experience and growth in the spiritual sense. If these planets are associated with selfish motivations, their effect is destructive in line with their particular characteristics.

Uranus destroys by becoming a hopelessly critical machine and stifling life by means of method and rigid systems. The classic Uranus disease is technophilia.

Neptune destroys by disintegration and the dissolution of boundaries. In practical terms, this means by addictions that slowly disintegrate the personality structure.

Pluto destroys the old to make way for the new. It acts destructively when the inner evolutionary process is opposed.

Pluto the Inner Principle

What Pluto is all about is really the higher, spiritual self, an individual spiritual entity, the image of the superior man that lies deep within us and which we can only access by intensive spiritual efforts. Pluto is inherent within a central, higher Will that is crucial for our motivation and represents our strongest, innermost driving force. Pluto indicates to what extent we are willing and able to change our nature. It can therefore strongly affect the person by causing a metamorphosis (structural transformation) during the person's life and bringing about changes.

As the central inner principle, Pluto enigmatically provides the most perfect vision of what is envisionable in terms of individuality right up to a transcendental idea of God. It is quite common, especially for the mystically inclined, to experience the inner self as the YOU, a higher being that is superior to us and whom we look up to. We then consciously communicate with this YOU, see it as a YOU and not as a part of ourselves, thus blocking ourselves spiritually.

We have not understood that we must identify with this YOU as a higher self or inner guide, so that we can transfer our own qualities into our lives for the benefit our fellow men.

The position of Pluto in the individual horoscope represents the spiritual paternal role model and is dependent on the figure or role that the father plays and the child observes. It tells us about the environmental influences on development of the paternal role model, specifically the exercise of the inner free will. For in the latter case, Pluto represents a force coming from deep inside us and wanting to grow. It is the power of the developing self, a quality unique to each individual. In the former case, it concerns a will imposed from outside.

The spirit changes the form
(metamorphosis)

Some of the Pluto symbols still used today

Monogram of the discoverer, Percival Lowell	The adoration of the spirit (Medality)	"Chemical marriage" the union of mind and spirit (Alchemy)	Mind, spirit, body (Ritual/ cultish attitude)

Form elements of the planetary symbols

Self, place	Spirit space	Form body	Soul sensitivity

One can say that Pluto magically penetrates the innermost being and destroys everything there that is alien; all masks, false motivations, fake ego forms and role functions are transformed in a kind of chemical smelting process. In this way it conducts both the great metamorphoses of our time, and also those of individuals, to enable a new structure to emerge corresponding to the inner principle.

Aspects to Pluto

Pluto's power depends on the sign in which it is located and on the aspects and its position in the house system. It has an enormous intensifying and exaggerating effect on the elements concerned. It is as though everything it comes into contact with is electrified. The effects of this can, of course, be positive or negative. When it comes to the evaluation of aspects, we must ascertain whether a real growth process is involved or if it is just that the "small self" is strongly inflated, in which case everything that gets in the way must be got rid of and in some cases the person is prepared to stop at nothing to achieve their goals.

Few or no aspects to Pluto are indicative of a weakness of will, and often the metamorphosing forces are powerful and break through with the force of a higher power. At this point though I must reiterate that the horoscope must be considered as a whole to really understand the person concerned. Only then is it possible to correctly evaluate his life situation and provide effective help.

Basically some aspects are more suited to Pluto and others less so. As a "hard planet", red, hard aspects are better suited (square and opposition) than soft blue aspects (trine, sextile). Pluto can cope just as well with the opposition as with the square. If there are sensitive planets at the other end of the hard aspects, their sensitivity often diminishes to the point of numbness. An exception is Jupiter, which is still able to function vigorously even in a square aspect. Soft Pluto aspects (trine and sextile) usually confer distinctly paranormal abilities on sensitive planets; at the very least there is a hypersensitivity

The Statue of Zeus at Olympia

of the sense organs. Conversely, hard planets are weakened and lose their inner "clout". There can also be evidence of self-satisfaction, conceitedness and pride.

A semi-sextile is a guarantee of long-term growth; it opens up a constant flow of information. Red-green aspects in particular give it a certain importance because a constantly regenerating motor function of the aligned planetary forces is stimulated, and this ceaseless activity leads either to the loss of power, restlessness, unrest or creativity.

The quincunx is called the decision, longing or will aspect. It represents the gap between reality and ambition. As Pluto is the spiritual will, and confronts a quincunx with people who require decisions from the horoscope owner, there is a kind of pressure to refine Pluto, to show its best side and to purify itself of its all too worldly ideas. In this situation, Pluto can develop its own will qualities and over the long term, show significant growth.

As Pluto intensifies everything it comes into contact with, it also strengthens the effect of planets with which it is in conjunction. Sensitive planets like Neptune, Jupiter, Moon and Mercury can find their receptivity magnified; we can almost "hear the grass growing". Hard planets like Sun, Saturn and Mars can be used to positive or negative effect as powerful tools.

Pluto in the First House

In the 1st house, the emphasis is on action rather than self reflection. This fire house, corresponding to the sign of Aries, harbours Martian and cardinal forces that push outwards and drive upwards. As this is where the individual constructs the self-image that he will show to the world, Pluto has a definite influence on the formation of the personality. People with this position feel that they are quite special and have exceptional power within them. This attitude is not necessarily wrong in itself, but it is up to the individual to show what he is really made of rather than just inflating his abilities and knowledge.

The person always believes that they are a powerful character. Unfortunately, this power is often misused to manipulate and patronise the environment because the person feels called to do so. There is a pronounced tendency to play the commander and "big shot", which is naturally misguided. Pluto is not at the YOU point, the DC, but at the I point. The subject is therefore the self, and this is where any criticism should be directed.

Pluto at the AC means that this person is constantly working on their self-image, and must undergo a lifelong process of metamorphosis. The powers with which to change and develop the self are available. If these energies are not used for the purpose of personal development, the person is almost forced to direct them towards the You and to use them in the manipulative way mentioned above. These are usually difficult partners; particularly in a business context one would do well to establish whether the person concerned has understood their Pluto, in which case they should be easy to get on with. Otherwise it would be better to keep your distance.

Basically it can be said that Pluto positions on the main axes indicate enormously strong potential that is generally misused because we tend to take the path of least resistance.

However, with the exercise of self control and self criticism extraordinary things can be achieved. A good example is the *Gründerzeit* (years of rapid industrial expansion in Germany at the end of the 19th century), when Pluto was in Aries (1821-1851). At this time, pioneers conjured up factories out of nothing, undeterred by obstacles. Their risk-taking enabled achievement of something great, but nothing ventured, nothing gained. Success is only possible though if the person is able to exercise sufficient self observation and self criticism. If these pre-requisites are lacking, mistakes will be made, and these people will be accused of being dictators and despots.

Pluto in the 1st house produces a typical born leader. However, if the aspect pattern does not indicate an equally pronounced leadership character, we have the situation where Pluto provides the leadership tendencies, yet the other tools required are lacking. Then the self image presented to the environment is nothing more than a mask.

However, if in the individual horoscope there is a clear individual character, the person may be able to achieve great things and be a success, something that is not only important to him personally but can be equally important for the development of many others.

The new planets always give rise to abilities and effects that concern not just individuals but the group. It is therefore particularly important that people with Pluto in the 1st house understand that the effects of this planet must be beneficial and good for the greater collective. "One person's spiritual growth benefits others," the old saying goes. This is especially true with Pluto in the 1st house.

Pluto in the Second House

The character that is born in the 1st house and first shouts: "here I am" to make the world take notice of him, gradually realises in the 2nd house that he is not alone in the world. This discovery is initially destabilising. There is a tendency to protect himself from the environment, to build a wall around himself. Where Pluto is concerned, the context is not a worldly one, but instead involves nourishing, protecting, preserving and caring for the inner self.

This is a fixed, social house. Aspects of socialisation are of primary importance: self preservation and self assertion, social adaptation and suffering, caring and commitment, dependency, constraints and lack of freedom; for in the 2nd house we must consider other people. Here our attitude towards society is defensive, passive and introverted; we are not trying to do anything more than keep our place. In this position Pluto can still cause great selfishness, which distorts the relationship of self to society.

The task of Pluto in the 2nd house is wholesale implementation of the ideas and substance it brings with it. In the 2nd house there is a great fund of personal substance, character, knowledge and skill, and Pluto wants to increase this knowledge, develop the talent and develop real skills. It asserts its power through what it "has" and what it "can do". This involves developing the inner resources of the character and placing less value on material things. The motivations should shift from the external to the internal world.

Often people with this setup are proud of the power and extent of their expertise and possessions. They feel strong and form a front with their equals, leading to a kind of clannish and elitist thinking that can unfortunately often be found among spiritually oriented people who gather together in groups and look down on others. This way of thinking creates a barrier between people and makes their desire to help others ineffective.

Elitist thinking is fundamentally a defensive attitude, because one feels small and weak when confronted with society as a whole. In order to cope people stick together, naturally in an elite group as Pluto wants to be superior; it is not satisfied with half measures. "Status-thinking" here reaches almost Saturnine proportions. Some people become distinctly materialistic, and want to become not just very rich, but super-rich: another kind of elitism, for possessing a great estate gives the feeling that they have risen above the masses. A superego imago of a millionaire and the like is often found here. Wealth impresses and Pluto in the 2nd house is particularly susceptible to it. If not born into a wealthy family, he feels cheated. Aristocrats can also be found here, the baron who had to sell his castle long ago and lost his fortune. Often such people are almost ridiculous caricatures because they cling to their "dignified" lifestyle, missing the opportunity to be a real human being in the process.

It is important with this Pluto position that clannish thinking and elitism does not predominate, but rather the ability to manage the laws of economics in the correct way, so that they are used for the good of mankind.

Pluto in the Third and Fourth Houses

The third and fourth houses represent our roots, the familiar place in which we exist and where we feel at home. It is a limited environment, a space where a child can understand the collective. Here we find those character traits that are conditioned by the environment. Pluto's ambitions in these houses also relate to the social environment, home, background, the group as a whole; all endeavours are concerned with this collective. One is able to protect and care for what is good and even make improvements. People with this Pluto position will basically work in some way (depending on sign) for the collective and try to structure it as well as possible. In this century democratic ideas have been particularly prominent in "civilised" nations: everybody's rights must be respected. This may be in a wider context, whereby Pluto forces people to go out onto the streets and fight for their rights, or may be in a more personal context, looking after one's own particular milieu (family, relatives, etc.) and wanting to ensure their well-being. Insufficient large-scale thinking, which Pluto really requires, can easily make one prone to pettiness or even fanaticism here. These misguided attitudes are then expressed by the separating off of one's own collective (family egoism), and include racism and other forms of caste thinking.

While intellectual, mental functions predominate in the 3rd house, which corresponds to Mercurial, airy Gemini, the 4th house is home to emotional receptivity and feelings. There is therefore an opposition between mind and emotions.

In the 3rd house, Pluto is interested in collective knowledge and education. The person tends to a certain intellectualism, which is more or less pronounced depending on their intelligence and ability. There may be a tendency to see things from a scientific or academic point of view. The thought norms of the collective prevail, so that the person is likely to be very conservative and want to defend and protect the status quo and be hostile to new ideas.

We should not neglect the positive side, which usually involves an interest in sociological, political and psychological issues. If aspects to Saturn are involved, there is also an interest in history. Pluto therefore gives one an interest in the social sciences that deal with the collective and its behaviour. This Pluto position also tells us about different ways of thinking. The city dweller is more flexible, tolerant and broad minded in their thinking than a villager, who is less complicated, but also more clear cut with a more fixed mindset.

The villager is therefore much less prone to moral lapses and decadent behaviour, whereas it is hard for the city dweller to find a clear moral code as there are too many options open to him. The sign in which Pluto is situated tells us about the person's thought structures as far as inner, personal ambitions and essential considerations are concerned. Three of the most restricting signs are Taurus, Cancer and Virgo; in Cancer the functioning is simple rather than narrow. Gemini, Leo and also Libra indicate somewhat broader thought structures.

In the 4th house sensations and feelings rule, not the mind. Here one is not interested in knowledge but in the emotional desire to belong. One is still concerned with the collective though, as one is looking for love, security and close relationships that provide a feeling of security. The 4th house type will have a clear dislike of anything different, alien, new and disturbing. Such conservatism can be healthy, but can also make one prone to exclusivity.

In these houses this effect is quite strong, as they are concerned not just with mental and intellectual issues in general, but specifically the attitude of the individual due to the influence of the collective, which can lead to a detrimental dependency. There is also a tendency to block external things and only accept those that belong to one's own collective. What is almost never found in the 3rd and 4th houses is moral courage. Pluto is particularly susceptible to this, for in here the individual "should" not assert himself intellectually, but should adapt instead. Anyone who sticks out by having an individual opinion and sensitivity is punished by the collective by being excluded.

Sacrificing oneself for the collective is typical of Pluto in these two houses. Here we see the hero of fairy tales, legends and stories. He is, however, not a real hero in the individual sense, but only in the name of the collective that gives him the strength and courage for his deeds and stands behind him. If this sacrifice is excessive, the person loses their individuality and is unable to live properly, leading to possible mental or physical health problems. While it is true that nature requires every individual to align himself to and work positively with the whole, this needs a certain self awareness and a minimum amount of self manifestation. If this minimum is lacking and the person has not acquired a certain amount of self confidence from his own achievements, he becomes – at least spiritually – ill, due to the inadequate development of his individuality.

Pluto is restricted in the 3rd and 4th houses and finds it hard to do its job. It even finds it difficult to get in touch with its inner essence. Particularly in the 4th house, the person is very suggestible and imagines things that are not really there at all, they say they receive waves of sympathy from others that make them feel strong, although they themselves cannot demonstrate any kind of substance. There are many such figures who are carried by the collective and are able to make a good living out of it, although they often do amoral things and are also criticised for this by the collective (for example, the Mafia).

The main positive thing and also the role of Pluto in the collective area is the pronounced need and inner wish to deal with the collective in the best and most beneficial way possible. This happens in the 3rd and 4th houses in different ways. In the former, there is more importance attached to knowledge and people may work as legislators or deal with future societal structures that are better than the existing one. For example, in all revolutions the leading group is composed of these people, who then go on to use their knowledge to offer the collective optimal opportunities and try to establish the best living conditions.

In the 4th house, the same problems are approached from a more emotional angle. Here the person is much more interested in personal wellbeing and in a wider sense also the security gained by taking refuge in the collective. They submerge themself in the masses and are no longer discernable as an individual, which can be both positive and negative. The feeling of domesticity and "embeddedness" is key though and represents the stimulating force. People with Pluto in the 4th house deliberately try to extend their sphere of influence from the home to – in extreme cases – the state, by creating a homely, cosy atmosphere where people feel comfortable.

In the 3rd and 4th houses, possible downsides are the classic superego functions. This is most clearly so in the 3rd house, because there we find precisely those ideas and thought patterns that most impress modern, relatively intelligent people and influence them most strongly. The most enduring of these are the behavioural structures taught to children. Feelings can quickly change when stimulated by a particular event, but it is much more difficult to change thought structures. If as a child we have become used to a certain way of thinking with all its associated fixed ideas, even at the age of 16, an age at which we make our first attempts to think for ourselves, it is difficult for us to get rid of them. For we perceive our thoughts not as something alien to ourselves, but identify with them, and think that they come from ourselves, which is typical of the superego. If the learnt thought structures are too dominant, the inner essence has no room to develop. This state leads in the short or long term to mental or spiritual illness, hence the need for constant self control and self criticism, as well openness and constant willingness to change.

An unfavourable characteristic (superego) that is particularly common is the stereotypical "patriarch", who needs his own family to behave like subjects in order to provide him with a minimum of self confidence. This attitude is further reinforced to become mask-like, if either Pluto lies at the IC or a weakly positioned Sun in the 4th house is looking for compensation.

Pluto in the Fifth House

If the 4th house is all about identifying with the collective, the next developmental goal in the 5th house is clearly the YOU point. One notices that the people encountered are actually individuals, not just a group. They are all different and should be dealt with accordingly.

As a social house, the 5th house is concerned with making individuals want to appear as nice as possible. Here one tries to charm people and shine with the whole personality to give a positive impression. Being nice is a much more effective way of controlling others than, for example, being cruel – cruelty makes people anxious and inspires more fear than affection, but if one receives sympathy and love one is on safer ground. This explains the certain cockiness we find in the 5th house. Having gone through the "collective bath", all one has to do now is make a good impression. An example is the stars who become famous at the age of 25 to 30 in show business.

However, Pluto is more interested in inner essence than show. There is a great danger of losing touch with oneself, i.e. searching in the external world, going outwards instead of developing inner qualities. The attraction is enormous, for one has the opportunity to directly and lastingly effect the environment. Pluto in the 5th house requires vigilance with respect to the self. One must constantly check whether one is really doing what one wants or whether one is in the process of successfully passing oneself by and becoming almost a victim of the public.

The 5th house therefore has a clear moral principle: one plays "catch as catch can"; everything is allowed that is not forbidden, when it comes down to it. Here one can easily do things that deep down inside one knows are not right for oneself, i.e. one cheats oneself. However, the fifth house is all about giving individual expression to our inner character. This must not be hypocrisy but real moral courage. Here it is not only possible, but essential. This inner quality is not dependent on popularity or approval, but is self-contained, as Pluto is self-affirming and therefore does not need approval from the environment.

The purpose of the 5th house is not to occupy and secure a place in society, but self actualisation. One should try to manifest one's own character in an appropriate way, and be motivated by the wish and will to participate in life. *I* want to be part of this world and want to act

The Colossus of Rhodes

in it in ways that suit *me* and allow me to make my own individual contribution. This has nothing whatever to do with the showiness mentioned above. However, it is not so easy to find a suitable form of self expression as, like all fixed houses, the 5th house is also a place of ordeals. Fixed behaviour, existing orders, prevailing opinions, certain expectations that people have of me, the pressure of my own ideas and principles all make it hard for me to really be myself. People with this Pluto position are therefore often pathologically sure of themselves and their greatness. Even if all other planetary constellations contradict this, this idea of the self still exists, but the person remains unfulfilled, which makes them feel misunderstood.

It is therefore helpful to remember that the 5th house is a social house. The key to success in the actualisation of personal essential qualities lies in showing consideration towards society, i.e. in belonging to the whole. One is a personality here (in a certain place) and now (at a specific time) and this fact brings certain fixed forms of behaving and thinking with it. One should put as much of oneself into life as one can in order to gain momentum, for one only makes a real contribution by doing more than just one's duty. This is the law of the 5th house: giving more than one thinks one can and more than one thinks that the environment can stand. This is where the opportunity for growth lies both for my fellow men and for myself.

Pluto in the Sixth House

The 6th house tends to be a place of suffering. Here we hope to find recognition and acceptance from the YOU. The issue of survival is key: we must find our "market niche". That is why this house is so fundamental in career matters, although admittedly less in terms of finding our vocation (where the 10th house is more influential). Here it is largely the environment that determines how we earn our living. We have to survive physically, which means that between the ages of 30 and 36 we must seriously look for a position where we can become established and best use our strengths. Now it is time for us to stand on our own two feet and we do not have too much time left to experiment. Very often in this house we must cut back, downsize big ideas and adapt to reality. In this process, it is quite easy for Pluto, who usually increases and intensifies things, to lose all sense of proportion, particularly when we act not according to inner convictions, but to the requirements of the environment. We can easily become a victim of the environment out of the need to please at any cost. With Pluto in the 6th house, one easily allows oneself to be overwhelmed with jobs and responsibilities. Although hard working, one is always overstretched and runs the risk of partially or completely losing oneself. In order to survive one does things that do not correspond to one's inner essence; a kind of "professional prostitution", the tragedy of many bad career choices. People working in the wrong job often do not allow their dissatisfaction to penetrate into their consciousness. They should instead take responsibility for their mistake and change their situation. However, they repress any self-questioning and become slowly but surely ill as their mental equilibrium disintegrates. A classic consequence of this is a heart attack in retirement. It happens because throughout life one has done the wrong thing, has not been true to oneself and can no longer find the strength to start the new phase of life that retirement represents.

Pluto in the 6th house asks us to do the right thing and search for as long as it takes to find the role in which our abilities are really needed. That is not an easy task; many people avoid it out of convenience, by selling themselves for temporary advantage. In the long run though, finding a job one loves makes one happier than allowing oneself to be prematurely forced into an unsuitable career path.

With Pluto in the 6th house, one must defend oneself against this kind of pressure. Although here the planet naturally finds itself in a place of suffering, it still has the ability to find its correct place in the community, by exercising freedom of choice and refusing to work in the wrong place. This sometimes needs more strength and courage than simply "sacrificing" oneself to the environment by being a self exploiting workaholic. With Pluto in the 6th house, a motivation of serving and helping does indeed always exist, but the willingness to sacrifice can here all to easily degenerate into a "selling out" of one's own developmental potential.

Herein lies a piece of philosophy that should not be ignored, even if one claims to be too busy. In the 6th house we are confronted with the harsh facts of reality as far as the issue of survival is concerned, and it is worth reiterating two essential points:

1. Knowing, nurturing and developing one's own abilities.
2. The insight that life is not just about survival, but also about being a social individual and as such making a positive contribution to society. This contribution should correspond exactly to one's own skills and abilities.

Bringing these two things together is Pluto's mission. Its position in the zodiac sign indicates my true nature, and only when I am myself can I become creatively active. The sort of person I am and what I am able to give must therefore be fully reconciled with my inner vocation.

The demands of the 6th house are difficult to fulfil because they involve hardship and struggle with oneself without looking for external encouragement. However, living life one's own life is the secret of a happy and satisfying existence.

Pluto in the Seventh House

In the 7th house one does not behave passively but actively. Here one can make decisions and even give orders, which admittedly does not make one popular with the environment but with Pluto at the DC there is a tendency to do this anyway. As in the other cardinal houses, there is an inherent fundamental self conception in the 7th house: one assumes certain pre-requisites without discussion and then gives orders first and asks questions later. Pluto is therefore in a dangerous place here, for the temptation is great to shape the world according to its own model. It is still – as in the 6th house – close to the YOU and must get on well with it. In the 7th house one tries to do this by conditioning the YOU. At the main axis, Pluto has a particular kind of power; it frequently uses force against its fellow men. This often happens with the justification typical of the 7th house that also corresponds to Libra: "for the sake of justice and truth". However, this behaviour and attitude inevitably bring negative consequences.

The general consensus is that the 7th house is very friendly, for it is concerned with partnerships. This is the house of the famous "scales of justice" with blindfolded eyes, holding the weighing scales and the sword. However, it is not unconditionally concerned with jurisdiction in the sense of bringing justice. What is meant is behaving in a prescribed way to the advantage of all parties concerned. This sounds like a rational calculation: the burden must be shared equally; everyone should receive the same amount and nobody should lose out.

This goal can be achieved by observing the letter of the law. We know only too well and from many examples that our "scales of justice" with blindfolded eyes sometimes treats people extremely unfairly and mistreats them because she sticks to the letter of the law and does not take the human reality of the people concerned sufficiently into consideration.

With Pluto in the 7th house, we also find fanatics of justice and truth who like to work with the sword. This position is therefore difficult, because Pluto is already all too willing to judge others. If one thinks that one must change other people, one has not understood

Pluto. Pluto is concerned with me, not other people, and with the need to change myself and my character. To consciously confront a YOU means accepting that this YOU also makes mistakes. One should therefore not try to tinker about with the YOU, but work on oneself in an attempt to implement one's ideal image of what a person should be like.

We can then influence the environment by example and – if we are very consistent with ourselves – have much more influence than if we had played the judge. If someone with Pluto in the 7th house tries to put pressure on other people, he has already overstepped a boundary, which is expressed in an ancient Chinese saying: "Power stops where force begins". With Pluto in the 7th house, I must repeatedly ask myself: do I manipulate others or do I use my strength to force them? Do I use force because that person does not want to do something or does not see what has to be done? I cannot and should not force him.

However, by using my personality to demonstrate another way of living and behaving, I possess the greatest possible power over him. For if he finds the example I set worthwhile, he has the possibility of emulating it without feeling forced or pressurised. That is important for Pluto. If Pluto lies at the low point of the 7th house, the tendency to order others about is less pronounced, for one quickly notices that it does not work. On the axis though, Pluto has plenty of opportunities and finds it more difficult to see that force should not be used, even in a subtle way.

In the 7th house one should not use personal power against others, otherwise it can lead to fighting and confrontation. It is not about upstaging others and being the best, but about attaining optimal coexistence, being together for each other. Each should make his contribution for the benefit of the whole: this is a particularly clear requirement for Pluto in the 7th house.

Pluto in the Eighth House

The 8th is another fixed house, and it is normally clear to people that society is a collection of individuals. It is not so much about the individuals themselves but rather about the system, the structure of society and the laws and legalities that govern human coexistence.

Pluto's influence is therefore directed toward the organisation and the establishment. Its strength, which can bring damage and destruction when directed at individuals, in the 8th house is oriented towards structures, which can be replaced or redeveloped.

It is typical here to attempt to change, improve and perfect one's own organisation, the personality. The word "purify" is crucial. One exercises self denial and self discipline, lives a healthy life, regulates and orders habits, i.e. works on the personality structure and tries in this way to change oneself. However, this is not the way to change our character. Although at certain times it is necessary to make our personality structure work like clockwork, if we concentrate too much on it, we waste time and energy without achieving anything in terms of personal development. That is the pitfall of the 8th house, that we mistake the form for the content, the structure for the essence. This then has a destructive effect on the environment, if we turn this conviction into a theory and want to impose it on others by force or want to judge others only according to their position of power in society, or their status – for example if someone has lots of money he is important and if he has no money he is worth nothing. The person with Pluto in the 8th house is often deluded by other people's status.

What is therefore the central meaning of Pluto in the 8th house? The 8th house lies exactly between the DC and the MC, two very different points. At the DC, we are convinced by the YOU as the authority, the self is pitted against the YOU and we allow ourself to be conditioned to a certain extent by the YOU. At the MC, exactly the opposite is true. Our individual properties and differentness are emphasised here. We want to acquire confidence and freedom by being autonomous and independent from the YOU. The 8th house is precisely where these two forces intersect: the influence of the DC is still effective and that of the MC can already be felt. We do not want to give up the many advantages we get from the YOU but also want to enjoy the freedom offered by the MC. This constant inner oscillation makes us want to try to build a structure or system in which both the above are present in quite specific proportions.

The solution is of course a compromise that can lead to a split in the character that can be managed but is difficult to live with.

Many people therefore have a double life, an official life and a private life. One is a façade allowing them to get on in life, and the other is more suited to intimate, liberal needs. Pluto in the 8th house encourages the person to overcome this "schizophrenia", meaning that a decision must be made. As the horoscope journey always goes forwards, they must decide in favour of individuality and freedom.

The benefits expected to result from systematic behaviour of the YOU must be renounced, even if this means losing out. Having the courage to be independent should, however, not mean walking over others, letting things stay as they are and ignoring one's duty to the YOU. One may neglect duties but not overall responsibility. Duties are not exactly substantial, but just necessary for things to work well. However, they are not necessarily good; duties can be a burden because they do not correspond to our innermost nature. Responsibility though is a substantial feeling of responsibility towards others, and one may even sacrifice personal freedom for the sake of fellow men. However, being good out of a sense of duty belies a certain profit motive in this attitude, for one does it not for others but for oneself.

Pluto in the 8th house therefore requires that one choose freedom and particularly the opportunity for free development of the individual, but not at the expense of others; one must know the difference between freedom and selfishness.

Pluto in the Ninth House

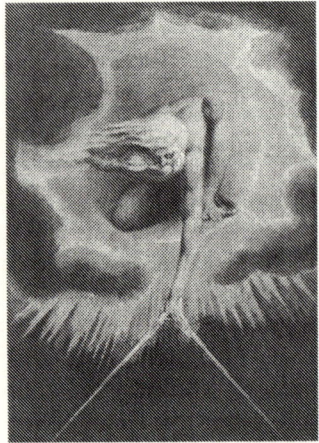

Logically, Pluto is in its "best" place in the 9th house, for here the main concern is individuality. However, wherever Pluto is, it always requires a certain discrimination leading to insights that turn one towards one's essential core. Even in the 9th house this discrimination is still necessary; it cannot be avoided anywhere.

In the 9th house, the important thing is not external, worldly authority, but inner authority. In principle, this Pluto is concerned with spiritual autonomy, for power and control over others have no place here.

The 9th house is flexible, mutable and as such a house of insight. Individuality is understood as spiritual autonomy; the aim should be independence of thought, that is a law unto itself. Work on the self always lies behind the positive effects of Pluto. If Pluto causes people to behave destructively, it is because they have not understood what Pluto actually requires of them.

In the individual area of the chart, Pluto requires that one is self-critical, i.e. that one is honest with oneself, which automatically also means being honest with other people. This is particularly important in the 9th house, for here the priority is clearly, unambiguously and uncompromisingly understanding connections, principles and laws. It is a basic pre-requisite that one should think transpersonally and not be preoccupied with petty personal problems and difficulties. Pluto requires one to turn towards others and to identify and solve their problems.

Pluto in the 9th house has great strength coming from the core being, and there is a temptation to use it for selfish ends. This can mean that dogmatic or even demagogic people can be found here, who try to force others to think in certain ways of their choosing. Such behaviour can degenerate into depriving others of their spiritual liberty.

Again, the mistake is to direct efforts outwards instead of inwards towards oneself. To start with, the transformative powers must always be used on oneself to change the structure of one's own mental perception, philosophy and possibly also ethics. Spiritual rigidity must not get in the way of growth towards greater insights. One's concept of life and of people must be very adaptable. A structural change should however only be undertaken when the change brings an improvement, an expansion of consciousness or perception. Only then can one start to think about wanting to change how other people think. The first priority should definitely be one's own capacity for spiritual growth, for otherwise one will tend to impose platitudes and stereotypes on the environment. An example that specifically illustrates this danger is the so-called "one-size-fits-all philosophy" that is particularly common when Pluto is in Cancer in the 9th house.

The 9th house should allow one to develop a spiritually-derived approach to the world and use insights elaborated by oneself, perhaps even with one's own methods. One's perceptions are constantly being expanded and one is challenged to think creatively.

Hence the need to beware of received, collective and undifferentiated ideas, which always carry the risk of being over-simplified. Indeed, this is often the case for relatively closed thought structures, which on closer examination only consist of a loose collection of simple truisms. Although they give people an answer to every question, however complex, they do not necessarily have valid answers for the big questions, instead providing the most convenient and least taxing explanation.

In the 9th house, one must acquire the ability to question and criticise everything, not in order to destroy but in order to discover the substance of things, forming a personal philosophy in a creative process from the insights gained from one's own intellectual efforts. This philosophy is the basis of spiritual autonomy and healthy, individual freedom that allows the person to make a positive contribution to mankind.

Pluto in the Tenth House

The 10th house is all about attitudes, actions and externally directed activities. There is a significant danger that Pluto can inflate the ego here. Particularly when Pluto is the most sensitive planet in the aspect structure, delusions of grandeur and excessive self importance can be models that inflate the ego.

The 10th house is also known as the house of authorities, leading to the possibility of false authorities in the case of unfavourable aspects. Strong aspects between Saturn or the Sun and Pluto are significant, for they tend to indicate a superego function.

As we know, the superego is external, but internalised. It is a model that we try to aspire to that does not necessarily correspond to our own character but instead is provided by the environment. We copy the power of something or someone stronger in order to enhance ourself. This happens particularly often with parents who consider their children to be extensions of themselves and try to turn them into what they would like to have been but could not be. This ambition is so strongly implanted in the child that over time they identify completely with it and are later convinced that this was their own idea.

For example, if Pluto is in the 10th house and the Sun is down in the 4th house, the father wanted to achieve through his son or daughter the self actualisation that he himself was unable to achieve. The Sun's position in the 4th house indicates that the father's self confidence was not allowed to blossom because of excessive conditioning from his collective. The father compensated for this through his child who then had to live out a superego, which required a lifetime's struggle on the child's part, with little chance of success. In extreme cases, it can lead to a loss of self, for example with Sun position at the DC, for the person concerned usually does not know themselves at all.

Columbus column, Barcelona

If Saturn is in opposition to Pluto, the mother has probably also manipulated the child, but not by trying to live through the child but by wanting to turn him into somebody important in life. This could be called the manipulation of the father model by the mother.

In the 10th house, the model is that of the leader, and one naturally aspires to take responsibility for others. Politicians often have Pluto in the 10th house, people who rise above the masses and those with an influential position within a collective. Pluto's role is to develop inner strength of character. Anyone with Pluto in the 10th house who wants to enforce their power by acquired stereotypical behaviour and games of political intrigue will one day be brought down from the throne on which he has placed himself. The 10th house is always concerned with developing a personal, self-acquired authority that is the expression of real individuality and an autonomous personality.

Pluto in the 10th house is naturally associated with the temptation to want to represent authority. In many cases, this affects those who are successful at an early age (stars, etc.). It often happens that the people concerned only notice after a certain time that their "stellar"

career cannot last forever, but somewhere along the line will fade away, for popularity provided by a fickle public can disappear very quickly.

Only someone in the 10th house who has learned self-mastery, who can be intellectually independent and who does not use manipulation to achieve self affirmation will gain a genuine authoritative charisma. Then he will convince by the sheer force of personality alone, by his presence, not because he strives for this effect, but because he controls himself intellectually. Without really trying, this person has real authority and possesses influence and power that he will use for the good of all.

Pluto in the Eleventh House

The 11th house is immediately associated with the term "friendship". This does not just mean some kind of acquaintance, but a bond based on mutual trust, with a stability that does not just depend on external interests. People who go "through thick and thin" for a while together but have ambitions for external success, are not necessarily also friends, for if the ambition fails or leads to disagreement, the so-called friend can suddenly become an enemy. We often find that in times of need, none of our so-called "friends" are around to help. Real friends are there for me at any time and stick by me, for they know me: they have my trust and I have theirs. That is something of great value.

Behind every friendship, there always lies a fundamental spiritual process. The extent to which this is conscious depends on the kind of person involved. My image of man determines my choice of friends. These are a chosen few out of the vast selection of people I can choose from.

It is not important here whether I have consciously chosen my friends, or whether we met "just like that": consciously or unconsciously my selection is based on my vision. In my friends, I search for actualisation of my ideal image of man. They must therefore possess at least a certain number of qualities that correspond to this image.

The model of the ideal person – the central theme of the 11th house – has different effects: firstly I choose certain friends, as described above, and secondly I try to make changes in the world in order to be able to actualise my ideals. As there are abundant opportunities for improvement in this world, in the 11th house numerous attempts are made to improve conditions for the people of tomorrow – here we usually think of the future. No house has as much influence as this one in the area of large-scale humanitarian planning.

As Pluto is a "super ideal" planet, which only wants perfection and is only interested in how it can be implemented, in the 11th house it likes to think on a grand scale, for it always exaggerates the characteristics of the house in which it is situated. It emphasises the world-improving tendencies of its subjects, leading them to develop a "transmission consciousness". This person has the feeling that they are not working "off their own bat", but that they are in a certain sense acting on orders, for a clearly definable authority. It can be a spiritual authority or its exact opposite: the whole of mankind. Whichever it is mainly depends on the overall structure of the horoscope.

Although this transmission consciousness is the danger of the 11th house, most people recognise here the real influence of Pluto. Egocentricity is therefore not really the problem, for it is not just that the ego identifies with the issue, but that one assumes oneself to be superior. Nevertheless, if it does happen, the transmission consciousness is exaggerated to a messianic complex. The ego identifies to such a strong extent with the greater order, the commanding authority, that it believes it is itself this higher power. This is how the phenomenon of thinking one is Christ arises! These cases are always linked to highly damaged Sun positions: one would be correct in suspecting that this is a compensative process, a compensation function for a very damaged self-confidence that is not strong enough to cope. Pluto has confronted us with a false personality or superego function yet again.

In extreme cases the person may even become a dictator who wants to bring about good by force and to force people to love with a sword. The problem with this "crusade mentality" is that the person wants to overcome feelings of low self esteem by compensating and misusing spiritual theories and arguments. This attitude can lead to devastating consequences, sometimes even criminal behaviour. However, such cases are extreme, and the vast majority of 11th house Pluto positions are definitely positive, as they indicate great commitment and readiness to sacrifice a great deal for one's ideas, so that some of them may even be realised.

An accurate indicator of possible ego emphasis is how strictly one makes perfectionist demands on one's fellow men.

In the 11th house, Pluto is mainly concerned with improving circumstances, with an other-worldly motivation that is clearly oriented towards this world. One is looking for the immanent God, for the part of God that is present in nature and therefore also in man. The motive for all actions is the love of goodness, which one consciously champions, thereby making one a model of true humanity for many people.

Pluto in the Twelfth House

In the 12th house, unlike the 11th, Pluto has an other-worldly orientation, but sometimes a worldly motivation. The energies run in almost exactly the opposite direction. Pluto wants to find the way back to the source. In this process, neither the person's type, construction nor their degree of spiritual maturity determine whether he is searching for something completely beyond the comprehensible and thereby mainly a "great YOU", or whether he wants to explore the unknown parts of himself. A well-positioned Pluto normally goes through both of these phases, first discovering the "great YOU" and then realising that in the process it has actually found its own original source that it can relate to.

However, Pluto in the 12th house may also construct its own secret spiritual kingdom into which it retreats when it can no longer cope with external conditions. In this imaginary world one thinks one can do anything and feels misunderstood by the world. One flees into this realm from the "big, bad world". But the "flight into the mind" is not the right way to solve problems, for that world is illusory and not truly spiritual. To be able to distinguish between these two things, one needs to have such good self-knowledge that one cannot fool oneself. Quite a few factors are required to be able to meet this demand alone.

Pluto in the 12th house is always deeply religious. It is up to the individual to what extent this is conscious, what form it takes and what kind of behaviour it leads to. In any case there are always undifferentiated, deeply religious sentiments or the feeling that a strong pull is being exerted. If these feelings are not intellectually differentiated, the individual may join a religious body. He will then adopt the behavioural norms of this community and uncritically subordinate himself to them. This process of conformity completely or partially restricts this person's characteristic religious nature, as it is then no longer able to function freely and spontaneously.

The more differentiated the person's normal, daily consciousness focuses on this theme and tries to gain an intellectual understanding of it, the less the above-described phenomenon will occur; i.e. it will become obvious that it is the content that really matters and not the form. The religion publicly embraced is therefore not important; what matters is having access to what lies behind it. When Pluto is in the 12th house, this process must begin no later than the end of puberty. Experience has shown that with this Pluto position, religious questions or visions usually arise already in early childhood.

The demands of Pluto are tough here and, once recognised, are unavoidable. In principle, people have three possibilities here. If they try to differentiate their essential experience as described above, they must be absolutely, uncompromisingly honest with themselves, as any attempt at self-deception inevitably means the end of the spiritual journey. Another possibility is complete rejection, turning away from these religious feelings and not wanting to know anything about them. In order to quell the need they still feel, they will devote themselves to a worldly career and external success as a kind of anaesthetic. The third possibility is an undifferentiated belief in one's own feelings, but no attempt is made to achieve a conscious experience. A genuine spiritual experience is therefore impossible, which in the long run leads to a certain spiritual calcification.

Pluto in the 12th house shows the environment an almost embarrassing need for its intimate sphere to remain untouched. Nobody should dare to disturb the person's feelings, whether they are human or religious. He is merely trying to protect his private space, and not trying to resolve spiritual issues any longer. This is really the worst and most undeveloped feature of this Pluto position.

The 12th house is on the existence axis in the horoscope, hence the need for me as a spiritual being to answer the questions: "What am I? Where do I come from?" or better still to experience them. The starting point for such efforts is almost always an existential fear, in most cases the fear of dying. However, typical 6th house fears concerning material existence can also cause a catapult effect into the 12th house and raise the issue of survival. Whatever the reason one begins to deal with spiritual issues, all that really matters is ultimately discovering true values and transferring them into real life, which Pluto, linked to our innermost original source, enables us to do thanks to its metamorphosing power.

□ □ □ □ □

Contacts and Resources

APA

The Astrological Psychology Institute (UK)

A MODERN APPROACH to SELF-AWARENESS and PERSONAL GROWTH

Astrology has become recognised as a valuable tool for the development of self awareness and human potential. Bruno and Louise Huber researched and developed this approach over many years, combining selective astrology with Roberto Assagioli's psychosynthesis. Our courses are based on their results and inspiration.

PERSONAL GROWTH Most of our Diploma students not only learn astrology, chart interpretation and astrological counselling skills, but find that the course helps develop their own self understanding and personal and spiritual growth.

COURSES We offer Foundation Modules to those new to astrology or to the Huber Method. Our Modular Diploma Course teaches the Hubers' psychological approach to chart interpretation for working with clients. Details are in our prospectus.

EVENTS Our programme of seminars, workshops and conferences includes annual workshops that are an integral part of the Diploma in Astrological Counselling.

CONJUNCTION Our magazine *Conjunction* contains articles, news and supplementary teaching materials.

API (UK) Enquiries and Membership
P.O. Box 29, Upton, Wirral CH49 3BG, England
Tel: 00 44 (0)151 605 0039; Email: api.enquiries@btopenworld.com
Website: www.api-uk.org

API(UK) Bookshop
Books and API(UK) publications related to the Huber Method.
Linda Tinsley, API(UK) Bookshop
70 Kensington Road, Southport PR9 0RY, UK
Tel: 00 44 (0)1704 544652, Email: lucindatinsley@tiscali.co.uk

API Chart Data Service
Provides colour-printed Huber-style charts and chart data.
Richard Llewellyn, API Chart Data Service
PO Box 29, Upton, Wirral CH49 3BG, UK
Tel: 00 44 (0)151 606 8551, Email: r.llewellyn@btinternet.com

Software for Huber-style Charts
AstroCora, MegaStar, Regulus, Regulus Light Special Huber Edition.
On CD: **Elly Gibbs** Tel: 00 44 (0)151-605-0039
Email: software.api@btinternet.com
Download: **Cathar Software** Website: www.catharsoftware.com

Publications on Astrological Psychology

THE COSMIC EGG TIMER
A practical introduction to Astrological Psychology
by Joyce Hopewell & Richard Llewellyn

An introduction and overview of the Huber approach. Offers a new and exciting way of using astrology, for all interested in finding out more about astrological psychology - and themselves! Using your own birth chart alongside this book you will gain insights into the kind of person you are, what makes you tick, and which areas of life offer you the greatest potential.

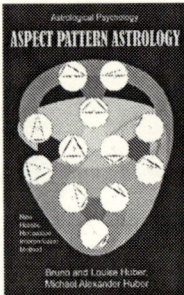

ASPECT PATTERN ASTROLOGY
Understanding motivation through aspect patterns

Essential reference on a key feature of the Huber approach. The pattern of the aspects reveals the structure and basic motivations of an individual's consciousness. Over 45 distinct aspect figures are identified, each with a different meaning. A systematic introduction to the practical use of this method, using many examples. Whether beginner or experienced astrologer, aspect patterns can provide immediate significant revelations about yourself and others.

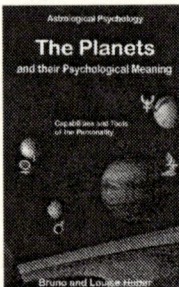

The Planets
and their Psychological Meaning

Shows how the positions of the planets are fundamental to horoscope interpretation. They represent basic archetypal qualities present in everyone, giving clues to psychological abilities and characteristics, growth and spiritual development. Comprehensive descriptions of each planet, based around fundamental principles aiming to stimulate interpretative abilities. Contains examples plus detailed descriptions of key personality planets Sun, Saturn, Moon in each of the astrological houses or signs.

* Books by Bruno & Louise Huber except where authors otherwise indicated.

A Modern Approach to Self Awareness and Personal Growth

MOON NODE ASTROLOGY

Combines psychological understanding with the concept of reincarnation, bringing a new astrological focus on the shadow personality and the individual's evolutionary process. Includes the psychological approach used with the Moon's Nodes, the Nodal Chart and the link with esotericism showing how earlier lives are reflected in the aspect structure and Nodal Chart. Covers the role of three charts in the individual's evolutionary process, the Nodal Chart symbolising the past, the Natal Chart the present, and the House Chart the impetus from the environment for development.

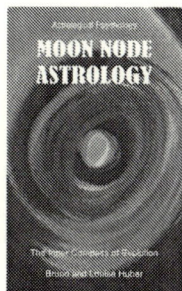

LifeClock

Revised, integrated edition. The horoscope is seen as a clock for the person's lifetime, with the Age Point indicating their age as the 'time' on the clock. Those trying it invariably find significant correspondences between indications in their birth chart and meaningful events in their lives. This deepens self understanding and provides impetus and insight to psychological and spiritual growth. A powerful tool for the helping professions, enabling quick identification of psychological sources of a client's problems.

ASTROLOGICAL PSYCHOSYNTHESIS
Astrology as a Pathway to Growth

Bruno Huber's introduction to this holistic approach to astrology, based on Assagioli's psychosynthesis, following the premise that every human being has a soul which is at the root of all developmental processes. It aims to help people to find their true self and work consciously towards integration and wholeness. The horoscope is used not just as an analytical tool, but also as an instrument to enhance the process of self-realisation and spiritual transformation. Three parts focus on intelligence, personality integration, love/ sexuality/ relationships.

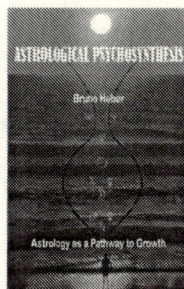

Published by HopeWell, PO Box 118, Knutsford, Cheshire WA16 8TG, UK

Printed in the United Kingdom
by Lightning Source UK Ltd.
126456UK00001B/100/A